Dyslexia: Biology,
Cognition and Intervention

Dyslexia: Biology, Cognition and Intervention

Edited by
Charles Hulme and Margaret Snowling

Whurr Publishers Ltd
London

© 1997 British Dyslexia Association

First published 1997
by Whurr Publishers Ltd
19B Compton Terrace,
London N1 2UN,
England

Reprinted 1997

British Library Cataloguing in Publication Data
A catalogue record for this book is available from the
British Library.

ISBN 1 86156 035 4

Printed and bound in the UK by Athenaeum Press Ltd,
Gateshead, Tyne & Wear

Contents

Contributors

Maricela Alarcón, Institute for Behavioral Genetics, University of Colorado, Boulder, CO, USA.

Lee Allard, Center for Molecular and Behavioral Neuroscience, Rutgers University, Newark, NJ, USA

Nanci Bell, Lindamood-Bell Learning Processes, San Luis Obispo, CA, USA

Ina Borstrøm, Department of General and Applied Linguistics, University of Copenhagen, Copenhagen, Denmark

Susan Curtiss, Department of Linguistics, University of California at Los Angeles, CA, USA

J.C. DeFries, Institute for Behavioral Genetics, University of Colorado, Boulder, CO, USA

Carsten Elbro, Department of General and Applied Linguistics, University of Copenhagen, Copenhagen, Denmark

Uta Frith, MRC Cognitive Development Unit, 4 Taviton Street, London, UK and University College London, UK

Usha Goswami, Department of Experimental Psychology, University of Cambridge, Cambridge, UK

Alexandra Gottardo, Birkbeck College, University of London, UK

Cathy Guttentag, Massachusetts General Hospital, Boston, MA, USA

Jennifer R. Hiemenz, Center for Clinical and Developmental Neuropsychology, University of Georgia, Athens, GA, USA

James Hodgson, Massachusetts General Hospital, Boston, MA, USA

John H. Hogben, Department of Psychology, University of Western Australia, Nedlands, WA, Australia

George W. Hynd, Center for Clinical and Developmental Neuropsychology, University of Georgia, Athens, GA, USA

Susan Lambrecht-Smith, Massachusetts General Hospital, Boston, MA, USA

Patricia Lindamood, Lindamood-Bell Learning Processes, San Luis Obispo, CA, USA

Phyllis Lindamood, Lindamood-Bell Learning Processes, San Luis Obispo, CA, USA

John L. Locke, Department of Human Communication Sciences, University of Sheffield, Sheffield, UK

Heikki Lyytinen, Department of Psychology and Niilo Mäki Institute, University of Jyväskylä, Finland

Paul Macaruso, Massachusetts General Hospital, Boston, MA, USA

Steve Miller, Scientific Learning Principles Corp., San Francisco, CA, USA

Kate A. Nation, Department of Psychology, University of York, York, UK

Richard K. Olson, Department of Psychology, University of Colorado, Boulder, CO, USA

Jerry Ring, Department of Psychology, University of Colorado, CO, Boulder, USA

Jennifer Roberts, Massachusetts General Hospital, Boston, MA, USA

Linda S. Siegel, University of British Columbia, Vancouver, Canada

Margaret J. Snowling, Department of Psychology, University of York, York, UK

Keith E. Stanovich, Ontario Institute for Studies in Education, University of Toronto, Toronto, Canada

Joy Stackhouse, Department of Human Communication Science, University College London, UK

Paula Tallal, Center for Molecular and Behavioral Neuroscience, Rutgers University, Newark, NJ, USA

Bill Wells, Department of Human Communication Science, University College London, UK

Barbara W. Wise, Department of Psychology, University of Colorado, Boulder, CO, USA

Preface

The chapters in this book represent a small selection of the papers presented to the Fourth International Conference of the British Dyslexia Association, held in York in April 1997.

In the 100 years since the first case of developmental dyslexia was described we have learned a great deal about the causes and consequences of the disorder. The dominant view today is that dyslexia is a form of language disorder that runs in families and can be effectively remediated if identified early. There is considerable agreement that phonological processing plays a critical role in the normal development of reading and that the core cognitive deficit in dyslexia is a phonological one. At the biological level, genes implicated in the development of dyslexia have been identified and behaviour geneticists have found that the phonological skills that underpin reading development are highly heritable.

As understanding increases, our questions become more specific, and there are still many unanswered questions concerning the causes of dyslexia, the factors which modify its expression, and the best ways of identifying and treating the disorder. This book brings together recent advances in understanding the biological bases of dyslexia, its antecedents in the pre-school years, its different cognitive manifestations and evidence concerning the efficacy of different types of interventions.

In the opening chapter, Uta Frith argues that there is compelling evidence that the cognitive cause of dyslexia is in phonological processing. However, the behavioural manifestations can differ according to the developmental history of the child and, in particular, the characteristics of the orthography in which he or she learns to read. The hypothesis of a core phonological deficit is consistent with findings of functional brain imaging studies comparing adults with a developmental history of dyslexia with controls of equivalent educational level.

The results of such studies indicate there is less left hemisphere activation during the completion of phonological processing tasks in dyslexic brains and, in particular, in the brain regions normally associated with the processing of phonological information.

Two chapters have as their focus the biological bases of dyslexia. John DeFries and his colleagues provide an update on their recent work from the perspective of behavioural genetics on the aetiologies of reading and spelling difficulties. Continuing the biological theme, George Hynd and Jennifer Hiemenz review evidence for differences in brain structure and function between dyslexic and normal readers.

Evidence from genetic studies has encouraged attempts to identify factors that will be predictive of reading failure amongst those children who are at genetic risk of dyslexia. If we could reliably predict reading difficulties from early cognitive indicators we would be in a very strong position to provide interventions to prevent the later development of reading problems. Following the pioneering work of Hollis Scarborough (1990), a number of such family studies are in progress internationally. In this book, John Locke and his colleagues, Heikki Lyttinen, Ina Borstrøm and Carsten Elbro, Uta Frith and Margaret Snowling and Kate Nation all make reference to such studies, at various stages of progress. The Finnish study, reported by Lyttinen, recruited infants born into dyslexic families. This study reveals differences in early speech perception skills and auditory evoked potentials to speech stimuli between at-risk children and babies born to control families. The Harvard study, reported by Locke and his colleagues, also recruited infants and, by analysing their babble, showed that at-risk infants show more restricted vocalisations than children deemed not at risk of reading problems. The London study, discussed by both Frith and Snowling and Nation, consisted of older children, tested just before their fourth birthday; these children showed early language difficulties including deficits in phonological processing and delayed vocabulary development. Converging evidence from the Danish study, reported by Ina Borstrøm and Carsten Elbro, shows that an intervention to develop phonemic awareness in children at risk of dyslexia is effective in warding off the development of reading difficulties.

Alongside the growing evidence of data on the phonological processing difficulties in dyslexia is continuing interest in individual differences. The long-standing debate concerning the role of visual factors in dyslexia (cf. Stein & Fowler, 1985; Lovegrove, Martin & Slaghuis, 1986) is reviewed by John Hogben who concludes that, although there is strong evidence of visual transient deficits in dyslexia, their status and role in the determination of reading problems remains equivocal. Keith Stanovich and his colleagues review recent research which attempts to establish the validity of different sub-types of dyslexia.

Their analysis suggests that the reading behaviour of the majority of dyslexic children is within the normal range; although a few children can be classified as displaying a 'hard' sub-type of phonological dyslexia, however. These children typically show greater difficulties on phonological awareness tasks than children who display a surface dyslexic pattern. Very similar conclusions are arrived at by Snowling and Nation, based on evidence from single-case studies of children with developmental dyslexia. These authors also point out that, whilst a child's phonological processing deficit undoubtedly places constraints on their reading development, the status of their other language skills will in turn affect prognosis. Thus, learning to read should be considered as the interaction between a child's processing skills and weaknesses with the teaching to which they are exposed. Goswami's chapter highlights that, among factors extrinsic to the child, the orthography of the language in which he or she learns to read will affect the manifestation of reading difficulties. Following extensive research with European languages, she concludes that the level of phonological awareness that is critical for reading development differs according to the way in which the phonology of a language is reflected in its orthography. In turn, different orthographies pose different demands for the dyslexic child.

The chapters by Tallal and her colleagues and by Stackhouse and Wells are both concerned with the interface between spoken and written language disorders. Because learning to read entails the creation of mappings between spoken and printed words, children with phonological difficulties affecting spoken language should be at particular risk of developing dyslexic difficulties. Reporting the educational outcome of pre-school children with language impairments, Tallal argues that this is indeed the case, and Stackhouse and Wells propose a clinical framework within which to assess the difficulties, with a view to intervention.

It is gratifying, given the growth in knowledge of the aetiologies of dyslexia, that there has been scientific validation of some methods of intervention for reading difficulties (see Snowling, 1996, for a review). The final chapters of the book are concerned with interventions designed to help overcome the reading difficulties found in dyslexia. Lindamood describes the methods she has pioneered to enhance the phonological awareness skills of poor readers and also to improve their comprehension strategies. These are used in centres internationally and validation data are reported. Wise and Olson review the large-scale Colorado computer remediation project pointing to both its strengths, which are considerable, and also to future developments planned to further refine and improve it. Finally, Borstrøm and Elbro describe the very exciting finding that classroom-based interventions for children at risk of dyslexia hold the possibility of preventing the development of reading difficulties in the school-age child.

References

Lovegrove, W., Martin, F. & Slaghuis, W. (1986). A theoretical and experimental case for a visual deficit in specific reading disability. *Cognitive Neuropsychology* 3, 225–267.

Scarborough, H.S. (1990) Very early language deficits in dyslexic children. *Child Development* 61, 1728–1743.

Snowling, M.J. (1996). Contemporary approaches to the teaching of reading. *Journal of Child Psychology and Psychiatry* 37, 139–148.

Stein, J. & Fowler, M.S. (1985). Effects of monocular occlusion on visuomotor perception and reading in dyslexic children. *Lancet* 69–73.

Charles Hulme and Maggie Snowling
York, 1997

Acknowledgements

The chapters in this book are based on a selection of papers presented at the Fourth International Conference of the British Dyslexia Association "Dyslexia: Biological Bases, Identification and Intervention" held at the University of York. We would like to thank our colleagues on the Conference Organising Committee for their help and support. We also thank the contributors for cheerfully meeting the very tight deadlines necessitated by our need to publish in time for the conference. Finally, we are very grateful to Ian Walker for his help in proof reading and compiling the indices.

Chapter 1
Brain, Mind and Behaviour in Dyslexia

UTA FRITH

Definitions of Dyslexia and their Paradoxes

Dyslexia is no longer a specialist medical term – it has been thoroughly adopted into everyday language. Everyone knows that dyslexics are not able to read properly and spell in a weird fashion. Dyslexics themselves talk poignantly about their difficulties with written language: 'Letters on a page appeared a meaningless jumble – with no more logic than alphabet spaghetti...I could make no connection between what I heard and what appeared on the page' (Sophy Fisher, *Independent*, Education, 7 November 1996).

There is one major problem with this everyday understanding of dyslexia: it has to do with the legacy of behaviourism. Only observable behaviour and not the unobservable mind was considered the proper object of scientific study. In one sense this view was a healthy stance against unscientific and indulgent speculation. In another sense, however, it acted as a straitjacket by ignoring the reasons underlying the behaviour. This was particularly limiting when trying to explain impairments of behaviour, such as reading difficulties.

The behaviourist era is waning but still casts a long shadow. Discussions about dyslexia are frequently constrained within a space which is entirely defined by surface behaviour: performance on reading, spelling and IQ tests, and differences between them. However, test scores are only the starting points for the scientific study of dyslexia. Whilst increasingly attacked, it must be acknowledged that the behavioural definition of dyslexia as unexpected reading failure, a 'discrepancy', has been extremely helpful. Objectively measurable performance elevates discussion of dyslexia from an unspecified complaint that may be in the mind of the beholder to a reality that is there for all to see. One point many critics have made is that for a discrepancy to be found the child has to have a relatively high IQ test score, which introduces a bias against diagnosing dyslexia in less able children (Siegel, 1992).

Furthermore, in many cases a discrepancy may be present at a particular point in time but not at later ages when reading has improved. A true behaviourist would claim that in this case dyslexia is no longer present. This contrasts with the claim of many dyslexics, namely that the quality of their reading remains slow, effortful and fragile. However, the main limitation of the behavioural definition of dyslexia is that it is easy to forget that the reason for the discrepancy has to be explained. Unexpectedly poor performance on tests is only a sign of an underlying problem; it is not the problem itself.

Levels of Explanation

The restriction of the discussion space to behavioural observations is no longer necessary. This space has been widened by cognitive neuro-science which insists that there is a place for the scientific study of the mind and brain, not just behaviour. There are cognitive abilities under-lying observable behaviour, and these are based on neural systems in the brain. Links between biological, cognitive and behavioural levels are needed for a better understanding of dyslexia. The behaviour can be explained by a cognitive dysfunction; the cognitive dysfunction can be explained by a brain dysfunction. This chain of causal links from brain to mind to behaviour has to be set within the context of environmental and cultural influences. Figure 1.1 lays out the discussion space, taking account of all these factors. This notation has been applied to a number of developmental disorders and has been described by Morton and Frith (1995).

As everyone knows, nature and nurture interact and they cannot be separated from each other. This is obviously true in the case of dyslexia,

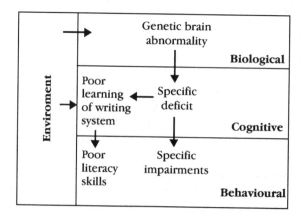

Figure 1.1 Basic causal modelling diagram

where the main effect of the disorder is on literacy, a supremely cultural phenomenon. Framed by both environmental and biological factors, the cognitive level sits in the middle of the space. The way to read the diagram is by starting from the top as follows:

(1) Biological conditions in interaction with environmental conditions can have adverse effects on brain development, causing developmental disorders such as dyslexia. Brain function varies from individual to individual, partly for genetic reasons, including predispositions to certain disorders, and partly for environmental reasons, including quality of nutrition or presence of toxins.

(2) The brain-based predisposition for dyslexia can lead to the subtle malfunction of one single mental component – or possibly several. The nature of the critical component(s) is a matter for theory, subject to rigorous empirical testing. For literacy problems to result the abnormality must compromise the learning of reading and writing skills. The effort involved in learning will depend on the complexity of the writing system as well as the effectiveness of the teaching. Cultural tools here interact with cognitive processes so that the grapheme–phoneme code of the alphabet becomes fully internalised.

(3) The cognitive deficit is reflected in a characteristic pattern of behavioural signs and symptoms. These will vary with age, ability, motivation and many other factors besides (not indicated in the diagram). The relevant factors are not only within the child, but also outside, such as social and physical conditions.

Biological and Environmental Factors in Explanations of Dyslexia

The quest for the 'underlying problem' has been pursued vigorously by brain researchers and geneticists as well as by researchers who are especially interested in social and educational factors. Both approaches have resulted in suggestions for possible causes of dyslexia. For instance, Galaburda (1989) demonstrated abnormal symmetry in the structure of the planum temporale (see also chapter by Hynd in the present volume); Livingstone et al. (1991) identified cellular migration abnormalities in the magnocellular system of the brain which have been related to behavioural findings by Cornelissen et al. (1995; see also chapter by Hogben in the present volume). Genetic linkage studies with dyslexic families have identified regions on chromosomes 15, 1 and most recently 6 (Cardon et al., 1994). On the other hand, possible interventions have been highlighted in studies which aimed to look directly at the causes of learning failure. For instance, poor sound categorisation ability was shown to be causally connected to poor reading performance (Bradley & Bryant, 1978; 1983). Hatcher, Hulme & Ellis. (1994) went on to show that reading failure could be effectively remediated by a combination of training with sounds and letters. However, the knowledge gained from these different approaches has not been well integrated, and in any case is not enough to provide a full explanation of dyslexia.

The Cognitive Level

There is a big gap between an individual child's behaviour and the activity of neurons or genes. There is also a big gap between an individual child's behaviour and methods of instruction. This gap is precisely the space that cognitive psychology has claimed as its own. Biological and sociocultural factors can only be part of a story which has to account for the developmental course of the disorder in a particular individual as well as for the differences between individuals. The promise of cognitive neuroscience is that the cognitive level will connect a range of known behavioural signs to a range of biological and environmental factors influencing development. This includes ideas about deficits in specific cognitive components as well as ideas about protection and risk factors inherent in general cognitive systems. Interactions between these systems might go some way towards explaining the individual differences typically found in developmental disorders.

Any theory proposing a cognitive deficit in dyslexia should be able to explain the cultural impact of the deficit. Dyslexia appears to be a different burden for the individual and for society in different countries. For instance, dyslexia is less of a handicap in Italy or Spain than it is in other European countries. An important question to answer is why learning to read English is so particularly challenging to the dyslexic child. A good theory should also make a link to brain processes. At the same time the identification of a faulty component must be able to explain patterns of behaviour that seem paradoxical to common sense. If there were no separable mental components, then behaviour would seem to be homogeneous and all of a piece. This is patently not what we observe. One of the most striking paradoxes in dyslexia is that a child may be 'unable to see meaning in a written page' and yet be highly intelligent and able to follow an academic career.

Paradoxes in behaviour give clues to the underlying causes of the behaviour. That is why dyslexia is one of the key disorders in the systematic investigation of the architecture of the mind and its basis in the brain. There are two opposite approaches that one might take: One is to identify the specific component that is responsible for the specific test failure, in the belief that such a component must exist if the behaviour suggests that everything else is working perfectly. The other approach is to doubt that there is a specific problem and to look for more general problems. Both of these paths have been taken by different theoreticians and the answer is by no means clear cut. In my view, the evidence favours the notion of a specific deficit. However, it remains to be seen just how specific the deficit is.

An Illustration of the Causal Modelling of Dyslexia with the Hypothesis of a Phonological Deficit Hypothesis

To reiterate the points made previously and originally by Morton and Frith (1995): When trying to explain a developmental disorder, we have to make a distinction between different levels of description. First, there is the biological level and the environmental level; it is here where we may look for causes and cures. Second, there is the behavioural level, where we can make our observations and assessments. Third, there is the cognitive level, which lies in between and makes links in all directions. It is here where the intuitive clinical impression can be captured that the presenting disorder is a distinct and recognisable entity despite variable symptoms. This notation should enable different theories about a disorder to be represented in a neutral fashion.

The diagram in Figure 1.2 illustrates the phonological deficit hypothesis. Of course, this is not a randomly chosen example. The proposal of a phonological deficit as the cognitive basis of dyslexia has such strong

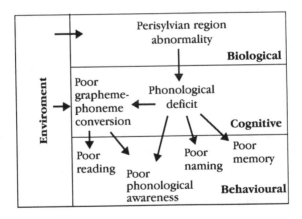

Figure 1.2 Example of causal modelling of dyslexia as a phonological deficit
*Note:*The specific cognitive deficit affects reading through its interaction with the demands of an alphabetic writing system. Learning this system requires the acquisition and internalisation of grapheme to phoneme decoding rules. The tests at the behavioural level are phoneme awareness, naming speed and auditory short-term memory. Other phonological tests could also have been included.

theoretical and empirical support that it has been widely accepted.

This figure uses the same basic diagram as Figure 1.1. Starting with the biological level, it is assumed that there is a brain abnormality which affects areas subserving phonological processing, that is the perisylvian region of the left hemisphere (Galaburda, 1989; Paulesu et al., 1996; Rumsey et al., 1992). Furthermore, the evidence for a genetic origin of dyslexia is increasingly compelling (Pennington, 1990).

We now need to make the crucial link from brain to cognition. If there is an abnormality at the neurological level in a specific brain system, then an abnormality in the mental processes subserved by this system would be expected. Of course, such a consequence is not inevitable: there may be protective factors. Also, there may be sufficient redundancy in the system to avert any further cognitive consequences. We are not talking about a deterministic cause, only a probabilistic one. Let us assume, however, that at least in certain cases, the neurological abnormality causes a weakness in a cognitive component of the phonological system.

Again we need to make a crucial link between levels. We assume that under certain circumstances, bearing in mind the existence of protective and risk factors, the cognitive deficit in the phonological system will give rise to problems in learning to speak and will be a major impediment in the acquisition of written language. This link has stood the test of time in a large number of studies. The target group usually consists of individuals who are clinically diagnosed as dyslexic using a discrepancy criterion, but not using any tests of phonological processing in the diagnostic procedure. The critical question is whether these individuals show impairments in tasks that involve phonological processing. The answer from an impressive number of studies has been yes, they do show such impairments. Listed below are some of the early findings that provided evidence for this conclusion and have proved to be particularly robust:

- Dyslexics are slow at rapid automatic naming (e.g. Denckla & Rudel, 1976).
- They are poor at verbal learning and memory (Nelson & Warrington, 1980).
- They are poor at non-word repetition (e.g. Snowling, 1981).
- They have poor phoneme awareness (Bradley & Bryant, 1978).
- They have difficulties in segmenting phonemes (e.g. Kamhi & Catts, 1986).
- They have difficulties in object naming (e.g. Snowling, Wagtendonk & Stafford, 1988).

These findings have all been replicated in many subsequent studies (see Snowling, 1995). The findings mentioned focus on speech processes and implicate accuracy of processing as well as speed and verbal memory. It remains to be seen whether these are separate problems or whether they are all different facets of the same problem.

Problems in Testing Phonological Competence

A future definition of dyslexia as a phonological deficit is an exciting possibility. For this to be acceptable, a great deal of work needs to be done. It would, for example, be necessary to construct sensitive as well as specific tests. That is, phonological impairments, no matter how subtle, must be identified in true dyslexics, but they should not be observed in individuals who are not dyslexic.

This remains an aim for the future, but its achievement might help to answer the vexed question of whether a specific cognitive deficit can be shown to exist in cases of low intelligence. A second issue that needs to be addressed is to what extent spoken-language processing is affected by literacy practice. Some phonological tests can be solved by virtue of being a proficient reader. This implies that a proficient reader who acquired reading skills by an abnormal route, that is, without an intuitively grounded phonological ability, would be able to achieve good performance on at least some phonological tests. Such a reader would have knowledge of phonology, rather like a music critic may have knowledge of music without being musical. In other words, phonological skills may be acquired in different ways and may mean different things (Perfetti et al., 1987). Phonological awareness in particular is promoted by learning an alphabetic script (Morais et al., 1979; Read et al., 1986). It therefore cannot be a fair test of an individual's phonological ability if that person has not had schooling. It remains to be seen to what extent other phonological skills, such as naming speed, verbal short-term memory and non-word repetition are similarly affected.

Tests always tap many different underlying abilities and are subject to many influences. The lesson from behaviourism is that we must be alert to the danger of mistaking a test score for the inferred underlying ability. A score, regardless of whether it is within the normal range or not, is only a pointer. Because many different influences govern behaviour, not just the single malfunctioning cognitive component, the behavioural signs and symptoms will often be obscured. At the very least they change with age, but they are also subject to active influences from such factors as remedial teaching. The problem at the behavioural level may be disguised and revealed only under stress.

The Relevance of Phonological Processing Ability to Learning to Read

It is not enough to pinpoint a cognitive deficit and find evidence for it in studies of psychological function. It is necessary for a link to be made to the major presenting symptom of dyslexia, namely the unusual and severe difficulties in learning to read and spell. The importance of phonology in learning to read is asserted by all current models (e.g. Goswami & Bryant, 1990; Share, 1995; van Orden, Pennington & Stone, 1990; Wagner & Torgesen, 1987). The main task for a child learning to read an alphabetic system is to understand how speech sounds are represented by letters and how to translate between written and spoken language (Liberman, Shankweiler & Liberman, 1989). How children acquire such an alphabetic strategy is a critical problem for explanation, and many theorists have directed their attention to this (see chapters in Gough, Ehri & Treiman, 1992). It is in acquiring this strategy that phonology is so crucial.

What is the alphabetic strategy? Skill in this strategy can be assessed in non-word reading tasks, where dyslexics show striking impairments (Rack, Snowling & Olson, 1992). Liberman et al. (1989) were among the first to emphasise that alphabetic scripts are based on the principle that the speech stream can be segmented into sub-syllabic components known as phonemes. Because speech is a continuous stream of sound, we are largely unaware of phonemes unless we have learned to read (Morais et al., 1979). Children, when they learn about the alphabetic principle, have to be introduced to this artificial mode of speech segmentation (Liberman et al., 1974). The idea that a phoneme maps onto a grapheme seems quite natural to those of us who are literate. To the beginning reader, however, it is a wholly new concept. Children approaching the task of reading have a phonological lexicon housing thousands of representations of words in their spoken vocabulary. They then have to make a huge leap in their awareness of speech sounds in order to appreciate the alphabetic code which underpins our writing system. This leap is easy to make for those with a well-functioning phonological system, but very hard for those who have some weakness in this system.

Evidence for a Cognitive Deficit which is Specific, Persistent and Universal

Most dyslexic children eventually learn to read and spell. Their performance changes and their test scores can appear normal for their age-group. However, no one who has experience of dyslexia would doubt that dyslexic children become dyslexic adults, regardless of the improvement they show in reading and the improvement they can show on certain phoneme awareness tests. Probably no one would doubt that dyslexia also exists in languages where orthography is so consistent that learning to read is relatively easy, even for dyslexic children. The important questions to ask are whether, in the case of the compensated dyslexic, good reading performance is produced in the same way as in the normal reader, and whether dyslexia in different languages reflects the same underlying problem. Furthermore, it is necessary to establish that this underlying problem is specific so that it does not preclude intact performance in other cognitive functions.

Persistence

The examples of change over time with learning and compensation and the existence of dyslexia in different languages show that it is highly misleading to think of dyslexia purely at the behavioural level. A definition of dyslexia in terms of reading test performance remains at a very superficial level. It is rather like defining an infection as an increase in body temperature. Raised temperature, however, is merely a sign of the infection, not the illness itself. Quite a different metaphor is needed when we talk about dyslexia. All the research evidence indicates that dyslexia is not a disease which comes with school and goes away with adulthood. It is not a temporary childhood affliction. It is a lifelong burden. Of course, this does not mean immutability and impossibility of affecting change – far from it. Change over time in a developing organism is inevitable – and dramatic changes in behaviour can be effected by education and its tools.

Longitudinal studies provide evidence for both the persistence of underlying problems and the change in the behavioural manifestation. An important prospective study, carried out by Scarborough (1990), showed that children who were later diagnosed as dyslexic showed subtle language impairments at age 2. These were manifested primarily in slower vocabulary and syntactic development. Gallagher, Frith & Snowling (submitted) also found that children who were at familial risk of dyslexia showed phonological impairments at age 3 compared with children from unaffected families. The children at risk of dyslexia found it difficult to repeat non-words with an unusual stress pattern (weak–strong as in the word balloon), but not those with a familiar strong–weak pattern (as in the word basket). They were also less able to recall nursery rhymes and, in those they did remember, they were less likely to notice and correct a deliberate non-rhyming error (Humpty Dumpty...had a great *tumble*). Vocabulary skills were also less well developed in this group, but not story-telling skills, or articulation. These findings indicate a central phonological rather than a peripheral impairment with wider repercussions for language acquisition in general. In this study it was also found that the children at risk of dyslexia knew significantly fewer letters than the comparison group, even though neither group had experienced any formal teaching. This inequality in letter knowledge before the start of reading instruction makes subsequent differences in reading ability more than likely.

The continuation of difficulties into adulthood even in those individuals who have compensated for their reading problems and who can achieve a normal score on both word and non-word reading tests has also been demonstrated (Paulesu et al., 1996). Increasingly, adults with dyslexia are being studied and phonological difficulties can be demonstrated (Bruck, 1992; Elbro, Nielsen & Petersen, 1994; Pennington et al.,

1990). This is particularly clear in novel and challenging phoneme manipulation tests, such as spoonerisms (John Lennon becomes 'lon jennon') and phonemic fluency (say as many words as you can in one minute starting with 'f'). Such a result has been found, for example, by Gallagher et al. (1996) who compared students preparing for university entrance exams with controls of the same intelligence and mathematics exam result. Whilst reading performance did not distinguish these groups, challenging phonological tests did.

Universality

If we define dyslexia as a phonological deficit regardless of difficulties with written language, then it should exist in many different languages regardless of the writing system, and even in pre-literate societies. However, if we define dyslexia primarily as a problem in the acquisition of written language, then we can probably identify the condition only in alphabetic writing systems. As argued above, these systems make very high demands on phonological ability. Other writing systems based on syllables or whole-word sounds or meanings would be equally difficult to learn for individuals with and without a phonological weakness.

A number of orthographic comparisons have been made. I will use the example of German, which has a more transparent orthography than English and in which children are taught in a systematic phonics-oriented fashion. Dyslexia is also diagnosed in German-speaking countries. However, the instruments used for diagnosis have to be different from those used in English-speaking countries. On the whole, German-speaking dyslexics do not make word or non-word reading errors. They can rely on a very consistent orthography to achieve correct pronunciations. Even with long words such as 'Schokoladentorte' the piecemeal sounding out of consonants and vowels or familiar consonant–vowel combinations, when put together, closely resemble the pronunciation of the whole-word sound. In German, the critical test is the time taken to decode a word or non-word. This time is significantly slower in the case of dyslexics. Even though individuals with dyslexia can in theory decode a novel word very accurately, they will often give up before the decoding process is finished (Wimmer & Frith, 1994). Landerl, Wimmer & Frith (submitted) showed that, despite the different manifestation of dyslexia in non-word reading in the two languages, German-speaking dyslexics have just as much difficulty with a phoneme manipulation task as English-speaking dyslexics.

Specificity

The notion of specificity arises because many abilities are well developed in dyslexics and the problems usually stand out as 'unexpected' in relation to their intelligence. In fact the discrepancy definition of dyslexia makes specificity a requirement for diagnosis. However, just how specific is the deficit is that is hypothesised to underlie dyslexia? Are there degrees of severity? Are there qualitative differences in the underlying problems such that different subtypes result? All these questions have yet to be resolved.

The phonological deficit hypothesis assumes that there is a degree of specificity, in that phonology but not semantics is targeted as the core problem, and output rather than input phonology (e.g. Snowling, 1987; Pennington et al., 1990). At the same time, non-verbal ability is presumed to be intact. This is justified on the basis of normal performance on a range of other scholastic achievements and IQ tests. However, research often uncovers the existence of other subtle problems which appear to be unrelated to verbal intelligence. For instance, Slaghuis, Lovegrove & Davidson (1993) pointed out that phonological weakness is often accompanied by subtle visual impairments. Nicolson and Fawcett (1995) report impairments on a wide range of abilities involving motor control. These possibilities will be discussed in more detail below.

The precise nature of the phonological deficit remains tantalisingly elusive. One possibility is that a single component in the phonological system is faulty; another is that crucial connections between the various components do not work (see below). The issue is even more complicated when we try to disentangle associated deficits in other brain functions. Thus a faulty pathway may affect different parts of the brain and may result in additional difficulties that may or may not influence language-related processes.

Evidence for a Link between Brain and Cognition: a Brain-imaging Experiment on Phonological Processing in Dyslexia

The phonological deficit hypothesis of dyslexia suggested a brain-imaging experiment on five well-compensated adult dyslexics, which was conducted by Paulesu et al. (1996). It is worth describing this experiment briefly as an illustrative example, as it shows how cognitive concepts and brain function can be studied together. The dyslexic volunteers taking part in the study had been assessed as children or adolescents when they had severe reading and spelling difficulties. All except one were university graduates. The normal control group consisted of graduates of the same age.

The tasks that the volunteers had to perform during the scan were extremely simple: rhyme judgement (does B rhyme with T?) and memory (was a target letter present in a previously seen series of six letters?). These tasks engage the phonological system even though nothing is heard and nothing is spoken. The letters were presented visually and the volunteers had to press a yes/no button. In order to make the rhyme judgement it was necessary to evoke the letter sounds internally and segment them in order to decide whether or not the final sound segment rhymed (the /ee/ sound in /b-ee/ and in /t-ee/ is the same). In the memory task, where it was necessary to judge whether or not a letter had been seen before, subjects silently rehearsed the names of the letters as they were presented. This rehearsal is apparently quite automatic and normally enhances memory performance.

During PET scanning blood flow is made visible by means of a radioactive tracer. Blood flow indirectly measures increases in neural activity at particular locations in the brain. An increase in activity was clearly seen in both groups during the critical tasks. It was not seen during two extremely similar control tasks which used non-verbal symbols instead of letters. Here the subject had to make a yes/no decision about whether one symbol was visually similar to another, and had to indicate whether a particular symbol was amongst the six preceding ones. The symbols were based on Korean letters and the subjects found them quite impossible to name. The tasks therefore did not involve any form of inner speech.

The difference in brain activity between phonological and visual tasks was very clear. The phonological tasks activated the phonological system of the brain which is situated in the left hemisphere around the perisylvian fissure. It is a large area composed of four major systems: Broca's area, Wernicke's area (superior temporal gyrus), the insula, and IPL (inferior parietal lobule). Broca's area is near the front of the brain, and if damaged, leads to severe loss of the ability to speak. Further back is Wernicke's area, damage to which results in loss of intelligible speech so that only gibberish is produced. In between these areas lies the insula, insult to which leads to the inability to repeat speech. Above lies an area which is thought to function as a phonological store, because if it is injured, the patient is unable to recall even short sequences of words or digits. All these areas were activated in concert by the normal volunteers during the phonological tasks. The dyslexics did not show such concerted activity in the system as a whole, and on closer inspection it was clear that they did not activate the insula at all. This experiment demonstrates that even compensated dyslexics show evidence of brain dysfunction. Doing very simple phonological tasks was no problem for these subjects and yet it appears that neural activity while performing these tasks is abnormal.

We can interpret the findings in the following way. The dyslexics could not easily evoke internal speech sounds. Thus they performed even simple phonological tasks very differently from normal individuals. This was because they could not rely on the fully coordinated action of all the areas of the language and speech system. This seemingly effortless coordination makes it easy for normal people to internally evoke, edit and compare speech sounds. It may well be that the insula is normally involved in this function. This study suggests that dyslexia might be due to a disconnection between language systems.

The findings from this brain-imaging study support the assumption of a specific failure in one particular brain system. A difference was shown in a specific region during specific tasks. In the tasks that used non-verbal symbols, dyslexics showed a normal pattern. However, in another brain imaging study, Eden et al. (1996) found that an area of the brain involved in the perception of visual motion was less active in dyslexics than in normals when the task was to detect whether random dots were or were not moving in a particular direction. This task has been shown to distinguish dyslexic from non-dyslexic individuals (Cornelissen et al., 1995). This mental function is difficult to link with the acquisition of reading skills, and suggests the possibility of correlated dysfunctions in other parts of the brain.

Associated Problems, Secondary Consequences and Other Causes of Dyslexia

The question posed at the beginning of this chapter was whether dyslexia can be explained by a specific deficit in one mental component alone, or whether the problem is in fact more general. This touches on a very important theoretical issue in the conception of the brain and the mind. It is widely held that the brain is structured in such a way that it contains many different specialised organs, just as the body does. Of course it goes without saying that all of these specialised organs have to be coordinated and have to work together. They are also influenced by the same general factors, for instance blood supply or temperature. At the same time it is important to acknowledge that during early development the brain is not as specialised as it is in the adult. However, the plasticity of the developing brain is limited. Speculatively, there may be a number of problems which are part and parcel of one and the same biological structure, resulting from some abnormality before differentiation into different brain components occurred. A consequence of this argument for the explanation of dyslexia is to look for other problems besides those connected with spoken and written language. The problems in visual motion detection might perhaps be explained in this way. Figure 1.3 illustrates this possibility.

Other more general theories have also been offered as explanations for the different areas of cognitive dysfunction seen in dyslexia. One of these focuses on problems of rapid temporal perception (Miller & Tallal, 1995). These problems might encompass different modalities, not just auditory perception. Another theory suggests weakness in motor

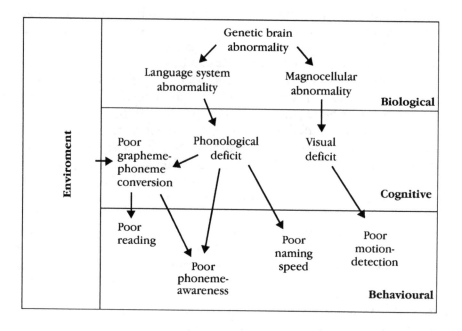

Figure 1.3 Example of causal modelling of dyslexia as a deficit in both visual and phonological systems based on the findings by Eden et al. (1996)
Note: The visual deficit is illustrated to lead to a marker symptom: poor motion detection. The causal link between a magnocellular deficit and impairment in motion detection is shown in the diagram as separate from the phonological deficit and not directly involved in the origin of reading problems.

control and time estimation, functions thought to be under the direct control of the cerebellum. These could also affect the motor and timing aspects of speech processing (Nicolson & Fawcett, 1995). Thus, phonological impairments would be explained as consequences of a more general deficit which also affects balance. This theory is illustrated in Figure 1.4.

Other candidates for specific cognitive causes of literacy failure include visual problems such as exaggerated effects of visual stress which can be alleviated by reducing glare (Wilkins, 1995). Visual memory failure is also plausible in the explanation of poor spelling, where the individual seems unable to remember a sequence of letters (Goulandris & Snowling, 1991). Sequential ordering problems and problems in the processing of visual word forms are other possibilities (Seymour, 1986).

Secondary consequences of reading failure, e.g. refusal and oppositional attitudes also need to be considered and distinguished from primary general problems. It is said that diagnosis itself is often the first therapeutic step in an otherwise misunderstood and misinterpreted

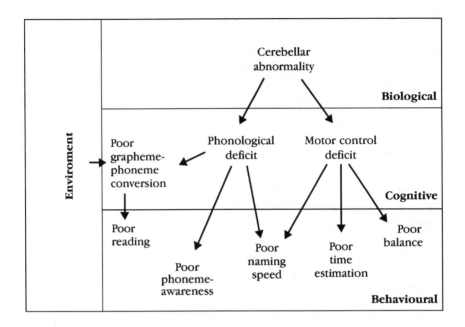

Figure 1.4 Example of causal modelling of dyslexia as a cerebellar abnormality based on the proposal by Nicolson and Fawcett (1995)
Note: This brain abnormality affects speech processing as well as more general motor control processes including time estimation. The effect of the abnormality on reading acquisition is illustrated as mediated by a phonological deficit which in turn is a consequence of a speech motor deficit.

pattern of problems. A better understanding of dyslexia could therefore have the very practical benefits of preventing the unnecessary spiral of failure, poor self-esteem and maladjustment. Presumably the damaging experience of failure can be avoided if dyslexia is diagnosed before the child experiences such failure.

Individual Variability and Compensation

In the preceding sections I have argued that dyslexia is a genetically based neuro-developmental disorder. But what does this imply for individual cases? Why does the disorder happen in a particular individual and what problems might it lead to in the individual's life? What can be done to prevent or remediate such problems as they occur? It is important to remember that we are only considering probabilities, not certainties. The notion of cause and effect as experienced by us when dealing with the mechanical world does not apply to the mental world. For instance, while highlighting a specific deficit in one mental component it is necessary to remember the effect of general cognitive systems that will play an important role in the alleviation or possible aggravation of the effects of a specific deficit. One general cognitive system is intelligence, another is planning and monitoring thought and action. Yet another is integration of information in the search for meaning. There are normal individual differences in all three of these systems, and these can be seen as protective or risk factors.

Influence of general cognitive factors

Even with the same phonological disorder one individual may adjust well and find ways of learning through different means; another may not cope well and may need constant support. Low general ability is obviously a limiting factor in the development of compensatory strategies. High ability on the other hand might well allow the extra resources needed to enhance the use of a general route when a specific route is blocked. Likewise, it is easy to see that a problem in the attention system could affect the learning of spoken and written language. Attention deficits lead to problems precisely when new skills have to be learned. An attention deficit would, however, result in poor learning and achievement in a whole range of school subjects, not just reading. If there were an additional phonological deficit, this would clearly aggravate the problem. In the case of information integration which appears to be another dimension where individual differences can be found, a strong tendency to extract gist would help in the effort involved when decoding individual words. Looking for overall meaning might well be a very effective means of overcoming a weakness in decoding (e.g. Frith & Snowling, 1983; Stanovich, West & Freeman, 1981) .

Influence of cultural factors

The single most important factor in the prevention and remediation of dyslexia is without doubt the protective influence of culture. This is not only through the fostering of positive attitudes towards written language and the provision of schools, and teachers trained in the art of teaching children with dyslexia. Culture also influences the outcome of dyslexia through the writing system it adopts, which in the case of a complex and inconsistent orthography can act as a risk factor. The phonology of a particular language may itself play a role in the ease or difficulty of learning to speak. Not all languages are equal in terms of the complexity of their phonology or their grammar. This aspect of cultural heritage in the development of language has hardly been explored. We may speak of dyslexia-friendly languages and writing systems and contrast them with those that are challenging for dyslexics. The arguments put forward in this chapter suggest that languages and writing systems can mitigate the outward symptoms of the underlying neurocognitive deficit, even if the deficit itself remains. The use of computer spell checkers, for example, has dramatically improved dyslexic spelling within one generation, within the same language, and without change of instructional methods.

Conclusions

There is a general consensus that dyslexia is a lifelong developmental disorder with a biological origin. There is some evidence for a genetic basis, and there is some evidence for a brain basis, although in both fields the work is only just beginning. There may be many different kinds of genes and different kinds of brain conditions interacting with environmental influences that are ultimately responsible for dyslexia. Cultural influences can be seen in the strikingly different behavioural manifestations of dyslexia in different countries. They can also be seen in the effectiveness of teaching and achievement of compensation. Whilst there is much variability in the behavioural signs, and presumed variability in the biological basis of dyslexia, the underlying cognitive deficit appears to be circumscribed, specific, persistent and universal. For these reasons it appears that the cognitive level of description provides a unifying theory of dyslexia. Such a theory is necessary to pull together the many different observational strands in this most intriguing and subtle disorder.

References

Bradley, L. & Bryant, P. (1978). Difficulties in auditory organization as a possible cause of reading backwardness. *Nature* **271**, 746–747.

Bradley, L. & Bryant, P. (1983). Categorising sounds and learning to read: a causal connection. *Nature* **303**, 419–421.

Bruck, M. (1992). Persistence of dyslexics' phonological awareness deficits. *Developmental Psychology* **28**, 874–886.

Cardon, L.R., Smith, S.D., Fulker, D.W., Kimberling, W.J., Pennington, B. F. & DeFries, J.C. (1994). Quantitative trait locus for reading disability on chromosome 6. *Science* **266**, 276–279.

Cornelissen, P., Richardson, A., Mason, A., Fowler, S. & Stein, J. (1995). Contrast sensitivity and coherent motion detection measured at photopic luminance levels in dyslexics and controls. *Vision Research* **35**, 1483–1494.

Denckla, M. & Rudel, R.G. (1976). Rapid 'automatized' naming (R.A.N.) dyslexia differentiated from other learning disabilities. *Neuropsychologia* **14**, 471–479.

Eden, G.F., VanMeter, J.W., Rumsey, J.M., Maisog, J.M., Woods, R.P. & Zeffiro, T.A. (1996). Abnormal processing of visual motion in dyslexia revealed by functional brain imaging. *Nature* **382**, 66–69.

Elbro, C., Nielsen, I. & Petersen D.K. (1994). Dyslexia in adults: Evidence for deficits in non-word reading and in the phonological representation of lexical items. *Annals of Dyslexia* **44**, 295–326.

Frith, U. & Snowling, M. (1983.) Reading for meaning and reading for sound in autistic and dyslexic children. *British Journal of Developmental Psychology* **1**, 329–342.

Galaburda, A. (1989). Ordinary and extraordinary brain development: Anatomical variation in developmental dyslexia. *Annals of Dyslexia* **39**, 67–79.

Gallagher, A.M., Frith, U. & Snowling, M. (submitted). Language processing skills in children at risk of developmental dyslexia.

Gallagher, A.M., Laxon, V., Armstrong, E. & Frith, U. (1996). Phonological difficulties in high-functioning dyslexics. *Reading and Writing* **8**, 499–509.

Goswami, U. & Bryant, P. (1990). *Phonological Skills and Learning to Read*. Hove, UK: Laurence Erlbaum.

Gough, P., Ehri, L. & Treiman, R. (1992). *Reading Acquisition*. Hillsdale, NJ: Lawrence Erlbaum.

Goulandris, N. & Snowling, M. (1991). Visual memory deficits: A plausible cause of developmental dyslexia? Evidence from a single case study. *Cognitive Neuropsychology* **8**, 127–154.

Hatcher, P.J., Hulme, C. & Ellis, A. (1994). Ameliorating early reading failure by integrating the teaching of reading and phonological skills: The phonological linkage hypothesis. *Child Development* **65**, 41–57.

Kamhi, A.G. & Catts, H.W. (1986). Toward an understanding of developmental language and reading disorders. *Journal of Speech and Hearing Disorders* **51**, 337–347.

Landerl, K., Wimmer, H. & Frith, U. (in press). The impact of orthographic consistency on dyslexia: A German–English comparison. *Cognition*.

Liberman, I.Y., Shankweiler, D. & Liberman, A.M. (1989). The alphabetic principle and learning to read. In D. Shankweiler & I.Y. Liberman (Eds.) *Phonology and Reading Disability*, pp. 1–34. Ann Arbor: University of Michigan Press.

Liberman, I.Y., Shankweiler, D., Fischer, F.W. & Carter, B. (1974). Explicit syllable and phoneme segmentation in the young child. *Journal of Experimental Child Psychology* **18**, 201–212.

Livingstone, M.S., Rosen, G.D., Drislane, F.W. & Galaburda, A. M. (1991). Physiological and anatomical evidence for a magnocellular defect in developmental dyslexia. *Proceedings of the National Academy of Science USA* **88**, 7943–7947.

Miller, S.L. & Tallal, P. (1995). A behavioral neuroscience approach to developmental language disorders: Evidence for a rapid temporal processing deficit. In D. Cicchetti & D.J. Cohen (Eds.) *Developmental Psychopathology*, Vol. 2, (pp 274-298.) New York: Wiley.

Morais, J., Cary, L., Alegria, J. & Bertelson, P. (1979). Does awareness of speech as a sequence of phones arise spontaneously? *Cognition* **7**, 323–331.

Morton, J. & Frith, U. (1995). Causal modelling: A structural approach to developmental psychopathology. In D. Cicchetti & D.J. Cohen (Eds.) *Manual of Developmental Psychopathology*, (pp. 357–390.) New York: Wiley.

Nelson, H. & Warrington, E.K. (1980). An investigation of memory functions in dyslexic children. *British Journal of Psychology* **71**, 487–503.

Nicolson, R.I. & Fawcett, A.J. (1995). Dyslexia is more than a phonological disability. *Dyslexia: An International Journal of Research and Practice* **1**, 19–37.

Paulesu, E., Frith, U., Snowling, M., Gallagher, A., Morton, J., Frackowiak, R.S.J. & Frith, C.D. (1996). Is developmental dyslexia a disconnection syndrome? Evidence from PET scanning. *Brain* **119**, 143–157.

Pennington, B. F. (1990). The genetics of dyslexia. *Journal of Child Psychology and Psychiatry* **31**, 193–201.

Pennington, B.F., VanOrden, G.C., Smith S.D., Grenn, P.A. & Haith, M.M. (1990). Phonological processing skills and deficits in adult dyslexics. *Child Development* **61**, 1753–1778.

Perfetti, C.A., Beck, L., Bell, L. & Hughes, C. (1987). Phonemic knowledge and learning to read are reciprocal: A longitudinal study of first grade children. *Merrill-Palmer Quarterly* **33**, 282–319.

Rack, J.P., Snowling, M. & Olson R.K. (1992). The nonword reading deficit in developmental dyslexia: a review. *Reading Research Quarterly* **27**, 28–53.

Read, C., Zhang, Y., Nie, H. & Ding, B. (1986). The ability to manipulate speech sounds depends on knowing alphabetic writing. *Cognition* **24**, 31–44.

Rumsey, J.M., Andreason, P., Zametkin, A.J., Aquino, T., King, A.C., Hamburger, S.D., Pikus, A., Rapoport, J.L., & Cohen, R.M. (1992). Failure to activate the left temporoparietal cortex in dyslexia. *Archives of Neurology* **49**, 527–534.

Scarborough, H. S. (1990). Very early language deficits in dyslexic children. *Child Development* **61**, 1728–1743.

Seymour, P.H.K. (1986). *Cognitive Analysis of Dyslexia*. London: Routledge & Kegan Paul.

Share, D.L. (1995). Phonological recoding and self-teaching: The sine qua non of reading acquisition. *Cognition* **55**., 151–218.

Siegel, L.S. (1992). An evaluation of the discrepancy definition of dyslexia. *Journal of Learning Disabilities* **25**, 618–629.

Slaghuis, W. L., Lovegrove, W.J. & Davidson, J.A. (1993). Visual and language processing deficits are concurrent in dyslexia. *Cortex* **29**, 601–615.

Snowling, M. (1981). Phonemic deficits in developmental dyslexia. *Psychological Research* **43**, 219–234.

Snowling, M. (1987). *Dyslexia: A Cognitive-Developmental Perspective*. Oxford: Blackwell.

Snowling, M. (1995). Phonological processing and developmental dyslexia. *Journal of Research in Reading* **18**, 132–138.

Snowling, M., van Wagtendonk, B. & Stafford, C. (1988). Object-naming deficits in developmental dyslexia. *Journal of Research in Reading* **11**, 67–85.

Stanovich, K.E. , West, R.F. & Freeman, D.J. (1981). A longitudinal study of sentence context effects in second grade children: tests of an interactive compensatory model. *Journal of Experimental Child Psychology* **32**, 185–199.

van Orden, G.C., Pennington, B.F. & Stone, G.O. (1990). Word identification in reading and the promise of subsymbolic psycholinguistics. *Psychological Review* **97**, 488–522.

Wagner, R. K. & Torgesen, J. K. (1987). The nature of phonological processing and its causal role in the acquisition of reading skills. *Psychological Bulletin* **101**, 192–212.

Wilkins, A. (1995). *Visual Stress*. Oxford: Oxford University Press.

Wimmer, H. & Frith, U. (1994). Reading difficulties among English and German children: Same cause – different manifestation. In U. Frith, G. Luedi, M. Egli & C.A. Zuber (Eds.) *Proceedings of the ESF Workshop on Contexts of Literacy*, 3, pp. 257—274. Strasbourg: European Science Foundation.

Chapter 2
Genetic Aetiologies of Reading and Spelling Deficits: Developmental Differences

J. C. DeFRIES, MARICELA ALARCÓN AND RICHARD K. OLSON

Results from previous twin studies provide evidence that reading difficulties are due in part to heritable influences (DeFries & Alarcón, 1996). For example, an early review by Zerbin-Rüdin (1967) included data from six case studies of twin pairs with 'congenital word-blindness', a small Danish twin study, and six pairs of twins from Hallgren's (1950) family study of specific dyslexia. The probandwise concordance rates (proportion of pairs in which both twins were affected) for the 17 identical (monozygotic [MZ]) and 34 fraternal (dizygotic [DZ]) twin pairs in the combined sample were 100% and 52%, respectively. Because MZ twins are genetically identical, whereas DZ twins share only about one-half of their segregating genes, on average, this result suggests that reading deficits may be highly heritable. However, case studies of concordant twin pairs are more likely to be reported than those of discordant pairs (Harris, 1986); thus, recruitment biases may have artificially inflated the concordance rates for the twin pairs included in Zerbin-Rüdin's (1967) review.

Bakwin (1973) subsequently used parental interviews, telephone calls and mail questionnaires to obtain reading history information from 338 same-sex twin pairs recruited through mothers-of-twin clubs. From this initial sample, Bakwin identified 31 pairs of MZ twins and 31 pairs of DZ twins in which at least one member of each pair had 'a reading level below the expectation derived from the child's performance in other school subjects' (p. 184). Although the ascertainment procedures employed in this study were different from those used in the studies reviewed by Zerbin-Rüdin (1967), the probandwise concordance rates for the twin pairs included in Bakwin's (1973) sample were only slightly lower, i.e. 91% and 45% for MZ and DZ twins, respectively.

More recently, Stevenson et al. (1984, 1987) reported results from the first twin study of reading disability in which children were administered standardised tests of intelligence, reading and spelling. The Schonell Graded Word Reading and Spelling Tests (Schonell & Schonell, 1960) and the Neale Analysis of Reading Ability (Neale, 1967) were administered to 285 pairs of 13-year-old twins ascertained from primary schools in the London area or by screening hospital records in five London boroughs. Resulting test scores were then used to diagnose these children for reading or spelling 'backwardness' (i.e., reading or spelling age more than 18 months below chronological age) and reading or spelling 'retardation' (18 months or more below the expected reading or spelling age predicted by IQ and chronological age). Rates of these disabilities were somewhat lower in MZ twins than in DZ twins (8.9%–14.2% versus 15.0%–25.5%, respectively), resulting in samples of 14 to 19 pairs of MZ twins and 27 to 43 pairs of DZ twins in which at least one member of each pair had a reading or spelling disability. For the various diagnostic categories, the probandwise concordance rates of MZ and DZ twin pairs were as follows: reading backward (Neale), 38% and 54%; reading backward (Schonell), 50% and 43%; reading retarded (Neale), 33% and 29%; reading retarded (Schonell), 35% and 31%; spelling backward, 59% and 41%; and spelling retarded, 50% and 33%. Based upon this result, Stevenson et al. (1987) hypothesised a developmental dissociation between reading and spelling deficits in children. Whereas genetic factors may be important as a cause of reading disability at younger ages, spelling difficulties appear to be more heritable than reading deficits at 13 years of age: 'In particular, the emergence of spelling as the most clearly genetically influenced literacy skill may well be due to developmental changes that would not have been found at an earlier age' (Stevenson et al., 1987, p. 243).

In order to assess possible developmental differences in the genetic aetiology of reading disability, Wadsworth et al. (1989) analysed composite reading scores from MZ and DZ twin pairs tested in the Colorado Twin Study of Reading Disability. The sample included 99 pairs of identical twins and 73 pairs of same-sex fraternal twins in which at least one member of each pair was diagnosed as being reading disabled (the proband) using objective criteria. However, instead of employing a comparison of concordance rates in MZ and DZ twin pairs to assess genetic aetiology, Wadsworth et al. (1989) used a statistically more powerful and versatile multiple regression methodology (DeFries & Fulker, 1985, 1988). A basic regression model that predicted a co-twin's score from the proband's score and the coefficient of relationship was fitted separately to data from younger (<11.5 years) and older (11.5 –20.2 years) twin pairs. Resulting estimates of h^2g, an index of the extent to which the deficit of probands is due to heritable influences, were 0.60 and 0.38 in the younger and older groups, respectively. Although these results indicated that genetic factors may be more important as a cause of reading problems in younger children, the difference between these two estimates of h^2g was not significant.

Wadsworth et al. (1989) also conducted a preliminary test of the Stevenson et al. (1987) hypothesis of a possible developmental dissociation between reading and spelling difficulties by fitting the basic regression model separately to word recognition, reading comprehension, and spelling sub-test scores of twin pairs in their sample. Tests for differential genetic aetiology as a function of age were non-significant for each of these measures, but differences in h^2g estimated from data of the younger and older twin pairs were somewhat larger for word recognition (0.57 vs 0.36) and reading comprehension (0.68 vs 0.31) than for spelling (0.63 vs 0.52). Thus, the results of this study tended to support the hypothesis of Stevenson et al. (1987) that genetic factors may be more salient as a cause of spelling difficulties than of reading deficits in older children. However, estimates of h^2g for a given measure should be obtained from samples in which at least one member of each twin pair has a deviant score for that measure (DeFries & Fulker, 1985, 1988); thus, more appropriate estimates of h^2g for the three sub-test scores would have been obtained if samples of twins had been reselected for deficits in the individual measures.

Subsequently, DeFries et al. (1991) fitted the basic regression model to spelling data from 100 pairs of MZ twins and 71 pairs of same-sex DZ twins tested in the Colorado Twin Study, and also to data from 12 pairs of MZ twins and 15 pairs of same-sex DZ twins tested in the London Twin Study of reading disability. For both samples, twin pairs included at least one member with a spelling score one standard deviation or more below the mean of the study sample and a Verbal or Performance IQ of at least 90. However, in the Colorado study, a positive school history of reading problems was an additional ascertainment criterion. Different spelling measures were also employed in the two studies. In the Colorado study, subjects were administered the Spelling sub-test of the Peabody Individual Achievement Test (PIAT) (Dunn & Markwardt, 1970), a test of spelling recognition. In contrast, the Schonell Spelling Test (Schonell & Schonell, 1960) used in the London study requires subjects to generate correct spellings of individual words. In spite of these procedural differences between the two studies, the resulting estimates of h^2g were remarkably similar, namely 0.62 and 0.61, respectively. This similarity of results obtained from two independent twin studies strengthens the evidence for a substantial genetic aetiology for spelling deficits. Moreover, because these h^2g estimates for spelling were somewhat higher than that reported by DeFries and Gillis (1991) for a composite measure of reading performance (0.50), the authors concluded that their results supported the suggestion of Stevenson et al. (1984) that spelling may be less susceptible than reading to environmental influences.

Since the preliminary developmental-genetic analysis of reading and spelling data from the Colorado Twin Study of Reading Disability (Wadsworth et al., 1989), the sample size in this ongoing study has almost doubled. Thus, the primary objective of the present study is to test the hypothesis that the genetic aetiologies of reading and spelling deficits change differentially as a function of age in this larger sample of twin pairs. In order to obtain appropriate estimates of h^2g for word recognition, reading comprehension and spelling in younger and older age-groups, as well as for a composite measure of reading performance, samples of twins were reselected with deficits in these individual measures. Finally, data from the co-twins of probands with both word recognition and spelling deficits were subjected to a repeated-measures analysis of variance to assess the statistical significance of an apparent differential change in the aetiologies of these two measures as a function of age.

Method

Sample

Because of the paucity of previous twin studies of reading disability, a new twin study (Decker & Vandenberg, 1985) was initiated in 1982 as part of a programme project (DeFries, 1985) supported by the National Institute of Child Health and Human Development (NICHD). In this ongoing study, now supported by the NICHD-funded Colorado Learning Disabilities Research Center (DeFries et al., in press), MZ and DZ twin pairs in which at least one member of each pair had a school history of reading problems, and a comparison group of twins with a negative school history, are being administered an extensive battery of tests including the WISC-R (Wechsler, 1974) or the WAIS-R (Wechsler, 1981), the Peabody Individual Achievement Test (PIAT) (Dunn & Markwardt, 1970), and various other psychometric tests.

In order to minimise the possibility of referral bias (Vogel, 1990), twin pairs are systematically ascertained from 27 cooperating school districts within the state of Colorado. First, without regard to their school achievement, all twin pairs in a school are identified by administrators and school personnel. Permission is then sought from parents of twins to review the school records of both members of each pair for evidence of reading deficits. If either member of a twin pair manifests a positive school history of reading problems (e.g. low achievement test scores, referral to therapists because of poor reading performance, etc.), both members of the pair are invited to complete an extensive battery of tests in the laboratories of J. C. DeFries and R. K. Olson at the University of Colorado, Boulder, and in B. F. Pennington's laboratory at the University of Denver.

Data from the PIAT Reading Recognition, Reading Comprehension and Spelling sub-tests are then used to compute a discriminant function score for each child employing coefficients estimated from an analysis of PIAT data obtained from an independent sample of 140 non-twin children with reading disabilities and 140 controls tested during an early phase of the program project (DeFries, 1985). Twin pairs are included in the proband (reading-disabled) sample if at least one member of the pair with a positive school history of reading problems is also classified as affected by the discriminat score; has a Verbal or Performance IQ of at least 90; shows no evidence of significant neurological, emotional or behavioural problems; and has no uncorrected visual or auditory acuity deficits. Control twins are matched to probands on the basis of age, gender and school district, have no school history of reading problems, and are classified as unaffected by the discriminant score.

Selected items from the Nichols and Bilbro (1966) twin questionnaire are used to determine zygosity. In doubtful cases, zygosity is confirmed by analysing blood samples. Twin pairs were reared primarily in middle-class homes in which American English is spoken, and ranged in age from 8;1 to 20;2 years at the time of testing.

As of 31 May 1996, a total of 195 pairs of MZ twins and 145 pairs of same-sex DZ twins met our criteria for inclusion in the proband analysis sample. In addition, a total of 187 pairs of MZ twins and 117 pairs of same-sex DZ twins comprised the control sample.

Referred or clinic samples of children with reading difficulties typically include three or four times as many boys as girls (Vogel, 1990). In contrast, the gender ratio in our proband sample does not differ substantially from 1:1. For example, our current sample of MZ and same-sex DZ twins includes 247 male probands and 225 female probands, a gender ratio of 1.10:1. Because female MZ twin pairs tend to be over-represented in twin studies (Lykken et al., 1978), this relatively low gender ratio in our proband sample may have been due in part to a differential volunteer rate for male and female MZ twin pairs. In agreement with this expectation, the gender ratio in our sample of MZ probands (0.93:1) is lower than that for the same-sex DZ probands (1.44:1). Nevertheless, both of these gender ratios are substantially lower than those typically found in referred samples of children with reading deficits; thus, the relatively high gender ratios observed in referred and clinic samples may be due in part to a referral bias (cf., Shaywitz et al., 1990; Vogel, 1990).

The probandwise concordance rate for reading disability in the 195 MZ twin pairs included in the present study is 0.67, whereas that for the 145 same-sex DZ pairs is 0.37, a highly significant difference ($p < 0.001$). Thus, the results obtained in this twin study also suggest that reading disability is partly a consequence of heritable influences.

Analyses

For categorical variables (e.g. presence or absence of a disease), a comparison of concordance rates in MZ and DZ twin pairs can provide prima facie evidence for a genetic aetiology; however, children with reading disability are identified in part because of deviant scores on continuous measures (e.g. reading performance) with arbitrary cut-off points (Stevenson et al., 1987). Transformation of a continuous measure of reading performance into a categorical variable obviously results in a loss of important information about reading performance. To analyse continuous data from twin pairs identified because of reading difficulties, DeFries and Fulker (1985, 1988) proposed a multiple regression analysis that provides a better test of genetic aetiology.

When MZ and DZ probands have been identified because of deviant scores on a continuous measure, the scores of their co-twins are expected to regress towards the mean of the unselected population. However, to the extent that the average deficit of the probands is due to genetic influences, this regression towards the mean should differ for the MZ and DZ co-twins. Because members of MZ twin pairs are genetically identical, whereas DZ pairs share only about one-half of their segregating genes on average, the scores of DZ co-twins should regress more towards the mean than those of MZ co-twins if the proband deficits are due in part to genetic influences. Thus, for both univariate and repeated-measures analyses, comparisons of MZ and DZ co-twin means provide tests for genetic aetiology. However, for univariate analyses of data from twin pairs in which at least one member has been ascertained because of deviant scores for a specific measure, fitting the following multiple regression model to data for that measure from both probands and co-twins provides a more general, statistically powerful and versatile test:

$$C = B_{1}P + B_{2}R + K \qquad (1)$$

where C symbolises the co-twin's score, P is the proband's score, R is the coefficient of relationship (1.0 for MZ twin pairs and 0.5 for DZ twins), B_{1} and B_{2} are regression weights and K is the regression constant.

When equation 1 is fitted to data from twin pairs (using double entry for concordant pairs; DeFries & Gillis 1991), B_{2} estimates twice the difference between the means of the MZ and DZ co-twins after covariance adjustment for any difference between the scores of the MZ and DZ probands. Consequently, B_{2} provides a test for genetic aetiology that is more general and statistically powerful than a comparison of MZ and DZ concordance rates (DeFries & Fulker, 1988).

Equation 1 can also be used to quantify the extent to which the proband deficit is due to genetic influences ($h^{2}g$). When data from twin pairs are transformed by expressing each score as a deviation from the mean of the unselected population and then dividing this deviation by the difference between the proband and control means, $B_2 = h^2g$ (DeFries & Fulker, 1988).

Equation 1 was first fitted to transformed discriminant function score data from all probands and their co-twins to assess the genetic aetiology of reading disability in the total sample. Subjects were then divided into the two age-groups previously analysed by Wadsworth et al. (1989), less than 11.5 years and 11.5–20.2 years. Equation 1 was then fitted to transformed data from each age-group separately to assess the genetic aetiology of reading deficits in older and younger twin pairs.

In order to test the significance of the difference between the estimates of h^2g obtained from analyses of data from the older and younger groups, the following extended model was fitted to data from both groups simultaneously:

$$C = B_{1P} + B_{2R} + B_{3A} + B_{4PA} + B_{5RA} + K \qquad (2)$$

where A symbolises age, PA is the product of the proband's score and age, and RA is the corresponding product of the coefficient of relationship and age. When A is a dichotomously coded variable (e.g. –0.5 for twin pairs less than 11.5 years of age and +0.5 for those greater than 11.5 years), the B_5 coefficient provides a direct test of the significance of the difference between the h^2g estimates in the younger and older groups. However, when each twin pair's actual age is used in equation 2 as a continuous variable, the B_5 coefficient tests for linear changes in h^2g across the entire age range of the sample.

Following the regression analyses of the discriminant function score data (a composite measure of reading/spelling performance), possible developmental differences in the aetiologies of individual reading and spelling measures were explored by fitting equations 1 and 2 to PIAT sub-test score data. In order to obtain estimates of h^2g for Reading Recognition, Reading Comprehension and Spelling, three samples of probands were reselected with scores at least 1.5 standard deviations below the mean of the controls for the relevant measure. All other ascertainment criteria for these samples were the same as those used to select the sample diagnosed on the basis of discrimination function score data.

Finally, the significance of a possible developmental difference in the aetiologies of word recognition and spelling deficits was tested by reselecting another sample of twins in which at least one member of each pair had a score 1.5 standard deviations or more below the control means for both measures. Transformed scores of the co-twins of these probands were then subjected to a repeated-measures analysis of variance, with two between-subjects factors (age and zygosity) and one within-subjects factor (measure, i.e. Reading Recognition and Spelling).

The three-way interaction between age, zygosity and measure provided a test of statistical significance for the differential change in genetic aetiology as a function of age for the two measures.

Because of the procedure used to ascertain each sample of twins, data from concordant pairs were double-entered for the regression analyses in a manner analogous to that used to calculate probandwise concordance rates (DeFries & Alarcón, 1996). In a corresponding manner, both members of each concordant pair were included as co-twins for the repeated-measures analysis of variance. Consequently, computer-provided tests of significance were adjusted for both the regression and repeated-measures analyses (Stevenson et al., 1993).

Results

Average discriminant scores of the MZ and same-sex DZ probands and their co-twins, expressed in standard deviation units from the mean of the control twins, are presented in Table 2.1. From this table it may be seen that the MZ and DZ proband means are highly similar, and over 2.5 standard deviations below the mean of the controls. Moreover, the MZ co-twins have regressed only 0.21 standard deviation units on average toward the control mean, whereas the DZ co-twins have regressed 0.94 standard deviation units. When equation 1 was fitted to the transformed discriminant function data, $B_2 = h^2g = 0.56$ ($p < 0.001$), suggesting that over half of the average reading performance deficit of probands is due to heritable influences.

Table 2.1 Mean discriminant scores (a composite measure of reading and spelling performance) of identical and same-sex fraternal twins in which at least one member of each pair is reading-disabled*

	Number of pairs	Mean	
		Proband	Co-twin
Identical	195	–2.72	–2.51
Fraternal	145	–2.65	–1.71

Note: * Expressed in standardised deviation units from the mean of the control twin pairs.

Estimates of h^2g for the discriminant function scores of the younger and older groups are presented in Table 2.2. The estimate of h^2g in the younger group (0.61) is somewhat larger than that estimated from data of the older group (0.49). Thus, this result also indicates that genetic factors may be somewhat less important as a cause of reading disability in older children. However, the difference between these two estimates of h^2g is not significant. When the extended model (equation 2) was fitted to the data from both groups simultaneously and age was coded dichotomously, $B_5 = -0.12$ ($p = 0.25$, one-tailed test). It is interesting to note that because age was coded as -0.5 and $+0.5$ for members of the younger and older groups and their data were separately transformed, B_5 exactly estimates the difference between h^2g in the two groups, i.e. $0.61 -0.49 = -0.12$. As expected, when age is entered in equation 2 as a continuous variable, the test for differential genetic aetiology is somewhat more powerful. However, the corresponding estimate of $B_5 = -0.03$ in this case is also non-significant ($p = 0.17$).

Table 2.2 Tests for genetic aetiology of reading disability in younger and older age groups

| Age range (years) | Number of twin pairs | | $B2 = h^2g$ | P |
	MZ	DZ		
8:1–11:5	110	84	0.61 ± 0.11	.001
11:5–20:2	85	61	0.49 ± 0.13	.001

Estimates of h^2g for Reading Recognition, Reading Comprehension and Spelling in the older and younger groups are presented in Table 2.3. Inspection of this table reveals possible developmental differences in the aetiologies of word recognition and spelling deficits. Whereas h^2g for Reading Recognition is higher in the younger group than in the older group (0.64 vs 0.47), the opposite pattern occurs for Spelling (0.52 vs 0.68). In contrast, little or no change in h^2g is evident for Reading Comprehension (0.40 vs 0.39). When equation 2 was fitted separately to these three data sets, the test for differential h^2g as a linear function of age was marginally significant for Reading Recognition ($p < 0.10$, one-tailed test) and Spelling ($p < 0.16$), but not for Reading Comprehension ($p = 0.27$). Nevertheless, these results tend to support the hypothesis of Stevenson et al. (1987) that spelling deficits are more heritable than reading deficits in older children.

Table 2.3 Tests for genetic aetiology of reading and spelling deficits in younger and older age groups*

| Age range (years) | Reading recognition | | Reading comprehension | | Spelling | |
	h^2g	$P \leq$	h^2g	$P \leq$	h^2g	$P \leq$
8:1–11:5	0.64 – 0.12	.001	0.40 – 0.14	.005	0.52 – 0.13	.001
11:5–20:2	0.47 – 0.14	.001	0.39 – 0.17	.026	0.68 – 0.18	.001

Note: * Numbers of MZ and DZ twin pairs range from 143–174 and 98–133, respectively.

Because the samples of twins selected for reading or spelling deficits were partly overlapping, we reselected twins in which at least one member of each pair had a score 1.5 standard deviations or more below the control means for both measures. Thus, in this sample, differences between the MZ and DZ co-twin means could be assessed in the older and younger groups for both measures, and the differential change in the pattern of MZ–DZ co-twin differences for the two measures could be evaluated for statistical significance using a repeated-measures analysis of variance.

Table 2.4 mean transformed* word recognition and spelling scores for co-twins of probands with both reading and spelling deficits

Age range (years)	Zygosity	Reading recognition	Spelling	Number of pairs
8:1–11:5	MZ	0.91	0.86	74
	DZ	0.53	0.56	56
11:5–20:2	MZ	0.94	0.87	47
	DZ	0.69	0.49	29

Note: * Co-twin scores divided by proband mean.

Mean transformed word recognition and spelling scores for co-twins of probands with both reading and spelling deficits are presented in Table 2.4. As depicted in Figure 2.1, the difference between the MZ and DZ co-twin means for Reading Recognition is larger for the younger group (0.91 – 0.53 = 0.38) than that for the older group (0.94 – 0.69 = 0.25). Because these MZ–DZ co-twin differences are functions of h^2g, this result also indicates that the heritable nature of the group deficit for word recognition is greater in younger subjects. In contrast, the difference between the MZ and DZ co-twin means for Spelling is somewhat smaller for younger children (0.86 – 0.56 = 0.30) than for older children (0.87 – 0.49 = 0.38). Thus, the pattern of decreasing genetic influence for word recognition and increasing genetic influence for spelling as a function of age is also evident in twin pairs in which the probands were selected with both reading and spelling deficits.

In order to test the significance of this apparent differential change in the aetiologies of word recognition and spelling deficits as a function of age, the co-twin data were subjected to a repeated-measures analysis of variance. As predicted by the Stevenson et al. (1987) hypothesis of a developmental dissociation between reading and spelling deficits, the three-way interaction involving age, zygosity and measure (word recognition versus spelling) is significant ($F = 4.20$, df = 1/203, $p < 0.05$). Thus, the results of this analysis provide additional evidence that the

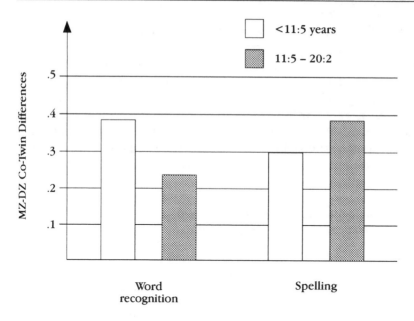

Figure 2.1 Differences between the means of the MZ and DZ co-twins of probands ascertained for both word recognition and spelling deficits

genetic aetiologies of reading and spelling deficits change differentially as a function of age.

Discussion

Results obtained from the London Twin Study (Stevenson et al., 1984, 1987) suggested that spelling difficulties at 13 years of age are due substantially to heritable influences, whereas genetic factors may be less salient as a cause of reading deficits at that age. In order to assess possible developmental differences in the genetic aetiology of reading disability, Wadsworth et al. (1989) conducted a preliminary analysis of composite reading scores from twin pairs tested in the Colorado Twin Study of Reading Disability. Resulting estimates of h^2g, an index of the extent to which the deficits of probands are due to heritable influences, were 0.60 and 0.38 in the younger (< 11:5 years) and older (11:5–20:2 years) groups, respectively. Although these results suggest that genetic factors may be less important as a cause of reading deficits in older children, the difference between the two h^2g estimates was non-significant. Wadsworth et al. (1989) also attempted a preliminary test of the Stevenson et al. (1987) hypothesis of a developmental dissociation between reading and spelling difficulties by fitting the basic regression model of DeFries and Fulker (1985) to reading and spelling sub-test scores of twin pairs with reading deficits. Although tests for differential genetic aetiology as a function of age were non-significant for each measure, differences in h^2g estimated from data of the younger and older groups were somewhat larger for reading than for spelling, again suggesting that genetic factors may be more salient as a cause of spelling difficulties than of reading deficits in older children. However, because the probands in this twin sample had been selected for a composite measure of reading performance, and not for the individual measures of reading or spelling deficits, the estimates of h^2g obtained for the various sub-test measures in that study were only approximate.

The sample size in the ongoing Colorado Twin Study of Reading Disability has almost doubled since the preliminary analysis of Wadsworth et al. (1989). Thus, the primary objective of the present study was to test the hypothesis that the genetic aetiologies of reading and spelling deficits in this enlarged twin sample change differentially as a function of age. Moreover, more appropriate estimates of h^2g for sub-test measures were obtained by reselecting samples of twins with reading or spelling deficits.

Discriminant function score data (a composite measure of reading/spelling performance) from 195 pairs of MZ twins and 145 pairs of same-sex DZ twins were subjected to multiple regression analysis (DeFries & Fulker, 1985, 1988). When the basic regression model was fitted to transformed data from the total sample, the h^2g estimate was 0.56 ($p < 0.001$), indicating that somewhat more than one-half of the proband deficit, on average, is due to heritable influences. When the same model was fit separately to data from younger (< 11:5 years) and older (11:5–20:2 years) twin pairs, resulting estimates of h^2g were 0.61 and 0.49, respectively. Although these results also indicate that genetic factors may be less important as a cause of reading/spelling deficits in older children, the difference between these two estimates of h^2g is non-significant ($p = 0.25$ when age was coded as a dichotomous variable, and $p = 0.17$ when age in years was entered as a continuous variable).

When the samples were reselected for reading or spelling deficits and the data were fitted to the basic regression model, resulting estimates of h^2g in the younger and older groups were as follows: Reading Recognition, 0.64 vs 0.47; Reading Comprehension, 0.40 vs 0.39; and Spelling, 0.52 vs 0.68. Thus, h^2g decreases as a function of age for word recognition, but increases for spelling. Moreover, the differences in h^2g as a function of age are marginally significant for both Reading Recognition and Spelling ($p < 0.10$ and $p < 0.16$, respectively); therefore, these results suggest that the aetiologies of word recognition and spelling deficits change differentially as a function of age.

The basic regression model was also fitted to an experimental measure of Time-Limited Word Recognition (TLWR) that requires a correct response within 2 seconds (Olson et al., 1994), and to the Wide Range Achievement Test (WRAT) (Jastak & Jastak, 1978) of spelling production. The resulting estimates of h^2g for these measures in the younger and older groups were as follows: TLWR, 0.64 vs 0.48; WRAT, 0.58 vs 075. The differences in heritability as a function of age were not significant for either measure, but the contrasting developmental pattern in reading and spelling was similar to that found for the PIAT tests. Thus, we have some confidence that the differential age pattern will replicate across both timed and untimed measures of word recognition, and both recognition and production measures of spelling.

Because the two samples of twins with Reading Recognition or Spelling deficits on the PIAT are partially overlapping, tests of differential h^2g in the two samples are not independent. Consequently, the significance of possible developmental differences in the aetiologies of reading and spelling deficits was assessed by subjecting MZ and DZ co-twin scores to a repeated-measures analysis of variance. For this analysis, another sample of twins was reselected in which at least one member of each pair had both reading and spelling difficulties. Inspection of the co-twin means in this sample revealed that the MZ–DZ co-twin difference (a function of h^2g) for Reading Recognition was larger in the younger group than in the older group, whereas the opposite pattern occurred for Spelling. Thus, the pattern of decreasing genetic influence for word recognition and increasing genetic influence for spelling as a function of age is also present in this sample in which probands were selected for both reading and spelling deficits. When the co-twin Reading Recognition and Spelling data for this sample were subjected to a repeated-measures analysis of variance, the three-way interaction involving age, zygosity and measure was significant ($p < 0.05$). Thus, as predicted by the Stevenson et al. (1987) hypothesis of a developmental dissociation between reading and spelling difficulties, the genetic aetiologies of the two measures change differentially as a function of age.

Stevenson et al. (1984) concluded that genetic influences on literacy problems are more appropriately studied through their impact on spelling ability than on reading measures. However, the results of the present study suggest that this dictum is more relevant to studies involving older children and adults than to those involving younger children. There are several reasons for postulating that spelling deficits in older children and adults may be less susceptible than reading to environmental influences (DeFries et al., 1991). First, the spelling performance of children with reading difficulties improves less over time than does reading (Rutter & Yule, 1975; Critchley & Critchley, 1978). Second, because there are fewer contextual clues to spelling versus word recognition, there is a greater scope for remediating reading difficulties. Third, the results obtained by Stevenson et al. (1987) and those of the present study both suggest that spelling deficits are more heritable than word-recognition difficulties in older children. Thus, because spelling may emerge as the most genetically influenced literacy skill during early adolescence, perhaps future twin studies and genetic linkage analyses of dyslexia in older children and adults should focus primarily upon spelling deficits.

In addition to locating the individual genes or quantitative trait loci (QTL) that cause dyslexia, genetic linkage analyses could also provide an alternative test for the differential aetiology of reading and spelling deficits. In our previous report of the possible localisation of a QTL for reading disability to a small region on the short arm of chromosome 6 (Cardon et al., 1994, 1995), a discriminant function score based on three PIAT sub-tests (Reading Recognition, Reading Comprehension and Spelling) was used for proband ascertainment. Subsequently, Gayan et al. (1995) subjected these three sub-tests, as well as four other measures of reading and language processes (non-word reading, orthographic coding, pig latin, and the TLWR experimental measure of word recognition), separately to QTL analysis. The subjects for this study were the 50 pairs of DZ twins included in the Cardon et al. (1994) study which had been genotyped for five informative DNA markers on the short arm of chromosome 6. The best evidence for linkage to chromosome 6 was obtained for PIAT Reading Recognition and the TLWR measure of word recognition (both $p < 0.001$). Although evidence for linkage was also obtained for PIAT Spelling, Reading Comprehension, and non-word reading in the same region of chromosome 6, the level of significance was lower ($p < 0.05$) for each of these measures. Thus, Gayan et al. (1995) concluded that the QTL for reading disability may differentially influence different measures of reading performance. In addition to influencing more than one character, the effects of a given gene may also vary as a function of age. Although the present sample of fraternal twins with DNA marker information is too small to conduct such analyses, eventually it may be possible to conduct genetic linkage analyses of both reading and spelling deficits in younger and older twins, and thereby assess the differential impact of individual genes on these measures at different ages.

The multiple regression analysis of twin data, sometimes referred to as 'DF analysis' (e.g. Plomin & Rende, 1991; Rodgers et al., 1994; Waller, 1994), is a versatile methodology. In addition to assessing the aetiology of group deficits, it can also be used to assess the aetiology of individual differences within the normal range of variation and to test the hypothesis that the aetiology of deviant scores differs from that of individual differences (DeFries & Alarcón, 1996). Moreover, it can be used to test hypotheses concerning the differential aetiology of a measure as a function of continuous covariates such as IQ (DeFries & Light, 1996), or categorical variables such as gender (DeFries et al., 1993) and sub-type (Olson et al., 1991; Casto et al., 1996). Although DF analysis was used to assess differential genetic aetiology as a linear function of age in the present study, it also facilitates tests for non-linear relationships. For example, Wadsworth et al. (1989) obtained some suggestive evidence for a possible differential genetic aetiology of reading deficits as a quadratic function of age by fitting an extended regression model that included age-squared terms to twin data. However, when such a model was fitted to reading performance data from the twin pairs tested in the present study, no evidence for a differential aetiology of reading disability as a quadratic function of age was obtained ($p = 0.90$).

Bivariate DF models may also be fitted to twin data to assess the aetiology of co-morbidity for conditions such as reading disability and mathematics deficits (Light & DeFries, 1995) or ADHD symptoms (Stevenson et al., 1993). For such bivariate analyses, probands are ascertained based on their scores for one measure (X), whereas their co-twins are measured for another variable (Y). When the basic DF regression model is fitted to such data (namely co-twins' Y scores are predicted from probands' X scores and the coefficient of relationship), the bivariate $B2$ term provides a measure of the extent to which the deviant scores of both measures are due to the same genetic influences (Light & DeFries, 1995).

Unfortunately, DF analysis does not readily accommodate tests of differential h^2g for different measures, especially when the samples of twins ascertained for such analyses are overlapping. However, because differences between MZ and DZ co-twin means are functions of h^2g, repeated-measures analyses of variance of co-twin scores can provide tests of differential genetic aetiology. If probands are identified because of their co-morbidity for two conditions (e.g. continuous measures of dyslexia and ADHD symptoms), the difference between the MZ and DZ co-twin means should be larger for the more heritable condition. Thus, when co-morbid probands are ascertained and the scores of their co-twins are subjected to a repeated-measures analysis of variance, the interaction between zygosity and measure could be used as a test for the differential genetic aetiology of the two conditions. In the present study, a three-way interaction involving zygosity, measure and age was used to test for a differential change in aetiology of word recognition and spelling deficits as a function of age.

In conclusion, the results of the present study provide evidence that the aetiologies of word recognition and spelling deficits change differentially as a function of age, i.e. reading difficulties appear to be more heritable in younger children (8–11:5 years) than in older children, whereas spelling deficits are more heritable in older children. Although this result suggests that spelling deficits may be more difficult to remediate than reading deficits in older children, novel teaching methods might still be highly efficacious (Wise & Olson, 1995).

Acknowledgements

This work was supported in part by programme project and center grants from NICHD (HD-11681 and HD-27802).

We gratefully acknowledge the invaluable contributions of the staff members of the many Colorado school districts from which the samples were ascertained and those of the families who participated in the study. We also thank Ms Kathy Huckfeldt for secretarial services.

References

Bakwin, H. (1973). Reading disability in twins. *Developmental Medicine and Child Neurology* **15**, 184–187.

Cardon, L.R., Smith, S.D., Fulker, D.W., Kimberling, W.J., Pennington, B.F. & DeFries, J.C. (1994). Quantitative trait locus for reading disability on chromosome 6. *Science* **266**, 276–279.

Cardon, L.R., Smith, S.D., Fulker, D.W., Kimberling, W.J., Pennington, B.F. & DeFries, J.C. (1995). Quantitative trait locus for reading disability: a correction. *Science* **268**, 5217.

Casto, S.D., Pennington, B.F., Light, J.G. & DeFries, J.C. (1996). Differential genetic aetiology of reading disability as a function of mathematics performance. *Reading and Writing* **8**, 295–306.

Critchley, M. & Critchley, E.A. (1978). *Dyslexia Defined*. London: Heinemann.

Decker, S.N. & Vandenberg, S.G. (1985). Colorado twin study of reading disability. In D.B. Gray & J.F. Kavanagh (Eds.) *Biobehavioral Measures of Dyslexia* (pp. 123–135). Parkton, MD: York Press.

DeFries, J.C. (1985). Colorado Reading Project. In D.B. Gray & J.F. Kavanagh (Eds.) *Biobehavioral Measures of Dyslexia* (pp. 107–122). Parkton, MD: York Press.

DeFries, J.C. & Alarcón, M. (1996). Genetics of specific reading disability. *Mental Retardation and Developmental Disabilities Research Reviews* **2**, 39–47.

DeFries, J.C. & Fulker, D.W. (1985). Multiple regression analysis of twin data. *Behavior Genetics* **15**, 467–473.

DeFries, J.C. & Fulker, D.W. (1988). Multiple regression analysis of twin data: Aetiology of deviant scores versus individual differences. *Acta Geneticae Medicae et Gemellologiae* **37**, 205–216.

DeFries, J.C. & Gillis, J.J. (1991). Aetiology of reading deficits in learning disabilities: Quantitative genetic analysis. In J.E. Obrzut & G.W. Hynd (Eds.) *Neuropsychological Foundations of Learning Disabilities: A Handbook of Issues, Methods and Practice* (pp. 29–47). Orlando, FL: Academic Press.

DeFries, J.C. Light, J.G. (1996). Twin studies of reading disability. In J.H. Beitchman, N. Cohen, M.M. Konstantareas & R. Tannock (Eds.) *Language, Learning and Behavior Disorders*. New York: Cambridge University Press.

DeFries, J.C., Gillis, J.J. & Wadsworth, S.J. (1993). Genes and genders: A twin study of reading disability. In A.M. Galaburda (Ed.) *Dyslexia and Development: Neurobiological Aspects of Extra-ordinary Brains* (pp. 187–204). Cambridge, MA: Harvard University Press.

DeFries, J.C., Stevenson, J., Gillis, J.J. & Wadsworth, S.J. (1991). Genetic aetiology of spelling deficits in the Colorado and London twin studies of reading disability. *Reading and Writing* **3**, 271–283.

DeFries, J.C., Filipek, P.A., Fulker, D.W., Olson, R.K., Pennington, B.F., Smith, S.D. & Wise, B.W. (in press). Colorado Learning Disabilities Research Center. *Learning Disabilities Quarterly*.

Dunn, L.M. & Markwardt, F.C. (1970). *Examiner's Manual: Peabody Individual Achievement Test*. Circle Pines, MN: American Guidance Service.

Gayan, J., Olson, R.K., Cardon, L.R., Smith, S.D., Fulker, D.W., Kimberling, W.J., Pennington, B.F. & DeFries, J.C. (1995). Quantitative trait locus for different measures of reading disability. *Behavior Genetics* **25**, 266.

Hallgren, B. (1950). Specific dyslexia: a clinical and genetic study. *Acta Psychiatrica and Neurologica Scandinavica*, Supplement **65**, 1–287.

Harris, E.L. (1986). The contribution of twin research to the study of the aetiology of reading disability. In S.D. Smith (Ed.), *Genetics and Learning Disabilities* (pp. 3–19). San Diego: College Hill Press.

Jastak, J. & Jastak, S. (1978). *The Wide Range Achievement Test – Revised*. Wilmington, DE: Jastak Associates.

Light, J.G. & DeFries, J.C. (1995). Comorbidity of reading and mathematics disabilities: genetic and environmental aetiologies. *Journal of Learning Disabilities* **28.**, 96–106.

Lykken, D.T., Tellegen, A. & DeRubeis R. (1978). Volunteer bias in twin research: the rule of two-thirds. *Social Biology* **25**, 1–9.

Neale, M.D. (1967). *Neale Analysis of Reading Ability*. London: Macmillan.

Nichols, R.C. & Bilbro, W.C. (1966). The diagnosis of twin zygosity. *Acta Genetica et Statistica Medica* **16**, 265–275.

Olson, R.K., Forsberg, H., Wise, B. & Rack, J. (1994). Measurement of word recognition, orthographic, and phonological skills. In G.R. Lyon (Ed.) *Frames of Reference for the Assessment of Learning Disabilities: New Views on Measurement Issues* (pp. 243–277). Baltimore, MD: Paul H. Brooks.

Olson, R.K., Rack, J.P., Conners, F.A., DeFries, J.C. & Fulker, D.W. (1991). Genetic aetiology of individual differences in reading disability. In L.V. Feagans, E.J. Short & L.J. Meltzer (Eds.) *Subtypes of Learning Disabilities* (pp. 113–135). Hillsdale, NJ: Lawrence Erlbaum.

Plomin, R. & Rende, R. (1991). Human behavioral genetics. *Annual Review of Psychology* **42**, 161–190.

Rodgers, J.L., Rowe, D.C. & Li, C. (1994). Beyond nature versus nurture: DF analysis of nonshared influences on problem behaviors. *Developmental Psychology* **30**, 374–384.

Rutter, M. & Yule, W. (1975). The concept of specific reading retardation. *Journal of Child Psychology and Psychiatry* **16**, 181–197.

Schonell, F.J. & Schonell, P.E. (1960). *Diagnostic and Attainment Testing*. Edinburgh: Oliver & Boyd.

Shaywitz, S.E., Shaywitz, B.A., Fletcher, J.M. & Escobar, M.D. (1990). Prevalence of reading disability in boys and girls. *Journal of the American Medical Association* **264**, 998–1002.

Stevenson J., Graham P., Fredman G. & McLoughlin, V. (1984). The genetics of reading disability. In C.J. Turner & H.B. Miles (Eds.) *The Biology of Human Intelligence* (pp. 85–97). Nafferton: Nafferton Books.

Stevenson, J., Graham, P., Fredman, G. & McLoughlin, V. (1987). A twin study of genetic influences on reading and spelling ability and disability. *Journal of Child Psychology* **28**, 229–247.

Stevenson, J., Pennington, B.F., Gilger, J.W., DeFries, J.C. & Gillis, J.J. (1993). Hyperactivity and spelling disability: testing for shared genetic aetiology. *Journal of Child Psychology* **34**, 1137–1152.

Vogel, S.A. (1990). Gender differences in intelligence, language, visual-motor abilities, and academic achievement in students with learning disabilities: A review of the literature. *Journal of Learning Disabilities* **23**, 44–52.

Wadsworth, S.J., Gillis, J.J., DeFries, J.C. & Fulker, D.W. (1989). Differential genetic aetiology of reading disability as a function of age. *Irish Journal of Psychology* **10**, 509–520.

Waller, N.G. (1994). A DeFries and Fulker regression model for genetic nonadditivity. *Behavior Genetics* **24**, 149–153.

Wechsler, D. (1974). *Examiner's Manual: Wechsler Intelligence Scale for Children – Revised*. New York: Psychological Corporation.

Wechsler, D. (1981). *Examiner's Manual: Wechsler Adult Intelligence Scale – Revised*. New York: Psychological Corporation.

Wise, B.W. & Olson, R.K. (1995). Computer-based phonological awareness and reading instruction. *Annals of Dyslexia* **45**, 99–122.

Zerbin-Rüdin, E. (1967). Kongenitale Worblindheit oder spezifische dyslexie [congenital word-blindness]. *Bulletin of the Orton Society* **17**, 47–56.

Chapter 3
Dyslexia and Gyral Morphology Variation

GEORGE W. HYND* & JENNIFER R. HIEMENZ

Developmental dyslexia is generally agreed to affect some 4% of the population and is associated with phonological and semantic/syntactic language deficits (Adams, 1990; American Psychiatric Association, 1994; Bruck, 1992). Although dyslexia may also be associated with emotional and behavioural difficulties, deficits in phonological and language processes seem to be central to explaining the problems dyslexic children have in learning to read (Hynd, Morgan, Edmonds, Black, Riccio & Lombardino, 1995). These core deficits in language skills are believed to be heritable and a loci on at least one candidate chromosome has been implicated (e.g., Cardon et al., 1994).

There has long been a presumption that dyslexia has a neurodevelopmental aetiology (Hynd & Semrud-Clikeman, 1989) and research in the past several decades has supported the view that, for many dyslexics, there is indeed evidence that the severe reading disability is related in some fashion to the development of neurological anomalies during fetal ontogeny (Galaburda, 1993).

This chapter addresses the progress that has been made in understanding the variability found in the brains of individuals who suffer from developmental dyslexia. As will be seen, there are different ways to approach the investigation of brain differences in this population, ranging from the post-mortem study of dyslexics' brains to the use of neuroimaging techniques in living subjects. This chapter will focus primarily on neuroimaging studies conducted in the past decade, although the seminal importance of the post-mortem studies cannot be ignored. Consequently, the post-mortem studies will be discussed briefly but the primary focus will be on the neuroimaging studies that

*Supported in part by a grant (RO1-HD26890-03) awarded to the first author from the National Institute of Child Health and Human Development (NICHHD), and the National Institutes of Health (NIH).

serve as a window to understanding variation in the language-related cortex in dyslexics.

First, however, it is appropriate to consider normal neurological development. Variations in the brains of dyslexics seem to emerge during known critical stages in fetal neuronal genesis and these variations in brain development may later produce, or be associated with, the reading and language deficiencies observed in dyslexia.

Neurodevelopmental Formation of Gyri and Sulci

Normal sequence of brain ontogeny

In the earliest stages of human prenatal development, the brain's surface is smooth and lacks sulci and gyri (the characteristic grooves and convolutions on the brain's surface). By birth, however, the adult gyral pattern is fully present. The sulcal/gyral patterns in the brain develop according to a well-documented timetable, in which the major sulci dividing the cerebral lobes appear first and the secondary gyri within the lobes appear later. This pattern of brain development seems to support the conceptualisation of gyri being related to the functional ontogeny and organisation of the brain. Understanding the scope and sequence of neural development helps us to understand the factors that may facilitate or impede the normal structural and functional development of the human brain. Whilst the focus here is on morphological asymmetries in the modern human brain, some evidence suggests that elements of these brain asymmetries existed in Australopithecus Africanus, in Neanderthal man (LeMay, 1976), and in the higher apes (though the functional implications of these limited studies are quite unclear; Corballis, 1983).

The process of neurulation, where the neural tube develops and closes, is generally completed by the sixth week of fetal gestation. At approximately 14 weeks of fetal gestation, the longitudinal fissure, which divides the brain into two cerebral hemispheres, and Sylvian fissure, dividing the parietal and frontal lobes from the temporal lobes, are present. At 16 weeks of gestation, the parieto-occipital sulcus, which differentiates the parietal from the occipital lobes, is present. Finally, at about 20 weeks, the central sulcus appears, dividing the frontal lobes from the parietal lobes (Dooling, Chi & Gilles, 1983; Chi, Dooling & Gilles, 1977a, b). Following a brief period of rapid increase in brain weight between the 24th to 26th weeks, the brain undergoes a rapid spurt in gyrification between the 26th and 28th weeks of fetal gestation that follows an orderly and symmetrical progression (Dooling et al., 1983; Hynd & Willis, 1988). It is during this period that the superior temporal gyrus and gyri in the temporo-parietal region become clearly evident.

The formation of gyri was originally thought to reflect a passive process resulting from the mechanical folding of the cortex during fetal development so that more cortical surface area could fit within the physical confines of the skull (Welker, 1990). However, we now know that the process of gyrification is a complex outcome of the formation of cortical connections during neuronal placement. While the brain is still smooth, or lissencephalic, the process of neuronal migration from the germinal matrix, located on the dorsolateral aspect of the lateral ventricles, to the cortex occurs. The arriving neurons migrate in waves to form layers, beginning with the deepest layer (VI) and terminating with the most superficial layer (II) so that they are arranged in columns. Once migration is completed, the cortical surface is primed for the formation of gyri. Gyri are formed when the cortical neurons form intracortical connections through arborisation and differential cell death. Neuronal differentiation, arborisation, synapse formation, glial cell proliferation, and laminar differentiation all seem to be more profuse in gyral crowns than in the walls of the sulci and occur according to different timetables depending on their location in the cortex (Welker, 1990). The combination of all of these processes produce the gyri and sulci that characterise the cortex.

Although each person's individual sulcal/gyral pattern varies slightly, historically no conclusive relationship has been found between the characteristic cortical folding and age, body weight or length, or brain weight (Zilles et al., 1988). However, gyral patterns themselves have been found to be modifiable in experimental studies (Dvorak, Feit & Jurankova, 1978). For example, pre-natal removal of a small region of cortex in the rhesus monkey led in one experiment to the development of abnormal gyral patterns (Welker, 1990). In another more recent study, Rosen, Sherman and Galaburda (1994) demonstrated that microgyria and cytoarchitectonic abnormalities may result from neonatal brain injury, possibly due to the release of a trophic factor during the recovery stage after injury. The cognitive and behavioural effects of experimentally altering gyral patterns has yet to be clearly understood although some experimental evidence suggests that auditory temporal processing deficits may result from induced hemispheric lesions during early development in rat pups (Fitch et al., 1994). Other studies with humans suggest that subtle neurodevelopmental variation in the brains of clinical populations, possibly under genetic or traumatic influences, may exist and could be related to the cognitive and behavioural characteristics we see in these populations (e.g. Andreasen et al., 1994).

Given that gyral patterns are indicators of the patterns of intracortical connections, patterns that are unusual or extreme are likely to be associated with deviations in cortical connections and by implication with cognitive or behavioural deficits. Thus, abnormal variations in gyral patterns in a particular area, for instance in the left central language zones, may be associated with deficits in functions associated with that area, such as language and related abilities (i.e. reading).

Sulcal/gyral asymmetries and language lateralisation

The re-emergence of interest in the examination of sulcal/gyral patterns in the human cortex came in the late 1960s, with a flood of research on the structural correlates of gross morphological asymmetries in the classical language areas. In early studies, anatomists began to document right–left asymmetries of the perisylvian region, specifically the length and angulation of the Sylvian fissure (Connolly, 1950; Cunningham, 1892). For example, Rubens, Mahowald and Hutton (1976) reported that asymmetries existed with regard to the angulation of the right and left Sylvian fissures. In contrast with the left Sylvian fissure, the right posterior Sylvian fissure angles sharply upward into the inferior parietal region such that in the right posterior Sylvian area there is a smaller parietal operculum, a shorter planum temporale, and a relatively larger inferior parietal region.

Historically, it was Geschwind and Levitsky (1968) who put forth the first strong evidence of neuroanatomical asymmetry in a post-mortem study of 100 adult brains. They reported that 65% of these brains had a left greater than right asymmetry of the superior surface of the planum temporale in the posterior area of the Sylvian fissure. As this figure corresponded to notions regarding the functional importance of right-handedness and language lateralisation, the logical conclusion was that for most humans this left greater than right planum asymmetry was related to both right-handedness and language lateralisation. This conclusion was supported by earlier, historically important, case studies by Broca, Wernicke, and others which linked language function and dysfunction to the left perisylvian area, particularly the region of the planum temporale which corresponds on the left to Wernicke's region (Witelson, 1982).

Following Geschwind and Levitsky's (1968) seminal publication, numerous studies have examined planum temporale asymmetries in relation to language lateralisation (e.g. Steinmetz et al., 1989;· Foundas et al., 1994). These studies have been thoroughly reviewed by Hynd and Semrud-Clikeman (1989) and more recently by Morgan and Hynd (in press). Significantly, the normal left larger than right asymmetry of the planum temporale seems to be associated with language lateralisation. For example, a recent study by Foundas and her colleagues examined the relationship between leftward asymmetry of the planum temporale as revealed on magnetic resonance imaging (MRI) scans and the results from Wada testing. Eleven subjects with language lateralised to the left hemisphere all had a leftward asymmetry of the planum temporale, whilst one subject with language lateralised to the right hemisphere (a non-right-handed person) had a strong rightward asymmetry of the planum temporale (Foundas et al., 1994). Thus, asymmetries of the planum temporale as revealed by MRI analyses do indeed seem to be related to functional language lateralisation.

The evidence for left-sided language dominance and its relationship to morphological asymmetries in the central language areas naturally led to the idea that language and reading disorders result from mixed or reversed hemispheric specialisation for language abilities (Hynd & Cohen, 1983; Witelson, 1982). It is from this perspective that other studies have investigated the link between gross brain morphological asymmetries and dyslexia, as the perisylvian area seems to be implicated in reading disability or dyslexia (e.g. Duara et al., 1991; Hynd et al., 1990; Kushch et al., 1993; Larsen et al., 1990; Leonard et al., 1993; Schultz et al., 1994; Semrud-Clikeman et al., 1991). These latter studies have employed morphometric analyses of MRI scans. They have produced theoretically interesting results which deserve consideration as they may shed light on the potentially important relationship between deviations in brain sulcal morphology and dyslexia.

Deviations in Planum Temporale Asymmetries and Dyslexia

Before reviewing neuroimaging studies of the brains of individuals with dyslexia, note must be made of several exceedingly important post-mortem studies by Galaburda and his colleagues (e.g. Galaburda & Kemper, 1979; Galaburda et al., 1985). Whilst Galaburda and his colleagues have continued their important post-mortem and anatomical research on the neurodevelopmental bases of dyslexia (Galaburda, 1993), two studies in particular paved the way for examining asymmetries of the planum temporale in developmental dyslexia using MRI.

Post-mortem findings in dyslexia

In a seminal study, Galaburda and Kemper (1979) examined plana asymmetry in a young man who had an unusually well-documented history of developmental dyslexia. Their subject had died as a result of a fall. Their post-mortem study revealed that in this case symmetrical plana existed as well as mild cortical dysplasias which were found in the left hemispheric limbic, primary and association cortices. Their finding of symmetrical plana was of interest because from the work of Geschwind and Levitsky (1968) it was known that asymmetry was the rule and that symmetry of the plana occurred in only some 11% of the normal population. Thus, they raised the question in this study, was symmetry or reversed asymmetry in the region of the plana related to the dyslexic syndrome? Later, Galaburda et al. (1985) examined three other brains of individuals with dyslexia ranging in age from 14 to 32 years, and also found symmetrical plana as well as neuronal ectopias and cytoarchitectonic dysplasias generally located in the perisylvian area of the left hemisphere.

It was concluded that these symmetrical plana were generally larger than normal asymmetrical plana and that dyslexics may suffer from an excess of language-related cortex, primarily in the right posterior Sylvian region. Also, whilst symmetrical plana are not pathognomonic of dyslexia, they may place an individual at risk for difficulties in learning to read, especially if genetic predispositions and neuronal/cytoarchitectonic abnormalities are present. Finally, the post-mortem results were important because they highlighted the fact that these morphological characteristics in the brains of dyslexics were related to prenatal neurodevelopmental variation that could only occur during the fifth to seventh month of fetal gestation. Other evidence published during this period provided confirmation that symmetry in the plana existed in additional dyslexic subjects and that these findings were not gender specific. It was on the basis of these studies that other investigators began employing MRI imaging techniques to examine asymmetry/ symmetry in the region of the plana in living patients.

MRI findings regarding plana morphology in developmental dyslexia

A number of studies have examined brain morphology differences in dyslexics employing both computed tomography (CT) and MRI (e.g. Duara et al., 1991; Haslam et al., 1981; Hier et al., 1978; Hynd et al., 1995; Kushch et al., 1993; Rosenberger & Hier, 1980; Rumsey et al., 1986). However, these studies did not specifically examine asymmetries in the region of the plana and are thus not reviewed here. Generally, these studies find morphological differences in the brains of dyslexics in the posterior regions of the brain or in other regions less well understood in regard to their importance to linguistic and cognitive deficits found to characterise dyslexics (Morgan & Hynd, in press).

A series of MRI investigations has specifically examined plana morphology in developmental dyslexia and deserves special attention because the link between the left plana and receptive language abilities and reading is so well documented (Galaburda, 1993; Hynd & Semrud-Clikeman, 1989). As will be seen, however, significantly different methodologies employed in measuring the plana support only general conclusions regarding the importance of plana asymmetries in dyslexia.

In 1990 two studies appeared that examined plana morphology in dyslexics. Larsen et al. (1990) studied plana asymmetry in 19 dyslexics compared with 18 normal control children. Using coronal MRI slices, they found that the length and area of the planum temporale was significantly more symmetrical in 70% of the dyslexics as contrasted with 30% of the normals. Further, they reported that the symmetrical plana in the dyslexics was attributed to a larger right planum based on contrasting the mean length of the plana for children with and without symmetrical plana.

Hynd and colleagues (Hynd et al., 1990) examined plana asymmetries in 10 dyslexic children, 10 attention deficit disorder with hyperactivity (ADD-H) children, and 10 diagnosed normal control children. The normal left larger than right (L > R) asymmetry of the planum temporale was found on examining lateral sagittal MRI slices in 70% of the normal and ADD-H children but only in 10% of the dyslexics. In this study, the degree of symmetry in the dyslexics was related to a smaller than normal left planum temporale, not a larger right plana. This study was unique in that a clinic control group of children was employed who did not have diagnosed reading or language problems (ADD-H), and diagnosed control children were employed. However, both the Larsen et al. (1990) and Hynd et al. (1990) studies only measured the temporal bank of the planum temporale and did not consider the morphology of the parietal bank. The parietal bank of the plana extends from the most posterior aspect of the Sylvian fissure up into the parietal region. Figure 3.1 shows the location of the temporal and parietal banks of the planum temporale.

Leonard and colleagues (1993) did examine both the temporal and parietal banks of the planum temporale in nine dyslexic teens and adults, 10 unaffected first- and second-degree relatives, and 12 controls using lateral sagittal MRI slices. This study was important because the temporal bank is thought to be important in linguistic processing whilst the parietal bank is believed to be vital in non-verbal or visuospatial processing. It should be pointed out that Leonard et al. (1993) suggested that, earlier, Geschwind and Levitsky (1968) only measured asymmetries of the temporal bank of the plana and did not include the parietal bank. Interhemispheric analyses indicated that all but one subject had a leftward asymmetry of the temporal bank and rightward asymmetry of the parietal bank. Each of their groups evidenced a small but insignificant leftward asymmetry when the total planum temporale was calculated by adding both the temporal and parietal bank measurements. Intrahemispheric contrasts suggested that in the left hemisphere all but two dyslexic subjects had larger temporal than parietal banks and the left intrahemispheric asymmetry coefficient was highly significant for all groups. However, the dyslexic group had a significantly smaller right hemispheric coefficient of asymmetry than the controls, which was thought to reflect a right parietal shift in neural tissue from the temporal to parietal bank. Interestingly, the dyslexics were found to have more cerebral anomalies than the controls (Leonard et al., 1993). Schultz et al. (1994) reported supportive findings as well.

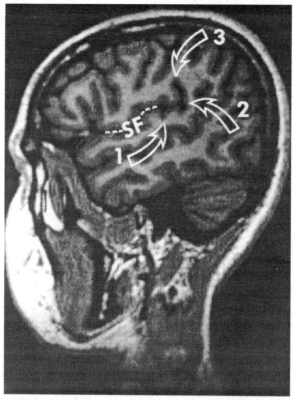

Figure 3.1 Sagittal MRI section (1.17 mm slice thickness) showing the topography of the planum temporale and planum parietal buried in the Sylvian fissure. The tip of arrow 1 points at the bottom of Heschl's sulcus, i.e. the anterior border of the planum temporale. The tip of arrow 2 points at the posterior end of the horizontal portion of the Sylvian fissure, i.e. the posterior border of the planum temporale and inferior border of the planum parietal. The tip of arrow 3 points at the upper end of the posterior ascending ramus of the Sylvian fissure, i.e. the upper border of the planum parietal. The planum temporale covers the inferior wall of the Sylvian fissure between arrows 1 and 2. The planum parietal covers the posterior wall of the Sylvian fissure between arrows 2 and 3 (From Jancke et al., 1994, with permission)

Plana morphology and linguistic/reading deficits in dyslexia

Whilst the left planum temporale is in Wernicke's region, which has long been recognised as being vitally important to language processing and comprehension (Kolb & Whishaw, 1990; Mayeux & Kandel, 1991), cytoarchitectonic evidence underscores its importance. As Rubens et al. (1976) have indicated, in order to draw an association between gross anatomical differences and their relative functional importance, it is necessary to have correlative cytoarchitectonic evidence. Evidence in this regard has been provided by Galaburda, Sanides and Geschwind (1978) who reported that asymmetries in the volume of area TPT, whose connectional organisation is believed to be important to language, corresponds closely with observed asymmetries of the planum temporale. Thus, not only is the left planum temporale part of the classical central language zone but it also appears to have unique cytoarchitectonic characteristics which probably underlie its functional importance in language, and perhaps reading ability.

In the study by Larsen et al. (1990), the relationship between plana asymmetry/symmetry and word decoding was examined. Of the five dyslexics classified as having pure phonological deficits, all had symmetrical plana. Of the four dyslexic children not characterised as having a specific phonological deficit, three had asymmetrical plana whilst one had symmetrical plana. Larsen et al. (1990) concluded that symmetry of the planum temporale was associated with phonological processing deficits. Semrud-Clikeman et al. (1991) used the same subjects as Hynd et al. (1990) and examined the relationship between neurolinguistic ability and plana variation. They reported that regardless of group membership, subjects with either symmetry or reversed asymmetry (L < R) of the plana had significantly lower verbal comprehension, naming, word recognition and reading comprehension scores.

Even more recently, correlations between the temporal and parietal banks of the plana and language and reading scores have been reported (Morgan et al., 1996). Whilst Morgan et al. did not find group differences in plana asymmetry similar to those found by Leonard et al. (1993) and Schultz et al. (1994), they did report that the left planum temporale length correlated positively with language scores for non-dyslexic subjects and that the right planum temporale length correlated negatively with linguistic measures among the dyslexics. Further, expressive and receptive language measures as well as performance on measures of reading attainment most frequently correlated with planum temporale measurements. Thus, it appears that leftward asymmetry of the planum temporale, especially the temporal bank, confers linguistic advantages.

Whilst these correlative relationships are theoretically consistent with what might be expected considering the known functional importance of the left planum temporale, it is still an unanswered question as to exactly how variation in plana asymmetry and cortical anomalies found at post-mortem by Galaburda et al. (1985) affect the development of language and reading skills.

How do variations in plana asymmetry and cortical anomalies affect the development of language and reading skills in dyslexia?

Hier et al. (1978) first suggested that alterations in patterns of asymmetry in developmental dyslexia may reflect 'the mismatch between hemispheric specialization for language and structural asymmetry of the hemispheres' (p. 92). This line of reasoning suggested to Hier et al.

(1978) that children with symmetry or reversed asymmetry were at risk for developing reading problems because the left hemisphere was not as structurally adapted for language as it was in individuals with normal patterns of asymmetry. This line of reasoning has been expanded upon more recently.

For example, Steinmetz and Galaburda (1991) suggested that symmetry affects an individual's ability to compensate for the cortical anomalies (focal dysplasias, ectopias, brain warts, polymicrogyri, etc.) that Galaburda et al. (1985) have documented in the brains of dyslexics at post mortem. Another possibility is that symmetrical plana reduce or inhibit in some fashion the nature and amount of cognitive strategies available to an individual at risk for dyslexia. It needs to be pointed out that these explanations acknowledge the importance, and perhaps primacy, of the cortical anomalies found in the brains of dyslexics. This view relegates symmetry or reversed asymmetry to a variation that may exacerbate the role of cortical anomalies in the acquisition and development of the linguistic and cognitive processes critical to fluent reading ability. In fact, it is argued that both symmetry and cortical anomalies are required for the development of developmental dyslexia. Humphreys, Kaufmann and Galaburda (1990) suggested that symmetry of the plana places individuals at risk for dyslexia because of the assumed alterations in cortical connections resulting from a failure of neurons in the right hemisphere to be pruned, which may interfere with cognitive processing. Galaburda (1989) provides some support for this idea because he found that cortical areas that are more symmetrical contain more neurons and have denser interhemispheric connections.

Unfortunately, however, the resolution of MRI procedures only allows a window from which one can view structural regions such as the planum temporale. Whilst regions of abnormal cortex such as those characterised by polymicrogyri (Galaburda & Kemper, 1979) may be visualised on MRI scans, the more focal cortical dysplasias and cytoarchitectonic abnormalities cannot at present be seen. Thus, MRI morphometry of the planum temporale is not only fraught with serious measurement difficulties (e.g. type of acquisition protocol, temporal and spatial resolution, plane of scan, measurement procedure; Plante & Turkstra, 1991), but it may also be incapable of examining whether both cortical anomalies and symmetry of the plana are necessary to produce the linguistic and reading deficits found in dyslexia.

Some tentative conclusions about planum temporale asymmetries and dyslexia

So, what can be concluded about the relationship between planum temporale morphology and developmental dyslexia? Several tentative conclusions seem warranted.

First, there exists a long history of inquiry about the importance of the region generally encompassing Wernicke's area, and more specifically the left planum temporale, and its involvement in the comprehension of language and written text (Hynd, 1989). There exists little doubt that this region of the cortex plays an important role in the language system of most individuals. Recent MRI and high-resolution positron emission tomography (PET) studies provide further evidence of the normal asymmetry and functional importance of the left planum temporale (e.g., Karbe et al., 1995).

Second, post-mortem studies by Galaburda and colleagues document an increased incidence of both symmetry in the planum temporale and the presence of focal cortical dysplasias in individuals with a history of developmental dyslexia (e.g. Galaburda et al., 1985). Experimental evidence suggests that some of the cytoarchitectonic and morphologic anomalies may be due to the influence of traumatic events during neurological development (Rosen et al., 1994) and that they may be related to deficits associated with language or reading impairment (Fitch et al., 1994).

Third, neuroimaging studies employing MRI suggest that a relationship exists between deviations from normal patterns of asymmetry of the planum temporale and the dyslexic syndrome (e.g. Hynd et al., 1990, Larsen et al., 1990; Leonard et al., 1993). Other evidence supports the conclusion that deviations in normal patterns of asymmetry of the planum temporale, and possibly length measurements of the planum, are associated with language and phonological coding deficits in developmental dyslexics (e.g. Larsen, et al., 1990; Morgan et al., 1996; Semrud-Clikeman et al., 1991).

Fourth, all of the evidence to date from both post-mortem and neuroimaging studies implicates deviations from normal neuronal development during fetal gestation, most likely between the fifth and seventh month. The focal dysplasias identified in the brains of dyslexics by Galaburda and colleagues (e.g. Galaburda et al., 1985; Humphreys et al., 1990) must first emerge during this critical period when neuronal genesis and migration are at a peak (Dooling et al., 1983). It is also likely that it is developments during this critical period (when gyri are forming rapidly) that eventually lead to the alteration in normal patterns of asymmetry of the planum temporale as observed in some of the MRI studies. Thus, whether under genetic or traumatic influences, it does appear that the features we associate with developmental dyslexia have their genesis during fetal ontogeny.

Finally, it is clear that our understanding of what constitutes the region known as the planum temporale has expanded to include both the structural and potentially the functional importance of both the temporal and parietal banks of the plana (Jancke et al., 1994; Leonard et al., 1993; Steinmetz, et al., 1990). Thus, in the context of the importance of this region of the brain in reading and language it seems that new avenues for developing a better understanding of brain structure and function in dyslexia may be available for inquiry.

Sulcal/Gyral Patterns in the Perisylvian Region in Dyslexia

Although virtually every area of the cerebral cortex could be quantitatively classified by the patterns of sulci and gyri, classification systems have been limited so far to the posterior perisylvian/parietal opercular region, an area that has received attention because of its involvement in language functions associated with Wernicke's region. Whilst two classification systems have been developed (Steinmetz et al., 1990; Witelson & Kigar, 1992), the one developed by Steinmetz et al. (1990) has received rather more attention and is the focus of discussion in this chapter.

Steinmetz et al. (1990) examined 80 post-mortem hemispheres and 40 hemispheres by MRI. They divided the Sylvian fissure into three parts: the posterior horizontal region (PHR), which is the main horizontal branch, the posterior ascending ramus (PAR), and the posterior descending ramus (PDR). Figures 3.1 and 3.2 illustrate these structures.

Type 1 in this system is the 'textbook' type of morphology, in which the PAR of the Sylvian fissure ascends posterior to the inferior postcentral sulcus. In Type 2, the Sylvian fissure lacks a PAR, so that the fissure remains horizontal. Type 3 morphology is characterised by an extra sulcus interposed between the postcentral sulcus and the PAR, creating an extra gyrus. In Type 4, the PAR is continuous with the postcentral sulcus, so that the supramarginal gyrus is absent (Steinmetz et al., 1990). Generally, it was found that Type 1 morphology was most frequently observed in both the left (67–65%) and right (82–85%) of the post-mortem and MRI cases, respectively. Type 2 was not observed at all in the right hemisphere but occurred in 10% and 25% of the left hemispheres, respectively. Type 3 morphology occurred in 21% of the left hemispheres in the post-mortem sample and 5% of the MRI sample. Type 3 morphology appeared in only 5% of the right hemispheres in the post-mortem sample and not at all in the MRI sample. Type 4 was present in 2% of the left hemispheres in the post-mortem sample and 5% of the MRI sample whereas it was present in the right in 13% of the post-mortem sample and 15% of the MRI sample. Figure 3.2 illustrates these different posterior Sylvian morphology types.

To date, only one published study has applied the Steinmetz et al. (1990) classification system to MRI of the brains of dyslexics. Leonard et al. (1993) compared the sulcal patterns of 10 individuals with dyslexia

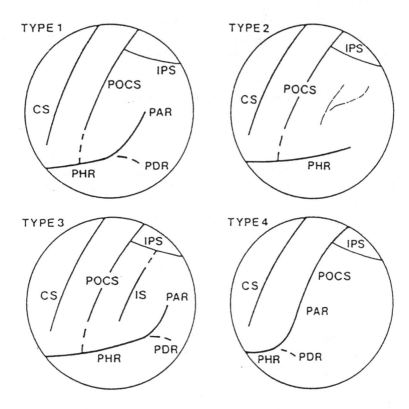

Figure 3.2 The four types of parietal opercular sulcus topography. Broken lines indicate inconstant sulcus segments. Abbreviations: CS – central sulcus; MS – marginal sulcus; PAOS – parieto-occipital sulcus; SF – Sylvian fissure; AHR – anterior horizontal ramus of the SF; AAR – anterior ascending ramus of the SF; PHR – posterior horizontal ramus of the SF; PAR – posterior ascending ramus of the SF; PDR – posterior descending ramus of the SF; PRCS – precentral sulcus; POCS – postcentral sulcus; IPS – intraparietal sulcus; IS – intermediate parietal opercular sulcus (From Steinmetz et al., 1990, with permission)

and nine normal individuals according to the Steinmetz et al. (1990) system. They found a greater incidence of Type 1 morphology in the left hemispheres of controls (90%) and a smaller incidence in either hemispheres of dyslexics (52%), as well as an increased incidence of Type 3 gyri in dyslexics in the left hemisphere (60%). Leonard et al. (1993) suggest that this increase in Type 3 morphology could be associated with learning disabilities, as first-degree relatives of dyslexic subjects also evidenced an increased incidence of Type 3 morphology in the left hemisphere, suggesting a familial component to sulcal morphology. Whilst this study is of critical importance in paving the way to examine possible links between sulcal pattern variation and dyslexia, the subjects in the Leonard et al. (1993) study were diagnosed primarily on reported history of reading problems. Because they were not subjected to a thorough clinical evaluation to document the presence of dyslexia there remains some doubt about the presence and severity of dyslexia in this sample.

To examine the possible relationship between sulcal morphology pattern type and the dyslexic syndrome in children, we examined posterior Sylvian fissure morphology according to the Steinmetz et al. (1990) method in 79 carefully diagnosed children using MRI. There were 14 diagnosed normal children, 27 dyslexics (reading ability at least two standard deviations below measured intelligence with a documented positive family history of reading problems), and 38 children diagnosed as having attention deficit hyperactivity disorder (ADHD). The children in the ADHD group served as a clinical control group. All children received a comprehensive two-day neuropsychological evaluation and an MRI scan (3D acquisition in the sagittal plane, 2.3 mm slices, 0% gap). All scans were read as normal by a neuroradiologist. No significant differences existed between groups on chronological age (9–12 years), gender, or race/ethnic background. Both the normal and ADHD children had normal reading achievement whilst the mean standard score on a measure of reading was 78 for the dyslexic children. Posterior Sylvian fissure morphology was classified according to the Steinmetz et al. (1990) method. Figure 3.3 shows MRI scans with each of the Steinmetz et al. (1990) sulcal morphology patterns.

In our sample of normal children, 60% had Type 1 morphology in the left hemisphere whereas 40% had Type 3. Therefore, in our sample of normal children it can be concluded that Types 1 and 3 are the most common sulcal patterns in the left hemisphere. In our dyslexic and ADHD subjects, Type 1 was most frequent in the left hemisphere (68%, 61% respectively). Of the ADHD children, 30% had Type 3 in the left whereas in the dyslexics Type 2 occurred in 16% as did Type 3 (16%). These differences were statistically significant ($\chi^2 = 33.49, p < 0.001$).

In the right hemisphere, and consistent with the normative data provided by Steinmetz et al. (1990), 90% of the normals had Type 1 and 10% had Type 3 morphology. The ADHD children had a similar incidence of Type 1 and 3 morphologies in the right. However, the dyslexics had a significantly reduced incidence of Type 1 (57%) morphology and had a higher incidence of Type 3 (37%).

These preliminary results give some support to the notion that gyral morphology patterns in this region of the brain, particularly in the left perisylvian parietal opercular region, may be associated with the reading and language deficits observed in dyslexia. Furthermore, there may be as Leonard et al. (1993) suggest, familial links in the manifestation of gyral morphology patterns as, in a very small sample of new families, there seems to be some association between the gyral morphology pattern in the affected parent and that shown by the child with diagnosed dyslexia (see Figure 3.4). As can be seen in Figure 3.4, out of five

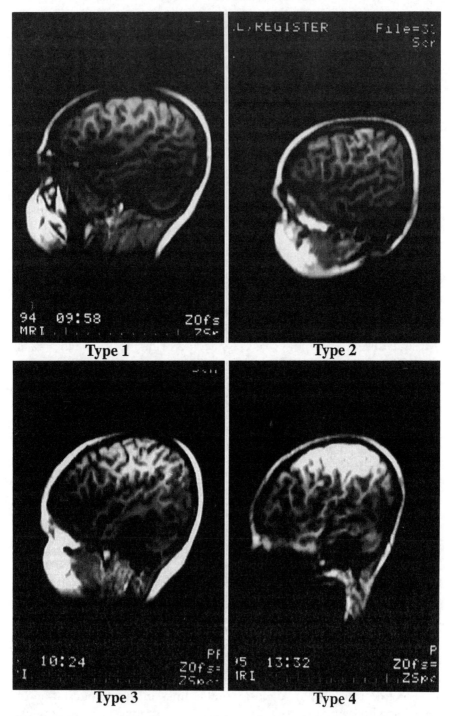

Figure 3.3 Four types of posterior Sylvian fissure (parietal opercular region) morphology according to the method of Steinmetz et al. (1990). See Figure 3.2 for a graphic representation of the sulcal morphology patterns illustrated on these MRI scans

cases where a clinically diagnosed affected parent and dyslexic child can be compared (cases 3, 6, 23, 33 and 72), there exists 60% agreement in sulcal morphology patterns across 10 hemispheres, most significantly so in the presence of Type 2 morphology pattern in the right hemisphere in three out of the five comparable cases.

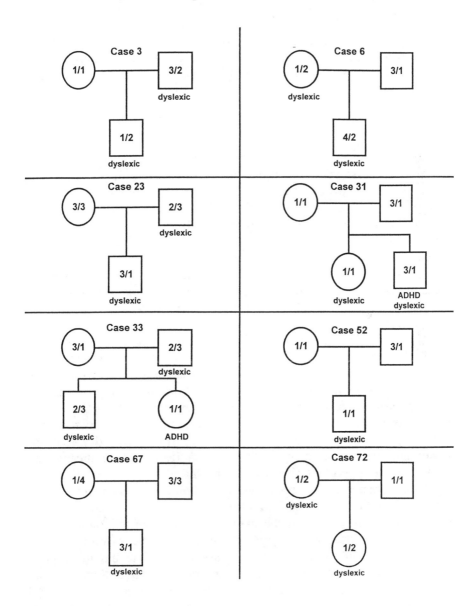

Figure 3.4 Dyslexic pedigree for eight families in which five families have one affected parent. Left/right gyral morphology patterns according to the method of Steinmetz et al. (1990) are noted

It is impossible to compare these results directly with those obtained in the Leonard et al. (1993) study because of the differences in the documented presence of dyslexia and because of the small samples. However, in each case, departures from the normative data of Steinmetz et al. (1990) seems to exist in the dyslexic subjects. Again, this raises the possibility that gyral morphology patterns may be associated with the unique neurolinguistic deficits dyslexic individuals often experience but it will remain for further, more comprehensive studies to address this issue fully. It is important to remember that these gyral patterns first emerge between the fifth and seventh month of fetal gestation and may be under genetic control or be responsive outcomes of traumatic influences.

Conclusions

Contrary to those who voiced the opinion that the brains of dyslexics would not reveal any evidence of the presumed neurobiological basis of severe reading problems (Critchley, 1964), the post-mortem and neuroimaging studies (MRI) reviewed here have been revealing. Can it be said that we now know what it is in the brains of dyslexics that 'causes' severe reading problems? Clearly, we cannot say with confidence that we know the neurobiological cause of dyslexia. However, there are some general conclusions that can be offered about the relationship between variability in brain morphology and the deficits observed in dyslexia.

All of the post-mortem studies to date have revealed the presence of focal cerebral dysplasias in the brains of developmental dyslexics (Galaburda et al., 1985). These focal dysplasias only appear during the period of neuronal genesis and placement occurring in the fifth to seventh month of fetal gestation. Generally, the placement of these focal dysplasias affects the regions of the cortex known to participate in the neurolinguistic system in the left cerebral hemisphere (Hynd & Semrud-Clikeman, 1989). Also, some of the MRI studies reveal significant variability in the region of the planum temporale in dyslexic subjects, particularly with regard to the length of the temporal and parietal banks (Morgan & Hynd, in press). Differences in MRI measurement procedures and discrepancies in the assessment of subjects' cognitive and reading skills probably contribute to the differences between studies, especially regarding patterns of plana asymmetry that may distinguish dyslexic from normal subjects. Finally, the more recent and exploratory examination of gyral patterns in the posterior perisylvian, parietal opercular region may offer some promise of showing whether these gyral pattern differences are unique to dyslexia and whether or not they are associated with familial dyslexia. Significantly more work needs to be accomplished in this arena, however.

Whilst these general conclusions seem justified, one critical issue remains largely unaddressed. How exactly does variability in the language-related cortex in dyslexia cause or relate to severe reading difficulties? Whilst some intriguing ideas have been advanced (Galaburda, 1993; Humphreys et al., 1990; Steinmetz & Galaburda, 1991), we still do not 'know' how variability in the posterior perisylvian region, or even focal neuronal abnormalities in the language cortex, affects the development and maintenance of phonological coding and other language abilities required for fluent reading ability. Perhaps functional MRI (fMRI) procedures will allow us an opportunity to examine this and related issues in a non-invasive fashion in living subjects.

Progress has been made in understanding the neurobiological basis of developmental dyslexia. Clearly, variation in prenatal neurogenesis seems highlighted in all of the studies considered here. For this reason, increased efforts to understand those factors, including genetic, environmental or traumatic influences, that contribute to brain variability in dyslexia are warranted.

One may well consider the research conducted to date as analogous to century-old efforts to document individual differences in intelligence, personality, aptitude and physical attributes. With regard to intelligence, for example, little scientific progress was made until Binet in France provided a conceptually well thought-out, and reliable, measure of cognitive development in children. Once the range of human cognitive abilities could be reliably measured and documented, research could move forward in better understanding those factors that characterised, discriminated and influenced the manifestation of cognitive ability over development. This may be analogous to our present position with regard to understanding the variability that characterises the brains of dyslexics. Within the next decade progress will be made in providing valid and reliable methods for discriminating the range of variability in normal brains and how and why the brains of dyslexics meaningfully differ. We have clearly embarked on a promising journey.

References

Adams, M.J. (1990). *Beginning to Read: Thinking and Learning about Print*. Cambridge, MA: MIT Press.

American Psychiatric Association (1994). *Diagnostic and Statistical Manual of Mental Disorders*, 4th edn. Washington, DC: American Psychiatric Association.

Andreasen, N.C., Flashman, L., Flaum, M., Arndt, S., Swayze, V., O'Leary, D.S., Ehrhardt, J.C. & Yuh, W.T.C. (1994). Regional brain abnormalities in schizophrenia measured with magnetic resonance imaging. *Journal of the American Medical Association* **272**, 1763–1769.

Bruck, M. (1992). Persistence of dyslexics' phonological awareness deficits. *Developmental Psychology* **28**, 874–886.

Cardon, L.R., Smith, S.D., Fulker, D., Kimberling, W.J., Pennington, B.F. & DeFries,

J.C. (1994). Quantitative trait locus for reading disability on chromosome 6. *Science* **226**, 276–279.

Chi, J.G., Dooling, E.C. & Gilles, F.H. (1977a). Gyral development of the human brain. *Annals of Neurology* 1, 86–93.

Chi, J.G., Dooling, E.C. & Gilles, F.H. (1977b). Left–right asymmetries of the temporal speech areas of the human fetus. *Archives of Neurology* **34**, 346–348.

Connolly, C.J. (1950). *External Morphology of the Primate Brain*. Springfield, IL: Charles C. Thomas.

Corballis, M. (1983). *Human Laterality*. New York: Academic Press.

Critchley, M. (1964). *Developmental Dyslexia*. London: Heinemann.

Cunningham, D.J. (1892). *Contribution to the Surface Anatomy of the Cerebral Hemispheres*. Dublin: Royal Irish Academy.

Dooling, E.C., Chi, J.G. & Gilles, F.H. (1983). Telencephalic development: Changing gyral patterns. pp. 94–104. In F.H. Gilles, A. Levitan & E.C. Dooling (Eds.) *The Developing Human Brain*. Boston, MA: John Wright.

Duara, R., Kushch, A., Gross-Glenn, K., Barker, W., Jallad, B., Pascal, S., Loewenstein, D.A., Sheldon, J., Rabin, M., Levin, B. & Lubs, H. (1991). Neuroanatomic differences between dyslexic and normal readers on magnetic resonance imaging scans. *Archives of Neurology* **48**, 410–416.

Dvorak, K., Feit, J. & Jurankova, Z., (1978). Experimentally induced focal microgyria and status verrucosus deformis in rats: Pathogenesis and interrelation histological and autoradiolographical study. *Acta Neuropathologia* **44**, 121–129.

Fitch, R.H., Tallal, P., Brown, C.P., Galaburda, A.M. & Rosen, G.D. (1994). Induced microgyria and auditory temporal processing in rats: A model for language impairment? *Cerebral Cortex* **4**, 260–270.

Foundas, A.L., Leonard, C.M., Gilmore, R., Fennell, E. & Heilman, K. (1994). Planum temporale asymmetry and language dominance. *Neuropsychologia* **32**, 1225–1231.

Galaburda, A.M. (1989). Ordinary and extraordinary brain development: Anatomical variation in developmental dyslexia. *Annals of Dyslexia* **39**, 67–80.

Galaburda, A.M. (Ed.) (1993). *Dyslexia and Development: Neurobiological Aspects of Extra-Ordinary Brains*. Cambridge, MA: Harvard University Press.

Galaburda, A.M. & Kemper, T.L. (1979). Cytoarchitectonic abnormalities in developmental dyslexia: A case study. *Annals of Neurology* **6**, 94–100.

Galaburda, A.M., Sanides, F. & Geschwind, N. (1978). Human brain. *Archives of Neurology* **35**, 812–817.

Galaburda, A.M., Sherman, G.F., Rosen, G.D., Abioitiz, F. & Geschwind, N. (1985). Developmental dyslexia: Four consecutive patients with cortical anomalies. *Annals of Neurology* **18**, 222–233.

Geschwind, N. & Levitsky, W. (1968). Human brain: Left–right asymmetries in temporal speech region. *Science* **161**, 186–187.

Haslam, R.H., Dalby, J.T., Johns, R.D. & Rademaker, A.W. (1981). Cerebral asymmetry in developmental dyslexia. *Archives of Neurology* **38**, 679–682.

Hier, D.B., LeMay, M., Rosenberger, P.B. & Perlo, V.P. (1978). Developmental dyslexia: Evidence for a subgroup with a reversal of cerebral asymmetry. *Archives of Neurology*, **35**, 90–92.

Humphreys, P., Kaufmann, W.E. & Galaburda, A.M. (1990). Developmental dyslexia in women: Neuropathological findings in three patients. *Annals of Neurology* **28**, 727–738.

Hynd, G.W. (1989). Learning disabilities and neuropsychological correlates: relationship to neurobiological theory. In D.J. Bakker & H. Van der Vlugt (Eds.) *Learning Disabilities*, Vol. 1: *Neuropsychological Correlates and Treatment*, (pp. 123–147). Amsterdam: Swets & Zeitlinger.

Hynd, G.W. & Cohen, M.J. (1983). *Dyslexia: Neuropsychological Theory, Research, and Clinical Differentiation*. Boston, MA: Allyn & Bacon.

Hynd, G.W. & Semrud-Clikeman, M. (1989). Dyslexia and brain morphology. *Psychological Bulletin* 106, 447–482.

Hynd, G.W. & Willis, W.G. (1988). *Pediatric Neuropsychology*. Boston, MA: Allyn & Bacon.

Hynd, G.W., Semrud-Clikeman, M., Lorys, A.R., Novey, E.S. & Eliopulos, D. (1990). Brain morphology in developmental dyslexia and attention deficit disorder/hyperactivity. *Archives of Neurology* 47, 919–926.

Hynd, G.W., Morgan, A.E., Edmonds, J.E., Black, K., Riccio, C.A. & Lombardino, L. (1995). Reading disabilities, comorbid psychopathology, and the specificity of neurolinguistic deficits. *Developmental Neuropsychology* 11, 311–322.

Hynd, G.W., Hall, L.J., Novey, E.S., Eliopulos, D., Black, K., Gonzalez, J.J., Edmonds, J.E., Riccio, C. & Cohen, M.J. (1995). Dyslexia and corpus callosum morphology. *Archives of Neurology* 52, 32–38.

Jancke, L., Schlaug, G., Huang, Y. & Steinmetz, H. (1994). Asymmetry of the planum temporale. *NeuroReport* 5, 1161–1163.

Karbe, H., Wurker, M., Herholz, K., Ghaemi, M., Pietrzyk, U., Kessler, J. & Heiss, W.-D. (1995). Planum temporale and Brodman's area 22: Magnetic resonance imaging and high-resolution tomography demonstrate functional left–right asymmetry. *Archives of Neurology* 52, 869–874.

Kolb, B. & Whishaw, I.Q. (1990). *Human Neuropsychology*, 3rd edn. New York: W.H. Freeman.

Kushch, A., Gross-Glenn, K., Jallad, B., Lubs, H., Rabin, M., Feldman, E. & Duara, R. (1993). Temporal lobe surface area measurements on MRI in normal and dyslexic readers. *Neuropsychologia* 31, 811–821.

Larsen, J.P., Hoien, T., Lundberg, I. & Odegaard, H. (1990). MRI evaluation of the size and symmetry of the planum temporale in adolescents with developmental dyslexia. *Brain and Language* 39, 289–301.

LeMay, M. (1976). Morphological cerebral asymmetries in modern man, fossil man, and non-human primate. *Annals of the New York Academy of Science* 280, 349–366.

Leonard, C.M., Voeller, K.K.S., Lombardino, L.J., Morris, M.K., Hynd, G.W., Alexander, A.W., Andersen, H.G., Garofalakis, M., Honeyman, J.C., Mao, J., Agree, O.F. & Staab, E.V. (1993). Anomalous cerebral structure in dyslexia revealed with magnetic resonance imaging. *Archives of Neurology* 50, 461–469.

Mayeux, R. & Kandel, E.R. (1991). Disorders of language: The aphasias. In E.R. Kandel, J.H. Schwartz & T.M. Jessell (Eds.) *Principles of Neural Science*, 3rd edn, pp. 839–851. New York: Elsevier.

Morgan, A.E. & Hynd, G.W. (in press). Dyslexia, neurolinguistic ability, and anatomical variation of the planum temporale. *Brain Imaging and Behavior*.

Morgan, A.E., Hynd, G.W., Hall, J., Novey, E.S. & Eliopulos, D. (1996). Planum temporale morphology and linguistic abilities. Manuscript under review.

Plante, E. & Turkstra, L. (1991). Sources of error in the quantitative analysis of MRI scans. *Magnetic Resonance Imaging* 9, 589–595.

Rosen, G.D., Sherman, G.F. & Galaburda, A.M. (1994). Radial glia in the neocortex of adult rats: Effects of neonatal brain injury. *Developmental Brain Research* 82, 127–135.

Rosenberger, P.B. & Hier, D.B. (1980). Cerebral asymmetry and verbal intellectual deficits. *Annals of Neurology* 8, 300–304.

Rubens, A.B., Mahowald, M.W. & Hutton, J.T. (1976). Asymmetry of the lateral

(Sylvian) fissures in man. *Neurology* 26, 620–624.

Rumsey, J.M., Dorwart, R., Vermess, M., Denckla, M.B., Kruesi, M.J.P. & Rapoport, J.L. (1986). Magnetic resonance imaging of brain anatomy in severe developmental dyslexia. *Archives of Neurology* 43, 1045–1046.

Schultz, R.T., Cho, N.K., Staib, L.H., Kier, L.E., Fletcher, J.M., Shaywitz, S.E., Shankweiler, D.P., Katz, L., Gore, J.C., Duncan, J.S. & Shaywitz, B.A. (1994). Brain morphology in normal and dyslexic children: The influence of sex and age. *Annals of Neurology* 35, 732–742.

Semrud-Clikeman, M., Hynd, G.W., Novey, E.S. & Eliopulos, D. (1991). Dyslexia and brain morphology: Relationships between neuroanatomical variation and neurolinguistic tasks. *Learning and Individual Differences* 3, 225–242.

Steinmetz, H. & Galaburda, A.M. (1991). Planum temporale asymmetry: in-vivo morphology affords a new perspective for neuro-behavioral research. *Reading and Writing: An Interdisciplinary Journal* 3, 331–343.

Steinmetz, H., Ebeling, U. Huang, Y. & Kahn, T. (1990). Sulcus topography of the parietal opercular region: An anatomic and MRI study. *Brain and Language* 38, 515–533.

Steinmetz, H., Rademacher, J., Jancke, L., Huang, Y., Thron, A. & Zilles, K. (1990). Total surface of temporoparietal intrasylvia cortex: Diverging left–right asymmetries. *Brain and Language* 39, 357–372.

Steinmetz, H., Rademacher, J., Huang, Y., Hefter, H., Zilles, K., Thron, A. & Freund, H. (1989). Cerebral asymmetry: MR planimetry of the human planem temporale. *Journal of Computer Assisted Tomography*, 13, 996–1005.

Welker, W. (1990). Why does cerebral cortex fissure and fold? A review of determinants of gyri and sulci. In E.G. Jones & A. Peters (Eds.) *Cerebral Cortex*, 8B, pp. 3–136. New York: Plenum Press.

Witelson, S.F. (1982). Bumps on the brain: Right–left anatomic asymmetry as a key to functional lateralization. In S.J. Segalowitz (Ed.), *Language Functions and Brain Organization*, pp. 117–143. New York: Academic Press.

Witelson, S.F. & Kigar, D.L. (1992). Sylvian fissure morphology and asymmetry in men and women: Bilateral differences in relation to handedness in men. *Journal of Comparative Neurology* 323, 326–340.

Zilles, K., Armstrong, E., Schleicher, A. & Kretschmann, H. (1988). The human pattern of gyrification in the cerebral cortex. *Anatomy and Embryology* 179, 173–179.

Chapter 4
How Does a Visual Transient Deficit Affect Reading?

JOHN HOGBEN

Transient versus Sustained Systems in Vision

Current understanding of the primate visual system relies heavily on the existence of two parallel pathways extending from the retina into the visual cortex. These pathways, known as the magnocellular and parvocellular, are most sharply distinguished at the level of the lateral geniculate nucleus (LGN), part-way between the retina and the cortex, where they are segregated into distinct layers of large (magnocellular) and small (parvocellular) cells. The properties ascribed to these pathways are so similar to the properties previously ascribed to the psychophysically defined transient and sustained channels in the visual system (e.g. Breitmeyer & Ganz, 1976; Kulikowski & Tolhurst, 1973) that many investigators treat the distinctions as equivalent. This has led people to equate the transient system with the operation of the magnocellular pathway and the sustained system with the parvocellular pathway (e.g. Breitmeyer & Williams, 1990), and assimilate ideas developed within the older transient/sustained framework into that of the more recent magnocellular/parvocellular distinction. In this chapter, the two sets of terms will be treated as synonymous, and the terminology used in any given context will reflect the tradition followed by the particular investigators.

For the purposes of this chapter, the important characteristics of the two systems are as follows. The transient (magnocellular) system responds preferentially to lower spatial frequency and higher temporal frequency stimulation, it responds to the onset and offset of stimuli, and its responses are both rapid and brief. It is insensitive to wavelength in the sense that it fails to signal differences between patches of colour of different hue but of the same luminance (equiluminant). The sustained (parvocellular) system, by contrast, exhibits responses that are slower and more enduring than those of the transient (magnocellular) system, it is sensitive to higher spatial frequencies (i.e. has higher spatial resolution), and is colour-selective, in that it distinguishes between patches of colour that are of different hue even though they may be of the same luminance.

At the level of the retina, parvocellular cells (which comprise about 80% of the ganglion cells) have a relatively higher density at the fovea, whereas the magnocellular cells (about 10%) are evenly distributed across the retina (Bassi & Lehmkuhle, 1990). At the LGN, parvocellular cells occupy the four dorsal layers and magnocellular cells the two ventral layers. Both sets of cells project to the primary visual cortex (striate cortex) and thence the parvocellular stream continues largely to the temporal cortex and the magnocellular largely to the parietal cortex (Merigan & Maunsell, 1993). The two streams are generally thought of as performing parallel analyses of visual input, although there is some cross-talk between them. Inhibitory interactions between the streams have been considered important and, in particular, transient-on-sustained inhibition has been assigned an important role in understanding phenomena of visual masking (Breitmeyer & Ganz, 1976).

Over more than a decade, evidence has accumulated that the visual systems of dyslexic or specifically reading-disabled subjects are characterised by a deficit in the transient, or magnocellular, system. On balance, this evidence appears strong and convincing although there is still no compelling theory of how such a deficit might affect the reading process. Until such a theory exists, sceptics will quite reasonably continue to argue either that there is no visual deficit, or that if it does exist it is an accidental concomitant of reading disability and plays no causal role (e.g. Hulme, 1988).

Evidence for a Transient Deficit in Developmental Dyslexia

There are several sources of evidence pointing to a transient, or magnocellular, deficit in dyslexia, mainly psychophysical but also physiological and histological. Foundations of the psychophysical evidence were laid by the Lovegrove group, and the main aspects are summarised by Lovegrove et al. (1986). These are differences in the contrast sensitivity function and the effects of flicker masking on these; differences in flicker sensitivity; and differences in visible persistence and the effects of flicker masking on these.

Two studies by Martin and Lovegrove (1984, 1988) best exemplify differences in contrast sensitivity between dyslexic and control subjects. The dyslexics were found to have lower contrast sensitivity, but only at lower spatial frequencies, where the magnocellular system is dominant. When the measurements were repeated in the presence of 6 Hz uniform field flicker (UFF), which is believed to reduce magnocellular sensitivity, contrast sensitivity was reduced at lower spatial frequencies, but only for control subjects. Uniform field flicker had no effect on the low spatial frequency contrast sensitivity of the dyslexic subjects, presumably because their magnocellular sensitivity is already depressed. Evans, Drasdo & Richards (1994) also found lower contrast sensitivity at low spatial frequencies in a large sample of dyslexic children. Mason et al. (1993) obtained corroborating evidence of depressed contrast sensitivity in disabled readers at a range of spatial frequencies. A further study by Borsting et al. (1996) classified adult dyslexic subjects on the Boder criteria, and found that dysphonetic dyslexics, but not dyseidetic dyslexics, showed lower contrast sensitivity to low spatial frequency gratings, especially when they were drifting at a relatively fast rate of 10 Hz.

Studies by Martin and Lovegrove (1987, 1988) established differences between dyslexic and control groups in flicker sensitivity. They examined sensitivity to 2 c/deg. gratings flickering at frequencies between 2 and 25 Hz, and found that the dyslexic subjects were less sensitive at all temporal frequencies, but with greater differences at higher temporal frequencies, consistent with a magnocellular system deficit. Brannan and Williams (1988) examined sensitivity for detection of flicker in a large (12.3 degree) visual field in 8- to 10-year-old good and poor readers and found the poor readers less sensitive at all rates of flicker from 4 to 24 Hz, but apparently with a greater difference at lower flicker rates.

A number of studies have demonstrated that dyslexic subjects and controls show a different slope of the function relating the duration of visible persistence to the spatial frequency of the display. For all subjects, the duration of visible persistence increases with spatial frequency. However, the slope is less for dyslexic subjects: at low spatial frequencies, they show greater visible persistence, whereas at higher spatial frequencies their persistence is the same as, or less than that of controls (Badcock & Lovegrove, 1981; Lovegrove, Heddle & Slaghuis, 1980; Slaghuis & Lovegrove, 1984). If the increase in visible persistence is understood as reflecting the decreasing influence of transient-on-sustained inhibition as spatial frequency increases, the greater visible persistence in dyslexics at low spatial frequencies is easily interpretable as a lesser degree of transient-on-sustained inhibition in their visual systems. When visible persistence was examined with the addition of 6 Hz uniform field flicker, Slaghuis and Lovegrove (1984) found that the control subjects developed more persistence at low spatial frequencies, with the outcome that their results resembled those of the dyslexic subjects without the flicker mask. It appears, therefore, that the uniform field flicker reduces the magnocellular sensitivity of the control subjects to the level of the lower magnocellular sensitivity in the dyslexics.

Some studies have failed to find evidence of a transient or magnocellular deficit in dyslexics, and have been reviewed by Hogben (1996) and Lovegrove (1996). It has been argued by Hogben (1996) that these studies share a common feature, in that they employed subjects who had been recruited from clinical populations rather than obtained by screening from school-wide populations. For example, Smith, Early & Grogan (1986) tested dyslexic boys from a private boarding school for dyslexic children and found that they failed to show differing reaction times from normal readers, as would have been expected from a transient deficit hypothesis. Gross-Glenn et al. (1995) tested a heterogeneous sample of people aged from 15 to 63 years, who had been diagnosed on 'psychometric and historical criteria' and found null results with several visual tasks. Walther-Mueller (1995) employed dyslexics who had been referred to the study by educational psychologists or by their parents. On four psychophysical tests, he found a mixture of results, which on balance he could not accept as support for a transient deficit. Cornelissen et al. (1995) examined subjects who had been referred to an orthoptic department because of their reading difficulties; they found no differences on a contrast sensitivity task performed under photopic conditions, but they did find differences in coherent motion detection, consistent with a magnocellular system deficit. Hogben argues that recruiting subjects from clinical populations such as these and verifying their reading disability on the basis of a variety of tests (choices involve real word versus non-word reading, accuracy versus comprehension or rate, passages versus word lists, etc.) allows for the assemblage of heterogeneous samples of subjects whose reading problems may have a variety of origins. It then becomes difficult to interpret the outcomes of experiments, particularly if they are in the direction predicted but the effect is too small to reach statistical significance. The best available evidence, partly confirmed by the results of a study by Borsting et al. (1996) is that it is those dyslexics with dysphonesis (Boder, 1971), or a difficulty with phonological decoding (Castles & Coltheart, 1993) who exhibit signs of a transient deficit.

How Might a Transient System Deficit Affect how Children Learn to Read?

Theory A: Transient-on-sustained inhibition

Two distinct theories have arisen to explain how a transient deficit could affect the development of reading. The first (which I shall call Theory A) arises from the hugely influential work of Breitmeyer and Ganz (1976), which introduced the new ideas of transient and sustained channels to a wider psychological audience.

Breitmeyer (1980) considered the hypothetical sequence of events that occur when an observer makes a saccade (eye movement) from one position to another. A saccade, according to Breitmeyer, not only serves to change visual fixations, it also activates 'transient channels that inhibit the sustained activity that would persist from a previous fixation' and provides 'a series of clear, unmasked, and temporally segregated frames of sustained activity, each one of which represents the pattern information contained in a single fixation interval' (p. 63). On this view, the visible persistence of a stimulus (the measurable excess period of visibility after removal of the stimulus) is due to activity in the sustained channels, and is controlled by inhibition of this sustained activity by the transient channels (transient-on-sustained inhibition). Without such inhibition, Breitmeyer argues, visible persistence would be dysfunctional and each fixation on a visual scene would be cluttered by the persisting contents of the previous fixation.

It has been argued that this is precisely the problem faced by the dyslexic: because the transient system is defective, it fails to inhibit the sustained system, and accordingly as the eyes move across the printed page, the contents of one fixation are carried into the next, causing clutter and confusion. The first formulation of this theory was apparently by Slaghuis and Lovegrove (1984), and it has remained a primary interpretation of the mechanism of dyslexia since then (e.g. Lovegrove et al., 1987; Williams & Lovegrove, 1992; Slaghuis & Pinkus, 1993).

A serious problem arises for this theory, however, from the research of Burr et al. (1982) and Burr, Morrone & Ross (1994). Burr et al. (1982) presented observers with horizontal luminance-modulated gratings during normal viewing and during horizontal saccades. The gratings, at a variety of spatial frequencies, were presented for a duration of 20 msec. As the gratings were parallel to the direction of the saccade, and extended well beyond its path, they produced no effective image motion. At low spatial frequencies, contrast threshold for detection of the grating was greatly elevated during a saccade, whereas at higher spatial frequencies there was no difference, or detection of the grating was slightly enhanced compared with when the eye was stationary. This selective loss of sensitivity strongly suggests that the magnocellular system is insensitive during saccades, whilst the parvocellular system is unaffected, or perhaps is slightly more sensitive.

Burr et al. (1994) repeated the earlier experiment, but either modulating the grating in luminance, as Burr et al. (1982) had done, or modulating it in colour (red and green) at equiluminance, so as to exclude operation of the magnocellular system as far as possible. Again, loss of sensitivity was found selectively at low spatial frequencies for luminance modulated gratings; but with the equiluminant colour-modulated gratings, there was no loss of sensitivity at any spatial frequency. In fact, sensitivity to the equiluminant gratings appeared to be slightly better during the saccade than otherwise. Thus, under conditions favouring the operation of the parvocellular system (equiluminance and high spatial frequency) there is no loss of sensitivity, and under conditions favouring the magnocellular system (luminance-modulated targets and low spatial frequency) sensitivity is severely depressed.

The difficulty for the transient-on-sustained inhibition theory of dyslexia (and indeed, for Breitmeyer's view of the role of transient and sustained channels in reading) is obvious. This evidence suggests that, far from the transient (or magnocellular) system inhibiting the sustained (or parvocellular) system during a saccade, the magnocellular system is barely functioning and the parvocellular system is at least as sensitive as when the eyes are stationary, and perhaps more so. Indeed, Burr et al. (1982) suggest that the parvocellular system may be more sensitive during a saccade for the very reason that the motion-dependent (magnocellular) system is depressed, and exerting less inhibition on the motion-independent (parvocellular) system.

Theory B: temporal precedence theory

A very different form of interaction between the transient and sustained systems is proposed by the second theory (Theory B). Rather than inhibitory interactions, Theory B postulates a two-stage process of analysis of the visual scene, the magnocellular system performing an early analysis, the output of which is fed into the parvocellular system for further elaboration. Williams, Brannan & Lartigue (1987) suggested this theory to account for the results of a visual search experiment. They proposed a 'transient/sustained theory of visual perception' in which

'the transient subsystem is a fast-acting early warning system that extracts large amounts of global information. The sustained subsystem, on the other hand, responds more slowly and subsequent to the transient response, and is dependent to an extent on the output of the transient subsystem. If the transient visual response of poor readers is sluggish then the temporal precedence of transient information is mitigated, and progression to the detail processing stage is interfered with' (p. 371).

Subsequent development of the theory added that the transient system operates preattentively and performs a global analysis, 'parsing the field into units and regions and coding the position and movement of objects in space. The transient system may function to direct the sustained subsystem to particularly salient areas where it might be most efficacious to perform a more detailed analysis of the shape and color of objects' (Williams & LeCluyse, 1990, p. 112).

Whereas, in Theory A, the dyslexic's problem is that the transient system is weak and fails to inhibit the sustained system, in Theory B the transient system is too slow, and fails to provide timely input and direction to the sustained system. What is the current state of neurophysiological evidence, and what empirical support is available in the form of psychophysical evidence, for this theory?

It would appear that current knowledge of the human visual system says rather little about the neurophysiological substrate of this theory. From a quite recent review (Merigan & Maunsell, 1993), it is clear that the extent and nature of interactions between the magnocellular and parvocellular pathways and their cortical continuations is anything but clear. The neat neurophysiological package needed by Theory B must be recognised for what it is: a conjecture about the way in which the system might work, rather than a description of current knowledge.

The primary empirical support for the temporal precedence theory comes from a study by Williams et al. (1987). These authors employed, as a model of reading, a visual search task (Neisser, 1967), in which a subject is required to search an array of letters from left to right and from top to bottom, and to respond as soon as a target letter is located. As long as the subject has followed the instructions, the time taken to locate the target increases with the target's depth in the array, and the subject's search rate can be calculated from the slope of the linear regression line relating search time to the target's position within the array. Williams et al. found that 8- to 10-year-old poor readers searched much more slowly than good readers of the same age or adult readers; and that when the stimulus display was blurred, the search rate of the poor readers improved dramatically, so that it was comparable to that of the other subject groups, whose performance was hardly affected by blur. They interpreted this as showing that the transient system of poor readers is sluggish and fails to provide timely input to the transient system, resulting in slow rates of visual search; but that when the stimulus is blurred the sustained response is slowed, leading to a re-establishment of the temporal precedence of the transient system.

Sharply discrepant results were found in a similar study by Hogben et al. (1996): reading disabled children and normal readers did not differ in their search rates, either with sharp or blurred displays, and blurring of the display had little effect for either group. Whilst any of a number of methodological differences between the two studies could account for the discrepant findings, it was suggested by Williams and May (1996) that the spacing between the letters used in the search arrays could have been the critical difference. Obviously, this rather severely limits the generality of the Williams et al. (1987) finding, and suggests that there is more to learn about the visual search task before we can arrive at confident conclusions about its relevance to reading and reading disability. Indeed, Williams et al. (1995) concluded that the important stimulus manipulation in their earlier study may not have been blurring itself, but the contrast reduction that accompanied the blur.

What is the evidence that the transient system of dyslexics is sluggish in its operation, as required by Theory B, rather than simply weak, as

Theory A suggests? The clearest test of this question may come from studies of metacontrast masking in dyslexic and normal readers.

Metacontrast is a form of visual masking in which perception of a brief target stimulus is impaired by presentation of another stimulus following it in time: it is a form of backward masking. What makes metacontrast different from other forms of masking, though, is that the masking stimulus is not physically superimposed on the target, but is presented either alongside it, or surrounding it. Furthermore, most masking is obtained not when the target and mask are presented simultaneously (with a stimulus onset asynchrony, or SOA, of zero), as one might expect, but when the mask is presented some time later, with an SOA of 50 to 100 msec, typically. This paradoxical backward causation was explained by Breitmeyer and Ganz (1976) in terms of inhibitory interactions between transient and sustained channels in the visual system. According to this account, maximum masking occurs at relatively long SOAs because the short-latency transient response to the mask inhibits the long-latency sustained response to the target, and it is only when the presentation of the mask is delayed relative to the target that the respective transient and sustained responses are brought into temporal registration within the visual system. The SOA at which maximum masking is obtained (SOAmax) serves, then, as an index of the differential latency of the transient and sustained systems. If they had the same latency, maximum masking would be observed at zero SOA; a large differential would mean that the mask would have to be substantially delayed in order to bring its transient response into temporal registration with the sustained response to the target.

Two sets of conflicting results have been reported in relation to metacontrast and dyslexia. First, Williams et al. (1989) compared groups of 8- to 11-year-old normal and disabled readers, and found that SOAmax was briefer for the reading disabled children (about 10 msec compared with 30 msec). In foveal presentation of the stimuli, there was no difference in magnitude of masking, suggesting that the only difference between the two groups was in the timing of the transient responses. The second study, by Edwards et al. (1996), compared two groups of adolescent boys and found just the opposite: the reading-disabled boys exhibited weaker metacontrast masking overall (as would be expected if their transient-on-sustained inhibition was weaker) but there was no sign of a change in SOAmax. The reason for this divergence of results is unknown, but we are continuing to examine metacontrast with a view to clarifying the issue, with samples of children varying in age from 8 to 15 years.

From the foregoing, it should be clear that support for Theory B is not strong. Its physiological basis is conjectural rather than factual, and the evidence from psychophysical studies in its favour is in dispute. Moreover, the characteristic forms of interaction between the transient and sustained systems required by Theory A and Theory B appear to be incompatible. Theory A requires the transient system to be inhibiting the sustained system; Theory B has the transient system feeding partial analyses of the visual scene to the sustained system, and directing it to perform more detailed analysis. It is clear in some cases that either theory can account for experimental results: for example, the ameliorating effects of blur on dyslexics' visual search rates can be interpreted in terms of Theory A as well as of Theory B. Following Williams and LeCluyse (1990), image blurring, through diminishing the contrast of high spatial frequency components of the stimulus, may decrease the visible persistence of the contents of a fixation, and thereby bypass the dyslexic's problem of insufficient transient-on-sustained inhibition. Alternatively, the weakened sustained response achieved by blurring the display may be sufficiently feeble that the dyslexic's weak transient-on-sustained inhibition is now sufficient to prevent the visual clutter that occurs with sharply focused images. If either of these possibilities makes quantitative sense, it is difficult to see to what extent Theory B is needed to account for the blur result in the first place.

Thus, perhaps it is unnecessary to have two theories; but if it is necessary, some hard theoretical work needs to be done to specify in what circumstances each theory applies, as their basic premises appear contradictory, rather than complementary.

Where is Theory C?

If current theories of how a transient deficit affects reading are found to be wanting, where would we look for another? One possibility is suggested by Whyte (1994) who speculates on a possible connection between attentional processes and dyslexia. Whyte draws attention to the relationship between a putative transient deficit in dyslexia and perceptual grouping effects (e.g. Solman & Cho, 1991; Williams & Bologna, 1985), and crowding effects (e.g. Hill & Lovegrove, 1993; Rayner et al.,1989).

An important pointer to the neurophysiology of attention may have been provided in a recent paper by He, Cavanagh & Intrilligator (1996), who showed that crowding or lateral masking of an adapting grating does not affect the capacity of that grating to raise the contrast threshold of a subsequently presented grating of the same orientation. Crowding blocks visual awareness of the adapting grating, but does not affect adaptation to it. Orientation-specific adaptation obviously takes place at or beyond the level of cortical area V1, the first site of orientation processing; and this experiment shows that visual awareness, and the 'crowding' that blocks it, occur at a higher level than this. A second experiment showed that the effect of crowding is more severe in the upper visual field. In a third experiment attentional requirements of the task were manipulated in the manner of Treisman (1986), and a simple feature discrimination (lines oriented at 45 deg. or 135 deg.) and a conjunction task (letter T at various orientations) were compared. Only the conjunction task, which imposes high attentional demands, showed an asymmetry between upper and lower visual fields. A fourth experiment employed an attentional tracking task, and again found that performance was better in the lower visual field. He et al. (1996) claim that under conditions of crowding, perception of the spatial details of an item is governed not by visual acuity but by the ability of attentional mechanisms to isolate the item. Noting that the dorsal parietal area has classically been associated with 'attentional processes', they suggest that the dorsal parietal area may control attentional resolution. Experimental approaches like this would appear to have the potential to provide basic knowledge that we can apply to our investigations of the fundamental bases of dyslexia.

Conclusions

The evidence reviewed shows that there is a consistent association between magnocellular deficits and problems in learning to read. The proper interpretation of this association remains a matter of considerable controversy, however.

The point has been made more than once that a magnocellular deficit appears to coincide with difficulties in phonological processing (e.g. Hogben, 1996; Lovegrove et al., 1989; Slaghuis et al., 1993). However, there is no clear suggestion about how these factors relate to one another, as Lovegrove et al. frankly acknowledged. The same goes for the suggestion that a magnocellular deficit is part of a more general deficit in the nervous system (e.g., Lehmkuhle et al., 1993; Livingstone et al., 1991). For example, Lehmkuhle et al. speculate that a magnocellular deficit 'creates a timing disorder that precludes the rapid and smooth integration of detailed visual information necessary for efficient reading' (p.995). Similarly, Livingstone et al. (1991) speculate that pathological factors impeding development of the magnocellular system may also affect development of the language areas of the brain (in which case, a magnocellular deficit would have no direct role in reading disability, but would merely serve as a pointer to another deficit that does have a causal role).

In summary, the best developed theory of how a magnocellular deficit affects reading seems to be denied by recent evidence on the functioning of the magnocellular and parvocellular system during saccades, and other views are too incomplete or too speculative to offer a convincing account. As noted above, even though the evidence for a visual deficit appears strong and convincing, a coherent theory is required to make the case that it is more than an accidental concomitant of, or a marker for, reading disability.

Acknowledgements

This research was supported by grants from the Australian Research Council and the Dyslexia-SPELD Foundation of Western Australia.

References

Badcock, D. & Lovegrove, W.J. (1981). The effect of contrast, stimulus duration and spatial frequency on visible persistence in normal and specifically disabled readers. *Journal of Experimental Psychology: Human Perception and Performance* 7, 496–505.

Bassi, C.J. & Lehmkuhle, S. (1990). Clinical implications of parallel visual pathways. *Journal of the American Optometric Association* **61**, 98–110.

Boder, E. (1971). Developmental dyslexia: prevailing diagnostic concepts and a new diagnostic approach. In H.R. Myklebust, (Ed.) *Progress in Learning Disabilities*, Vol. II (pp. 293–321). New York: Grune & Stratton.

Borsting, E., Ridder, W.H., Dudeck, K., Kelley, C., Matsui, L. & Motoyama, J. (1996). The presence of a magnocellular defect depends on the type of dyslexia. *Vision Research* **36**, 1047–1053.

Brannan, J.R. & Williams, M.C. (1988). The effects of age and reading ability on flicker threshold. *Clinical Vision Sciences* **3**, 137–142.

Breitmeyer, B.G. (1980). Unmasking visual masking: a look at the 'why' behind the veil of the 'how'. *Psychological Review* **87**, 52–69.

Breitmeyer, B.G. & Ganz, L. (1976). Implications of sustained and transient channels for theories of visual pattern masking, saccadic suppression, and information processing. *Psychological Review* **83**, 1–36.

Breitmeyer, B.G. & Williams, M.C. (1990). Effects of isoluminant-background color on metacontrast and stroboscopic motion: interactions between sustained (P) and transient (M) channels. *Vision Research* **30**, 1069–1075.

Burr, D.C., Morrone, M.C. & Ross, J. (1994). Selective suppression of the magnocellular visual pathway during saccadic eye movements. *Nature* **371**, 511–513.

Burr, D.C., Holt, J., Johnstone, J.R. & Ross, J. (1982). Selective suppression of motion sensitivity during saccades. *Journal of Physiology* **333**, 1–15.

Castles, A. & Coltheart, M. (1993). Varieties of developmental dyslexia. *Cognition* **47**, 149–180.

Cornelissen, P., Richardson, A., Mason, A., Fowler, S. & Stein, J. (1995). Contrast sensitivity and coherent motion detection measured at photopic luminance levels in dyslexics and controls. *Vision Research* **35**, 1483–1494.

Edwards, V.T., Hogben, J.H., Clark, C.D. & Pratt, C. (1996). Effects of a red background on magnocellular functioning in average and specifically disabled readers. *Vision Research* **36**, 1037–1045.

Evans, B.J.W., Drasdo, N. & Richards, I.L. (1994). An investigation of some sensory and refractive visual factors in dyslexia. *Vision Research* **34**, 1913–1926.

Gross-Glenn, K., Skottun, B.C., Glenn, W., Kushch, A., Lingua, R., Dunbar, M., Jallad, B., Lubs, H.A., Levin, B., Rabin., M., Parke, L.A. & Duara, R. (1995). Contrast sensitivity in dyslexia. *Visual Neuroscience* **12**, 153–163.

He, S., Cavanagh, P. & Intrilligatar, J. (1996). Attentional resolution and the locus of visual awareness. *Nature* **383**, 334–337.

Hill, R. & Lovegrove, W.J. (1993). One word at a time: a solution to the visual deficit in SRDs? In S.F. Wright & R. Groner (Eds.) *Facets of Dyslexia and its Remediation*, Studies in Visual Information Processing, 3. Amsterdam: North-Holland/Elsevier.

Hogben, J.H. (1996). A plea for purity. *Australian Journal of Psychology* 48.

Hogben, J.H., Pratt, C., Dedman, K. & Clark, C.D. (1996). Blurring the image does not help disabled readers. *Vision Research* 36, 1503–1507.

Hulme, C. (1988). The implausibility of low-level visual deficits as a cause of children's reading disabilities. *Cognitive Neuropsychology* 5, 369–374.

Kulikowski, J.J. & Tolhurst, D.J. (1973). Psychophysical evidence for sustained and transient detectors in human vision. *Journal of Physiology, London* 232, 149–162.

Lehmkuhle, S., Garzia, R.P., Turner, L., Hash, T. & Baro, J.A. (1993). A defective visual pathway in children with reading disability. *New England Journal of Medicine* 328, 989–996.

Livingstone, M.S., Rosen, G.D., Drislane, F.W. & Galaburda, A.M. (1991). Physiological and anatomical evidence for a magnocellular defect in developmental dyslexia. *Proceedings of the National Academy of Sciences, USA* 88, 7941–7947.

Lovegrove, W. (1996). Dyslexia and a transient/magnocellular pathway deficit: The current situation and future directions. *Australian Journal of Psychology* 48.

Lovegrove, W., Martin, F. & Slaghuis, W. (1986). A theoretical and experimental case for a visual deficit in specific reading disability. *Cognitive Neuropsychology* 3, 225–267.

Lovegrove, W.J., Heddle, M. & Slaghuis, W.L. (1980). Reading disability: spatial frequency specific deficits in visual information store. *Neuropsychologia* 18, 111–115.

Lovegrove, W.J., Bowling, A., Badcock, D. & Blackwood, M. (1980). Specific reading disability: differences in contrast sensitivity as a function of spatial frequency. *Science* 210, 439–440.

Lovegrove, W., Pepper, K., Martin, F., Mackenzie, B. & McNicol, D. (1989). Phonological recoding, memory processing and visual deficits in specific reading disability. In Smith, D. & Vickers, P.L. (Eds) *Human Information Processing: Measures, Mechanisms, and Models*. Amsterdam: Elsevier.

Lovegrove, W., Martin, F., Bowling, A., Blackwood, M., Badcock, D. & Paxton, S. (1982). Contrast sensitivity functions and specific reading disability. *Neuropsycholgia* 20, 309–315.

Martin, F. & Lovegrove, W.J. (1984). The effects of field size and luminance on contrast sensitivity differences between specifically reading disabled children and normal children. *Neuropsychologia* 22, 73–77.

Martin, F. & Lovegrove, W.J. (1987). Flicker contrast sensitivity in normal and specifically disabled readers. *Perception* 16, 215–221.

Martin, F. & Lovegrove, W.J. (1988). Uniform-field flicker masking in control and specifically-disabled readers. *Perception* 17, 203–214.

Mason, A., Cornelissen, P., Fowler, S. & Stein, J. (1993). Contrast sensitivity, ocular dominance and specific reading disability. *Clinical Vision Sciences* 8, 345–353.

Merigan, W.H. & Maunsell, J.H.R. (1993). How parallel are the primate visual pathways? *Annual Review of Neuroscience* 16, 369–402.

Neisser, U. (1967). *Cognitive Psychology*. Appleton-Century-Crofts.

Rayner, K., Murphy, L.A., Henderson, J.M. & Pollatsek, A. (1989). Selective attentional dyslexia. *Cognitive Neuropsychology* 6, 357–378.

Slaghuis, W. & Lovegrove, W. (1984). Flicker masking of spatial-frequency-dependent visible persistence and specific reading disability. *Perception* **13**, 527–534.

Slaghuis, W.L., Lovegrove, W.J. & Davidson, J.A. (1993). Visual and language processing deficits are concurrent in dyslexia. *Cortex* **29**, 601–615.

Slaghuis, W. & Pinkus, S.Z. (1993). Visual backward masking in central and peripheral vision in late-adolescent dyslexics. *Clinical Vision Sciences* **8**, 187–199.

Smith, A.T., Early, F. & Grogan, S.C. (1986). Flicker masking and developmental dyslexia. *Perception* **15**, 473–482.

Solman, R.T. & Cho, H.-S. (1991). Color-mediated grouping effects in good and disabled readers. *Ophthalmic and Physiological Optics* **11**, 320–327.

Tallal, P. (1980). Auditory temporal perception, phonics, and reading disabilities in children. *Brain and Language* **9**, 182–198.

Treisman, A. (1986). Properties, parts, and objects. In K.R. Boff, L. Kaufman & J.P. Thomas (eds), *Handbook of Perception and Human Performance*. Chichester: Wiley.

Walther-Mueller, P.U. (1995). Is there a deficit of early vision in dyslexia? *Perception* **24**, 919–936.

Whyte, J. (1994). Attentional processes and dyslexia. *Cognitive Neuropsychology* **11**, 99–116.

Williams, M.C. & Bologna, N. (1985). Perceptual grouping in good and poor readers. *Perception & Psychophysics* **38**, 367–374.

Williams, M.C. & LeCluyse, K. (1990). Perceptual consequences of a temporal processing deficit in reading disabled children. *Journal of the American Optometric Association* **61**, 111–121.

Williams, M.C. & Lovegrove, W. (1992). Sensory and perceptual processing in reading disability. In J. Brannan (ed.), *Applications of Parallel Processing in Vision*. Amsterdam: Elsevier.

Williams, M.C. & May, J.G. (1996). On a failure to replicate: methodologically close, but not close enough. A response to Hogben et al. *Vision Research* **36**, 1509–1511.

Williams, M.C., Brannan, J.R. & Lartigue, E.K. (1987). Visual search in good and poor readers. *Clinical Vision Sciences* **1**, 367–371.

Williams, M.C., Molinet, K. & LeCluyse, K. (1989). Visual masking as a measure of temporal processing in normal and disabled readers. *Clinical Vision Sciences* **2**, 137–144.

Williams, M.C., May, J.G., Solman, R. & Zhou, H. (1995) The effects of spatial filtering and contrast reduction on visual search times in good and poor readers. *Vision Research* **35**, 285–291.

Chapter 5

The Development of Developmental Dyslexia

JOHN L. LOCKE, JAMES HODGSON, PAUL MACARUSO,
JENNIFER ROBERTS, SUSAN LAMBRECHT-SMITH, AND
CATHY GUTTENTAG

A century has passed since the first formal reports of developmental dyslexia began to appear (Critchley, 1970; Hinshelwood, 1900, 1917; Kerr, 1896; Morgan, 1896; Orton, 1925). Though we have certainly learned a great deal about dyslexia over the intervening years, there is still much progress to be made. One indication of the limits of our knowledge may be the range of hypotheses that purport to identify the primary cause of this puzzling disorder. Examples of those proposals include: low-level deficits in the visual system (e.g. Lovegrove, 1991; Lovegrove, Martin & Slaghuis, 1986; but cf. Hulme, 1988); defects in a general faculty of 'temporal order processing' (e.g., Tallal, 1984; Wolff, Michel & Orret, 1990; but cf. Studdert-Kennedy & Mody, 1995); impairments in the formation of general cognitive skills (e.g, Nicolson & Fawcett, 1990); and deficits in the control of eye movements (e.g., Pavlidis, 1983; but cf. Olson, Kliegl & Davidson, 1983).

The task of discovering the causes of reading impairment from the evidence provided by performance on standardised and experimental tasks is a daunting challenge both to our theoretical sophistication and to our methodological dexterity. We are therefore driven to take up promising modes of investigation even when they are expensive, effortful and slow to produce results. The project described here certainly qualifies on all three counts but we expect the results to be worth the work.

Of the many different deficit models that have been proposed as explanations of dyslexia, one has been particularly successful. It holds that dyslexia is at its core a linguistic deficit whose primary impact is on the phonological system (e.g., Bradley & Bryant, 1983; Frith, 1985, and this volume; Gleitman & Rozin, 1977; Gough & Hillinger, 1980; Liberman et al., 1974; Pennington et al., 1990; Rack et al., 1992; Share

& Stanovich, 1995; Snowling et al., 1986b; Stanovich, 1992). Many studies have reported reasonably strong correlations between measures of phonological function in children who are just embarking on reading instruction and their later levels of reading achievement (e.g., Bradley & Bryant, 1983; Lundberg, Olofsson & Wall, 1980; Stanovich, Cunningham & Cramer, 1984; Wagner & Torgesen, 1987). Another source of support for the phonological deficit hypothesis comes from the clinical profiles that are typical of 'classical' developmental dyslexia (Frith, 1985). These children, quite independently of any other feature of their perceptual, linguistic or intellectual profiles, have a difficult time with the task of learning the correspondences between orthographic and phonological units.

There are a number of important differences to be found among the many models that share a commitment to the linguistic hypothesis. For example, some models emphasise the metalinguistic character of the deficit. Children with dyslexia usually demonstrate serious difficulty in consciously decomposing spoken words into the hierarchy of phonological elements that are most directly represented by the orthographic system (e.g., Byrne & Fielding-Barnsley, 1990; Gough, Juel & Griffith, 1992; Treiman, 1992). This particular problem may dissociate relatively freely from the functioning of the linguistic system itself. Obstructions of metaphonological insight can be found as readily in individuals who are otherwise linguistically adroit as in those who have overt spoken-language impairments.

The universal impression among readers of alphabetic orthographies is that phonemes are as perceptually self-evident as the letters that represent them. That impression, however, has been shown to be wrong. Having command of a spoken language does not directly enable a speaker to discern the phonemic constituents of spoken words (Morais, 1991; Morais et al., 1979, 1986; Read et al., 1986). It seems that phonemic awareness is not acquired unless the speaker is also exposed to an alphabetic orthography, or some close approximation to one. Thus, we have come to recognise that phonemic and orthographic knowledge are acquired in concert, each reciprocally facilitating advances in the other (Bradley & Bryant, 1991; Ehri, 1984; Morais, 1991; Stanovich, 1992). The unexpected obscurity of the very segments that the writing system encodes provides a plausible answer to the fundamental question that has accompanied dyslexia from its first description; namely, how can it be that otherwise capable children cannot learn a small number of letter–sound correspondences? The answer may be that dyslexia reflects an impediment to the 'unnatural' metalinguistic insight into the phonological structure of words (Gough & Hillinger, 1980).

A second and closely related view also attributes dyslexia to a basic phonological impairment, but one of a rather different sort. On this account the focal impairment is not an obstruction to metalinguistic insight *per se*, but may instead reflect a subtle but nonetheless significant defect in the representation of speech or in the dedicated perceptual mechanisms that create and manipulate them. A number of studies have attempted to test whether individuals with reading problems have difficulty in perceiving speech accurately (e.g., Brady, Shankweiler & Mann, 1983; Brandt & Rosen, 1980; Bryson & Werker, 1989; Godfrey et al., 1981; Mody, Studdert-Kennedy & Brady 1995; Reed, 1989; Snowling et al., 1986b; Tallal, 1984; Werker, Bryson & Wasserberg, 1989; Werker & Tees, 1987). The results of these studies have been rather mixed, with some reporting small but significant group differences in such features as the slope of categorial boundaries between phones, or in the accuracy of perception of speech sounds in noise, whilst others find relatively little difference between good and poor readers.

Deficits affecting the representation of speech (i.e. phonological representations) are considered to have broad implications, leading to deficient performance on a range of tasks that rely on them. Examples include rapid serial naming (e.g., Wolf, 1986), repetition of complex multisyllabic nonsense words (e.g., Brady, Poggle & Rapala, 1989), and general cognitive tasks such as retaining lists of words in short-term memory (see Brady, 1991; Torgesen, 1988 for reviews). Children with developmental dyslexia have been shown to be deficient in each of these phonological domains (see Fowler, 1991, for a review).

A third type of linguistic deficit model seeks to link dyslexia to a wider range of language dysfunctions which extend beyond the phonological domain. These include impaired lexical representations, syntactic analysis and semantic integration (Aram & Nation, 1980; Bentin, Deutsch & Liberman, 1990; Bishop & Adams, 1990; Kamhi & Catts, 1989; Scarborough, 1990, 1991; Siegel & Ryan, 1988; Yuill & Oakhill, 1991). In the majority of these models, written language impairment is treated as a consequence of a developmental deficit in spoken language. Whilst it is not uncommon to find that children who have histories of difficulty in spoken language development have also had problems in the acquisition of literacy (Bishop & Adams, 1990), it is not at all uncommon to find that even severely dyslexic children have an impressive command over spoken language. In short, 'specific language impairment' and dyslexia dissociate rather freely. Neither condition can be cast as either a necessary or a sufficient condition for the occurrence of the other. Nevertheless, it is reasonable to suppose that more complex relationships between learning to talk and learning to read might hold.

The study we report here represents an attempt to evaluate the various linguistic hypotheses in a longitudinal study of the language development of young children from the onset of linguistic activity through the first few years of formal education. A longitudinal design is needed because the critical periods of advancement in the two domains of interest, the development of spoken and written language, occur at different times. Spoken language development begins well before children become competent talkers, perhaps even before birth (e.g. Mehler et al., 1988). By the time they are old enough to enter school, and hence to begin the process of becoming literate, the bulk of the linguistic system has been acquired (Locke, 1993; Pinker, 1994, 1995). But as we are not yet able to establish a diagnosis of dyslexia until reading problems have emerged, a study that aims to relate dyslexia to any but the most enduring features of language function must adopt a longitudinal design that encompasses the relevant parts of the development of both modalities.

There is also the problem of determining who to study. Given that the incidence of dyslexia is usually estimated to be somewhere around 3–8% in the population at large, a large sample would be needed to be sure that a reasonable number of children whose language development is recorded will also be diagnosed with dyslexia. Dyslexia has been shown to be highly heritable (DeFries et al., 1991; Lubs et al., 1994). Therefore, the sample problem is partially solved by recruiting young children from families with histories of dyslexia. This could increase the odds of including children who are later diagnosed with dyslexia by as much as an order of magnitude.

With dyslexia, as with almost any other neurocognitive disorder, it is usually better to begin intervention as early as possible. Though direct evidence is scant, there is a long-standing interest in discovering reliable predictors that will allow children at serious risk of dyslexia to be identified well before they enter school. The hope is that allowing parents, educators and clinicians to get a head start in addressing the core problems that dyslexia entails will reduce the damage caused by the experience of early academic failure, and perhaps minimise the pernicious accumulation of negative effects that often build throughout the course of education (Stanovich, 1986).

The importance of early identification of young children who are likely to be dyslexic follows from the expectation that the greatest benefits of remediation are likely to accrue if begun before too much of the neural and cognitive plasticity that children enter the world with is lost to maturation (e.g., Merzenich et al., 1993). The brain develops very rapidly during the first few months and years of life (Greenough, Black & Wallace, 1987), reaching roughly 95% of its adult volume by middle childhood (Caviness et al., 1996). Disorders of developmental origin raise special problems for the concept of plasticity, but even so, many of us believe that if we could detect the linguistic precursors of developmental dyslexia well before children begin their formal education, we might be able to achieve much greater success in treatment than we currently do (e.g. Scarborough, 1990).

There have been few longitudinal studies of the linguistic development of children at genetic risk of dyslexia. Scarborough's (1990) pioneering study found on retrospective analysis that children at genetic risk for dyslexia could be divided into those who did experience significant reading difficulty (65% of her sample) and those who did not. The latter group was indistinguishable from a matched group of control children on a range of measures. At the earliest ages, the children destined for dyslexia showed significantly lower performance on measures of syntactic complexity of utterances and accuracy of phonological production. Unexpectedly, the measures of vocabulary and phonemic discrimination did not produce group differences. At later ages, beginning at 3 years and becoming more stark at 5 years, differences in receptive vocabulary and object naming increased. Phonemic awareness and letter knowledge also emerged as reliable discriminators.

Thus, Scarborough's findings suggest that there may be important signs in spoken language development that can be used to anticipate dyslexia in individual children. The study reported here extends the advances she has made.

Method

To identify infants and young children who were at risk for developmental dyslexia, we attempted to locate dyslexic adults with young children. On purely statistical grounds, about half of these infants would be expected to have dyslexia themselves (e.g. DeFries et al., 1991; Lubs et al., 1994). We approached adults who had (a) an attested lifelong history of reading and writing difficulty and (b) a medically normal infant between 9 months and 3 years of age. Referrals were obtained from teachers at a large school for dyslexic students. Subjects were also contacted by public postings around the Boston area and word of mouth. All subjects lived in Massachusetts within a 60-mile radius of Boston.

Children born to a dyslexic parent (or parents) were labelled the potentially dyslexic (PD) group. There were 30 PD children (15 males, 15 females) in this study. Also recruited for the study were children whose parents, siblings, and other relatives had no known history of difficulty in learning to read and write. Originally there were 29 control children (14 males, 15 females) but one female control was eliminated once we discovered that she had sustained a head injury as an infant.

Every effort was made to match control children to PD children in terms of age of entry into the study. More than half of the children in each group (57% PD, 54% control) entered the study before 24 months of age. All children in the study had developmentally insignificant medical histories and no known permanent hearing problems.

There were eight families with one PD child and 11 families with two PD siblings in the study. Ten control families had one child, six had two siblings, and two had three siblings in the study. For the PD families, 12 had a dyslexic father, five had a dyslexic mother, and three had two affected parents.

Parents of the PD and control children were administered a short battery of tests to assess their reading and spelling skills. The battery included the Phonetic Analysis and Fast Reading sub-tests of the *Stanford Diagnostic Reading Test*, and the Reading and Spelling sub-tests of the *Wide Range Ach2gievement Test*. The dyslexic parents had considerably more difficulty on these tests than the control parents. For instance, 18 of the 23 dyslexic parents who took the Phonetic Analysis sub-test scored below the 30th percentile, whereas none of the 36 control parents scored below the 50th percentile on this test. More generally, 87% of the dyslexic parents scored below the 50th percentile on two or more sub-tests compared with only 3% of the control parents. These results show that in most cases the dyslexic parents demonstrated difficulties on standardised tests of reading and spelling, although a few did well on the standardised tests perhaps stemming from remedial training (Finucci, Gottfredson & Childs, 1986; Lefly & Pennington, 1991; Pennington et al., 1986; Pennington et al., 1990; Scarborough, 1984).

Children entering the study were seen on a regular schedule with frequency of visits depending on the child's age. Children between 6 months and 2 years were seen every two months. From 2 to 3 years of age children were seen every four months, and from 3 to 5 years of age every six months. These sessions contained formal testing (including standardised and experimental measures) and play activities designed to elicit speech samples. Children's pre-literacy skills were assessed once before entering kindergarten and once before entering first grade. The specific tests given and measures collected at various stages in the study are described in the sections below.

Results

Standardized measures

The Bayley Scales of Mental Maturity were administered once to children between 6 and 40 months. Nineteen PD children (mean age: 14 months) and 17 controls (mean age: 14 months) received the Bayley Scales. The PDs had a mean Mental Development Index (MDI) of 121.6 compared with a mean MDI of 119.5 for the controls, and a mean Psychomotor Development Index (PDI) of 105.5 compared with a mean PDI of 111.4 for the controls. Analysis by t-test revealed no significant differences between groups for the two Bayley indices.

The Differential Ability Scales (DAS) was administered once to children between the ages of 2 and 5 years. Twenty-nine PD children (mean age: 42 months) and 26 controls (mean age: 42 months) received the DAS. The PDs obtained a mean General Conceptual Ability (GCA) score of 117.4 whereas the control GCA mean was 124.5. A t-test revealed that the control mean is significantly higher than the PD mean ($t = 2.10$,

$p < 0.05$). It should be noted, however, that both groups performed well above the normed average of 100.

In addition to the overall GCA score on the DAS, children younger than 40 months receive a special non-verbal cluster score, whereas older children get both a non-verbal and verbal cluster score. A significant group difference was found on mean verbal cluster scores for older children (PD: 116.2; controls: 127.1) ($t = 2.35$, $p < 0.05$) but not on mean non-verbal cluster scores for both older and younger children. An examination of individual sub-tests reveals significantly lower scores for the PD children relative to controls on two verbal sub-tests, comprehension of verbal commands ($t = 3.08$, $p < 0.01$) and confrontation naming of objects ($t = 2.20$, $p < 0.05$).

The Sequenced Inventory of Communication Development (SICD) was given once between the ages of 6 and 48 months. Twenty-four PDs (mean age: 19 months) and 21 controls (mean age: 18 months) received the SICD. On this measure, the PDs scored on average two months above age level on the receptive profile score (RCA) and one month above age level on the expressive profile score (ECA). The control subjects averaged three months above age level on both the RCA and ECA scores. A look at the data for individual subjects reveals that 42% of the PD children (10 of 24) obtained negative ECA scores (i.e. scored below their chronological age) whereas only 19% of the controls (four of 21) did. The number of PD children and controls with negative RCA scores were seven and four, respectively.

The MacArthur Infant and Toddler Scales of Vocabulary Development were also administered. These scales reflect parental estimates of vocabulary using a checklist approach. The Infant Scale (8–16 months) was administered every two months, and the Toddler Scale (16–30 months) every two months up to 24 months and every four months thereafter. The results reported in Table 5.1 are based on the first administration of each scale. Fourteen PD children (mean age: 12 months) and 8 controls

Table 5.1 Number of children scoring in different percentile ranges on the MacArthur scales

Percentile ranges	PD			Control		
	<25	25–75	>75	<25	25–75	>75
Infant scale:						
Phrases	2	8	4	2	2	4
Comprehension	3	9	2	2	1	5
Production	3	7	4	3	2	3
Early gestures	1	7	6	1	5	2
Late gestures	1	8	5	1	4	3
Toddler scale:						
Word Production	6	8	6	4	8	5

(mean age: 12 months) received the Infant Scale, and 20 PD children (mean age: 20 months) and 17 controls (mean age: 19 months) received the Toddler Scale. Percentiles rather than raw scores are shown in the table because children were not completely age matched across groups.

For the Infant Scale measures the distributions of PD and control children across percentile ranges are quite similar. The only discrepancies occur for phrases understood and verbal comprehension in which relatively fewer PD children compared with controls scored in the upper quartile. The two groups show nearly identical distributions in word production on the Toddler Scale. (Scores from other components on the Toddler Scale are associated with percentile ranges that are too broad to be meaningful.)

In summary, results from the standardised measures reveal relatively few differences between the PD and control children. There were significant differences between groups in overall GCA and on two verbal subtests (comprehension and confrontation naming) on the DAS. However, we should emphasise that the PD children scored above normed averages on these measures. Also, slight discrepancies favouring the control children were seen on the expressive component of the SICD and on two comprehension measures from the MacArthur Scales.

Speech samples

Two types of analyses were conducted on the speech samples collected in this study. The first type was a phonetic analysis of vocalisations produced by children between the ages of 6 and 18 months, and the second type examined the syntactic output of children between ages 2 and 5 years.

Speech samples were obtained during sessions in which children were engaged with the examiner and one (or both) parents in free play. The sessions were video and audio recorded by an assistant. Sessions lasted up to 50 minutes, depending upon the time it took for a child to produce approximately 100 utterances.

Phonetic analysis

Each child participated in one, two, three or four play sessions used for phonetic analysis. There were 13 PD and 12 control children whose speech samples were included in phonetic analysis. Both groups averaged 15 months of age when the speech samples used in this analysis were obtained.

Transcriptions were performed independently by six research assistants. Utterances were transcribed into a computerised database (Logical International Phonetic Program, or LIPP) that employed conventional phonetic symbols. Utterances were defined as non-vegetative vocalisations – that is, spontaneous vocalisations other than crying, fussing, grunting, laughing, whispering, moaning and so forth – that were separated from other vocal events by silence or some sort of prosodic boundary. If an utterance contained one or more canonical syllables (where the consonant was other than a glottal or glide), these consonantal and vocalic segments were transcribed along with any glottals or glides that also happened to be present. If an utterance included a word, its vocalic constituents, along with any glottals or glides, were transcribed even if the infant's form of the word contained no syllables.

To establish reliability, pairs of coders prepared transcriptions for three 50-utterance samples. For these samples inter-coder agreement was found to be 94% for consonants, 93% for vowels and 72% for total consonants. The reliability indices are based on a program developed by D. K. Oller in which some disagreements (e.g., between fricatives and sonorants) are weighted more than others (e.g., between nasals and semi-vowels). Although it is possible that transcribers occasionally guessed the family reading history of an infant, this seems not to have systematically biased their transcriptions to an appreciable degree.

In the analyses to be reported, the number of utterances was equated across the PD and control children. This number ranged from 66 to 480 and averaged 260. The total sample contained 6500 utterances. The first analysis revealed that, on average, the control subjects produced 1.24 consonant-like segments per utterance. Although the PD group produced just 0.94 consonants per utterance, the difference fell short of significance ($t = 1.388; p = 0.169$).

A second analysis was conducted to determine the incidence of consonant cluster production in the two groups. For the PD group, it was found that 6.9% of all utterances included clusters, compared with 10.9% clusters among control subjects. This effect was not significant ($t = 1.150; p = 0.268$).

In a segment inventory analysis, the actual sounds perceived and transcribed for the two groups were compared. For both groups, the six most frequent sounds comprised just over 65% of the total sample and was achieved by the same group of stops and nasals: [d, b, m, n, g, t].

Phonetic transcriptional analyses suggest that articulatory gestures with similar properties (e.g. alveolar closures and high front vowels) tend to occur adjacently in the babbled syllables of prelexical infants (Davis & MacNeilage, in press), a tendency that has also been observed in the speech of 2- to 3-year-old children (Davis & MacNeilage, 1990; Stoel-Gammon, 1983). An analysis was conducted to see if these CV co-occurrence constraints applied equally to control and potentially dyslexic subjects. We added up all the cases where alveolars preceded front vowels, labials preceded mid-vowels and velars preceded back vowels and divided this sum by the total frequency with which segments of these places of articulation preceded all vowels. This analysis revealed a co-occurrence proportion of 45.2% for PDs and 45.5% for the controls.

Clearly, these figures exceed chance (33%) but do not differ from each other. Whether, with continued development, co-occurrence constraints relax earlier in control than potentially dyslexic subjects remains a possibility, but cannot be learned from these data.

Both groups appear to have developed vocal behaviour in a fairly typical way. Both groups produced more stops, nasals and glides than fricatives, affricates and liquids, and they produced more consonants singletons than clusters. PD and control subjects also appeared to share a disposition to produce syllables with apical closures and front vowels. The differences observed between groups were in the predicted direction, i.e. there were signs of delays in the PD group that fell short of significance. As some of our subjects are approaching school age, we expect soon to learn whether there are more pronounced developmental phonetic differences among PD infants who actually experience difficulty in learning to read.

Syntactic patterns

Speech samples collected between ages 2 and 5 were used to assess the syntactic patterns of the children. The video recordings were used for these transcriptions. Non-verbal gestures were also coded in the transcriptions along with unintelligible speech, interjections and no responses. The transcription format is based on Codes for the Human Analysis of Transcripts (CHAT) system taken from the Child Language Data Exchange System (CHILDES) project (MacWhinney, 1991). CHAT transcriptions were carried out by one of the authors (Jennifer Roberts) and several graduate assistants.

From these transcriptions we derived measures of syntactic complexity using the Index of Productive Syntax (IPSYN) developed by Scarborough (1990). It contains separate measures for production of noun phrases, verb phrases, questions, negations and sentence structure. Here we report findings from speech samples collected around 30 months of age. There were 19 PD children and 10 controls. We found that at older ages many children achieved high scores and thus the IPSYN was less sensitive to individual differences.

Although the control group outscored the PD children on each IPSYN sub-scale and total IPSYN score (see Table 5.2), we failed to find significant group differences using independent t-tests ($p > 0.30$). Scarborough (1990, 1991) reported significantly poorer IPSYN scores based on early speech samples of dyslexic children in comparison with non-dyslexic controls. In the present study we are comparing children of dyslexic parents with children of non-dyslexic parents, and at this point we remain uncertain about the reading status of the children. Perhaps group differences in productive syntax will emerge when analyses are restricted to PD children who turn out to be dyslexic.

Table 5.2 Mean IPSYN scores (and standard deviations) for PD and control children at 30 months

Factor	PD		Control	
	Mean	SD	Mean	SD
Noun phrase	15.9	5.2	16.5	4.9
Verb phrase	14.4	7.3	16.8	8.0
Questions/Negations	14.2	7.1	17.3	8.6
Sentence structure	7.4	4.4	8.7	4.2
Total	51.8	22.3	59.3	23.8

Rhyme discrimination task

Though the phoneme represents the level of phonological structure that corresponds most directly to letters of an alphabetic orthography, at least two higher levels of phonological structure have been shown to be important in reading development. One of these is the syllable, a phonological unit that consists of a vocalic centre (nucleus), together with any initial or final consonants (onset and coda, respectively). The syllable itself can be divided into a pair of constituents often referred to as the onset and rime (for reviews see Goswami & Bryant, 1990; Treiman, 1992). The onset, which is optional, consists of any syllable-initial consonants. The rime consists of the vocalic nucleus, normally a vowel, and any post-vocalic consonants. Thus, a single syllable word like *stand*, contains the onset /st/ and the rime, /ænd/. The traditional concept of rhyme is satisfied when two words have different onsets but identical rimes. This sub-division of the syllable has played a major role in recent considerations of phonological awareness and reading development (Bryant et al., 1990a, 1990b; Kirtley et al.,1989; MacLean, Bryan & Bradley, 1987).

Phonemic awareness is usually achieved at roughly the same time that children begin to read. In fact, it is now widely thought that there is a reciprocal relationship between the development of stable phonemic segmentation skills and the acquisition of knowledge about the alphabetic writing system (e.g., Morais, 1991; Bradley & Bryant, 1991). Higher levels of sublexical phonological structure, such as the syllable and the onset and rime, are believed to be more readily accessible and thus may be available to children, explicitly or implicitly, before reading instruction (e.g., Kirtley et al., 1989). If the phonological impairment that is thought to underlie dyslexia also affects the child's capacity to decompose speech into these other levels of sublexical phonological structure, then children who are destined to have difficulty in reading might also show less facility with syllables or onsets and rimes than their peers.

Research aimed at evaluating the relationship between success in early reading development and facility with supraphonemic phonological units has tended to employ methods that rely rather heavily on the metaphonological competence of the child. For example, the 'oddity task' developed by Bryant, Bradley and their colleagues (Bradley & Bryant, 1983; Kirtley et al., 1989) is quite challenging to pre-schoolers, even when steps are taken to reduce the extraphonological demands of the task (MacLean et al., 1987). In its most frequent implementation, the child hears three or four monosyllabic words and is asked to identify the one word in this set that does not share a certain phonological unit. This may be the word's onset, rime, nucleus (vowel) or coda (final consonant(s)). Training is usually limited to a very small number of initial trials, often only two or three, in which the experimenter provides feedback. Then a relatively small set of trials, often 10–12, follows without any further feedback. The child is thus asked to make a relatively complex negative decision in which the common component of the same items has to be discerned and the item without that feature identified and reported. For younger children, simple pictures are sometimes used to ease the memory load that task performance imposes (e.g., MacLean et al., 1987). Performance on these tasks has been shown to predict reading success in the first few years of school, but the task is rarely mastered by children under 4:6 years of age. Nevertheless, few believe that younger children are unable to appreciate rhymes. The impediment to successful performance is probably linked to task difficulty and the child's capacity to employ solidly metalinguistic strategies.

Whilst these more formal and challenging measures of phonological awareness are quite effective for some purposes, the relatively late emergence of children's ability to perform them constrains their usefulness for early assessment. One of our goals was to develop a rhyme discrimination task that would be less formal and perhaps more sensitive to the tacit phonological intuitions of younger children. A task of this type might serve as a fairly reliable form of assessment of phonological insight.

Children were introduced to a puppet, Ryan Lion, who was particularly fond of pictures of things that sounded alike. A series of training trials was given in which a card with a picture of an object on it was placed in Ryan's lap. Then two additional cards were shown to the child, one with a picture of an object whose name rhymed with the object in Ryan's picture and another object whose name did not. The child was told the names of the two objects and was asked which of the two pictures Ryan would choose. Rhyming pictures had a star affixed to the back. When the child had chosen a card by name or by touching it, the card was turned over to see if it carried a star. During the practice phase, the experimenter gave free-form feedback to the child.

Sixteen trials were then administered with feedback being provided only by checking the back of the card. If the correct item was chosen, the experimenter responded by saying 'Yes, x and y sound alike.' If the foil was selected, the experimenter said 'No, x and y sound alike' as she turned over the correct card. The correct and incorrect choices were randomly ordered with regard to order of presentation and spatial location. Each child received a score representing the number of trials out of 16 on which the rhyming target was selected. A criterion for success was considered to be 13/16 (81% correct).

The rhyme discrimination test was administered at three-month intervals starting at age 3. Testing was continued until a child achieved a perfect score on two consecutive occasions.[2] The analysis of interest here is one which compares the proportions of children achieving criterion within each of four age bands, 3:0–3:6 years, 3:6–4:0 years, 4:0–4:6 years and 4:6–5:0 years. Table 5.3 presents those results. In the youngest group, there was no difference in rate of success for PD versus control children. Four of the 16 PD children reached criterion as did five of 14 controls. When tested between ages 3:6 and 4;0 years, however, differences did emerge. Only five of 16 children in the PD group attained criterion, whereas 11 of 14 controls did (χ^2 (1) = 6.592, p < 0.02). For the age span 4:0–4:6 years, there was again a significant difference between groups (χ^2 (1) = 4.981, p < 0.05). Whilst all but one of the 14 control children achieved criterion, only 11 of 16 children from the PD group did. By the time the children were between 4:0 and 5:0 years, the group differences had waned (χ^2 (1) = 2.917, 0.10 > p > 0.05). All 14 of the control children had reached criterion, as had 13 of the 16 PD children.

These results suggest that children from families with positive histories of written language disorder are, as a group, less facile in a task that taps phonological awareness at the level of onset and rime. More specifically, their performance shows a delay in their mastery of this task. Neither group shows much skill in identifying the rhyming word in the period from 3:0 to 3:6 years. During the following year (3:6–4:6), the children from families without dyslexia did significantly better than the group with positive family histories. By the final six months in which the rhyme task was administered (4:6–5:0), the PD group had begun to close the gap, though a marginally significant difference still remained.

The PD group cannot, of course, be considered uniform, given that a significant proportion of those children are expected not to have dyslexia. It is therefore important to know how these group differences are distributed within each cohort. Whilst we only have very preliminary evidence regarding which of the children in the study will have significant difficulty learning to read, preliminary indications suggest that the poorer performance of the PD group may come from a subset of the children included. In the control group, there were also two children

---

[2] Several children in each group were given the test during every home visit as a test of the consistency of mastery. None of these children ever made more than one error out of 16 trials after they had attained their first perfect score.

whose performance suggested that they might have specific difficulty with metaphonological tasks. The true significance of the differences reported here will be established only if they are predictive of later reading performance.

Table 5.3 Proportion of children in PD and Control groups who achieved criterion (81% correct) on the Rhyme Discrimination Task

Age (years)	3–3:6	3:6–4	4–4:6	4:6–5
Group:				
PD	0.250	0.313	0.688	0.813
Control	0.357	0.786	0.929	1.00
	n.s.	$p < 0.02$	$p < 0.05$	$0.10 > p > 0.05$

Verbal short-term memory

A number of studies have shown that dyslexic children experience difficulties on short-term memory tasks (see Brady, 1991; Jorm & Share, 1983; Torgesen, 1988, for reviews). Their difficulties usually show up on tasks involving material that can be coded in verbal form, but not on tasks involving non-verbal material (e.g., Katz, Shankweiler & Liberman, 1981; McDougall et al., 1994). The problem is not that dyslexics fail to make use of verbal (phonological) codes on short-term memory tasks, but that they seem to make less efficient use of these codes (see Olson et al., 1984). The verbal short-term memory limitations of dyslexics are seen as one facet of a broader linguistic impairment at the phonological level (e.g., Fowler, 1991; Stone & Brady, 1995).

Verbal short-term memory is implicated at various stages in the reading process. For instance, reading unfamiliar words requires temporary storage of phonological segments as part of the decoding process. Short-term memory resources are also needed to retain word identity and order information for sentence-level syntactic and semantic processing (e.g., Perfetti, 1985; Stanovich, 1982). Longitudinal studies have shown a relationship between early measures of verbal short-term memory and later reading success (e.g., Mann & Liberman, 1984; see Wagner & Torgesen, 1987, for a review).

In this component of our study we consider whether the PD children show early signs of verbal short-term memory limitations relative to the controls. Beginning at 2:6 years of age, children were administered a short-term memory test every six months until the age of 5. The test had eight two-, three- and four-item strings evenly divided into word and non-word trials. Maintaining non-words in short-term memory is expected to be more difficult than words, given that words should benefit from the activation of stored lexical information. In addition, some of the strings contained items that were phonologically related (e.g., 'ride rock rain') whereas on other trials unrelated items were used (e.g., 'pig ball moon sock'). Trials were presented in a fixed order, starting with two-item strings and ending with four-item strings.

For this test the children were introduced to two puppets, 'Pete' and 'Repeat', and were asked to play the role of Repeat who says everything that Pete says. The children were told that Pete sometimes says make-believe words like 'lote'. After a set of simple practice items, the 24 strings were presented. The examiner said each item at a rate of approximately one word per second.

The results reported here are based on the first and second administrations of the short-term memory test. Twenty-seven PD children and 21 controls received an initial administration of the short-term memory test. Mean ages for the PDs and controls were 43 and 42 months, respectively. Results from the first administration are given in Table 5.4. The values in the table reflect mean percentage of items responded to correctly. An item was scored correct if it was pronounced accurately and produced in the correct serial position taken from the beginning or end of the string.

Table 5.4 Mean percentage correct (and standard deviations) on the first administration of the short-term memory task

Item	PD		Control	
	Mean	SD	Mean	SD
Words	61.5	13.2	74.3	11.9
Non-words	40.7	14.1	54.0	19.6

An analysis of variance showed a significant group difference in mean percentage correct ($F(1,46) = 11.5, p < 0.01$) with the control children outperforming the PDs. The word/non-word difference was also significant ($F(1,46) = 110.3, p < 0.01$), but there was no interaction between these two variables.

A second set of analyses was conducted on data collected from children administered the test a second time. In this case there were 19 PDs and 17 controls (mean age 46 months for both groups). Although the word/non-word difference remained significant ($F(1,34) = 157.7$, $p < 0.01$), the group difference was no longer significant. The PD and control means were 70.2 and 73.2 for word trials, and 44.5 and 52.7 for non-word trials, respectively.

Overall, analyses of data from the short-term memory task reveal that at the youngest ages the PD children showed significantly poorer performance than the controls. However, the group difference failed to reach significance at the second testing session. The fact that there was no interaction between word vs non-word and group indicates that PD children did not show less (or more) benefit from activating stored phonological representations than controls (see McDougall et al., 1994, for a related outcome with older children).

Pre-literacy measures

A pre-literacy battery of tests was administered to all children in the summer prior to kindergarten entry and again before entry into first grade. Twenty-four PD children (mean age: 64.6 months) and 19 controls (mean age: 61.9 months) received the battery before kindergarten, and 18 PD children (mean age: 76.3 months) and 11 controls (mean age: 73.4 months) received the battery again before grade 1. The battery consists of tasks designed to assess oral language skills, metaphonological abilities, and alphabetic knowledge.

To test *auditory discrimination*, we asked the children to decide whether pairs of words (or nonsense items) sounded the same (e.g., 'car' 'car') or different (e.g., 'dog' 'door'). Although both PD children and controls performed well on this task at pre-kindergarten (PD mean: 87.0%; control mean: 93.0%), a significant group difference was found ($t = 2.37$, $p < 0.05$). The group difference was no longer significant before first grade (PD mean: 90.9%; control mean: 93.9%).

In a test of *speech repetition* the children were asked to repeat individual mono- and multisyllabic words (e.g., 'refrigerator') and nonsense items (e.g., 'felizopter'). The items were selected from a study by Brady et al. (1989). The two groups obtained high scores on this task both at pre-kindergarten (PD mean: 90.9%; control mean: 95.1%) and before first grade (PD mean: 93.6%; control mean: 95.9%). Group differences were not significant.

Comprehension of spoken sentences containing *complex syntactic structures* (e.g., relative clauses) was assessed with a two-choice sentence/picture matching task (see Smith et al., 1989). An example of a sentence from this task is 'The man is touching the lady who is carrying a suitcase'. No significant group differences in accuracy were found at pre-kindergarten (PD mean: 69.5%; control mean: 71.9%), and prior to grade 1 (PD mean: 72.7%; control mean: 76.1%).

A test of *serial rapid naming* (e.g., Wolf, 1986) was administered using both colours and objects. Children were asked to say aloud the names of 50 pictured items as rapidly as possible. Although the PD children were somewhat slower than controls in mean naming speed (seconds) at pre-kindergarten (PD colour: 87.6; control colour: 78.6; PD object: 93.8; control object: 80.5), group differences were not significant. No differences between groups were seen before first grade (PD colour: 65.8; control colour: 62.5; PD object: 69.6; control object: 65.9).

One test of metaphonological ability was a *rhyme production* task. Children were asked to produce as many rhymes as they could for 10 spoken target words. At pre-kindergarten the control group (mean: 48.8) produced a significantly greater number of rhymes than the PD children (mean: 34.3) ($t = 3.09$, $p < 0.01$). The difference in rhyme production was again evident before grade 1 (PD mean: 51.9; control mean: 65.5) but the difference failed to reach significance (owing to high within-group variability).

We used a *delete initial consonant* task as a second index of metaphonological ability. Children were presented with a spoken word (e.g., 'feet') and asked to say the word that remains when the initial sound is taken away (e.g., 'eat'). This task proved to be very difficult for pre-kindergarten children, particularly in the PD group. For instance, 14 out of the 23 PD children (and nine out of the 19 controls) failed to produce any correct responses. However, improvements were seen in both groups prior to Grade 1. Ten out of 17 PD children and seven out of 11 controls achieved a success rate of 90% or better.

To assess knowledge of the alphabet we administered a set of letter recognition tasks. No significant mean differences between groups were found in reciting the alphabet, both at pre-kindergarten (PD: 21.5; control: 25.1) and prior to Grade 1 (PD: 25.7; control: 23.1). A significant mean difference was found at pre-kindergarten in providing the names of the 26 letters presented in random order (PD: 19.8; control: 24.9; $t = 3.08$, $p < 0.01$). The PD children caught up with the controls prior to Grade 1 (PD: 24.7; control: 25.8). In generating the sounds associated with consonant letters, the PD children again scored below the controls at pre-kindergarten (PD: 55.2%; controls: 74.0%) but the difference failed to reach significance (owing to large within-group variability). Both groups performed well on this task prior to first grade (PD: 92.6%; controls: 97.0%).

In summary, clear differences between PD and control children were found on pre-literacy measures collected before entry into kindergarten. PD children scored significantly below controls in auditory discrimination (although they achieved high performance levels), rhyme production and naming letters. They also appeared to have more difficulty than controls in deleting initial consonants and producing sounds associated with consonant letters. In each case group differences no longer emerged when measures were collected prior to entry into first grade. We also found that in both assessments the PD children did not differ from controls in speech repetition, comprehension of complex syntax, rapid naming of colours and objects, and reciting the alphabet.

Discussion

In this final section we will first review the main findings of this study in respect of prominent claims about underlying impairments contributing to dyslexia. We then mention some of our plans for further analyses once we have gathered sufficient reading outcome measures from the PD and control children.

First, the results of standardised testing conducted at early ages support a commonly held view that areas of weakness in children of dyslexic parents are not likely to be found on tests of general cognitive and motor skills (e.g. Pennington et al., 1992; Siegel, 1989; Stanovich, 1991). The PD children performed like controls on the Bayley Scales and on the non-verbal sub-tests of the DAS.

There were some indications in these data that PD children show a general language impairment that extends beyond the phonological domain (e.g. Bishop & Adams, 1990; Scarborough, 1990, 1991; Siegel & Ryan, 1988). Although parental reports of vocabulary growth on the MacArthur Scales failed to reveal any clear differences between groups, a greater percentage of PD children than controls had negative expressive language scores on the SICD. In addition, significant group differences favouring the controls were found on two of the verbal sub-tests of the DAS: verbal comprehension, in which children must follow spoken commands, and name vocabulary, a confrontation naming task. The latter finding is consistent with differences Scarborough (1990) reports between dyslexic and non-dyslexic groups in her retrospective analysis of performance on the Peabody Picture Vocabulary Test (PPVT) and on the Boston Naming Test. We did not directly replicate Scarborough's finding of a significant difference on her measure of syntactic competence (IPSYN, Scarborough, 1991), but that may be due to important differences between the studies. The syntactic comparison that Scarborough conducted was a retrospective one, comparing children who were diagnosed as dyslexic with those with no reading problem. At this stage in our study, we are only able to compare children with family histories of dyslexia with children from families that do not report such a history. Whether our retrospective assessment will agree with hers must be left for the future. Finally, results on the pre-literacy battery show no group discrepancies in comprehension of sentences containing complex syntactic structures.

More support was found for a narrower claim that PD children are likely to experience difficulties in processing phonological information (e.g. Fowler, 1991; Stone & Brady, 1995). This was evident on the verbal short-term memory task, in which PD children, when tested at young ages, scored significantly below same-age controls in recall of both word and non-word strings. Group differences favouring the controls were also obtained in pre-kindergarten assessment of auditory discrimination (although both groups produced high scores). In contrast with these findings and somewhat unexpectedly, we failed to see group differences in speech repetition (Brady et al., 1989) and serial rapid naming (e.g., Wolf, 1986).

The developmental phonetic differences that occurred during the late-babbling period were in the predicted direction, the PDs displaying fewer consonant-like segments and segment clusters per utterance, though at non-significant levels. This is a disappointing result, which appears to be related to high intra-group variability and the presence of conspicuous outliers. However, there are several areas that we intend to examine in the future. One is the level of phonetic complexity of subjects who actually experience difficulty in the acquisition of literacy skills. The other area relates to consonant–vowel co-occurrence constraints. Both groups, it will be recalled, displayed a tendency to produce syllables comprising harmonious consonantal and vocalic gestures in an early stage of phonetic development. Whether the truly dyslexic subjects in our sample were slower to dissociate these gestures in development is a question we also expect to pursue.

Much theoretical and empirical weight has been attached to the importance of phonological awareness in reading acquisition (Adams, 1990; Bradley & Bryant, 1983; Gough & Hillinger, 1980; Liberman et al., 1977). One of our strongest outcomes is the clear discrepancy between PD and control children in demonstrating awareness of rhyme between the ages of 3:6 and 4:6 years. Similarly, the rhyme production task on the pre-literacy battery also produced significant group differences favouring the controls. Finally, more PD children than controls had diffi- culty with the phoneme awareness task that required them to delete initial consonants (though group differences did not reach significance). This task is one of the more difficult phonological awareness tasks (Stanovich et al., 1984). Children often do poorly on it before they have had much reading experience. The performance of both groups improved and the difference between them declined when these phoneme awareness measures were collected again at later ages. These results suggest that there may be time-sensitive periods in which metaphonological indices of future reading disturbances can most readily be detected.

Finally, a few of the pre-literacy battery measures directly assessed knowledge of letters and their sounds. Two of these indices showed group differences although only one was significant. The PD children were significantly poorer than controls at providing letter names at pre- kindergarten. This finding is consistent with previous reports which found letter naming to be a good predictor of later reading success (e.g., Share et al., 1989).

We would like to conclude this discussion by mentioning our future plans. We have begun to collect reading outcome measures for both PD and control children, a number of whom are now completing first and second grades. They are too few in number to present here, but we expect to be able to report on them soon. In the next phase of the study, we will re-categorise children on the basis of reading outcomes and carry out retrospective comparisons of dyslexic and non-dyslexic children on the array of data we have collected from them over the years (Scarborough, 1990). The comparisons of interest will obviously include dyslexic and non-dyslexic children, but we are also interested in comparing unaffected children from families with histories of dyslexia with children from the control group whose family histories are negative. Preliminary analyses lead us to expect that children who are ultimately diagnosed with dyslexia will present performance profiles consistent with the problem areas identified for PD children in this study. However, it is also possible that some of the group differences we found are not related to reading ability and thus may not be replicated when children are grouped on that basis. Characterising the performance profile typical of dyslexic children generally is one aim of our continuing investigation. But at the same time, we believe that the most fruitful approach to understanding the cognitive and linguistic precursors to developmental dyslexia will involve analyses of performance on a case-by-case basis. We are eagerly awaiting the chance to conduct these explorations.

References

Adams, M.J. (1990). *Beginning to Read: Thinking and Learning about Print*. Cambridge, MA: MIT Press.

Aram, D. & Nation, J. (1980). Preschool language disorders and subsequent language and academic difficulties. *Journal of Communication Disorders* 13, 229–241.

Bentin, S., Deutsch, A. & Liberman, I.Y. (1990). Syntactic competence and reading ability in children. *Journal of Experimental Child Psychology* 48, 147–172.

Bishop, D.V.M. & Adams, C. (1990). A prospective study of the relationship between specific language impairment, phonological disorders and reading retardation. *Journal of Child Psychology and Psychiatry* 31, 1027–1050.

Bradley, L. & Bryant, P. (1983). Categorizing sounds and learning to read – a causal connection. *Nature* 301., 419–421.

Bradley, L. & Bryant, P. (1991). Phonological skills before and after learning how to read. In S. Brady & D. Shankweiler (Eds.) *Phonological Processes in Literacy* (pp. 37–46). Hillsdale, NJ: Erlbaum.

Brady, S. (1991). The role of working memory in reading disability. In S. Brady & D. Shankweiler (Eds.) *Phonological Processes in Literacy* (pp. 129–152). Hillsdale NJ: Erlbaum.

Brady, S., Poggie, E. & Rapala, M. (1989). Speech repetition abilities in children who differ in reading skills. *Language and Speech* 32, 109–122.

Brady, S., Shankweiler, D. & Mann, V. (1983). Speech perception and memory coding in relation to reading ability. *Journal of Experimental Child Psychology*, 35, 345-367.

Brandt, J. & Rosen, J.L. (1980). Auditory phonemic perception in dyslexia: Categorical identification and discrimination of stop consonants. *Brain and Language* 9, 324–337.

Bryant, P.E., MacLean, M. & Bradley, L. (1990a). Rhyme, language and children's reading. *Applied Psycholinguistics* 11, 237–252.

Bryant, P.E., MacLean, M., Bradley, L. & Crossland, J. (1990). Rhyme and alliteration, phoneme detection and learning to read. *Developmental Psychology* 26, 429–438.

Bryson, S.E. & Werker, J.F. (1989). Toward understanding the problem in severely disabled readers, Part I: Vowel errors. *Applied Psycholinguistics* 10, 1–12.

Byrne, B. & Fielding-Barnsley, R. (1990). Acquiring the alphabetic principle: A case for teaching recognition of phoneme identity. *Journal of Educational Psychology* 82, 805–812.

Caviness, V.S., Kennedy, D.N., Richelme, C., Rademacher, J. & Filipek, P.A. (1996). *Cerebral Cortex* 6, 726–736.

Critchley, M. (1970). *The Dyslexic Child*, 2nd edn. Springfield, IL: Charles C Thomas.

Davis, B.L. & MacNeilage, P.F. (1990). Acquisition of correct vowel production: A quantitative case study. *Journal of Speech and Hearing Research* 33, 16–27.

Davis, B.L. & MacNeilage, P.F. (in press) Serial organization of babbling: A case study. *Language and Speech*.

DeFries, J.C., Olson, R.K., Pennington, B.F. & Smith, S.D. (1991). Colorado Reading Project: An update. In D.D. Drake & D.B. Gray (Eds.) *The Reading Brain: The Biological Basis of Dyslexia* (pp. 53–87). Parkton, MD: York Press.

Ehri, L.C. (1984). How orthography alters spoken language competencies in children learning to read and spell. In J. Downing & R. Valtin (Eds.) *Language Awareness and Learning to Read* (pp. 119–147). New York: Springer-Verlag.

Ehri, L.C. (1992). Reconceptualizing the development of sight word reading and its relation to recoding. In P. Gough, L. Ehri & R. Treiman (Eds.) *Reading Acquisition* (pp. 107–143). Hillsdale NJ: Erlbaum.

Ehri, L. & Wilce, L.S. (1985). Movement into reading: is the first stage of printed word learning visual or phonetic? *Reading Research Quarterly* 20, 163–179.

Finucci, J.M., Gottfredson, L.S. & Childs, B. (1986). A follow-up study of dyslexic boys. *Annals of Dyslexia* 35, 117–136.

Fowler, A.E. (1991). How early phonological development might set the stage for phoneme awareness. In S. Brady & D. Shankweiler (Eds.) *Phonological Processes in Literacy* (pp. 97–117). Hillsdale, NJ: Erlbaum.

Frith, U. (1985). Beneath the surface of developmental dyslexia. In K. Patterson, J. Marshall & M. Coltheart (Eds.) *Surface Dyslexia*. Hillsdale, NJ: Erlbaum.

Gleitman, L. & Rozin, P. (1977). The structure and acquisition of reading, I: Relations between orthographies and the structure of language. In A. Reber & D. Scarborough (Eds.) *Toward a Psychology of Reading*. Hillsdale, NJ: Erlbaum.

Godfrey, J.J., Syrdal-Lasky, A.K., Millay, K.K. & Knox, C.M. (1981). Performance of dyslexic children on speech perception tests. *Journal of Experimental Child Psychology* 32, 401–424.

Goswami, U. & Bryant, P. (1990). *Phonological Skills and Learning to Read*. Hove, UK: Erlbaum.

Gough, P. & Hillinger, M.L. (1980). Learning to read: An unnatural act. *Bulletin of the Orton Society* 30, 179–196.

Greenough, W.T., Black, J.E. & Wallace, C.S. (1987). Experience and brain development. *Child Development* 58, 539–559.

Hinshelwood, J. (1900). *Letter-, Word-, and Mind-Blindness*. London: Lewis & Son.

Hinshelwood, J (1917). *Congenital Word Blindness*. London: Lewis & Son.

Hulme, C. (1988). The implausibility of low-level visual deficits as a cause of children's reading difficulties. *Cognitive Neuropsychology* 5, 369–374.

Jorm, A.F. & Share, D.L. (1983). Phonological reading and reading acquisition. *Applied Psycholinguistics* 4, 103–147.

Kamhi, A. & Catts, H. (Eds.) (1989). *Reading Disabilities: A Developmental Language Perspective*. Boston: Allyn & Bacon.

Katz, R.B., Shankweiler, D. & Liberman, I.Y. (1981). Memory for item order and phonetic recoding in the beginning reader. *Journal of Experimental Child Psychology* 32, 474–484.

Kerr, J. (1896). School hygiene in its mental, moral and physical aspects. *Journal of the Royal Statistical Society* 60, 613–680.

Kirtley, C., Bryant, P.E., MacLean, M. & Bradley L. (1989) Rhyme, rime and the onset of reading. *Journal of Experimental Child Psychology* 48, 224–245.

Lefly, D.L. & Pennington, B.F. (1991). Spelling errors and reading fluency in compensated adult dyslexics. *Annals of Dyslexia* 41, 143–162.

Lieberman, P., Meskill, R.H., Chatillon, M. & Schupack, H. (1985). Phonetic speech perception deficits in dyslexia. *Journal of Speech and Hearing Research* 28, 480–486.

Leonard, L., Nippold, M., Kail, R. & Hale, C. (1983). Picture naming in language impaired children: differentiating lexical storage from retrieval. *Journal of Speech and Hearing Research* 26, 609–615.

Liberman, A.M. (1992). The relation of speech to reading and writing. In R. Frost & L. Katz (Eds), *Orthography, Phonology, Morphology and Meaning* (pp. 167–178). Amsterdam: Elsevier.

Liberman, I.Y., Shankweiler, D., Fischer, F.W. & Carter, B. (1974). Explicit syllable and phoneme segmentation in the young child. *Journal of Experimental Child Psychology* 18, 201–212.

Liberman, I.Y., Shankweiler, D., Liberman, A.M., Fowler, C.A. & Fisher, F.W. (1977). Phonetic segmentation and decoding in the beginning reader. In A. S. Reber & D.L. Scarborough (Eds.) *Toward a Psychology of Reading*.

Locke, J.L. (1993). *The Child's Path to Spoken Language*. Cambridge, MA: Harvard University Press.

Lovegrove, W. (1991). Is the question of the role of visual deficits as a cause of reading disabilities a closed one? *Cognitive Neuropsychology* 8, 435–442.

Lovegrove, W., Martin, F. & Slaghuis, W. (1986). A theoretical and experimental case for a visual deficit in specific reading disability. *Cognitive Neuropsychology* 3, 225–267.

Lubs, H., Gross-Glenn, K., Duara, R., Feldman, E., Skottun, B., Jallad, B., Kushch, A. & Rabin, M. (1994). Familial dyslexia: genetic, behavioral and imaging studies. In A. J. Capute, P. J. Accardo & B.K. Shapiro (Eds.) *Learning Disabilities Spectrum: ADD, ADHD and LD* (pp. 85–105). Parkton MD: York Press.

Lundberg, I., Olofsson, A. & Wall, S. (1980). Reading and spelling skills in the first school years predicted from phonemic awareness skills in kindergarten. *Scandinavian Journal of Psychology* 21, 159–173.

McDougall, S., Hulme, C., Ellis, A. & Monk, A. (1994). Learning to read: the role of short-term memory and phonological skills. *Journal of Experimental Child Psychology* 58, 112–133.

MacLean, M., Bryant, P.E. & Bradley, L. (1987). Rhymes, nursery rhymes and reading in early childhood. *Merrill-Palmer Quarterly* 33, 255–282.

MacWhinney, B. (1991). *The CHILDES project*. Hillsdale, NJ: Lawrence Erlbaum.

Mann, V.A. & Liberman, I.Y. (1984). Phonological awareness and short-term memory: can they presage early reading problems? *Journal of Learning Disabilities* 17, 592–599.

Mehler, J., Jusczyk, P., Lambertz, G., Halstead, N., Bertoncini, J. & Amiel-Tison, C. (1988). A precursor of language acquisition in young infants. *Cognition* 29, 143–178.

Merzenich, M.M., Schreiner, C., Jenkins, W. & Wang, X. (1993). Neural mechanisms underlying temporal integration, segmentation, and input sequence representation: Some implications for the origin of learning disabilities. In P. Tallal, A.M. Galaburda, R. R. Llinas & C. von Euler (Eds.) *Temporal Information Processing in the Nervous System: Special Reference to Dyslexia and Dysphasia. Annals of the New York Academy of Sciences* **682**, 1–22.

Mody, M., Studdert-Kennedy, M. & Brady, S.A. (1995). Speech perception deficits in poor readers: auditory processing or phonological coding?

Morais, J. (1991). Constraints on the development of phonemic awareness. In S. Brady & D. Shankweiler (Eds.) *Phonological Processes in Literacy* (pp. 5–28). Hillsdale, NJ: Erlbaum.

Morais, J., Bertelson, P., Cary, L. & Alegria, J. (1986) Literacy training and speech segmentation. *Cognition* **24**, 45–64.

Morais J., Cary, L., Alegria, J. & Bertlesen, P. (1979). Does awareness of speech as a sequence of phones arise spontaneously? *Cognition* **7**, 323–331.

Morgan, J. (1896). A case of congenital word blindness. *British Medical Journal* **2**, 1378.

Nicolson, R.I. & Fawcett, A.J. (1990). Automaticity: A new framework for dyslexia research? *Cognition* **30**, 159–182.

Olson, R.K., Klieg, R. & Davidson, B.J. (1983) Eye movements in reading disability. In K. Rayner (Ed.), *Eye Movements in Reading: Perceptual and Language Processes* (pp. 467–479). New York: Academic Press.

Olson, R.K., Davidson, B.J., Kliegl, R. & Davies, S.E. (1984). Development of phonetic memory in disabled and normal readers. *Journal of Experimental Child Psychology* **37**, 187–206.

Orton, S.T. (1925). 'Word blindness' in school children. *Archives of Neurology and Psychiatry* **14**, 581–613.

Pavlidis, G.T. (1983). The 'dyslexia syndrome' and its objective diagnosis by erratic eye movements. In K. Rayner (Ed.), *Eye Movements in Reading: Perceptual and Language Processes* (pp. 441–466). New York: Academic Press.

Pennington, B.F., Gilger, J.W., Olson, R.K. & DeFries, J.C. (1992). The external validity of age-versus IQ discrepancy definitions of reading disability: Lessons from a twin study. *Journal of Learning Disabilities* **25** (9), 562–573.

Pennington, B.F., Van Orden, G.C., Kirson, D. & Haith, M.M. (1991). What is the causal relation between verbal STM problems and dyslexia? In S. Brady & D. Shankweiler (Eds.) *Phonological Processes in Literacy* (pp. 173–186). Hillsdale, NJ: Erlbaum.

Pennington, B.F., Van Orden, G.C., Smith, S.D., Green, P.A. & Haith, M.M. (1990). Phonological processing skills and deficits in adult dyslexics. *Child Development* **61**, 1753–1778.

Pennington, B.F., McCabe, L.L., Smith, S.D., Lefly, D.L., Bookman, M.O., Kimberling, W.J., & Lubs, H.A. (1986). Spelling errors in adults with a form of familial dyslexia. *Child Development* **57**, 1001–1013.

Perfetti, C.A. (1985). *Reading Ability.* New York: Oxford University Press.

Pinker, S. (1994). *The Language Instinct: How the Mind Creates Language.* New York: William Morrow.

Pinker, S. (1995). Language acquisition. In L. Gleitman & M. Liberman (Eds.) *An Invitation to Cognitive Science*, Vol. **1**: *Language* (pp. 135–182). Cambridge MA: MIT Press.

Rack, J., Snowling, M. & Olson, R.K. (1992). The nonword reading deficit in developmental dyslexia: A review. *Reading Research Quarterly* **27**, 29–53.

Read, C., Zhang, Y.-F., Nie, H.-Y., & Ding, B.-Q. (1986). The ability to manipulate speech sounds depends on knowing alphabetic writing. *Cognition* 24, 31–44.

Reed, M.A. (1989). Speech perception and the discrimination of brief auditory cues in reading disabled children. *Journal of Experimental Child Psychology* 48, 270–292.

Scarborough, H.S. (1984). Continuity between childhood dyslexia and adult reading. *British Journal of Psychology* 75, 329–348.

Scarborough, H.S. (1990). Very early language deficits in dyslexic children. *Child Development* 61, 1728–1743.

Scarborough, H.S. (1991). Early syntactic development of dyslexic children. *Annals of Dyslexia* 41, 207–220.

Share, D.L., McGee, R. & Silva, P.A. (1989). IQ and reading progress: A test of the capacity notion of IQ. *Journal of the American Academy of Child & Adolescent Psychiatry* 28, 97–100.

Share, D. & Stanovich, K. (1995). Cognitive processes in early reading development: Accommodating individual differences into a model of acquisition. *Issues in Education* 1, 1–57.

Siegel, L. (1989). IQ is irrelevant to the definition of learning disabilities. *Journal of Learning Disabilities* 22, 469–478.

Siegel, L.S. & Ryan, E.B. (1988). Development of grammatical-sensitivity, phonological and short-term memory skills in normally achieving learning disabled children. *Developmental Psychology* 24, 28–37.

Smith, S., Macaruso, P., Shankweiler, D. & Crain, S. (1989). Syntactic comprehension in young poor readers. *Applied Psycholinguistics* 10, 429–454.

Snowling, M. (1987). *Dyslexia: A Cognitive Developmental Perspective.* Oxford, UK: Blackwell.

Snowling, M., Goulandris, N., Bowlby, M. & Howell, P. (1986a). Segmentation and speech perception in relation to reading: A developmental analysis. *Journal of Experimental Child Psychology* 41, 487–507.

Snowling, M., Stackhouse, J. & Rack, J. (1986b). Phonological dyslexia and dysgraphia – a developmental analysis. *Cognitive Neuropsychology* 3, 309–339.

Stanovich, K.E. (1982). Individual differences in the cognitive processes of reading, II: Text-level processes. *Journal of Learning Disabilities* 15(9), 549–554.

Stanovich, K.E. (1986). Matthew effects in reading: some consequences of individual differences in the acquisition of literacy. *Reading Research Quarterly* 21, 360–406.

Stanovich, K.E. (1988). The right and wrong places to look for the cognitive locus of reading disability. *Annals of Dyslexia* 38, 154–177.

Stanovich, K.E. (1991). Discrepancy definitions of reading disability: has intelligence led us astray? *Reading Research Quarterly* 26(1), 7–29.

Stanovich, K.E. (1992). Speculations on the causes and consequences of individual differences in early reading acquisition. In P.B. Gough, L.C. Ehri & R. Treiman (Eds.) *Reading Acquisition* (pp. 307–342). Hillsdale, NJ: Erlbaum.

Stanovich, K.E. (1993). Dysrationalia: a new specific learning disability. *Journal of Learning Disabilities* 26(8), 501–515.

Stanovich, K.E., Cunningham, A.E. & Cramer, B.B. (1984). Assessing phonological awareness in kindergarten children. *Journal of Experimental Child Psychology* 38, 175–190.

Stoel-Gammon, C. (1983). Constraints on consonant–vowel sequences in early words. *Journal of Child Language* 10, 455–457.

Stone, B. & Brady, S. (1995). Evidence for phonological processing deficits in less skilled readers. *Annals of Dyslexia* 45, 51–78.

Studdert-Kennedy, M. & Mody, M. (1995). Temporal processing deficits in dyslexia: a critical review of the evidence. Unpublished manuscript.

Tallal, P. (1984). Temporal or phonetic processing deficit in dyslexia? That is the question. *Applied Psycholinguistics* **5**, 167–169.

Torgesen, J.K. (1988). Studies of children with learning disabilities who perform poorly on memory span tasks. *Journal of Learning Disabilities* **21**, 605–612.

Treiman, R. (1992). The role of intrasyllabic units in learning to read and spell. In P.B. Gough, L.C. Ehri & R. Treiman (Eds.) *Reading Acquisition* (pp. 65–106). Hillsdale, NJ: Erlbaum.

Wagner, R.K. (1988) Causal relations between the development of phonological processing abilities and the acquisition of reading skills: a meta-analysis. *Merrill-Palmer Quarterly* **34**, 261–279.

Wagner, R. & Torgesen, J. (1987). The nature of phonological processing and its causal role in the acquisition of reading skills. *Psychological Bulletin* **101**, 192–212.

Werker, J.F., Bryson, S. & Wasserberg, K. (1989). Toward understanding the problem in severely disabled readers, Part II: Consonant errors. *Applied Psycholinguistics* **10**, 13–30.

Werker, J. & Tees, R. (1987). Speech perception in severely disabled and average reading children. *Canadian Journal of Psychology* **41**, 48–61.

Wolf, M. (1986). Rapid alternating stimulus naming in the developmental dyslexias. *Brain and Language* **27**, 360–379.

Wolf, M. (1991). Naming speed and reading: the contribution of the cognitive neuro-sciences. *Reading Research Quarterly* **26**, 123–141.

Wolff, P.M., Michel, G.F. & Ovrut, M. (1990). The timing of syllable repetitions in developmental dyslexia. *Journal of Speech and Hearing Research* **33**, 281–289.

Yuill, N. & Oakhill, J. (1991). *Children's Problems in Test Comprehension: An Experimental Investigation*. Cambridge, UK: Cambridge University Press.

Chapter 6
In Search of the Precursors of Dyslexia: A Prospective Study of Children at Risk for Reading Problems

HEIKKI LYYTINEN

It is well known that a high proportion of dyslexic individuals have relatives experiencing reading problems (e.g., Gilger et al., 1991; Hallgren, 1950; Lubs et al., 1991; Lubs et al., 1993; Vogler, DeFries & Decker, 1985). Familial transmission makes it possible to investigate dyslexia prospectively. In our own prospective Study, the Jyväskylä Longitudinal Study of Dyslexia (JLD), children born to families with a dyslexic parent and at least one other close dyslexic relative have been followed from birth. In this early report we illustrate the screening and identification of the parents whose children we are following, describe the data collected for the prospective follow-up and outline some comparisons between the at-risk children and children from control families in the first 2 years of life.

The only comparable study from which results are available for children who have started reading is Hollis Scarborough's (1991) study. In this study the at-risk children were followed from 2:6 years to 8 years. In our study the assessment of the children is wider than in Scarborough's study and has included measures of motor skills and attention-related behaviours as well as a number of measures of cognition (especially of perceptual skills) and learning. Many of these measures have been implicated as correlates of dyslexia or causative factors in the development of the disorder. Environmental variables, especially the child's learning environment and his or her interaction with parents, are assessed in standardised laboratory sessions and by way of video recordings at home.

Why include such a large number of variables in our study? And why have we selected children of families with relatives who have various kinds of difficulties with reading as seen in their inaccurate and/or slow reading and not necessarily only those whose problems are explicitly phonological? These decisions are interrelated. It is relatively well-documented that difficulties in learning to read English are closely connected to the development of phonological skills and phonemic awareness. However, the developmental course leading to the poor learning of these skills is not well known. Thus it may not be sufficient to observe the development of phonological skills in isolation. These skills may be related to innate (genetic) factors but they surely interact with other perceptual and learning factors, and environmental effects may be substantial. Appropriate environmental stimulation — the opportunity to learn the basic language skills and to find the necessary motivation (e.g., to play with language and to become interested in reading) are apparently important prerequisites for learning to read. Related difficulties may therefore be found in the perceptual, attentional and motor prerequisites of everyday activities in the child's environment. These may affect, for example, the accuracy of speech perception, skills of speech production and comprehension, and different kinds of learning involved in reading acquisition. Such difficulties may slow down or disturb processes leading to the automatisation of skills or to the natural integration between modalities and the flow of sensory and motor information. Such difficulties may, especially if mild, remain unnoticed and may become increasingly difficult to detect in older children because they have been compensated for. A wide-ranging assessment of early skills is therefore important if we are to identify the early origins of children's difficulties with phonological and reading skills.

Accurate early diagnosis of the child's difficulties should enable us to provide rational ways of helping the child to overcome them. Early intervention will be important in helping to avoid the possible adverse emotional and motivational effects of the child's learning difficulties.

Identification of Families for the Study

The study was initiated in 1993 by screening for the occurrence of dyslexia among the approximately 3000 mothers who become pregnant each year in central Finland. More than 90% of Finnish mothers expecting a baby visit a publicly funded maternity clinic at least once during their pregnancy. As the first step in the screening process a short questionnaire was distributed (when the mothers visited the clinic) to all these families from 1993 to early 1996 asking whether the mother or father had experienced reading problems. The mother was also asked to provide her address if she thought the family would consider participating in a study in which the child's development would be followed in detail. Families without any history of reading problems were also encouraged to participate as a control group.

A more comprehensive second questionnaire was sent to all 4089 parents who gave their address in the first questionnaire. This means that almost one-quarter of all those families who had a birth during these years were willing to participate. The questionnaire covered a range of areas relevant to the identification of reading problems among family members and close relatives. Most items focused on early language learning, school achievements with special emphasis on reading and language and foreign language acquisition. Participation in support teaching and special education was explored in detail. Later experiences concerning present reading skills, reading habits and interests were also covered. Questions concerning the respondents' knowledge of their close relatives focused on language-related issues and reading and spelling skills in particular.

We used this questionnaire to select those parents we thought most likely to have dyslexic children. From the 300 parents reporting the most consistent signs of reading and spelling problems in themselves, more than half also identified at least one close relative who had reading problems and on this basis they were selected for the standardised in-lab reading assessment.

The Individual Assessments of Reading and Reading-related Skills

Individual reading assessments were used to place parents into the control or dyslexic groups. These assessments involved two tests:

1. Reading aloud. The test consisted of two texts of 218 and 128 words, respectively, resulting in scores for the number of errors made and reading time.
2. Spelling. The test consisted of 10 words and 10 non-words with 6–14 letters and 2–7 syllables. These items were spelled without imposing a time limit. The score was the number of errors made.

To be included in the dyslexic group at least one of the parents' reading scores had to be more than one standard deviation below the mean of the normal group of the same age (mean 31 years). In addition each subject had to score more than one standard deviation below the mean of the age- and education-matched normal group on at least two of the following five tests:

Phonological skills

3. Reading single non-words. This task consisted of 60 items with 4, 6 or 8 letters and 2–4 syllables. The subjects read the items on the computer screen which activated a voice key. The scores were the number of correct responses and the mean reaction time.

4. Lexical decision task. This task consisted of 30 items with 12–22 letters and 5–9 syllables. All stimuli were presented in an inflected form and pseudowords were created by adding an inflection which was not grammatically acceptable. The scores were the number of correctly identified items and the mean reaction time.

Orthographic skills

5. Reading tachistoscopically presented masked words and pseudowords. The task consisted of 40 words and 12 pseudowords presented for 80 msec before masking by a word/pseudoword. The subject had to pronounce both the target and the masking stimulus. The score was the number of correctly pronounced target words and pseudowords.

6. Lexical decision on tachistoscopically presented words and pseudowords. The task consisted of 21 words and 21 pseudowords of 4, 6, or 8 letters and 2–4 syllables. The items were presented for 60 msec. The subject responded by pushing one of two buttons. The scores were the number of correct decisions and the mean reaction time.

7. Hyphenation. Hyphenation is identical to syllabification in Finnish which is learned early because syllables are separated by stress patterns in Finnish speech. The rules of hyphenation are simple with very few exceptions and the teaching of reading is heavily based on syllable-based segmentation of words during spelling. The hyphenation task consisted of 24 words of 4, 6 or 8 letters and 2–4 syllables, half of them representing frequent and half of them rare words. The word was first presented on the screen and then the letters of the word were shown letter by letter below the word. The subject was asked to push a button between every two letters where there should be a hyphenation mark. The score was the number of correct hyphenations.

Phonological awareness

Four tasks tapping phonological manipulation skills (not used in selecting subjects but of interest here) were included among the tests of the individual test battery. These were tasks consisting of:

8.   phoneme deletion;
9.   syllable reversal;
10 & 11. rhyme recognition tasks.

Additionally sensory speed was assessed using simple or multiple choice RT tasks using visual imperative stimuli. Also auditory and visual working memory were assessed. None of these tests was used for placing individuals in the at-risk group.

Following this screening procedure 86 children were selected as coming from at-risk families. At least one parent of these families has a documented reading deficit and he or she had identified at least one close relative with poor reading skills. Also included was a further sample of 20 'compensated' parents. All of them were able to identify at least two close relatives with poor reading skills and had a school history of multiple indices of reading difficulties. However, for these parents, the individual assessment failed to show any reliable indications of a reading problem at the time of testing.

A comparison group of the same size ($n = 100$) was selected from the children of parents reporting a normal reading history (including the close relatives) and showing normal reading-related skills in the individual assessment. The families representing the at-risk and control groups were matched in terms of the mother's education. Only parents with a Raven's Progressive Matrices IQ exceeding 80 were included (for more details of the subject selection see Lyytinen et al., 1995).

Overview of the Reading Status of the Parents Screened for the Study

Using the questionnaire data, all the 4089 parents were classified into three categories of reading difficulty and familial background using composite scores for the reading status of each subject and his or her identification of relatives with reading difficulties. Self-reported reading status and familial background of reading problems were closely associated.

A substantially higher proportion of those who reported having relatives with reading difficulties reported that they themselves had reading problems. Similarly, parents who reported reading problems also frequently reported indications of reading problems among their relatives. The number of normal readers who have no relatives with reading difficulties was higher then expected. However, the probability that a normal reader would report many signs of dyslexia among their relatives was relatively low.

Of those parents who rated themselves as having reading difficulties, 48% identified multiple indications of problems amongst their relatives. For those parents who reported not having reading problems themselves only 9% reported reading problems in their relatives. Similarly, only 3% of parents who did not report relatives with reading problems reported multiple problems of their own. In contrast, 23% of parents who reported having reading difficulties reported multiple problems amongst their relatives.

Approximately half of the parents who self-reported many indicators of having reading problems fulfilled our criteria for dyslexia in the detailed reading assessment, whereas, from the parents identified as possibly having reading problems on the basis of our questionnaire measures, the prevalence of familial dyslexia confirmed with individual reading assessment was only 2.9 %.

Heterogeneity of the Reading-related Skills of Poor Reading Adults

A detailed analysis of the first 52 index parents (Lyytinen et al., 1995) reveals that 14 of the subjects had several low scores (five or more scores, more than 2 standard deviations below the norm) among the measures described above. The majority of the others had only a few low scores among sub-skills in addition to poor reading and spelling scores. As expected the most common difficulty was in reading non-words where only a few cases were as good as or better at reading non-words than they were at reading words (in Finnish, which is a highly regular orthography, this is unusual as the differences in accuracy or speed between reading words and non-words is relatively small). The clearest cluster of difficulties, as one might expect, was in phonological skills. This was the defining characteristic of a subgroup of 10 subjects. Twelve of the subjects had a 'double' deficit as shown by low scores on both phonological and orthographic variables. The difficulties of nine of the subjects were merely in orthographic skills. Ten of the subjects had particular problems with segmentation, making a number of errors in hyphenating Finnish words. In Finnish, hyphenation rules are very explicit and almost without exception Finnish secondary school children very seldom show any difficulties with hyphenation (which is used to mark syllable boundaries). Six subjects could not be clearly identified as belonging to any of these subgroups.

Surprisingly there were many adult dyslexics who did not show any clear difficulty in phonemic manipulation skills or in non-word reading. Most of these subjects were extremely slow readers (without being slow in tests containing tasks unrelated to reading) and could not recognise even highly familiar words rapidly.

Search for Differences between At-risk and Control Children in the First Two Years of Life

The follow-up of infants was initiated by paediatric and neurological (Brazelton, 1973) examinations immediately after birth. No clinically significant problems were found in any of the subjects and the EEG recordings made immediately after birth were normal. Psychophysiological recordings including brain event-related potentials (ERPs), heart rate (HR) and crying elicited by the detachment of the electrodes was performed at age 3–9 days. In this early ERP study an attempt was made to examine how the infant's brain discriminates small auditory differences. This was done by recording so-called mismatch negativity response (MMN) (see Näätänen, 1992; Näätänen & Alho, 1995) to deviant (in terms of pitch or duration) stimuli presented among sinusoidal tones and language stimuli in separate experiments. The deviant tones were presented infrequently among streams of stimuli repeated frequently (for details, see Leppänen et al., in press). The MMN has been shown to be a potentially sensitive measure of central auditory skill (like absolute pitch discrimination (Lang et al., 1990) or dysfunction (e.g. Kraus et al., 1996a, 1996b; Maiste et al., 1996) at a later ages. Although some minor differences between groups could be found, none of these very early measures has thus far been shown to be reliable enough to be used as a potential indicator of group membership. Heart rate measures containing measures of tonic (vagal tone, cf. Porges & Bohrer, 1990) and phasic responses to stimuli used in the ERP study have not revealed any differences between the groups, but the sample that has been analysed to date is still small and we have no way of determining which of the at-risk infants will actually develop into dyslexic children. The crying data, where the spectral components are analysed, are under examination (for the first report illustrating the normative values of the whole group see Michelsson et al, submitted).

The parents have agreed to complete a relatively extensive set of structured observation forms constructed as a diary during the first 16 months after birth. These observations include measures of early vocalisation, motor and temperamental behaviour. Parents also executed a number of simple 'tests' on their babies with the help of guidelines illustrated using a videotape. Some of the families had an opportunity to use camcorders lent to them monthly during the first 1:6 years for recording vocalisation and early language. Parents were asked to note the earliest age of occurrence of the vocalisation of certain sounds (like aa-, ii-), the production of sustained sounds, cooing, imitations, reduplicated babbling and the combination of syllables (variated babble). It is of interest that none of the above language measures has thus far shown any reliable differences between the at-risk and control groups of infants although the measures seem to be reliable and provide results consistent with test-based assessments. The preliminary findings do indicate, however, reliable differences in the attainment of a number of motor skills with small delays in development amongst the at-risk group.

At six months the families spent a day in the laboratory where a number of behavioural and ERP measures were taken. These tests focused on auditory and linguistic skills and included a differential conditioning of head turning for assessing the discrimination of quantity (or duration) in a segment of a nonsense word (ata-atta). The two ends of the dimension of lengthening the silent period between the vowel a- and the consonant t-sounds of the non-word were used as discriminative stimuli, i.e., as CR- (never followed by the US) or as CR+ (always followed by the US; a drumming rabbit). The anticipatory head turns (CRs) were recorded to assess discrimination and categorical perception. The results reveal an interesting difference between the at-risk and control groups in the perception of quantity at 6 months of age. The control children showed reliably less generalisation and thus more distinct categorisation of the short and long consonant (typical of Finnish) than the at-risk children.

Leppänen and Lyytinen (submitted) report preliminary findings showing interesting group differences in ERPs (MMN). These were elicited by similar stimuli to those used to condition head-turn responses. The results reveal laterality differences with the at-risk group showing higher ERP amplitudes from the right hemisphere to the critical (deviant) linguistic stimuli whilst controls respond with larger left hemisphere amplitudes to the same stimuli.

The other measures collected at the age of 6 months include assessments of visual recognition memory, which have been shown to predict later IQ (for a review see Colombo, 1993 and Rose & Feldman, 1995). Environmental variables were also assessed from the interaction between parents and their children in laboratory sessions during the first three years.

Vocabulary (MacArthur Communicative Development Inventory, CDI), symbolic play and the basic language measures included in the Reynell Developmental Scale (RDLS) and in the Revised Bayley Scales comprised the language-related measures assessed before the age of two years. The CDI was presented first at 12 months and then at 14 and 18 months. It provides scores of vocabulary comprehension and production at 12 months and additionally symbolic gestures at 14 months. The Reynell Scale was presented at 18 and 30 months. It provides scores of verbal comprehension and expressive language. The Bayley Scales were presented at 24 months and provide three language-related scores.

At the time of writing this report only part of the sample has reached an age above 6 months. Therefore few analyses are yet available. Lyytinen et al. (in press b) examined the parents' skills in evaluating the early vocalisation of their child. Relatively good agreement between laboratory measures and parental ratings was found. This encourages us to use the quite comprehensive assessment data collected by the parents. In a second paper the relationships between symbolic play and early language skills (Lyytinen et al., in press a) have been explored. We have found that those babies who have failed to speak before 18 months of age (according to the parental ratings) also show much lower levels of symbolic play in the laboratory. The Reynell comprehension scores also correlate reliably with both parental and symbolic play measures at this age.

The later stages of the follow-up consist largely of laboratory observations of language development at ages 12 and 18 months and a home visit at 28 months. An extensive programme for assessing language, cognitive and motor skills is now being initiated at the age of 42 months. It will involve the assessment of word repetition, rapid naming and phonological manipulation skills such as the segmentation of compound words, and the skills necessary to segment spoken words.

Conclusions

Any attempt to explore the early precursors of dyslexia is bound to face problems. The first problem is in the selection of parents of the at-risk children who are to be followed. We have little evidence about the possible determinants of very early skills which may form the foundations of reading acquisition. We did not restrict our interest to those parents who showed both poor reading skills and had a clear phonological deficit although phonological difficulties are generally supposed to be central to explanations of reading difficulties. We also included in the at-risk group parents whose reading difficulties may have reflected different (non-phonological) problems.

One further problem is the question of the course of development of any early skills which might be connected to the much later acquisition of reading skills. It is quite likely that variations in early language milestones will fail to be connected in any direct and straightforward way to later reading skills. Delays are often observed in a child's first speech, and much of early language development may depend upon latent developmental processes. This is why multiple measures of development may be needed, including, for example, a follow-up of motor development. The most likely candidates as precursors of dyslexia, given our present understanding of reading development, are measures of phonological development. However, the developmental 'distance' between early phonological skills and the later phonemic awareness skills that seem critical for learning to read may require both theoretical and empirical bridges to help connect them (see also Chapter 1 by Frith and Chapter 9 by Snowling and Nation, this volume). Phonological abilities constitute a relatively heterogeneous set of skills at least at the age when they start to mature fully. However, the beginnings of phonological development can be assessed from a relatively early age and some of the first indications of perceptual skills relevant to phonological variations may exist at this stage. Accordingly, we have repeated our assessment of auditory perception at a few days of age and at 6 months and have been able to observe interesting perceptual differences between the at-risk group and controls by the age of 6 months. To our surprise our other language measures have failed to show any comparable group differences in the follow-up study so far. However, we must remember that only part of the whole sample has yet been analysed in detail.

Possible environmental influences related to parent–child interaction patterns and their effects on temperamental and ability-based compensatory factors are also of interest. These may have a role as protective factors in a proportion of individuals who are congenitally at risk of dyslexia. Environmental factors may also help some people compensate later in life for an early reading problem. That such a 'compensated' subgroup exists was shown by our present screening study of the parent population (for a comparable finding see Gilger et al., 1996). A substantial number of our parents showed that they have had compensatory resources or needed environmental support. It is hoped that factors affecting such compensation in development will also be identified from our sample of children. The identification of compensatory processes encourages us in our belief that dyslexia may not necessarily be a lifelong disorder (e.g., Kamhi, 1992) and that early identification may help to overcome it.

Acknowledgements

A number of other people have been involved in the work described in this chapter including S. Leinonen, L. Kaukiainen, P. Leppänen, K. Eklund, K. Michelsson, A. Poikkeus, M. Laakso, M. Leiwo, D.T. Ahonen and P. Lyytinen. A number of external researchers have contributed substantially to different components of the project: Professor Jeffrey Gilger (University of Kansas) and Professor Dennis Molfese (University of Southern California) earn a special mention here. The study is supported by the Academy of Finland.

References

Brazelton, T.B. (1973). *Neonatal Behavioral Assessment Scale.* London: Spastics International Medical Publications.

Colombo, J. (1993). *Infant Cognition: Predicting Later Intellectual Functioning.* Newbury Park, CA: Sage Publications.

Gilger, J.W., Hanebuth, L., Smith, S.D. & Pennington, B.F. (1996). Differential risk for developmental reading disorders in the offspring of compensated versus noncompensated parents. *Reading and Writing* 8, 407– 417.

Gilger, J.W., Pennington, B. F. & DeFries, J. C. (1991). Risk for reading disability as function of parental history in three family studies. *Reading and Writing* 3, 205–217.

Hallgren, B. (1950). Specific dyslexia (congenital word-blindness): A clinical and genetic study. *Acta Psychiatrica et Neurologica Supplement* 65, 1–287.

Kamhi, A.G. (1992). Response to historical perspectives: A developmental language perspective. *Journal of Learning Disabilities* 25, 48–52.

Kraus, N., McGee, T.J., Carrell, T.D., Zecker, S.G., Nicol, T.G. & Koch, D.B. (1996a). Auditory neurophysiologic responses and discrimination deficits in children with learning problems. *Science* 273, 971–973.

Kraus, N., Mobic, T., Carrell, T. & Charm, A. (1996b). Neurophysiological basis of speech discrimination. *Ear & Hearing* 16, 19–37.

Kuhl, P.K., Williams, K.A., Lacerda, F., Stevens, K.N. & Lindblom, B. (1992). Linguistic experience alters phonetic perception in infants by 6 months of age. *Science* **225**, 606–608.

Lang, H., Nyrke, T., Ek, M., Aaltonen, O., Raimo, I. & Näätänen, R. (1990). Pitch discrimination performance and auditive event-related potentials. In C. H. M. Brunia, A.W.K. Gaillard & A. Kok (Eds.) *Psychophysiological Brain Research*, Vol. 1 (EPIC IX Noordwijk, 28 May to 3 June 1989, pp. 249–298). The Netherlands: Tilburg University Press.

Leppänen, P.H.T., Eklund, K.M. & Lyytinen, H. (in press) Event-related potentials to change in newborns. *Developmental Neuropsychology* **2**.

Leppänen, P.H.T. & Lyytinen, H. (submitted). Auditory ERPs and language related disorders. *Audiology and Neuro-otology*.

Lubs, H.A., Rabin, M., Carland-Saucier, K., Wen, X.L., Gross-Glenn, K., Duara, R., Levin, B. & Lubs, M., L. (1991). Genetic bases of developmental dyslexia: Molecular studies. In J. E. Obrzut & G.W. Hynd (Eds.) *Neuropsychological Foundations of Learning Disabilities* (pp. 49–75). London: Academic Press.

Lubs, H.A., Rabin, M., Feldman, E., Jallad, B.J., Kushch, A., Gross-Glenn, K., Duara, R. & Elston, R.C. (1993). Familial dyslexia: Genetic and medical findings in eleven three-generation families. *Annals of Dyslexia* **28**, 44–60.

Lyytinen, H., Leinonen, S., Nikula, M., Aro, M. & Leiwo, M. (1995). In search of the core features of dyslexia: Observations concerning dyslexia in the highly ortho-graphically regular Finnish language. In V. M. Berninger (Ed.) *The Varieties of Orthographic Knowledge, II: Relationship to Phonology, Reading, and Writing* (pp.177–204). Dordrecht, Netherlands: Kluwer.

Lyytinen, P., Poikkeus, A.-M. & Laakso, M.-L. (in press a). Language and symbolic play in toddlers. *International Journal of Behavioral Development*.

Lyytinen, P., Poikkeus, A.-M., Leiwo, M., Ahonen, T. & Lyytinen, H. (1996). Parents as informants of their child's vocal and early language development. *Early Child Development and Care* **126**, 15–25.

Maiste, A.C., Wiens, A., Hunt, M.J., Schert, M. & Picton, T., W. (1996). Event-related potentials and categorical speech sounds. *Ear & Hearing* **16**, 68–90.

Michelsson, K., Eklund, K., Leppänen, P. & Lyytinen, H. (submitted). Crying in healthy newborn infants: Sound spectrographic analysis. *Developmental Medicine and Child Neurology*.

Näätänen, R. (1992). *Attention and brain function*. Hillsdale, NJ: Lawrence Erlbaum.

Näätänen, R. & Alho, K. (1995). Mismatch negativity – a unique measure of sensory processing in audition. *International Journal of Neuroscience* **80**, 317–337.

Porges, S.W. & Bohrer, R.E. (1990). The analysis of periodic processes in psychophys-iological research. In J. T. Cacioppo & L.G. Tassinary (Eds), *Principles of Psychophysiology: Physical, Social, and Inferential Elements* (pp. 708-753). Cambridge: Press Syndicate of the University of Cambridge.

Rose, S. A. & Feldman, J.F. (1995). Prediction of IQ and specific cognitive abilities at 11 years from infancy measures. *Developmental Psychology* **31**, 685–696.

Scarborough, H. S. (1991). Early syntactic development of dyslexic children. *Annals of Dyslexia* **44**, 207–220.

Vogler, G.P., DeFries, J.C. & Decker, D.J. (1985). Family history as an indicator of risk for reading disability. *Journal of Learning Disabilities* **18**, 419–421.

Chapter 7
Progress in the Search for Dyslexia Subtypes

KEITH E. STANOVICH, LINDA S. SIEGEL and
ALEXANDRA GOTTARDO

The field of reading disabilities has so far made very little progress toward defining separable groups of disabled readers – that is, subgroups who are behaviourally, genetically and physiologically different from each other. This is surprising because there is enormous face validity to the idea that different reading-disabled individuals have different underlying cognitive deficits.

The field *has* made what might be termed 'negative progress', however, in that it has finally extricated itself from some overly restrictive and empirically unverified assumptions that characterised its early history. For example, from the very beginning of research on reading disability, it was assumed that poor readers who were of high intelligence formed a group who were cognitively and neurologically different. We are here referring to the early history of the field in which the definition of reading disability or dyslexia was tied to the notion of aptitude/achievement discrepancy (Ceci, 1986; Reynolds, 1985; Shepard, 1980; Siegel, 1989; Stanovich, 1991, 1993b, 1994). Early investigators who pioneered the study of the condition then known as congenital word-blindness (e.g., Hinshelwood, 1917) were at pains to differentiate reading-disabled children with high intelligence from other poor readers. Similarly, the term dyslexia has often been reserved for children displaying discrepancies between intelligence and reading ability. In the 1960s, 1970s and 1980s, proponents of the generic term learning disabilities – coined largely as a school service-delivery category (Kirk, 1963; Lerner, 1985) – continued the tradition of assuming that there were important aetiological, neurological and cognitive differences between high-IQ and low-IQ poor readers.

One might have thought that at least researchers would have begun with the broadest and most theoretically neutral definition of reading disability – reading performance below some specified level on some well-known and psychometrically sound test – and then proceeded to investigate whether there were poor readers with differing cognitive profiles within this broader group. Unfortunately, the history of reading disabilities research does not resemble this logical sequence. Instead, early definitions of reading disability *assumed* knowledge of differential cognitive profile (and causation) within the larger sample of poor readers and defined the condition of reading disability in a way that actually served to *preclude* empirical investigation of the unproven theoretical assumptions that guided the formulation of these definitions in the first place!

It was not until the mid-1970s that we had the data from the ground-breaking epidemiological comparison of poor readers with and without reading-IQ discrepancy conducted by Rutter and Yule (1975), and only in the last decade have their data been supplemented by that from other investigations of a similar type. Recent data – some from our own laboratory – have indicated that, contrary to some of the foundational beliefs in the reading disabilities field, the phenotypic indicators of poor reading (difficulties in phonological coding and weak phonological sensitivity) seem not to be correlated in any reliable way with degree of discrepancy between intelligence and reading achievement; nor do reading-disabled children with high and low IQs seem to differ greatly in other information-processing operations that support word recognition (Felton & Wood, 1992; Fletcher, 1992; Fletcher et al., 1992; Fletcher et al., 1994; Francis et al., 1996; Fredman & Stevenson, 1988; Hurford et al., 1994; Maughan et al., 1994; Pennington et al., 1992; Rispens, van Yeren & van Duijn, 1991; Schuerholz et al., 1995; Share et al., 1987; Shaywitz et al., 1992; Siegel, 1988, 1989, 1992; Stanovich & Siegel, 1994; Taylor, Satz and Friel, 1979). Recent evidence thus suggests that if there is a special group of reading-disabled children who are behaviourally, cognitively, genetically and/or neurologically 'different', it is becoming increasingly unlikely that they can be easily identified by examining achievement/IQ discrepancies.

Are there other, more promising, cognitive tools for identifying different types of poor readers? The classic subtyping literature in our field is not encouraging on this score (see Fletcher & Morris, 1986; Lyon, 1987; McKinney, 1984; Morris & Satz, 1984; Satz, Morris & Fletcher, 1985; Speece & Cooper, 1991; Torgesen, 1991). This older subtyping work is, in retrospect, disappointing because much of it was purely empirical and not grounded in extant theory, and some of it was grounded in theory but the theories have become dated and do not reflect the latest work in human information processing or cognitive psychology.

An Alternative Basis for Subtypes: Information Processing Theories of Word Recognition

There is, however, a body of subtyping work that is not subject to *either* of these criticisms. This work has grown up around the study of the acquired dyslexias and the attempt to conceptualise them within the framework of theories of adult word recognition. In the early 1980s, researchers (e.g., Coltheart et al., 1983; Temple & Marshall, 1983) began to present cases of developmental dyslexics whose performance patterns mirrored those of certain classic acquired dyslexic cases (Beauvois & Derouesne, 1979; Coltheart, Patterson & Marshall, 1980; Marshall & Newcombe, 1973; Patterson, Marshall & Coltheart, 1985) and to interpret these cases of developmental dyslexia within the functional cognitive architecture assumed by dual-route theory[1] (Carr & Pollatsek, 1985; Coltheart, 1978; Humphreys & Evett, 1985).

The extrapolation from the acquired dyslexia literature to the interpretation of the performance patterns of developmental cases proved controversial, however (see Ellis, 1979, 1984; Frith, 1985; Snowling, 1983). For example, Bryant and Impey (1986) criticised the authors of the developmental case studies for not including control groups of normal readers as a context for their case descriptions. Recently, Castles and Coltheart (1993) have tried to answer these criticisms – first by demonstrating that their dual-route subtypes can be defined by reference to the performance of normal controls, and then by showing that the subtypes so defined are not at all rare in the dyslexic population.

Castles and Coltheart (1993) analysed the exception word and nonword reading performance of 53 dyslexic individuals and 56 non-dyslexic chronological age controls. They were motivated by a desire to distil subgroups that were relatively skilled at sublexical processing ('phonic' reading or decoding: indexed by the reading of pseudowords) relative to lexical processing ('whole word' or sight word reading:

[1.] Although current theorising in this field has been immensely influenced by connectionist models of word recognition (Hinton & Shallice, 1991; Manis et al., 1996; Metsala & Brown, in press; Plaut et al., 1996; Plaut & Shallice, 1994; Seidenberg, 1993, 1994; Seidenberg & McClelland, 1989), we will retain dual-route nomenclature throughout this discussion. However, our adherence to this nomenclature is largely driven by explicative convenience and historical precedent rather than by a desire on our part to advance a strong position on particular microdebates in the dual-route versus connectionist literature (see Besner et al., 1990; Coltheart et al., 1993; Plaut & Shallice, 1994; Seidenberg, 1993, 1994). Instead, from the standpoint of the reading disability theorist standing outside these debates, it seems quite possible that many of these disputes arise from attempts to characterise performance at different levels of analysis (Fodor & Pylyshyn, 1988; McCloskey, 1991; Smolensky, 1988, 1989). The data patterns described remain of importance to theories of reading disability whether verbally characterised in the representational language of dual-route theory or the sub-symbolic language of connectionist theory.

indexed by the reading of irregular or exception words) and vice versa (or, to use the terms popularised in Olson's [e.g., Olson et al., 1989] influential studies, subgroups characterised by relatively unique deficits in phonological coding and orthographic coding). Castles and Coltheart (1993) argued that subtypes of reading disability could be identified based on the *relative* imbalances on the two tasks. They defined their subtypes by running a regression line with 90% confidence intervals through the exception word by pseudoword plot for the control children. This regression line and confidence intervals are then superimposed upon the scatterplot of the performance of the dyslexic sample. Subjects falling below the lower confidence interval in this plot and *not* its converse (the pseudoword by exception word plot) have been labelled as surface dyslexics: they are unusually impaired on exception word reading relative to their performance on pseudowords when the relationship among these two subskills in the normal population is used as the benchmark. An analogous but opposite regression outlier criterion defines the phonological dyslexia subtype.

Using this procedure, Castles and Coltheart (1993) defined 16 surface dyslexics and 29 phonological dyslexics. They thus argued that the vast majority of dyslexics in their sample (45 out of 53) displayed some type of dissociation and they concluded that

'The results reported here support the notion that a clear double dissociation exists between surface and phonological dyslexic reading patterns, with some children displaying a specific difficulty reading via the lexical procedure in the absence of any difficulty with the sublexical procedure and others showing precisely the reverse pattern...it would seem that these reading patterns are not rare phenomena, but are quite prevalent in the developmental dyslexic population' (p. 174).

However, interpretation of the Castles and Coltheart (1993) data is problematic for a reason argued by Bryant and Impey (1986) almost 10 years ago: the lack of reading-level controls. If relative efficiency of the lexical and sublexical procedures is bound up with the overall level that the reader has attained, then extrapolating from the reading patterns of children at a higher reading level is an inappropriate way of defining abnormal patterns of processing skills at a lower reading level.

A reanalysis of the Castles and Coltheart (1993) data (Anne Castles is thanked for providing the raw data from their study which allowed us to conduct a series of replots and reanalyses) serves to confirm these fears. When the performance of the Chronological Age (CA) controls on exception words is plotted against reading age and the performance on pseudowords is plotted against reading age, both variables display statistically significant quadratic trends ($p < 0.001$ in the case of pseudowords). In precisely the range of reading ages where the reading- disabled sample resides, the slope relating performance to reading age is steeper.

Another way of viewing this problem is to note that when the entire sample is considered, the slope of the function relating exception word performance to reading age (in months) is steeper for the reading-disabled sample than for the CA controls (0.260 versus 0.128). However, when the range of reading ages is restricted to the lower range (< 117 months) where there is overlap between the CA controls and reading-disabled sample, there is no difference in slopes (0.260 versus 0.310). Similarly, when the entire sample is considered, the slope of the function relating pseudoword performance to reading age (in months) is steeper for the reading-disabled sample than for the CA controls (0.305 versus 0.114). However, when the range of reading ages is restricted to the lower range (< 117 months) where there is overlap between the CA controls and reading-disabled sample, there is no difference in slopes (0.305 versus 0.378).

In short, the difference in the growth functions when the entire sample of CA controls is compared with the sample of dyslexics is simply a function of the differing distributions of the two samples across the reading age continuum. The steeper slope displayed by the dyslexics is not a function of being dyslexic – it is simply a property of these particular pseudowords and exception words being given to children of these particular reading levels. When reading at the same level, control children display exactly the same slope (this of course is a variant of the arguments for reading-level controls that have appeared in the literature before; see Bryant & Goswami, 1986; Bryant & Impey, 1986; Snowling, 1983). In fact, we can easily see that a regression line dominated by high reading-age control children is an inappropriate one for the dyslexic children by simply pondering the fact that it is equally inappropriate for *normal* children of reading ages similar to the dyslexics. This shows that extrapolating from the reading patterns of children at a higher reading level is an inappropriate way of defining abnormal patterns of processing skills at a lower reading level. In fact, if Figure 5 and Figure 6 in the Castles and Coltheart (1993) paper (the plots of exception word reading by pseudoword reading for the non-dyslexics and dyslexics, respectively) are superimposed upon each other, the dyslexic subjects are virtually outside the normal space.

In a recent study, Manis et al. (1996) added an important context for the Castles and Coltheart type of analysis – a reading-level control. They found that 12 of the 17 phonological dyslexics defined by a chronological age comparison also qualified for that subtype based on regression lines derived from a reading-level (RL) control sample. However, when the performance of the 15 chronological age defined surface dyslexics was examined, only *one* qualified for this subtype label when a reading-level control group was employed.

It can be shown that a similar pattern obtains in the Castles and Coltheart (1993) data as well. Given that theirs was a CA match investigation, it might be wondered how this was possible. It is possible because, as in many other studies, there is enormous variability around the point of the CA match (as identified by a statistic such as the mean). The CAs in their study spanned seven and a half years (90 months to 179 months) and the reading ages spanned seven years (78 months to 163 months). More importantly, however, at the lower reading ages, there is overlap between the groups. We thus formed matched reading-level groups of 17 non-dyslexic children and 40 dyslexic children from the Castles and Coltheart data – a comparison not examined in their original paper.

Table 7.1 indicates that although the match was less than perfect (there was almost three months' difference in reading age), the difference was not statistically significant. The reading-level controls outperformed the dyslexics on all three stimulus types. The difference was much larger on pseudowords and the interaction between stimulus type and subject group was highly significant ($p < 0.001$). The dyslexics named about the same number of pseudowords as exception words, whereas the RL controls named about six more pseudowords than exception words – a very large difference. Thus, the reading-level match from the Castles and Coltheart data replicates the classic finding of a dyslexic pseudoword reading deficit in an RL match (Rack, Snowling & Olson, 1992; Stanovich & Siegel, 1994).

Table 7.1 Mean differences between the reading-level matched dyslexics ($n = 40$) and the non-dyslexics ($n = 17$) in the Castles & Coltheart (1993) study

Variable	Dyslexics	Controls	t value
Reading age	101.0	103.9	1.34
Exception words	13.0	14.9	2.17*
Pseudowords	13.8	20.6	3.61***
Regular words	22.5	26.0	2.80**

Note: * = $p < 0.05$; ** = $p < 0.01$; *** = $p < 0.001$, all two-tailed.

Figure 7.1 illustrates one of the plots that identifies the subtypes, but this time using only the RL control group as a benchmark rather than the full CA-matched control group. The number of pseudowords read correctly is plotted against the number of exception words read correctly. The performance of the reading-disabled children is represented by Xs and the performance of the non-disabled RL-matched group is represented by squares. The regression line and confidence intervals displayed in the figure are based on the data from the 17 RL-controls (the squares). This plot in part identifies the phonological subtype (children low on pseudoword reading relative to exception word reading). There are 15 phonological dyslexics according to this criterion.

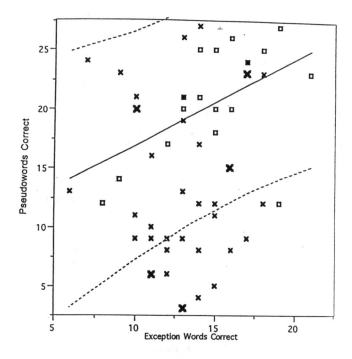

Figure 7.1 Performance on pseudoword reading plotted against exception word reading for the reading-disabled children (Xs) and RL controls (squares) in the Castles and Coltheart(1993) data. The regression line and confidence intervals were derived from the data of the RL controls. Larger Xs indicate two individuals with reading disability with the same scores and filled squares indicate that two individuals, one from each group, have the same scores.

Figure 7.2 displays the performance of the dyslexics plotted so as to identify surface dyslexics (children low on exception word reading relative to pseudoword reading). The number of exception words read correctly is plotted against the number of pseudowords read correctly. The performance of the reading-disabled children is again represented by Xs and the performance of the non-disabled RL-matched group is represented by squares. The regression line and confidence intervals displayed in the figure are again based on the data from the 17 RL-controls (the squares). Figure 7.2 indicates that the Castles and Coltheart (1993) data patterns themselves converge with the findings of Manis et al. (1996): most surface dyslexics disappear when a reading-age control is employed – only two are left in the Castles and Coltheart sample. Thus, a reanalysis of the original Castles and Coltheart (1993) data replicates the trend demonstrated by Manis et al (1996). When an RL control group is used, surface dyslexics defined by a CA match are almost completely eliminated, but phonological dyslexia (deficient non-word reading in relation to reading age) remains a common pattern.

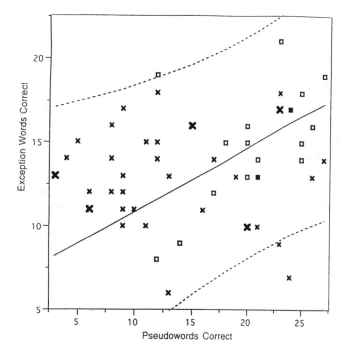

Figure 7.2 Performance on exception word reading plotted against pseudoword reading for the reading-disabled children (Xs) and RL controls (squares) in the Castles and Coltheart (1993) data. The regression line and confidence intervals were derived from the data of the RL controls. Larger Xs indicate two individuals with reading disability with the same scores and filled squares indicate that two individuals, one from each group, have the same scores.

Replication of the Subtype Patterns in a Younger Sample

We have conducted a subtype analysis of the Castles and Coltheart type on a sample of children who were considerably younger than those studied by Manis et al. (1996) and those examined in the *post hoc* analyses of Castles and Coltheart (1993). Our study extended beyond their findings in three ways. First, our dyslexics and RL controls were considerably younger than the children in the other studies. Thus, we examined whether the results generalise to earlier reading levels and how early the subtypes can be reliably identified. The dyslexics in our *post hoc* reanalysis of the Castles and Coltheart (1993) study were 137.9 months old and those in the Manis et al. (1996) investigation were 149.2 months old, whereas ours were 107.5 months old. The RL controls in both of the other two investigations were 102.0 months old, whereas ours were 88.9 months old.

Second, both the Castles and Coltheart (1993) and the Manis et al.

(1996) studies examined samples that *varied* widely in age. In contrast, our dyslexics, as well as their CA controls, were all third graders and our RL controls were all first and second graders. Finally, in our battery, unlike in the Castles and Coltheart (1993) study, we had a variety of other tasks which can provide some converging evidence for the existence of subtypes (see also Manis et al., 1996).

Recall that Castles and Coltheart (1993) defined their dyslexic subtypes by plotting pseudoword performance against exception word performance (and vice versa) and examining the 90% confidence intervals around the regression line determined from the CA control group. A phonological dyslexic is a child who is an outlier when pseudowords are plotted against exception words but is within the normal range when exception words are plotted against pseudowords. Surface dyslexics are defined by the opposite pattern. Figure 7.3 displays the data from our 68 third-grade reading-disabled children and plots exception word reading against pseudoword reading. The regression line and confidence intervals from the 44 CA controls in our sample is also displayed. All four groups that are defined by conjoining the results of this with the converse plot not shown (pseudoword performance

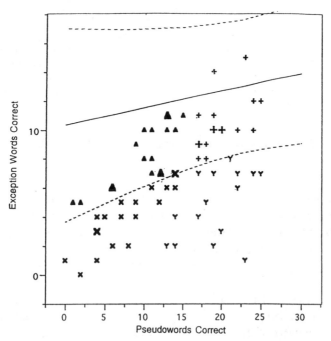

Figure 7.3 Performance on exception word reading plotted against pseudoword reading for the reading-disabled children in the present study. The regression line and confidence intervals were derived from the data of the CA controls. Y = surface dyslexics, ▲ = phonological dyslexics, ✖ = low on both, + = low on neither. Larger points indicate two individuals with the same scores.

against exception word performance) are indicated. Specifically, the points labelled with Ys are the surface dyslexics (low in the exception word by pseudoword plot and in the normal range on the converse plot), the triangles are the phonological dyslexics (low in the pseudoword by exception word plot and in the normal range on the converse plot), the Xs are subjects who are low on both measures, and the crosses represent individuals who are low on neither.

One interesting difference between our results and those involving the CA controls in the Castles and Coltheart (1993) and Manis et al. (1996) investigations concerns the fact that Manis et al. (1996) found that only 9.8% of their sample were outside the regression criterion on both measures, and Castles and Coltheart (1993) found only 5.7% of their sample low on both. In contrast, in our younger sample, 27.9% of the dyslexics (19 out of 68 children) were low on both types of stimuli. Perhaps these findings indicate that, with development, there is increasing dissociation between lexical and sublexical processes in dyslexic children.

Table 7.2 displays the comparisons between the 23 reading-level controls and the 68 dyslexics in our sample. The groups were matched closely on their WRAT reading raw scores. The dyslexics scored somewhat higher on the WRAT spelling subtest and on the Woodcock Word Identification subtest, perhaps indicating some degree of regression in the matched groups. The sample can be more closely matched on these variables at a cost in sample size but it does not materially affect the results. The older dyslexics were superior in arithmetic performance, a common finding in an RL match (see Stanovich & Siegel, 1994). On two measures of pseudoword reading (the Woodcock Word Attack and some experimental pseudowords of the type used by Coltheart & Leahy, 1992)

Table 7.2 Mean differences between the dyslexics ($n = 68$) and the reading-level controls ($n = 23$)

Variable	Dyslexics	RL controls	t value
WRAT Reading (raw)	51.2	51.0	0.12
WRAT Spelling (raw)	33.1	31.4	1.86
Woodcock Word Ident (raw)	46.8	42.6	1.83
WRAT Arithmetic	23.5	20.3	5.72**
Woodcock Word Attack (raw)	12.1	15.5	−2.25*
Rosner AAT	16.8	21.1	−2.16*
Wordlikeness choice	11.8	11.8	0.01
Exception words	6.9	6.4	0.52
Regular words	8.4	9.2	−0.73
Pseudowords	13.9	16.8	−2.05*

Note: * = $p < 0.05$; ** = $p < 0.001$, all two-tailed.

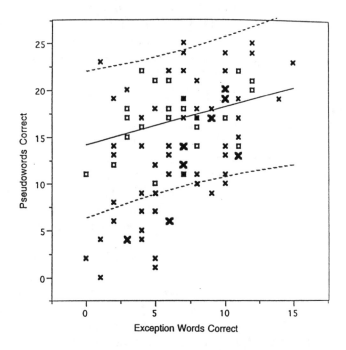

Figure 7.4 Performance on pseudoword reading plotted against exception word reading for the reading-disabled children (Xs) and RL controls (squares) in the present study. The regression line and confidence intervals were derived from the data of the RL controls. Larger Xs indicate two individuals with reading disability with the same scores and filled squares indicate that two individuals, one from each group, have the same scores.

we replicated the finding of a dyslexic deficit in an RL match. On a measure of phonological sensitivity (the Rosner Auditory Analysis Test), the dyslexics displayed a significant deficit, consistent with previous research (Bowey, Cain & Ryan, 1992; Bradley & Bryant, 1978; Bruck, 1992; Bruck & Treiman, 1990; Olson et al., 1990). On a measure of orthographic processing (a wordlikeness choice task, see Siegel et al., 1995) the two groups displayed no difference; nor were any differences displayed on a set of exception and a set of regular words. These exception words and the experimental pseudowords were used to define the dyslexic subgroups in our study.

Figure 7.4 displays the performance of the dyslexics plotted so as to identify phonological dyslexics (children low on pseudoword reading relative to exception word reading). The number of pseudowords read correctly is plotted against the number of exception words read correctly. The performance of the reading-disabled children is represented by Xs and the performance of the non-disabled RL-matched group is represented by squares. The regression line and confidence

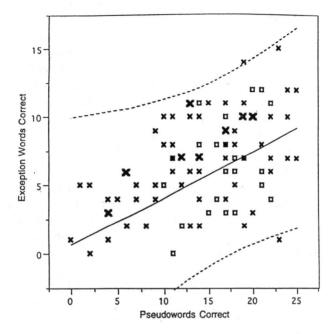

Figure 7.5 Performance on exception word reading plotted against pseudoword reading for the reading-disabled children (Xs) and RL controls (squares) in the present study. The regression line and confidence intervals were derived from the data of the RL controls. Larger Xs indicate two individuals with reading disability with the same scores and filled squares indicate that two individuals, one from each group, have the same scores.

intervals displayed in the figure are based on the data from the 23 RL controls (the squares in Figure 7.4).

Figure 7.5 shows the performance plotted so as to identify surface dyslexics (children low on exception word reading relative to pseudoword reading). The number of exception words read correctly is plotted against the number of pseudowords read correctly. The performance of the reading-disabled children is again represented by Xs and the performance of the non-disabled RL-matched group is represented by squares. The regression line and confidence intervals displayed in the figure are again based on the data from the 23 RL-controls (the squares).

Seventeen children were identified as phonological dyslexics by employing these two scatterplots and regressions. Figure 7.5 indicates that, consistent with the findings from the older sample of Manis et al. (1996) and our reanalysis of the Castles/Coltheart data presented above, surface dyslexics virtually disappear when a reading-age control is employed – only one is left in our sample. This is consistent with the two found in the Castles/Coltheart sample and one found in the Manis et al. sample. In contrast, substantial numbers of phonological dyslexics in RL-control comparisons were identified in all the samples.

In light of the similarity in the data patterns of the RL comparisons in all four of these studies, it is interesting to note that the original Bryant and Impey (1986) study – the first to analyse the patterns revealed in the surface and phonological dyslexic case studies in the context of reading-level controls – obtained a similar outcome. The one pattern of HM, the phonological dyslexic of Temple and Marshall (1983), that Bryant and Impey could not match to a child in their RL control group was HM's non-word reading. In contrast, Bryant and Impey were able to find a match in their RL control group for every pattern displayed by CD, the surface dyslexic. Likewise, the four acquired surface dyslexic cases studied by Birnboim (1995) displayed many performance similarities to second-grade reading-level controls. In short, the results from case studies of developmental phonological and surface dyslexia are entirely consistent with the patterns displayed in three studies with larger-scale sampling of reading-disabled children.

The results of all of these analyses suggest that the surface dyslexics defined by CA comparisons appear to be children with a type of reading disability that could be characterised as a developmental lag. In contrast, phonological dyslexia defined by comparison with a CA control group seems to reflect true developmental deviance. This conclusion is reinforced by examining performance comparisons between the surface dyslexics and RL controls on the other variables contained in our performance battery (see also Manis et al., 1996). Table 7.3 presents these comparisons and it is apparent that on only one variable (WRAT Spelling) were the two groups significantly different. The two groups of children performed similarly on several tasks not used to define the

Table 7.3 Mean differences between the surface dyslexics ($n = 15$) and the RL controls ($n = 23$)

Variable	Dyslexics	Controls	t value
WRAT Reading (raw)	53.1	51.0	0.96
WRAT Spelling (raw)	33.7	31.4	2.09*
Woodcock Word Ident (raw)	46.4	42.6	1.09
Woodcock Word Attack (raw)	15.4	15.5	−0.04
Exception words	4.8	6.4	−1.66
Regular words	11.3	9.2	1.45
Pseudowords	19.2	16.8	1.96
Rosner AAT	21.5	21.1	0.17
Wordlikeness choice	11.2	11.8	−0.69
Syntactic processing (z score)	0.256	0.235	0.12
Working memory (z score)	0.090	0.310	−1.03

Note: * = $p < 0.05$.

dyslexic subtypes (Rosner AAT, wordlikeness choice task, two subtests of the Woodcock), as well as measures of syntactic processing and verbal working memory that were included in this study. The latter two measures add to the picture of developmental lag that seems to characterise the surface subtype: these children had syntactic processing skills and verbal memory skills commensurate with their reading-level controls.

Comparisons of the phonological dyslexics (from the CA match, in order to be comparable with the surface dyslexia results) to RL controls are in marked contrast with those involving the surface dyslexics. Table 7.4 indicates that here there were several significant differences between the groups. The phonological dyslexics were markedly inferior on not only the experimental pseudowords which in part defined the group, but also on the Woodcock Word Attack subtest (not used to define the groups). Their phonological problems were further indicated by a significant deficit in phonological sensitivity as indicated by their performance on the Rosner Auditory Analysis Test. They were significantly *better* at reading exception words. One very interesting finding that serves to confirm the developmental deviancy of this group in the phonological/language domain was that phonological dyslexics performed significantly worse than these younger controls on the measures of syntactic processing skill and verbal working memory, perhaps indicating that these tasks are in part tapping their core phonological deficit (Bruck, 1992; Goswami & Bryant, 1990; Olson, 1994; Rack et al., 1993; Shankweiler et al., 1995; Share, 1995; Snowling, 1991, 1995; Stanovich, 1988, 1991; Stanovich & Siegel, 1994).

These results present a consistent picture of developmental deviancy and developmental lag that appears to characterise the phonological

Table 7.4 Mean differences between the phonological dyslexics ($n = 17$) and the RL controls ($n = 23$)

Variable	Dyslexics	Controls	t value
WRAT Reading (raw)	49.9	51.0	-0.58
WRAT Spelling (raw)	32.0	31.4	0.50
Woodcock Word Ident (raw)	46.8	42.6	1.28
Woodcock Word Attack (raw)	7.9	15.5	−5.07***
Exception words	8.3	6.4	2.04*
Regular words	7.2	9.2	−1.68
Pseudowords	9.9	16.8	−5.71***
Rosner AAT	13.9	21.1	−3.16**
Wordlikeness choice	12.2	11.8	0.51
Syntactic processing (z score)	−0.473	0.235	−3.15**
Working memory (z score)	−0.172	0.310	−2.30*

Note: * = $p < 0.05$; ** = $p < 0.01$; *** = $p < 0.001$, all two-tailed.

and surface subtypes, respectively. In our thinking about subtypes, it is also important not to ignore the 'deviant on both' group – the children below the CA control group confidence intervals for *both* pseudowords and exception words. As noted previously, this group was much larger in our sample of younger subjects (27.9% of the dyslexics) than in the Manis et al. and Castles/Coltheart samples who were 2:6 to 3:6 years older. We conjecture that this 'deviant on both' group are perhaps phonological dyslexics of the future, a hypothesis supported by the results displayed in Table 7. 5, which compares the performance of the phonological dyslexics to that of the deviant on both group. Here we see that the 'both deviant' group shares *all* of the phonological deficits of the phonological dyslexics – they are equally impaired at reading pseudowords and in phonological sensitivity. They share the syntactic processing problems and verbal working memory deficits – deficits which may well arise from processing problems at the phonological level (see Gottardo et al., in press; Shankweiler et al., 1992). The differences between the groups arise because the phonological dyslexics are better at reading words, particularly exception words.

Conclusions

Given that IQ-based discrepancies have been shown to have low returns for the field as mechanisms for demarcating conceptually interesting subtypes (Fletcher et al., 1994; Francis et al., 1996; Siegel, 1988, 1989, 1992; Stanovich, 1991, 1993b, 1994; Stanovich & Siegel, 1994), it appears that Castles and Coltheart (1993) are correct that the search for subtypes should proceed from psychological mechanisms that

Table 7.5 Mean differences between the phonological dyslexics (n = 17) and the 'deviant on both' group (n = 19)

Variable	Phonological	Both	t value
WRAT Reading (raw)	49.9	47.1	1.69
WRAT Spelling (raw)	32.0	30.7	1.18
Woodcock Word Ident (raw)	46.8	40.6	2.43*
Woodcock Word Attack (raw)	7.9	8.0	0.08
Exception words	8.3	3.9	6.23***
Regular words	7.2	4.4	2.85**
Pseudowords	9.9	7.7	1.58
Rosner AAT	13.9	13.3	0.32
Wordlikeness choice	12.2	10.7	1.86
Syntactic processing (z score)	−0.473	−0.308	0.61
Working memory (z score)	−0.172	−0.352	0.76

Note: * = p < 0.05; ** = p < 0.01; *** = p < 0.001, all two-tailed.

closely underpin the word recognition process (see Baron & Strawson, 1976; Byrne et al., 1992; Murphy & Pollatsek, 1994). In this chapter, we have explored the implications of reading disability subtypes so defined. Phonological dyslexia appears to reflect true developmental deviancy – that is, the pattern of linguistic and information-processing strengths and weaknesses displayed does not match those found in reading-level controls. In contrast, surface dyslexia has consistently – from the original analysis of Bryant and Impey (1986) to the samples analysed here – resembled a form of developmental delay. Interestingly, when trying to simulate surface dyslexia with a connectionist network, Plaut and Shallice (1994) reported that damaging the network did not work as well as simply examining the undamaged network at an earlier point in its learning curve. They found that 'a much better match to fluent surface dyslexia is found in the behaviour of the *undamaged* network earlier in learning, before it has mastered the entire training corpus' (p. 24).

We would conjecture that the two subtypes might separate when other methods of differentiating subtypes are employed – for example, response to treatment, genetic analyses, and neurological investigation. That is, it is hypothesised that phonological dyslexia will be more refractory to treatment than surface dyslexia (see Vellutino et al., in press), will have a higher heritability, and will more clearly display brain anomalies. Based on the data from our investigation, we also speculate that the 'deviant on both' subtype will be more similar to phonological dyslexia than to surface dyslexia in these characteristics.

How might a younger child deviant on both stimulus types develop into a phonological dyslexic? Some children in the both-deviant group might continue to practice reading and to receive considerable exposure to print (Stanovich, 1993a; Stanovich & Cunningham, 1993; Stanovich et al., 1995). This print exposure may result in these children having relatively less seriously impaired orthographic processing mechanisms (Siegel et al., 1995; Stanovich & Siegel, 1994; Zivian & Samuels, 1986). It may also result in these children building exception word recognition abilities (which depend on orthographic representations in the mental lexicon; see Ehri, 1992; Perfetti, 1992; Stanovich, 1990; Stanovich & West, 1989). However, their more seriously impaired phonological processing abilities will likely not develop at the same rate (Manis, Custudio & Szeszulski, 1993; Olson, 1994; Snowling, 1980), thus resulting in greater dissociation between phonological coding ability and exception word fluency at more advanced stages of development (see also Manis et al., 1996).

Consider how the two subtypes might also arise through different combinations of relative phonological impairment and experience with print. Low print exposure might not have very dire consequences for a reader with high levels of phonological coding skill. When such a reader *does* open a book, phonological coding enables the reading process –

irrespective of the inadequately developed orthographic lexicon. However, the situation is probably different for a reader with somewhat depressed phonological skills (and we must never forget that even the surface dyslexics have phonological processing problems to some degree). Without efficiently functioning phonological coding processes, a system designed for compensatory processing would actually draw more on orthographic knowledge – but in the case of the surface dyslexic, that orthographic knowledge may be lacking in part due to inadequate exposure to print.

Thus, surface dyslexia may arise from a milder form of phonological deficit than that of the phonological dyslexic, but one conjoined with exceptionally inadequate reading experience. This is a somewhat different interpretation of surface dyslexia (see also Manis, et al., 1996) from the common one of differential impairment in a dual-route architecture (Castles & Coltheart, 1993). As Snowling, Bryant & Hulme (1996) note: 'Many poor readers have low levels of exposure to print (Stanovich, 1993) – lack of reading experience may cause dyslexic children to resemble surface dyslexic patients. Arguably, what such children lack is the word-specific knowledge that is normally acquired by reading. In our view, it is misleading to describe such children as having an aberrant "lexical" but intact "sub-lexical" mechanism' (p. 6).

In contrast, the phonological dyslexic pattern might become more apparent when a more severe pathology underlying the functional architecture of phonological coding (Castles & Coltheart, 1993; Coltheart et al., 1993; Coltheart et al., 1980; Coltheart et al., 1983; Patterson et al., 1985; Plaut & Shallice, 1994) is conjoined with relatively high levels of exposure to print. The latter would hasten the development of the orthographic lexicon (which is critical for the processing of exception words) but the former would be relatively refractory to direct remediation efforts (Lovett et al., 1990; Lovett et al., 1994; Vellutino et al., in press) and result in relatively slow growth in the ability to read pseudo-words (Manis et al., 1993; Olson, 1994; Snowling, 1980).

References

Baron, J. (1979). Orthographic and word-specific mechanisms in children's reading of words. *Child Development* 50, 60–72.

Baron, J. & Strawson, C. (1976). Use of orthographic and word-specific knowledge in reading words aloud. *Journal of Experimental Psychology: Human Perception and Performance* 2, 386–393.

Beauvois, M. F. & Derouesne, J. (1979). Phonological alexia: three dissociations. *Journal of Neurology, Neurosurgery, and Psychiatry* 42, 1115–1124.

Berndt, R., Reggia, J. & Mitchum, C. (1987). Empirically derived probabilities for grapheme-to-phoneme correspondences in English. *Behavior Research Methods, Instruments, & Computers* 19, 1–9.

Besner, D., Twilley, L., McCann, R. & Seergobin, K. (1990). On the association between connectionism and data: Are a few words necessary? *Psychological Review* 97, 432–446.

Birnboim, S. (1995). Acquired surface dyslexia: The evidence from Hebrew. *Applied Psycholinguistics* 16, 83–102.

Bowey, J. A., Cain, M. T. & Ryan, S. M. (1992). A reading-level design study of phonological skills underlying fourth-grade children's word reading difficulties. *Child Development* 63, 99–1011.

Bradley, L. & Bryant, P. E. (1978). Difficulties in auditory organization as a possible cause of reading backwardness. *Nature* 271, 746–747.

Bruck, M. (1992). Persistence of dyslexics' phonological awareness deficits. *Developmental Psychology* 28, 874–886.

Bruck, M. & Treiman, R. (1990). Phonological awareness and spelling in normal children and dyslexics: The case of initial consonant clusters. *Journal of Experimental Child Psychology* 50, 156–178.

Bryant, P. E. & Goswami, U. (1986). Strengths and weaknesses of the reading level design: A comment on Backman, Mamen, and Ferguson. *Psychological Bulletin* 100, 101–103.

Bryant, P. & Impey, L. (1986). The similarities between normal readers and developmental and acquired dyslexics. *Cognition* 24, 121–137.

Byrne, B., Freebody, P. & Gates, A. (1992). Longitudinal data on the relations of word-reading strategies to comprehension, reading time, and phonemic awareness. *Reading Research Quarterly* 27, 141–151.

Carr, T. H. & Pollatsek, A. (1985). Recognizing printed words: a look at current models. In D. Besner, T. G. Waller, & G. E. MacKinnon (eds), *Reading Research: Advances in Theory and Practice*, 5, pp. 1–82. Orlando, FL: Academic Press.

Carroll, J. B., Davies, P.,& Richman, B. (1971). Word Frequency Book. Boston, MA: Houghton Mifflin.

Castles, A. & Coltheart, M. (1993). Varieties of developmental dyslexia. *Cognition* 47, 149–180.

Ceci, S. J. (1986). *Handbook of Cognitive, Social, and Neuropsychological Aspects of Learning Disabilities*, 1, Hillsdale, NJ: Erlbaum.

Coltheart, M. (1978). Lexical access in simple reading tasks. In G. Underwood (Ed.), *Strategies of Information Processing*, (pp. 151–216). London: Academic Press.

Coltheart, M., Patterson, K. & Marshall, J. C. (1980). *Deep Dyslexia*. London: Routledge & Kegan Paul.

Coltheart, M., Curtis, B., Atkins, P. & Haller, M. (1993). Models of reading aloud: Dual-route and parallel-distributed-processing approaches. *Psychological Review* 100, 589–608.

Coltheart, M., Masterson, J., Byng, S., Prior, M. & Riddoch, J. (1983). Surface dyslexia. *Quarterly Journal of Experimental Psychology* 35A, 469–496.

Coltheart, M. & Leahy, J. (1992). Children's and adults' reading of nonwords: Effects of regularity and consistency. *Journal of Experimental Psychology: Learning, Memory, and Cognition* 18, 718–729.

Ehri, L. C. (1992). Reconceptualizing the development of sight word reading and its relationship to recoding. In P. B. Gough, L. C. Ehri & R. Treiman (Eds.) *Reading Acquisition*, (pp. 107–143). Hillsdale, NJ: Erlbaum.

Ellis, A. W. (1979). Developmental and acquired dyslexia: Some observations on Jorm. *Cognition* 7, 413–420.

Ellis, A. W. (1984). The cognitive neuropsychology of developmental (and acquired) dyslexia: A critical survey. *Cognitive Neuropsychology* 2, 169–205.

Felton, R. H. & Wood, F. B. (1992). A reading level match study of nonword reading skills in poor readers with varying IQ. *Journal of Learning Disabilities* **25**, 318–326.

Fletcher, J. M. (1992). The validity of distinguishing children with language and learning disabilities according to discrepancies with IQ: Introduction to the Special Series. *Journal of Learning Disabilities* **25**, 546–548.

Fletcher, J. M., Francis, D. J., Rourke, B. P., Shaywitz, B. A., & Shaywitz, S. E. (1992). The validity of discrepancy-based definitions of reading disabilities. *Journal of Learning Disabilities* **25**, 555–561.

Fletcher, J. M. & Morris, R. (1986). Classification of disabled learners: Beyond exclusionary definitions. In S. J. Ceci (Ed.) *Handbook of Social, and Neuropsychological Aspects of Learning Disabilities*, **2**, pp. 55–80. Hillsdale, NJ: Erlbaum.

Fletcher, J. M., Shaywitz, S. E., Shankweiler, D., Katz, L., Liberman, I., Stuebing, K., Francis, D. J., Fowler, A. & Shaywitz, B. A. (1994). Cognitive profiles of reading disability: Comparisons of discrepancy and low achievement definitions. *Journal of Educational Psychology* **86**, 6–23.

Fodor, J. A. & Pylyshyn, Z. W. (1988). Connectionism and cognitive architecture: A critical analysis. *Cognition* **28**, 3–71.

Francis, D. J., Shaywitz, S. E., Stuebing, K., Shaywitz, B. A. & Fletcher, J. M. (1996). Developmental lag versus deficit models of reading disability: A longitudinal, individual growth curves analysis. *Journal of Educational Psychology* **88**, 3–17.

Fredman, G., & Stevenson, J. (1988). Reading processes in specific reading retarded and reading backward 13-year-olds. *British Journal of Developmental Psychology* **6**, 97–108.

Frith, U. (1985). Beneath the surface of developmental dyslexia. In K. Patterson, J. Marshall & M. Coltheart (eds), *Surface Dyslexia*, pp. 301–330. London: Erlbaum.

Goswami, U. & Bryant, P. (1990). *Phonological Skills and Learning to Read*. Hove, UK: Lawrence Erlbaum.

Gottardo, A., Stanovich, K. E. & Siegel, L. S. (in press). The relationships between phonological sensitivity, syntactic processing, and verbal working memory in the reading performance of third-grade children. *Journal of Experimental Child Psychology*.

Hinshelwood, J. (1917). *Congenital Word-blindness*. London: Lewis.

Hinton, G. & Shallice, T. (1991). Lesioning an attractor network: Investigations of acquired dyslexia. *Psychological Review* **98**, 74–95.

Humphreys, G. W. & Evett, L. J. (1985). Are there independent lexical and nonlexical routes in word processing? An evaluation of the dual-route theory of reading. *Behavioral and Brain Sciences* **8**, 689–740.

Hurford, D. P., Johnston, M., Nepote, P., Hampton, S., Moore, S., Neal, J., Mueller, A., McGeorge, K., Huff, L., Awad, A., Tatro, C., Juliano, C. & Huffman, D. (1994). Early identification and remediation of phonological-processing deficits in first-grade children at risk for reading disabilities. *Journal of Learning Disabilities* **27**, 647–659.

Kirk, S. (1963). Behavioural diagnosis and remediation of learning disabilities. *Paper presented at the Conference on the Exploration into the Problems of the Perceptually Handicapped Child, Fund for the Perceptually Handicapped Child, Evanston, IL.*

Lerner, J. (1985). *Learning Disabilities*, 4th edn. Boston, MA: Houghton Mifflin.

Lovett, M., Warren-Chaplin, P., Ransby, M. & Borden, S. (1990). Training the word recognition skills of reading disabled children: Treatment and transfer effects. *Journal of Educational Psychology* **82**, 769–780.

Lovett, M. W., Borden, S., DeLuca, T., Lacerenza, L., Benson, N. & Brackstone, D. (1994). Treating the core deficits of developmental dyslexia: Evidence of transfer of learning after phonologically- and strategy-based reading training programs. *Developmental Psychology* 30, 805–822.

Lyon, G. R. (1987). Learning disabilities research: False starts and broken promises. In S. Vaughn & C. S. Bos (Eds.) *Research in Learning Disabilities*, pp. 69–85. Boston, MA: College-Hill Press.

Manis, F. R., Custodio, R. & Szeszulski, P. A. (1993). Development of phonological and orthographic skill: a 2-year longitudinal study of dyslexic children. *Journal of Experimental Child Psychology* 56, 64–86.

Manis, F. R., Seidenberg, M. S., Doi, L. M., McBride-Chang, C. & Peterson, A. (1996). On the bases of two subtypes of developmental dyslexia. *Cognition* 58, 157–195.

Marshall, J. C. & Newcombe, F. (1973). Patterns of paralexia: A psycholinguistic approach. *Journal of Psycholinguistic Research* 2, 175–199.

Maughan, B., Hagell, A., Rutter, M., & Yule, W. (1994). Poor readers in secondary school. *Reading and Writing: An Interdisciplinary Journal* 6, 125–150.

McCloskey, M. (1991). Networks and theories: The place of connectionism in cognitive science. *Psychological Science* 2, 387–395.

McKinney, J. (1984). The search for subtypes of specific learning disability. *Journal of Learning Disabilities* 17, 43–50.

Metsala, J. L. & Brown, G. D. A. (in press). Normal and dyslexic reading development: the role of formal models. In C. Hulme & R.M. Joshi (Eds.) *Reading and Spelling: Develpment and Disorder* Hillsdale, NJ: Erlbaum.

Morris, R. & Satz, P. (1984). Classification issues in subtype research: an application of some methods and concepts. In R. Malatesha & H. Whitaker (Eds.) *Dyslexia: A Global Issue*, pp. 59–82. The Hague: Martinus Nijhoff.

Murphy, L. & Pollatsek, A. (1994). Developmental dyslexia: Heterogeneity without discrete subgroups. *Annals of Dyslexia* 44, 120–146.

Olson, R. K. (1994). Language deficits in 'specific' reading disability. In M. Gernsbacher (Ed.) *Handbook of Psycholinguistics*, (pp. 895–916). San Diego, CA: Academic Press.

Olson, R. K., Wise, B., Conners, F., Rack, J. & Fulker, D. (1989). Specific deficits in component reading and language skills: Genetic and environmental influences. *Journal of Learning Disabilities* 22, 339–348.

Olson, R. K., Wise, B., Conners, F. & Rack, J. (1990). Organization, heritability, and remediation of component word recognition and language skills in disabled readers. In R. Carr & B. A. Levy (Eds) *Reading and its Development: Component Skills Approaches* (pp. 261–322). New York: Academic Press.

Patterson, K., Marshall, J. C. & Coltheart, M. (1985). *Surface Dyslexia*. London: Erlbaum.

Pennington, B. F., Gilger, J., Olson, R. K. & DeFries, J. C. (1992). The external validity of age- versus IQ-discrepancy definitions of reading disability: Lessons from a twin study. *Journal of Learning Disabilities* 25, 562–573.

Perfetti, C. A. (1992). The representation problem in reading acquisition. In P. B. Gough, L. C. Ehri & R. Treiman (Eds.) *Reading Acquisition*, pp. 145–174. Hillsdale, NJ: Erlbaum.

Plaut, D. C., McClelland, J. L., Seidenberg, M. S. & Patterson, K. (1996). Understanding normal and impaired word reading: Computational principles in quasi-regular domains. *Psychological Review* 103, 56–115.

Plaut, D. & Shallice, T. (1994). *Connectionist Modelling in Cognitive Neuropsychology: A Case Study*. Hove, UK: Erlbaum.

Rack, J. P., Hulme, C. & Snowling, M. J. (1993). Learning to read: A theoretical synthesis. In H. Reese (Ed.) *Advances in Child Development and Behavior*, (pp. 99–132). San Diego, CA: Academic Press.

Rack, J. P., Snowling, M. J. & Olson, R. K. (1992). The nonword reading deficit in developmental dyslexia: A review. *Reading Research Quarterly* 27, 28–53.

Reynolds, C. R. (1985). Measuring the aptitude-achievement discrepancy in learning disability diagnosis. *Remedial and Special Education* 6, 37–55.

Rispens, J., van Yeren, T. & van Duijn, G. (1991). The irrelevance of IQ to the definition of learning disabilities: Some empirical evidence. *Journal of Learning Disabilities* 24, 434–438.

Rutter, M. & Yule, W. (1975). The concept of specific reading retardation. *Journal of Child Psychology and Psychiatry* 16, 181–197.

Satz, P., Morris, R. & Fletcher, J. M. (1985). Hypotheses, subtypes, and individual differences in dyslexia: some reflections. In D. B. Gray & J. F. Kavanagh (Eds.) *Biobehavioral Measures of Dyslexia*, (pp. 25–40). Parkton, MD: New York Press.

Schuerholz, L. J., Harris, E., Baumgardner, T., Reiss, A., Freund, L., Church, R., Mohr, J. & Denckla, M. B. (1995). An analysis of two discrepancy-based models and a processing-deficit approach in identifying learning disabilities. *Journal of Learning Disabilities* 28, 18–29.

Seidenberg, M. S. (1993). A connectionist modeling approach to word recognition and dyslexia. *Psychological Science* 4, 299–304.

Seidenberg, M. S. (1994). Language and connectionism: the developing interface. *Cognition* 50, 385–401.

Seidenberg, M. S. & McClelland, J. L. (1989). Visual word recognition and pronunciation: a computational model of acquisition, skilled performance, and dyslexia. In A. M. Galaburda (Ed.) *From Reading to Neurons*, (pp. 256–305). Cambridge, MA: MIT Press.

Shankweiler, D., Crain, S., Brady, S. & Macaruso, P. (1992). Identifying the causes of reading disability. In P. B. Gough, L. C. Ehri & R. Treiman (Eds.) *Reading Acquisition*, (pp. 275–305). Hillsdale, NJ: Erlbaum.

Shankweiler, D., Crain, S., Katz, L., Fowler, A., Liberman, A., Brady, S., Thornton, R., Lundquist, E., Dreyer, L., Fletcher, J., Stuebing, K., Shaywitz, S. & Shaywitz, B. (1995). Cognitive profiles of reading-disabled children: comparison of language skills in phonology, morphology, and syntax. *Psychological Science* 6, 149–156.

Share, D. L. (1995). Phonological recoding and self-teaching: Sine qua non of reading acquisition. *Cognition* 55, 151–218.

Share, D. L., McGee, R., McKenzie, D., Williams, S. & Silva, P. A. (1987). Further evidence relating to the distinction between specific reading retardation and general reading backwardness. *British Journal of Developmental Psychology* 5, 35–44.

Shaywitz, B. A., Fletcher, J. M., Holahan, J. M. & Shaywitz, S. E. (1992). Discrepancy compared to low achievement definitions of reading disability: Results from the Connecticut Longitudinal Study. *Journal of Learning Disabilities* 25, 639–648.

Shepard, L. (1980). An evaluation of the regression discrepancy method for identifying children with learning disabilities. *Journal of Special Education* 14, 79–91.

Siegel, L. S. (1988). Evidence that IQ scores are irrelevant to the definition and analysis of reading disability. *Canadian Journal of Psychology* 42, 201–215.

Siegel, L. S. (1989). IQ is irrelevant to the definition of learning disabilities. *Journal of Learning Disabilities* 22, 469–479.

Siegel, L. S. (1992). An evaluation of the discrepancy definition of dyslexia. *Journal of Learning Disabilities* 25, 618–629.

Siegel, L. S., Share, D. & Geva, E. (1995). Evidence for superior orthographic skills in dyslexics. *Psychological Science* 6, 250–254.

Smolensky, P. (1988). On the proper treatment of connectionism. *Behavioral and Brain Sciences* 11, 1–74.

Smolensky, P. (1989). Connectionist modeling: Neural computation/mental connections. In L. Nadel, L. A. Cooper, P. Culicover & P. M. Harnish (Ed.) *Neural Connections, Mental Computation*, (pp. 49–67). Cambridge, MA: MIT Press.

Snowling, M. J. (1980). The development of grapheme–phoneme correspondence in normal and dyslexic readers. *Journal of Experimental Child Psychology* 29, 294–305.

Snowling, M. J. (1983). The comparison of acquired and developmental disorders of reading – a discussion. *Cognition* 14, 105–118.

Snowling, M. J. (1991). Developmental reading disorders. *Journal of Child Psychology and Psychiatry* 32, 49–77.

Snowling, M. J. (1995). Phonological processing and developmental dyslexia. *Journal of Research in Reading* 18, 132–138.

Snowling, M. J., Bryant, P. E. & Hulme, C. (1996). Theoretical and methodological pitfalls in making comparisons between developmental and acquired dyslexia: some comments on Castles and Coltheart (1993). *Reading and Writing* 8, 443–451.

Speece, D. & Cooper, D. (1991). Retreat, regroup, or advance? An agenda for empirical classification research in learning disabilities. In L. Feagans, E. Short & L. Meltzer (Eds.) *Subtypes of Learning Disabilities*. Hillsdale, NJ: Erlbaum.

Stanovich, K. E. (1988). Explaining the differences between the dyslexic and the garden-variety poor reader: The phonological-core variable-difference model. *Journal of Learning Disabilities* 21, 590–612.

Stanovich, K. E. (1990). Concepts in developmental theories of reading skill: cognitive resources, automaticity, and modularity. *Developmental Review* 10, 72–100.

Stanovich, K. E. (1991). Discrepancy definitions of reading disability: has intelligence led us astray? *Reading Research Quarterly* 26, 7–29.

Stanovich, K. E. (1993a). Does reading make you smarter? Literacy and the development of verbal intelligence. In H. Reese (Ed.) *Advances in Child Development and Behavior*, 24, pp. 133–180. San Diego, CA: Academic Press.

Stanovich, K. E. (1993b). Dysrationalia: A new specific learning disability. *Journal of Learning Disabilities* 26, 501–515.

Stanovich, K. E. (1994). Does dyslexia exist? *Journal of Child Psychology and Psychiatry* 35, 579–595.

Stanovich, K. E. & Cunningham, A. E. (1993). Where does knowledge come from? Specific associations between print exposure and information acquisition. *Journal of Educational Psychology* 85, 211–229.

Stanovich, K. E. & Siegel, L. S. (1994). The phenotypic performance profile of reading-disabled children: A regression-based test of the phonological-core variable-difference model. *Journal of Educational Psychology* 86, 24–53.

Stanovich, K. E. & West, R. F. (1989). Exposure to print and orthographic processing. *Reading Research Quarterly* 24, 402–433.

Stanovich, K. E., West, R. F. & Harrison, M. (1995). Knowledge growth and maintenance across the life span: The role of print exposure. *Developmental Psychology* 31, 811–826.

Taylor, H. G., Satz, P. & Friel, J. (1979). Developmental dyslexia in relation to other childhood reading disorders: Significance and clinical utility. *Reading Research Quarterly* 15, 84–101.

Temple, C. M. & Marshall, J. C. (1983). A case study of developmental phonological dyslexia. *British Journal of Psychology* **74**, 517–533.

Torgesen, J. K. (1991). Subtypes as prototypes: Extended studies of rationally defined extreme groups. In L. Feagans, E. Short & L. Meltzer (Eds.) *Subtypes of Learning Disabilities*, pp. 229–246. Hillsdale, NJ: Erlbaum.

Vellutino, F. R., Scanlon, D. M., Sipay, E., Small, S., Pratt, A., Chen, R. & Denckla, M. (in press). Cognitive profiles of difficult to remediate and readily remediated poor readers: Toward distinguishing between constitutionally and experientially based causes of reading disability. *Journal of Educational Psychology*.

Zivian, M. T & Samuels, M. T. (1986). Performance on a word-likeness task by normal readers and reading-disabled children. *Reading Research Quarterly* **21**, 150–160.

Note

Portions of this chapter are adapted from material that has appeared in *Journal of Educational Psychology* and in B. Blachman (Ed.) (1997). *Foundations of Reading Acquisition and Dyslexia: Implications for Early Intervention*. Mahwah, NJ: Erlbaum. This research was supported by grant no. 0GP0001607 from the Natural Sciences and Engineering Research Council of Canada to Keith E. Stanovich. Anne Castles is thanked for kindly providing the raw data from their study.

Chapter 8
Learning to Read in Different Orthographies: Phonological Awareness, Orthographic Representations and Dyslexia

USHA GOSWAMI

Phonological skills – a child's awareness of the sound structure of spoken words, and ability to manipulate those structures – appear to be an important predictor of learning to read in virtually every orthography that has been studied. The relationship between phonological skills and reading holds for highly transparent orthographies, such as German and Spanish, for less transparent orthographies, such as English and French, and for orthographies that are wholly or partly logographic, such as Chinese and Japanese (e.g. Caravolas & Bruck, 1993; Cossu et al., 1988; Gombert, 1992; Huang & Hanley, 1995; Lundberg, Olofsson & Wall, 1980; Mann, 1986; Naslund & Schneider, 1991; Porpodas, 1993; Schneider & Naslund, in press; Wimmer et al., 1991; Wimmer, Landerl & Schneider, 1994).

In this chapter, I will discuss the connection between phonological skills, the development of orthographic representations, and reading development and dyslexia. The first part of the chapter will consider whether phonological development follows the same sequence in children who are growing up in different linguistic environments. The second part of the chapter will consider whether the nature of the phonological deficit is similar in dyslexic children who are growing up in these different linguistic environments, and the third will examine the kinds of connections that children make between phonology and orthography in different linguistic environments, and whether these connections lead to different orthographic representations. I will conclude by considering whether cross-linguistic differences in orthographic representations can throw any light on the nature of the phonological difficulties experienced by dyslexic children who are learning to read different languages.

The Sequence of Phonological Development

Levels of phonological awareness

Phonological skills were initially measured at the levels of the *syllable* and the *phoneme*. Syllabic awareness refers to children's ability to detect constituent syllables in words. For example, a word like *president* has three syllables, and a word like *dinner* has two. Phonemes are the smallest sounds that change the meanings of words: *cap* and *map* differ by a single phoneme (the initial phoneme), and so do *cap* and *cup* (the medial phoneme). We now know that phonological awareness can also be measured at a level that is intermediate between the syllable and the phoneme. This is the level of *onsets* and *rimes*.

Onset-rime awareness is the ability to detect that a single syllable is made up of two units, the onset, which corresponds to any phonemes before the vowel, and the rime, which corresponds to the vowel sound and to any following phonemes. Words like *sing*, *bring* and *spring* have onsets consisting of one, two and three phonemes respectively (corresponding to the spelling patterns *s*, *br* and *spr*). All of these words have a two-phoneme rime (corresponding to the spelling pattern *ing*). Words like *sea* and *free* have single-phoneme rimes, words like *beak* and *light* have two-phoneme rimes, and words like *gold* and *gulp* have three-phoneme rimes. These examples show that onset-rime awareness and phonemic awareness are not always distinct. Onsets can often be single phonemes, and so can rimes. Nevertheless, many rimes and a number of onsets correspond to phonological units that consist of more than one phoneme.

Measuring phonological awareness

Psychologists have devised a number of different tasks to measure the development of phonological knowledge. Three widely used measures of phonological skills are the *tapping* task, in which children are given a wooden dowel and required to tap out the number of sounds in words at different phonological levels, the *oddity* task, in which children have to listen to a group of spoken words and then select the word that has a different sound from the others, and the *same/different judgement* task, in which children listen to pairs of words and have to judge whether they share a sound or not. One advantage of these tasks is that they can be administered at any or all of the three phonological levels: syllable, onset-rime and phoneme.

For example, Liberman and her colleagues used the *tapping* task to measure the development of phonological awareness at the syllable and phoneme levels. They used words that had either one syllable or phoneme (*dog, I*), two syllables or phonemes (*dinner, my*), or three syllables or phonemes (*president, book*). The children, who were aged from 4 to 6 years, were asked to tap once with a wooden dowel for each of the syllables or phonemes in the words, and a criterion of six consecutive correct responses was set as evidence for segmentation ability. Liberman et al. found that 46% of the 4-year-olds in their study could segment the words into syllables, whereas 0% of this age group reached the criterion for phonemes. For the 5-year-olds, the figures were 48% and 17%, respectively. High levels of success on the phoneme task were only observed in the 6-year-olds, who had been learning to read for about a year (the mean age of this group was 6:11). Among the 6-year-olds, 90% succeeded in the syllable task, and 70% could segment the stimuli into phonemes.

Bradley and Bryant (1983) used the *oddity* task to measure the development of onset and rime awareness. They developed two versions of this task, one (based on sets of three words) for 4-year-olds, and one (based on sets of four words) for 5-year-olds. In the oddity task, the children were given a group of words and were asked to spot the 'odd word out' that differed in terms of either its initial sound (bus, bun, *rug*), its medial sound (*pin*, bun, gun) or its final sound (*doll*, hop, top). These triples of words differed in terms of single phonemes, too, but related research showed that the oddity judgements were made on the basis of shared onsets (the initial sound task) or rimes (the medial and final sound tasks; see Kirtley et al., 1989, for evidence that children solve the oddity task by thinking about onsets and rimes). Bradley and Bryant found that 4- and 5-year-olds were very proficient at the oddity task, performing at above-chance levels in all versions, although rime awareness was easier than onset awareness. In later work, Bryant and his colleagues showed that even 3-year-olds are aware of rimes (e.g. Maclean, Bryant & Bradley, 1987).

The *same/different judgement* task was used to measure the development of phonological awareness at all levels (syllable, onset-rime and phoneme) by Treiman and Zukowski (1991). They asked children to listen to two words spoken by the experimenter, and then say whether the two words shared a sound at either the beginning or the end. The children were aged 4, 5 and 6 years. The beginning version of the task could be performed on the basis of either shared syllables (*hammer, hammock*), shared onsets (*broom, brand*) or shared initial phonemes (*steak, sponge*). The end version of the task could be performed on the basis of either shared final syllables (*compete, repeat*), shared rimes (*spit, wit*) or shared final phonemes (*smoke, tack*). Treiman and Zukowski also used a criterion of six consecutive correct responses as evidence that the children could perform the different tasks. They found that the criterion on the syllable tasks was reached by 100% of 4- and 6-year-old children, and by 90% of the 5-year-olds. The criterion on the onset-rime version of the task was reached by 56% of the 4-year-olds, 74% of the 5-year-olds and 100% of the 6-year-olds. Performance with the phoneme version of the task was less impressive. Here the criterion was reached by only 25% of the 4-year-olds, 39% of the 5-year-olds and 100% of the 6-year-olds. The 6-year-olds had been learning to read for about a year, and they were the only group to show equivalent levels of performance at the three phonological levels.

From these studies, it seems that the development of phonological awareness progresses from the syllable level via the onset-rime level to the phoneme level. Many other studies have reached similar conclusions (see Goswami & Bryant, 1990, for a review). An awareness of syllables, onsets and rimes appears to develop long before children go to school and begin learning to read. An awareness of phonemes appears to develop as reading is taught. It is important to remember, however, that the development of onset-rime awareness *in itself* involves the development of phoneme awareness, as many words have single-phoneme onsets. The general conclusion that onset-rime awareness precedes phonemic awareness in most English-speaking children (Kirtley et al., 1989) refers to the *awareness of every constituent phoneme in words*, rather than to the awareness of any particular phoneme such as the initial phoneme.

Cross-linguistic studies

It is quite plausible, however, that a different sequence of phonological development might be found in children who are growing up in different linguistic environments. Differences in the phonological input provided by different languages may affect the development of children's awareness of different phonological levels. This hypothesis can be tested by looking at studies of the development of phonological awareness in languages other than English. So far, relatively little work of this kind exists, but surprisingly the studies that have been carried out to date appear to show that the developmental sequence of syllabic and onset/rime awareness preceding an awareness of phonemes is consistent across linguistic environments. We will consider three studies of this kind, choosing examples that have used the same phonological awareness tasks as the English studies discussed above. Our examples come from Italian, German and Czech.

The tapping task was used to measure phonological awareness in Italian children in a study carried out by Cossu et al. (1988). In a replication of the study carried out by Liberman et al. (1974), they asked preschool Italian children (aged 4 and 5 years) and older children already at school (7- and 8-year-olds) to tap once for each syllable in words like *gatto*, *melone* and *termometro*, and once for each phoneme in words like *mi*, *per* and *sale*. The criterion for phonological awareness was again set at six consecutive correct responses. The criterion at the syllable level was reached by 67% of the 4-year-olds, 80% of the 5-year-olds, and 100% of the school-age sample. The criterion in the phoneme task was reached by 13% of the 4-year-olds, 27% of the 5-year-olds and 97% of the school-age sample, respectively. Italian children thus showed a remarkably similar response pattern to American children. They showed good syllabic awareness prior to entering school and poor phonemic awareness until reading was taught.

Wimmer et al. (1994) developed a version of the oddity task to measure the development of onset and rime awareness in German children. The onset task was made up of sets of words like Bach, Bahn, *Dach*, and Bad, and the rime tasks were made up of sets of words like Mund, rund, *Mond*, Hund (middle sound different) and Meer, *Mehl*, sehr, leer (end sound different). The children were tested in their first month of schooling, which meant that they were aged on average 6;11. Wimmer et al. found that the onset task was more difficult than the rime tasks (40% correct vs. 60% correct respectively), which was similar to Bradley and Bryant's findings for English children. All the German children also performed at levels well above chance on all of the tasks. For German children, as for English children, onset and rime awareness appear to be present before reading is taught.

Finally, the same/different judgement task was used to measure the development of onset and phoneme awareness in Czech-speaking children by Caravolas and Bruck (1993). They asked the children to judge whether two spoken nonsense words shared the same beginning sound. The shared sound was always the initial phoneme, but in some cases the initial phoneme *was* the onset (*semp*, *soold*), and in others it was part of the onset (*krin*, *klav*). The first task was an onset awareness task, and the second task was a phoneme awareness task. Caravolas and Bruck tested three age-groups of children: 4-year-olds, 5-year-olds, and 7-year-olds. They found that the Czech children were significantly better at the onset task than at the phoneme task, although the performance differences were small in magnitude. The number of items solved correctly in each task for the 4-year-olds was 46% and 43% (onset task and phoneme task, respectively, both at chance level), 59% and 54% (5-year-olds, onset task and phoneme task), and 94% and 91% (7-year-olds, onset task and phoneme task). Similar levels of overall performance were found in a control group of Canadian English-speaking children. Thus children from both language groups appeared to follow the developmental pattern of onset awareness being easier than phoneme awareness.

From these three studies, it is possible to conclude that the sequence of phonological development is similar for children who are growing up in different linguistic environments. However, it is important to emphasise that rather few studies of this kind exist, and so it is too early to draw any strong conclusions. Caravolas and Bruck had initially hypothesised that Czech children would show a greater awareness of complex (= two-phoneme) onsets than English children, because complex onsets are more frequent in Czech than in English, and they did find some evidence for this in a sound isolation task in which the children had to isolate the first sound in nonsense words like *saul* and *slau*. We thus need to identify the phonological awareness tasks that are most sensitive to subtle cross-language differences, and then to use these tasks as the basis for our comparisons. The hypothesis that differences in the phonological input provided by different languages affect the development of phonological awareness at different phonological levels is a fascinating one, and has hardly begun to be explored.

Phonological Deficits in Dyslexia

If the sequence of phonological development is similar for children who are growing up in different linguistic environments, then it seems plausible to propose that the nature of the phonological deficit should be similar in dyslexic children who are growing up in these different linguistic environments. On the other hand, it is quite possible that the sequence of phonological development could be the same across different linguistic environments, but that the relationship between phonological awareness at the different levels and progress in reading and spelling could differ depending on the phonology of the language that is being learned and the orthographic units that this phonology makes salient. We will first consider the nature of the phonological deficit in studies of dyslexia carried out in English, and then examine whether similar relationships hold in other languages.

Phonological deficits and dyslexia in English

Studies of phonological awareness in English-speaking dyslexic children that use a reading level match design have revealed deficits at two of the three linguistic levels, onsets and rimes and phonemes. Studies of syllabic awareness in dyslexic children have typically found a deficit in comparison with chronological age-matched controls, but not in comparison with reading-level matched controls, a control group that offers a more stringent test of a causal hypothesis (although not a conclusive one; see Bryant & Goswami, 1986). However, it is important to point out that we still lack adequate *developmental* evidence on the nature of these phonological deficits. It may be that dyslexic children are following the same sequence of phonological development as non-dyslexic children, but far more slowly. On such a hypothesis, very young dyslexic children should also show a deficit at the syllabic level in comparison with reading-level matched controls, whereas older dyslexic children should eventually develop awareness of phonological structures at the onset-rime level. Unfortunately, studies that measure the phonological development of the *same* dyslexic children *longitudinally* are rather rare.

Evidence that dyslexic children do not show a phonological deficit at the syllable level in comparison with reading-level matched controls comes from a study by Swan (1995). She used a length-judgement task to compare syllabic awareness in a group of 12-year-old dyslexic children, a group of 12-year-old normally reading children, and a group of 10-year-old reading-level controls. Using a series of monosyllabic and polysyllabic names, she contrasted two names at a time by showing the children pictures of the words, and then asking them to compare the length of the picture names. For example, the children might be shown a picture of a *chain* and a picture of an *audience*, and asked 'Are both names the same length?'. Swan found that the dyslexic children performed at a similar level to the reading-level controls but at a lower level than the chronological-age controls in this length-judgement task. However, when she took word-finding difficulties into account, and adjusted the dyslexic children's scores for picture-naming performance, then the deficit in comparison with the chronological-age control group disappeared. We return to this remarkable finding later.

Studies examining whether dyslexic children show a phonological deficit at the onset-rime level in comparison with reading-level matched controls have produced mixed results. In a landmark study of this kind, Bradley and Bryant (1978) produced evidence that 10-year-old dyslexic children were significantly worse in the oddity task than a 7-year-old reading-level matched control group. However, in a more recent study, Bruck and Treiman (1990) found that 10-year-old dyslexic children performed at the same level as a 7-year-old reading-level matched control group in an onset-deletion task, in which the children had to delete onsets from spoken nonsense words (e.g. *plut* becomes *ut*). Once again, we are faced with the possibility that some phonological-awareness tasks may be more sensitive than others (see Yopp, 1988).

In a more recent study using the oddity task, Bowey, Cain & Ryan (1992) found that 9-year-old poor readers *were* significantly worse at recognising the odd word out in triples like 'deck, neck, fit' than 7-year-old normally developing readers. Finally, Swan (1995) used a same/different judgement task to compare onset-rime awareness in a group of 11-year-old dyslexic readers, a group of 11-year-old normally reading children, and a group of 9-year-old reading-level controls. The children were asked to judge whether pairs of words presented pictorially shared either an onset (e.g., *crust, cross*) or a rime (e.g., *coat, goat*). Swan found that the dyslexic children performed at a similar level to the reading-level controls, but at a lower level than the chronological-age controls. Once again, however, when she took word-finding difficulties into account and adjusted the dyslexic children's scores for picture-naming performance, then the deficit in comparison with the chrono-logical-age control group disappeared (see also Swan & Goswami, 1996).

Evidence that dyslexic children show a phonological deficit at the phoneme level in comparison with reading-level matched controls is perhaps easiest to find. Studies using a variety of different phonological awareness tasks have presented a very consistent picture of a phono-logical deficit at the phoneme level in dyslexia, in comparison with *both* reading-level and chronological-age matched controls. This is true whether the phonemic deficit is measured using an oddity task (e.g. Bowey et al., 1992), a same/different judgement task (e.g. Bruck & Treiman, 1990), a 'Pig Latin' task (in which the initial phoneme in a spoken word must have the segment 'ay' added and be moved to the end, as in *pat* to *atpay*, Olson et al., 1990), or a nonsense word reading task (e.g. Rack et al., 1992). The phoneme deficit found in dyslexia also seems to persist into adulthood, whereas the persistence of the onset-rime deficit is less clear (e.g. Bruck, 1992).

Does the phonemic deficit persist when word-finding difficulties in dyslexia are taken into account? This is an important question, as we have seen from the work of Swan that dyslexic children's phonological deficit at the syllabic and onset-rime levels appears to vanish in compar-ison with even chronological-age controls when picture-naming ability is controlled for. Swan (1995) examined this question by giving 11-year-old dyslexic readers, 11-year-old normally reading children and 9-year-old reading-level controls two phonemic-awareness tasks, a same/different judgement task and a tapping task. The children had to judge whether pairs of words like *crust* and *cloud* shared a phoneme, or had to tap out the number of phonemes in a word like *flag*. Prior to adjusting performance for word-finding difficulties, Swan found a phonemic deficit in the dyslexic group in comparison with both the reading-level and chronological-age control groups. However, once picture-naming skills were taken into account, the dyslexic children performed at a similar level to the reading-level control group. The deficit in comparison with the chronological-age control group remained robust, however (see also Swan & Goswami, 1996).

The connection between word-finding difficulties and English dyslexic children's performance on phonological awareness tasks is clearly in need of some explanation. Swan's findings suggest that, at least in some relatively old groups of dyslexics, difficulties in retrieving the phonology of words on demand *account for* phonological difficul-ties at the syllabic and onset-rime levels, but not for phonological diffi-culties at the phonemic level. Again, it is worth emphasising that further research is needed, and that the *developmental* picture is not yet clear. Nevertheless, one possibility is that the fundamental difficulty for dyslexic children lies in developing high-quality segmentally organised phonological representations of words (see Fowler, 1991; Snowling & Hulme, 1989; Swan & Goswami, 1996), rather than in performance in phonological awareness tasks *per se*. If a high-quality phonological representation for a particular word exists, as for words that can be picture-named without difficulty, then phonological analysis at the syllable and onset-rime levels is no more difficult for dyslexic children than for controls. Phonological analysis at the *phonemic* level, however, still presents difficulties.

This 'phonological representations' account of the phonological deficit in dyslexia is consistent with recent views of lexical development. It has been suggested that during linguistic development lexical items (i.e. words) are gradually restructured from initially fairly holistic representations into representations that are increasingly detailed and organised segmentally, with this organisation narrowing from the level of the syllable to the level of onsets and rimes and finally to the level of phonemes (e.g. Walley, 1993). This gradual lexical reorganisation and restructuring may be significantly helped by learning to read, particularly in terms of reorganisation at the phonemic level (e.g. Morais, Alegria & Content, 1987). Thus, according to a 'phonological representations' account of the phonological deficit in dyslexia, dyslexic children may be delayed or handicapped in developing high-quality phonological representations and in restructuring those representations at the different linguistic levels, and their reading difficulties may contribute to this developmental problem (Swan, 1995; Swan & Goswami, 1996).

Phonological deficits and dyslexia in other languages

One way to examine the underlying nature of the phonological deficit in dyslexia is to study the nature of this deficit in dyslexic children who are growing up in different linguistic environments. As noted earlier, it is quite possible that the sequence of phonological development could be the *same* across different linguistic environments. In this case, we would expect dyslexic children who are growing up in different linguistic environments to also show phonological deficits at the onset-rime and phonemic levels in comparison with reading-level controls. However, it was also noted earlier that the relationship between phonological awareness at the different levels and problems in reading and spelling could differ depending on the phonology of the language that is being learned and the orthographic units that this phonology makes salient. As the phonology of many languages makes the phoneme the most salient unit of analysis (in English the most salient unit of analysis is the rime; see Kessler & Treiman, 1996), children growing up in these linguistic environments may show particularly marked deficits at the phonemic level.

De Gelder and Vrooman (1991) have some relevant data. They gave a group of 11-year-old Dutch dyslexic children phonological awareness tasks at the syllabic, onset-rime and phonemic levels, and compared their performance with a group of normally progressing 8-year-old children matched for reading level and a group of normally progressing 11-year-olds. The syllabic task required the children to delete specified syllables in nonsense words (e.g. *olan* to *o*), the onset-rime task was a same/different judgement task, and the phoneme task was a phoneme deletion task (e.g. *kur* to *ur*). De Gelder and Vrooman found that the dyslexic group performed at a similar level to the reading-age matched control group in the syllable and onset-rime tasks, but showed a significant deficit in the phoneme deletion task. The dyslexic children's performance in the syllable and onset-rime tasks was also comparable to the chronological-age matched controls, suggesting no phonological difficulties at all at these two phonological levels (recall that English dyslexic children only performed at levels comparable to their chronological-age controls on syllable and onset-rime tasks once word-finding difficulties had been taken into account). In contrast with the findings reported by Bruck (1992) in English, the phonemic deficit found in Dutch dyslexics did not persist into adulthood.

Another relevant data set comes from a study of dyslexia in German, carried out by Wimmer (1993). Wimmer studied a large group of 74 German dyslexic children, aged between 8 and 10 years, and compared them with a group of chronological-age controls. Comparison of the oldest dyslexic children with the youngest chronological-age controls enabled an approximate reading-level match. The children were given a rhyme-oddity detection task, a phoneme-substitution task (substituting /i/ for any other vowel, so that *Anna ist krank* becomes *Inni ist krink*), and a nonsense word reading task, among others. Wimmer found that the dyslexic children performed at equivalent levels on the rhyme-oddity task and the phoneme-substitution task to the reading-level control group, although their performance was in general poorer than that of their chronological-age matched peers. However, they were significantly slower than the reading-level control group in the nonsense word reading task, although not significantly less accurate. These younger German dyslexics thus differed from the older Dutch dyslexics in performing at a lower level than their chronological-age controls in the rhyme-awareness task, although again it may be that the oddity task is a more sensitive measure than the same/different judgement task. However, the German group were similar to their Dutch counterparts in showing a deficit on a reading-level match in a phonemic task (nonsense word reading). As German dyslexic adults were not tested, we cannot ascertain whether the phonemic deficit revealed in the nonsense word reading task persisted into adulthood.

There are at least two aspects of the Dutch and German data that deserve further comment. First, it is notable that the only phonological difficulties that are found on a reading-level match in dyslexic children who are learning to read in these more transparent languages are phonemic ones (both Dutch and German are transparent in the sense that letter-sound mappings are highly predictable). This is consistent with the proposal that the relationship between phonological awareness and problems in reading and spelling may differ depending on the phonology of the language that is being learned and the orthographic units that this phonology makes salient. As both the Dutch and the German orthographies operate at the level of the phoneme, it is phonemic difficulties that particularly characterise Dutch and German dyslexic readers. Second, however, it seems that these phonemic difficulties do not particularly affect reading *accuracy*, but instead affect reading *speed*. We can thus propose that the very transparency of the German orthography allows children better conscious access to phonological structures at the phonemic level, thereby facilitating the process of sublexical reorganisation of phonological representations at this level. By adulthood, there is no phonemic deficit in dyslexia (at least in Dutch), although decoding difficulties in terms of reading speed remain.

Obviously, this proposal is consistent with the notion introduced earlier that a 'phonological representations' account may provide the best explanation of the phonological deficit in dyslexia. If dyslexic children are delayed or handicapped in developing high-quality phonological representations and in restructuring those representations at the different linguistic levels, then this should lead to deficits in phonological awareness tasks irrespective of the language that is being learned. However, if their reading difficulties *contribute* to their difficulty in restructuring their phonological representations, particularly at the phonemic level, then this process of restructuring should be easier in transparent orthographies in which the decoding process is straightforward (like Dutch and German) than in less transparent orthographies (like English) in which the decoding process is less straightforward. In English, the use of 1:1 mappings between letters and sounds only sometimes leads to accurate decoding, whereas in German and Dutch it always leads to accurate decoding. Thus Dutch and German dyslexic children may eventually develop phonological awareness at the phonemic level at least in part *because* of this orthographic transparency.

At the moment, this account can only be suggestive, as we lack sufficient data from dyslexic children in languages other than English. For example, word-finding difficulties have not been reported in dyslexic children from other countries, although such difficulties are frequently reported in English dyslexic children (e.g., Denckla & Rudel, 1976). Because word-finding difficulties can provide an index of the adequacy of a child's phonological representations (e.g. Swan, 1995), the absence of such difficulties in dyslexic children who are learning to read more transparent orthographies could be taken to indicate that the 'phonological representations' account does not provide the best available explanation of the data.

However, the apparent absence of this effect may simply mean that no one has looked for it. In a recent study, Wolfgang Schneider, Barbara Scheurich and I gave a confrontation naming task to a group of 10-year-old German dyslexics and compared their performance on this task with groups of age-matched and reading-matched controls. We found that there *was* a picture-naming deficit in German dyslexic children, in comparison with *both* the chronological- and reading-age controls, and that this deficit was particularly marked on long, low-frequency names, which would be consistent with a phonological account of the deficit (Goswami, Scheurich & Schneider, work in progress). Swan has reported a similar phonological component in the word-finding difficulties of English dyslexics, who are also particularly handicapped in naming pictures with long, low-frequency names (Swan, 1995; Swan & Goswami, in press). If further converging evidence is found across languages, then it may be that the 'phonological representations' account provides the best explanation of the causal deficit in dyslexia irrespective of the language that is being learned. It would then be the very transparency of orthographies like German and Dutch that enables dyslexic children who are learning to read these orthographies better conscious access to phonological structures at the phonemic level, which would in turn improve the quality of initially inadequate phonological representations and facilitate the process of sublexical reorganisation. This facilitation would not be available to dyslexic children who are learning to read English, who would thus need to focus on phonological structures at other linguistic levels, such as the rime.

Orthographic Representations in English and Other Orthographies

If it is true that the transparency of orthographies like German and Dutch provides dyslexic children who are learning to read these orthographies with better conscious access to phonological structures at the phonemic level, then one important question is whether the orthographic representations developed by these children do in fact show evidence of being organised at the phonemic level. If dyslexic children's orthographic representations are actually holistic 'whole word' recognition units, or only represent larger phonological units like onsets and rimes, then the hypothesis outlined above cannot be correct. So far, to my knowledge, no one has examined the nature of the orthographic representations that are developed by dyslexic children who are learning to read orthographies other than English. However, we do have evidence about the orthographic representations that are developed by normally progressing children who are learning to read such orthographies, and we also have evidence about the nature of the orthographic representations that are developed by normally progressing and also dyslexic English children. These data are consistent with the hypothesis that the orthographic representations developed by children who are learning to read very transparent orthographies such as Greek, German and Spanish reflect organisation at the phonemic level, whilst the orthographic representations developed by children who are learning to read English reflect organisation at the onset-rime level.

Orthographic representations in English

One way of trying to examine the phonological units that are coded in children's orthographic representations is to study nonsense word reading. Nonsense words can be matched in terms of the phonological assembly processes that they require, but can be spelled in such a way that they either have rimes that are familiar from real words (as in the English example *dake*, analogous to cake and make), or that they have rimes that use familiar grapheme–phoneme correspondences but are unfamiliar as units in themselves (as in the English example *daik*: the rime *aik* is found in no English words). Other examples of nonsense words that contrast rime familiarity are *fape* (cape) vs. *faip*, and *murn* (turn) vs. *mirn*. If children's orthographic representations code rime units as well as grapheme–phoneme correspondences, then words like *dake* should be easier to read than words like *daik*, as children can read a nonsense word like *dake* by using a rime analogy. In contrast, children can only read the phonologically matched nonsense word *daik* by assembling grapheme–phoneme correspondences. By measuring the magnitude of any difference in reading accuracy and reading speed between nonsense words with familiar rimes (e.g. *dake*) and nonsense words with unfamiliar rimes (e.g. *daik*), we can gain some insights into the nature of children's orthographic representations.

Table 8.1: Accuracy of nonsense word reading in English: nonsense words with familiar (*dake*) vs. unfamiliar (*daik*) rimes

List type (% correct)		Age (years)
dake	*daik*	
56.3	36.2	7
64.1	48.2	8
91.7	78.9	9

When such comparisons are made, then children who are learning to read English show a marked advantage for reading nonsense words with familiar rimes (like *dake*) compared with nonsense words with unfamiliar rimes (like *daik*). In a study of 7-, 8- and 9-year-old English readers carried out by Goswami, Gombert and Fraca de Barrera (in press), this advantage was found in terms of both reading accuracy and reading speed, with the accuracy advantage for nonsense words like *dake* being as large as 20% for the youngest readers (see Table 8.1). The fact that nonsense words like *dake* were read faster and more accurately than matched nonsense words like *daik*, even though the nonsense word lists were matched for lower-level variables like positional bigram frequency, suggests that the orthographic representations developed by young readers of English represent rime-level information as well as, and perhaps more strongly than, grapheme–phoneme level information. These orthographic representations obviously represent some grapheme–phoneme level information, as otherwise children would be *unable* to read nonsense words with unfamiliar rimes (like *daik*). Nevertheless, if the orthographic representations developed by English children were organised in terms of grapheme–phoneme level information only, then we would expect no accuracy or speed differences in reading nonsense words with familiar vs. unfamiliar rimes.

Orthographic representations in English dyslexic children

One important consideration for the argument being developed here is how dyslexic children would fare in reading nonsense words with familiar vs. unfamiliar rimes. Although the nonsense word deficit is one of the most robust findings in research in dyslexia (see Rack, Snowling & Olson, 1992), and is usually significant in reading-level match studies as well as in chronological-age match designs, there have been some reports of failures to find a nonsense word deficit in dyslexia when using a reading-level match (e.g. Treiman & Hirsh-Pasek, 1985). Inspection of the nonsense word stimuli used in such studies sometimes reveals that the nonsense words have highly familiar rimes, differing from real words by only a single onset, as was the case in Treiman and Hirsh-Pasek's study (they used nonsense words that were all analogues of real words). This could imply that dyslexic children, too, develop orthographic representations in which rime units are highly salient, and there is some evidence that is consistent with this notion (Treiman, Goswami & Bruck, 1990).

The real test of this idea, however, would be to give dyslexic children matched nonsense words like *dake* and *daik* to try to read aloud, and then to see whether they show the same accuracy and speed advantages in reading nonsense words with familiar rimes that are found in normally progressing readers. Along with Louise Dalton, I have recently conducted such a study (Goswami & Dalton, work in progress). In our study, we compared the performance of a group of 10-year-old dyslexic children who were reading at an 8-year-old level with a group of normally progressing 8-year-old readers, giving both groups lists of nonsense words like *dake* vs. *daik* to read aloud. We found no difference at all between the performance of the two groups. Both groups found nonsense words with familiar rimes like *dake* easier to read than matched nonsense words with unfamiliar rimes like *daik*, with the dyslexic children reading on average 61% of the former and 51% of the latter correctly, and both groups also showed similar patterns of reading speed for the two nonsense word types, with nonsense words like *dake* being read more quickly. Thus English dyslexic children, like normally developing English readers, develop orthographic representations that give a special salience to rime units. Grapheme–phoneme coding is also developing, but appears to progress more slowly (in fact, in our studies normally reading *adults* still show an advantage for reading nonsense words like *dake* compared with nonsense words like *daik*, suggesting that rime units continue to play a salient role in orthographic representations in adulthood, Goswami, Gombert & Fraca de Barrera, in press).

Orthographic representations in more transparent orthographies

As noted above, if the orthographic representations developed by English children were organised at the grapheme–phoneme level, then we would expect no accuracy or speed differences in reading nonsense words with familiar vs. unfamiliar rimes. Both nonsense word types could be decoded by the sequential application of grapheme–phoneme correspondences. This rationale leads to a clear prediction about the performance of children who are learning to read highly transparent orthographies. If such children develop orthographic representations that give priority to the phoneme, then we would expect nonsense words like *daik* to be decoded as quickly and as easily as nonsense words like *dake*. We would even expect nonsense words that have rimes that are unfamiliar *phonologically* as well as orthographically to be simple to decode. English examples of such stimuli are nonsense words like *faish* and *zoip*. Although it is possible to decode these nonsense words by applying grapheme–phoneme correspondences, they neither rhyme with any real English words nor share familiar spelling units for rimes. Accordingly, English children find such nonsense words particularly difficult to decode (e.g. Goswami, Porpodas & Wheelwright, in press).

Along with colleagues in Greece, Germany, Venezuela and France, I have been using this matched nonsense word technique to compare the orthographic representations developed by children who are learning to read in English, French, Spanish, German and Greek (Goswami, Gombert & Fraca de Barrera, in press; Goswami, Porpodas &

Wheelwright, in press; Goswami & Schneider, in preparation). Although it is difficult to devise nonsense words with unfamiliar rimes (like *daik*) in more transparent orthographies, we have managed by studying words of more than one syllable (Greek), thereby focusing on the entire unit following the onset (the spelling pattern for the *rhyme*), or by studying nonsense words that are unfamiliar in terms of rhyme phonology as well as rime orthography, like *faish* and *zoip* (Spanish). I will briefly describe some of the findings from these studies. However, to preview our results, it seems that children who are learning to read different orthographies do indeed develop somewhat different orthographic representations from children who are learning to read English. Children who are learning to read transparent scripts appear to develop orthographic representations that are underpinned by phonemic units from the *beginning* of learning to read.

Nonsense word reading in English vs. Greek

Greek is a highly transparent orthography. Because the relationship between graphemes and phonemes is so predictable in Greek, rime-level coding would not be expected to confer any functional advantage to a young reader. As nothing is gained in terms of decoding accuracy by focusing on rime units, children learning to read Greek should focus on grapheme–phoneme relations from the beginning of learning to read, and hence would not be expected to find nonsense words like *dake* easier to read than nonsense words like *daik*.

The same logic used in English of comparing children's reading of lists of nonsense words like *dake* vs. *daik* was thus used to compare children's orthographic representations in English and Greek (Goswami, Porpodas & Wheelwright, in press). Groups of 7-, 8- and 9-year-old readers from the two countries were given lists of the two nonsense word types to decode, and reading accuracy and reading speed were compared across the two orthographies. Although the very transparency of Greek made stimuli like *daik* difficult to create (there is only one way to spell most rimes), we were able to devise a contrast by using bi- and tri-syllabic words that incorporated the few Greek phonemes that could be represented by more than one letter. Examples of the Greek stimuli are *cleei* (*blei*, analogous to *plei*) and *claiu* (also sounds like *blei*). Examples of the English stimuli are *bomic* (analogous to *comic*) and *bommick*.

The results of this cross-linguistic comparison are given in Table 8.2. As can be seen, the English children found nonsense words like *bomic* much easier to read than nonsense words like *bommick*, whereas the Greek children showed equivalent decoding accuracy for both word types. Inspection of the reaction time data showed that the English children were also significantly faster in decoding nonsense words like

Table 8.2: Accuracy of nonsense word reading: English vs. Greek familiar rhymes (*bomic*) vs. unfamiliar rhymes (*bommick*)

Language	List type (% correct)		Age (years)
	bomic	*bommick*	
English	38.8	23.2	7
	72.4	56.3	8
	86.5	75.0	9
Greek	88.8	89.9	7
	84.9	85.4	8
	94.5	90.9	9

bomic, whereas the Greek children showed no significant difference in reading speed between the two word types. Thus, whereas nonsense words that share familiar spelling segments with real words (*bomic*) are decoded faster and with greater accuracy by children who are learning to read a non-transparent orthography such as English, the same is not true of children who are learning to read a transparent orthography such as Greek. This implies that the most salient units in the orthographic representations developed by young readers of Greek are grapheme–phoneme units, and that orthographic sequences that reflect rhymes have no representational status.

Nonsense word reading in English vs. Spanish

Spanish, like Greek, is a highly transparent orthography. Unlike Greek, its transparency is such that nonsense words with unfamiliar rimes like *daik* are impossible to devise. However, a third type of nonsense word can be created to measure orthographic representations in Spanish, by varying orthographic and phonological familiarity *together*. These nonsense words are unfamiliar in terms of *both* orthography and phonology at the level of the rime, as in the English examples *faish* and *zoip*. If Spanish children, like Greek children, attend to grapheme–phoneme relations from the beginning of learning to read, then they should find nonsense words with unfamiliar orthography and phonology like *zoip* no more difficult to decode than nonsense words with familiar orthography and phonology like *dake*. On the other hand, if children are learning something *specific* about the orthographic–phonological relations that operate in their particular orthography, then we might expect differences in reading nonsense words like *dake* and nonsense words like *zoip*.

Comparisons between these two kinds of nonsense word were made across English and Spanish by Goswami, Gombert and Fraca de Barrera (in press). In our study, English and Spanish 7-, 8- and 9-year-old readers were given lists of the two types of nonsense words to decode (examples of the Spanish stimuli are *duez* (analogous to *juez*) and *muet* (no orthographic or phonological analogy). The two types of nonsense words were equated across lists for their constituent grapheme–phoneme correspondences. Decoding accuracy and reading speed were again used as dependent measures. The accuracy data from this cross-linguistic comparison are given in Table 8.3.

Table 8.3: Accuracy of nonsense word reading: English vs. Spanish familiar rime words (*dake*) vs. unfamiliar rime words (*zoip*)

Language	List type (% correct)		Age (years)
	dake	*zoip*	
English	28.7	11.8	7
	66.2	33.3	8
	59.9	50.7	9
Spanish	95.8	94.3	7
	94.3	94.3	8
	94.8	92.2	9

As the table shows, a strong advantage in reading nonsense words like *dake* compared with nonsense words like *zoip* was found in English, but no comparable advantage was found in Spanish. This provides further evidence that children who are learning to read highly transparent orthographies develop orthographic representations that code grapheme–phoneme relations from the beginning of learning to read. When reading speed was examined, however, the Spanish children did show a significant effect of orthographic and phonological familiarity, taking significantly longer to read nonsense words like *zoip* accurately than nonsense words like *dake*. This suggests that the Spanish children *were* learning something specific about the orthographic–phonological relations that operated in their particular orthography, but that this learning did not affect the accuracy of their decoding. The hypothesis that children who are learning to read highly transparent orthographies develop orthographic representations that give priority to the phoneme is thus supported by these cross-linguistic data.

Conclusion

The first part of this chapter considered whether phonological development follows the same sequence in children who are growing up in different linguistic environments. The developmental sequence found in English-speaking children is that an awareness of syllables, onsets and rimes precedes an awareness of phonemes, with the development of phonemic awareness being partly dependent on being taught to read. A survey of the available cross-linguistic data showed that it was possible to conclude that the sequence of phonological development was similar for children who were growing up in other linguistic environments. However, a note of caution was sounded as different phonological tasks appeared to give rather different results, and it was noted that the hypothesis that differences in the phonological input provided by different languages affect the development of phonological awareness at different phonological levels has not really been thoroughly tested.

The second part of the chapter considered whether the nature of the phonological deficit was similar in dyslexic children who were growing up in different linguistic environments. In particular, it was noted that the relationship between phonological awareness at the different levels and progress in reading and spelling could differ depending on the phonology of the language that was being learned and the orthographic units that this phonology made salient. The comparison of studies carried out with English, Dutch and German dyslexic children suggested that whereas English dyslexic children showed phonological deficits at both the onset-rime and the phonemic levels, the Dutch and German dyslexic children showed a phonological deficit at the phonemic level only. It was suggested that the fundamental difficulty for dyslexic children may lie in developing high-quality segmentally organised phonological representations of words, and that a process of gradual lexical reorganisation and restructuring was necessary for this segmental organisation to occur. It was suggested that this restructuring, particularly at the phonemic level, may be significantly helped by learning to read, and that the transparency of the orthography being learned could affect this process. In particular, children learning to read highly transparent orthographies like German and Dutch may gain better conscious access to phonological structures at the phonemic level, because this level is unambiguously represented by the orthography.

The third part of this chapter examined the kinds of connections that children make between phonology and orthography in different linguistic environments, and whether these connections lead to different orthographic representations. It was argued that if the transparency of orthographies like German and Dutch provides dyslexic children who are learning to read these orthographies with better conscious access to phonological structures at the phonemic level, then the orthographic representations that are developed by normally progressing children in these orthographies should show evidence of being organised at the phonemic level. Nonsense word reading studies in English, Spanish and Greek were reviewed, and it was concluded that whereas the orthographic representations developed by dyslexic and normally progressing English children showed evidence of being organised in terms of onsets and rimes as well as phonemes, the orthographic representations developed by normally progressing Greek and Spanish children showed evidence of grapheme–phoneme organisation only from the earliest phases of development. Cross-linguistic data are therefore consistent with the possibility that orthographic transparency affects the process of sublexical reorganisation of phonological representations at the phonemic level that is so critical for reading progress in all orthographies. Although further work is needed, the proposal that the fundamental deficit in dyslexia lies in the development of high-quality phonological representations and in the restructuring of those representations at the different linguistic levels appears consistent with many of the current data.

Acknowledgements

I would like to thank the teachers and children of the many primary schools in Cambridge who participated in this research, and also Moon Hall School, Surrey, for allowing us to test dyslexic children. I thank Jean Emile Gombert, Costas Porpodas, Wolfgang Schneider, Denise Swan and the teachers and children of participating schools in France, Germany, Greece and Venezuela for fruitful collaborations. Support for this research was partly provided by a Medical Research Council Project Grant (G9326935N) and a Von Humboldt Research Fellowship.

References

Bradley, L. & Bryant, P.E. (1978). Difficulties in auditory organisation as a possible cause of reading backwardness. *Nature*, **271**, 746-747.

Bradley, L. and Bryant, P.E. (1983). Categorising sounds and learning to read: A causal connection. *Nature* **310**, 419–421.

Bowey, J.A., Cain, M.T. & Ryan, S.M. (1992). A reading-level design study of phonological skills underlying fourth grade children's word reading difficulties. *Child Development* **63**, 999–1011.

Bruck, M. (1992). Persistence of dyslexics' phonological awareness deficits. *Developmental Psychology* **28**, 87–886.

Bruck, M. & Treiman, R. (1990). Phonological awareness and spelling in normal children and dyslexics: The case of initial consonant clusters. *Journal of Experimental Child Psychology* **50**, 156–178.

Bryant, P.E. & Goswami, U. (1986). The strengths and weaknesses of the reading level design. *Psychological Bulletin* **100**, 101–103.

Caravolas, M. & Bruck, M. (1993). The effect of oral and written language input on children's phonological awareness: a cross-linguistic study. *Journal of Experimental Child Psychology* **55**, 1–30.

Cossu, G., Shankweiler, D., Liberman, I.Y., Katz, L. & Tola, G. (1988). Awareness of phonological segments and reading ability in Italian children. *Applied Psycholinguistics* **9**, 1–16.

De Gelder, B. & Vrooman, J. (1991). Phonological deficits: beneath the surface of reading acquisition. *Psychological Review* **53**, 88–97.

Denckla, M.B. & Rudel, R.G. (1976). Naming of object drawings by dyslexic and other learning-disabled children. *Brain & Language* **3**, 1–15.

Fowler, A. (1991). How early phonological development might set the stage for phoneme awareness. In S. Brady and D. Shankweiler (Eds.) *Phonological Processes in Literacy*. Hillsdale, NJ: Lawrence Erlbaum.

Gombert, J.E. (1992). *Metalinguistic Development*. Hemel Hempstead, Herts: Harvester Wheatsheaf.

Goswami, U. & Bryant, P.E. (1990). *Phonological Skills and Learning to Read*. Hillsdale, NJ: Lawrence Erlbaum.

Goswami, U., Gombert, J.E. & Fraca de Barrera, L. (in press). Children's orthographic representations and linguistic transparency: Nonsense word reading in English, French and Spanish. *Journal of Applied Psycholinguistics*.

Goswami, U., Porpodas, C. & Wheelwright, S. (in press). Children's orthographic representations in English and Greek. *European Journal of Educational Psychology*.

Huang, H.S. & Hanley, R.J. (1995). Phonological awareness and visual skills in learning to read Chinese and English. *Cognition* **54**, 73–98.

Kessler, B. & Treiman, R. (1996). Syllable structure and the distribution of phonemes in English syllables. Manuscript submitted for publication.

Kirtley, C., Bryant, P., MacLean, M. & Bradley, L. (1989). Rhyme, rime and the onset of reading. *Journal of Experimental Child Psychology* **48**, 224–245.

Liberman, I.Y., Shankweiler, D., Fischer, F.W. & Carter, B. (1974). Explicit syllable and phoneme segmentation in the young child. *Journal of Experimental Child Psychology* **18**, 201–212.

Lundberg, I., Olofsson, A. & Wall, S. (1980). Reading and spelling skills in the first school years predicted from phonemic awareness skills in kindergarten. *Scandanavian Journal of Psychology* **21**, 159–173.

MacLean, M., Bryant, P.E. & Bradley, L. (1987). Rhymes, nursery rhymes and reading in early childhood. *Merrill-Palmer Quarterly* **33**, 255–282.

Mann, V.A. (1986). Phonological awareness: The role of early reading experience. *Cognition* **24**, 65–92.

Morais, J., Alegria, J. & Content, A. (1987). The relationship between segmental analysis and literacy: An interactive view. *Cahiers de Psychologie Cognitive* **7**, 415–438.

Naslund, J.C. & Schneider, W. (1991). Longitudinal effects of verbal ability, memory capacity and phonological awareness on reading performance. *European Journal of Psychology of Education* **6**(4), 375–392.

Olson, R., Wise, B., Connors, F. & Rack, J. (1990). Organisation, heritability and remediation of component word recognition and language skills in disabled readers. In T. Carr & B.A. Levy (Eds.) *Reading and its Development: Component Skills Approaches*. San Diego, CA: Academic Press.

Porpodas, C. (1993). The relation between phonemic awareness and reading and spelling of Greek words in the first school years. In M. Carretero, M. Pope, R.J. Simons & J.I. Pozo (Eds.) *Learning and Instruction*, 3, (pp. 203–217). Oxford: Pergamon Press.

Rack, J., Snowling, M. & Olson, R.K. (1992). The nonword reading deficit in developmental dyslexia. *Reading Research Quarterly* **27**, 29–53.

Schneider, W. & Naslund, J.D., (1996). The impact of early phonological processing skills on reading and spelling in school: Evidence from the Munich Longitudinal

Study. In F.E. Weinert & W. Schneider (Eds.) *Individual development from 3 to 12: Findings from the Munich Longitudinal Study.* Cambridge: CUP.

Snowling, M. & Hulme, C. (1989). A longitudinal case study of developmental phonological dyslexia. *Cognitive Neuropsychology* **6**, 379–401.

Swan, D. (1995). The relationship between picture naming and phonological awareness deficits in developmental dyslexia. Unpublished PhD manuscript, University of Cambridge.

Swan, D. & Goswami, U. (in press). Picture naming deficits in developmental dyslexia: the phonological representations hypothesis. *Brain & Language.*

Swan, D. & Goswami, U. (1996). Phonological awareness deficits in developmental dyslexia and the phonological representations hypothesis. Manuscript submitted for publication.

Treiman, R., Goswami, U. & Bruck, M. (1990). Not all nonwords are alike: Implications for reading development and theory. *Memory and Cognition* **18**, 559–567.

Treiman, R. & Hirsh-Pasek, C. (1985). Are there qualitative differences between dyslexic and normal readers? *Memory and Cognition* **13**, 357–364.

Treiman, R. & Zukowski, A. (1991). Levels of phonological awareness. In S. Brady and D. Shankweiler (Eds.) *Phonological Processes in Literacy.* Hillsdale, NJ: Lawrence Erlbaum.

Walley, A. (1993). The role of vocabulary development in children's spoken word recognition and segmentation ability. *Developmental Review* **13**, 286–350.

Wimmer, H. (1993). Characteristics of developmental dyslexia in a regular writing system. *Applied Psycholinguistics* **14**, 1–33.

Wimmer, H., Landerl, K., Linortner, R. & Hummer, P. (1991). The relationship of phonemic awareness to reading acquisition: more consequence than precondition but still important. *Cognition* **40**, 219–249.

Wimmer, H., Landerl, K. & Schneider, W. (1994). The role of rhyme awareness in learning to read a regular orthography. *British Journal of Developmental Psychology* **12**, 469–484.

Yopp, H.K. (1988). The validity and reliability of phonemic awareness tests. *Reading Research Quarterly* **21**, 253–266.

Chapter 9
Language, Phonology and Learning to Read

MARGARET J. SNOWLING and KATE A. NATION

Since Vellutino's (1979) seminal review of dyslexia, the field has been dominated by theories that view spoken-language skills as critical to reading development. More specifically, there is strong evidence that phonological (speech) processing skills are intimately related to learning to read. The work of numerous investigators has shown that children's reading abilities can be predicted from their pre-school phonological awareness (Bradley & Bryant, 1983; Lundberg, Frost & Peterson, 1988; Muter et al., in press) and, in contrast, dyslexic children have phonological processing deficits (Snowling, 1995; Stanovich & Siegel, 1994). There is also converging evidence that training phonology has beneficial effects on reading attainment, particularly when it is linked to orthographic instruction (Bradley & Bryant, 1983; Hatcher, Hulme & Ellis, 1994; Tunmer, 1994).

Although there is still considerable debate concerning the mechanisms that account for the relationship between phonology and learning to read, the most widely held hypothesis is that children who do well on tests of phonological awareness are quick to understand how phonemes and graphemes relate in the orthography, and to use this knowledge of letter–sound rules as a self-teaching device (Share, 1995). An alternative view is that children who are aware of the rhyming relationships between spoken words can use orthographic relationships between words to read new words by analogy to familiar ones (Goswami, 1990). A rather different view is that learning to read involves setting up a system of *connections* between orthography and phonology (Seidenberg & McClelland, 1989) and, according to this hypothesis, children who have well-specified phonological representations are at an advantage during this process (Snowling & Hulme, 1994). Arguably, having well-specified representations allows a child to set up fine-grained links between the orthographic representations corresponding to written words and the phonological forms of spoken words (Hulme, Snowling & Quinlan, 1991). The knowledge embedded in these mappings will then generalise to allow the child to read new words without access to conscious rules.

From this 'connectionist' perspective on learning to read, dyslexic children are seen as having deficits at the level of phonological representations which compromise their ability to set up mappings between orthography and phonology (Hulme & Snowling, 1992). Converging evidence that dyslexic children have deficits in the representation of phonological information and not just in the conscious awareness of such information comes from the finding that their language difficulties extend to speech perception, speech production, verbal short-term memory and object naming skills (see Snowling, 1995 for a review). The strength of the evidence is such that Stanovich (1988) has argued that dyslexia is a core phonological deficit. The proposal is that when dyslexic children come to learn to read, their phonological representations are 'fuzzy'. At the least, this causes a delay in the acquisition of reading (cf. Manis et al., 1996; Stanovich, this volume). Very often, however, atypical development of phonological reading and spelling strategies ensues (cf. Rack, Snowling & Olson, 1992).

Notwithstanding the crucial role of phonological skills, it is also important to consider the other language skills that children bring to the task of learning to read. Plausibly, strengths and weaknesses in semantic and syntactic skills — in addition to phonological skills — will be related to the progress that children make in reading, especially if we consider aspects of reading beyond word recognition, namely reading comprehension. A good way of thinking about this is within a framework provided by Gough and Tunmer (1986). According to Gough and Tunmer, reading can be predicted by the product of two sets of skills: decoding and linguistic comprehension. Describing reading in this way reveals that there are three types of poor reader. We have discussed dyslexic children who have poor decoding but good comprehension skills. In marked contrast, some 10% of children have normal decoding skills but poor comprehension (Nation & Snowling, in press). Finally, generally poor readers have difficulties with both decoding and comprehension.

In this chapter, we will discuss the adequacy of the 'phonological representations' hypothesis as an explanation of the cognitive causes of dyslexia. We begin by briefly reviewing some recent evidence in its support (see the chapter by Frith, this volume, for a fuller discussion). We next examine two critical issues: the extent to which the hypothesis can account for individual variation amongst dyslexic readers, and the problem of accounting for normal reading development in some children with spoken-language problems. Finally, we report a study investigating the use of semantic context in dyslexic readers and suggest semantic processing capacities can compensate for phonological processing weaknesses when reading. Overall, the evidence suggests that differences in phonological skill provide a reasonable account of individual differences both in dyslexia and in normal reading development. However, a second source of variance, in semantic skill, contributes to differences in the behavioural manifestations of dyslexia between individuals.

Phonological Processing Deficits in Dyslexia

One of the strengths of the phonological representations hypothesis of dyslexia is that it provides a reasonable account of the difficulties experienced by dyslexic individuals across the life-span (Morton & Frith, 1995). To date, the majority of research had focused on dyslexia in the school-age child. However, in recent years, there has been a growth of interest both in the precursors of dyslexia in the pre-school years (see chapters by Elbro, Frith, Lyttinen and Locke in the present volume), and in the manifestation of dyslexia in adults.

A pioneering study by Scarborough (1990) was concerned with the early language skills of children born into dyslexic families, who themselves went on to be dyslexic. On the basis of her findings, Scarborough claimed that the language deficits associated with dyslexia change with time. Thus, 2-year-olds who later became dyslexic had greater difficulty with speech production and more limited use of syntax in conversation with their mothers than control children who did not go on to develop reading problems. At 3 years, the dyslexic pre-schoolers had poorer vocabulary and weaker naming skills than their peers and at 5 years, they showed the classic limitations of phonological awareness and letter-knowledge.

We have recently reported findings converging with those of Scarborough (1990) from a study of 71 children at genetic risk of dyslexia, compared with 37 children from control families in which there was no history of reading failure (Gallagher et al., submitted). All of the children were seen before their fourth birthday and assessed on a battery of language tasks which targeted expressive language, vocabulary development and phonological processing, and included tests of pre-literacy skills, including letter knowledge. Although it is not yet possible to ascertain which of these children will go on to become dyslexic, group differences at 45 months are instructive and will be summarised here.

The children at risk of dyslexia did not differ from the controls in non-verbal ability, as measured by the Draw a Man test. However, they were somewhat poorer on all of the language measures. Significant differences emerged between the groups on tests of expressive and receptive vocabulary, although there were no group differences in the children's articulation skills, or in their ability to retell a story. Importantly, the at-risk children were worse at repeating novel words, especially those with phonological structures comprising late-acquired forms, namely, two-syllable non-words with stress on the last syllable, [e.g., be'mur]. In addition, their knowledge of nursery rhymes, a test known to predict reading achievement, was poor and, strikingly, they already knew fewer letters than control children.

To summarise, we found that the at-risk children differed from controls in vocabulary development, phonological awareness and letter-knowledge. The finding that at-risk children had specific difficulty in repeating novel phonological forms with unusual patterns of stress strongly suggests that they were delayed in their phonological development. Arguably, non-word repetition is an excellent measure of how easy it is to set up new phonological representations. Consistent with the phonological representations hypothesis, children at risk of dyslexia appear to have difficulties with the creation of phonological representations long before they begin to read. It is reasonable to suspect, therefore, that they will come to the task of learning to read with poorly specified phonological representations. In turn, this will place limitations on their ability to establish mappings between orthography and phonology when learning to read (cf. Ehri, 1992; Rack et al., 1994).

Higher in the age spectrum, we carried out a study of the cognitive skills of university students with self-reported dyslexic difficulties (Snowling et al., 1997). When compared with age-matched peers of a similar educational level, the dyslexic readers had persisting difficulties with basic reading and spelling processes; their word-recognition skills were limited and they had problems with phonological reading and spelling strategies. We also observed deficits on a range of tests of phonological processing skill and phonological awareness. Thus, at a developmental stage where phonological skills can be assumed to asymptote, the dyslexic students did not exhibit error-free performance. They were slower on a speeded naming task than controls, and their memory span for non-words was impaired. They had difficulties with tasks requiring rhyme production and phoneme deletion and they were particularly disadvantaged on a spoonerism task (cf. Bruck, 1992; Gallagher et al., 1996; Pennington et al., 1990).

Arguably, the range of difficulties exhibited could be concomitants of poorly specified phonological representations. If the recall of non-words depends upon how easily new representations can be established, then the memory data suggest ongoing difficulties with this process. The possession of poorly specified representations should limit the speed of access to these representations in digit-naming tasks, and also compromise the ability to integrate them, as assessed by tests of rhyme production, phoneme deletion and spoonerisms (see Stackhouse & Wells, this volume, for a similar argument). Thus, even when dyslexic individuals reach an adult level of reading skill, they have persisting diffi-culties that point to underlying deficiencies at the level of phonological representations. More speculatively, this difficulty may relate to func-tional differences in brain processing between dyslexic and normal readers (cf. Paulesu, Frith et al., 1996; Frith, this volume).

Dyslexia as a Core Phonological Deficit?

The argument presented so far is consistent with what might be described as a 'unitary view' of dyslexia. A serious objection to this view comes from advocates of the 'sub-types' account of dyslexia (Castles & Coltheart, 1993). It is an implicit assumption of the sub-types view that delayed phonological development can only account for one form of dyslexia, namely phonological dyslexia. Other types of reading problem, for example surface dyslexia, may, in contrast, be attributable to visual deficits (Stein & Fowler, 1985).

However, it could be argued that just as normal readers vary in the reading strategies they use, so do dyslexic children. Although it is impor-tant to understand the causes of individual differences in reading, the possibility of defining true sub-types that are stable and unchanging with development seems remote. Furthermore, there is increasing evidence for the hypothesis that delayed phonological development is the cause of dyslexia, but that its behavioural manifestations differ between children as a function of the severity of their phonological processing impairments (Snowling et al., 1994a).

We explored the issue of individual differences in dyslexia in the context of a longitudinal study following the progress of 20 dyslexic children over two years (Snowling et al., in press). One of the main aims of this study was to investigate the cognitive skills underlying two so-called subtypes of dyslexia, namely, developmental phonological dyslexia, characterised by a selective non-word reading deficit, and developmental surface dyslexia, characterised by a selective deficit in reading irregular words.

It is important to make clear at the outset that the classification of dyslexic children into 'sub-types' was not straightforward for three reasons. First, the variation between dyslexic children was not signifi-cantly more marked than the variation we found amongst the normal readers (of the same reading age) in the control group. Second, many dyslexic children showed features of more than one sub-type and third, some children 'moved' between subtypes during the two years in which we followed them.

Because we considered it important to take account of normal varia-tion when identifying pure cases of phonological or surface dyslexia (Snowling, Bryant & Hulme, 1996), we decided to use an approach based on regression. Thus, we carried out two regressions at each point in time. First, we regressed non-word reading on Reading Age and second, irregular word reading on Reading Age. This allowed us to predict, for our clinical cases, the levels of non-word and irregular word reading that could reasonably be expected of them, given their Reading Age.

Our next step was to identify the children who had significant discrepancies between their expected and actual levels of performance in non-word reading (phonological dyslexia) and in irregular word reading (surface dyslexia). Out of our sample of 20, we identified just two children who resembled developmental phonological dyslexics and two resembling developmental surface dyslexics, whose reading profile remained stable over time. All four children were above average in intelligence and, at the beginning of the study, they were all reading at least 18 months behind expectation, at between the 6- and 7-year levels. They progressed at similar rates, making less than average progress over time.

To validate our classification procedure, we administered independent tests of regular, irregular and non-word reading two years after the start of the study. To examine the regularity effect in reading, we asked the children to read a corpus of words varying in frequency and regularity (after Seymour, 1986). When reading these words, the two phonological dyslexics showed a normal pattern of performance, whereas the two surface dyslexics exhibited an exaggerated regularity effect; although they could read regular words adequately, they had a very obvious deficit in irregular word reading and frequently made errors suggesting they were relying heavily upon 'sounding-out' as a strategy, e.g. BROAD → 'brode'. To examine the use of phonological strategies in reading and spelling, we asked the children to read and to spell a graded list of non-words. As expected, the phonological dyslexics, but not the surface dyslexics, had very poor non-word reading and non-word spelling.

Thus, the classification of the dyslexic children into stable 'sub-types' was possible in the case of these four children. The two children classified as developmental phonological dyslexics were faster readers than the surface dyslexics but, when they did not recognise a word, they had difficulty in decoding it, as evidenced by their poor non-word reading. The two surface dyslexic cases had adequate non-word reading abilities, though their reading of irregular words was impaired and their reading responses were slow.

To assess the extent to which phonological dyslexia is associated with phonological deficits and surface dyslexia with visual deficits, we also examined the performance of the four dyslexic cases on a range of processing tasks tapping phonological and visual abilities. Contrary to the sub-types view, there were very few differences between the performance of the children on the processing tasks. They did not differ in Digit

Span, rhyme oddity, word repetition or naming, or indeed on any of the visual processing tasks they were given. The only significant differences to emerge were in rhyme production and non-word repetition, where the phonological dyslexics had greater difficulty. They also differed in their spelling performance; here the phonological dyslexics made a very high proportion of dysphonetic errors, whereas the surface dyslexics made a high proportion of phonetically acceptable errors.

Arguably, the ability to produce strings of rhyming words, to repeat novel words and to spell words phonetically are all indices of how easy it is to access phonological representations of words. If this hypothesis is correct, then phonological representations are less easily accessed by children who resemble developmental phonological dyslexics than children who resemble developmental surface dyslexics.

Importantly, unlike the phonological dyslexics who did worse than RA controls on some of the phonological tasks, the developmental surface dyslexic children always performed at the same level as younger Reading Age-matched controls. It is inappropriate from a developmental perspective, therefore, to conclude that they were 'normal' for their age. Rather, they performed in line with reading skill, suggesting the development of these processing abilities was delayed. Finally, we found no support for the popular hypothesis that surface dyslexia is associated with visual processing deficits (cf. Stein & Fowler, 1985).

To summarise, we found relatively few differences between children who could be described as phonological dyslexics and those who could be described as surface dyslexics. The differences were in non-word repetition, phonological awareness and in the phonetic accuracy of their spellings. These differences suggest phonological dyslexics have more difficulty in accessing phonological representations of speech than surface dyslexics, and are consistent with the hypothesis that dyslexic children have less well-specified phonological representations than normally developing readers of the same age. These findings are also consistent with the view that the severity of a child's phonological processing impairment determines the qualitative nature of their reading and spelling performance — the severity hypothesis (Snowling et al., 1994a).

Our proposal, therefore, is that developmental phonological dyslexia characterises children with more severe phonological deficits who have poorly specified phonological representations. When these children come to learn to read, they are forced to develop mappings between orthographic and phonological representations that are coarse-grained. Formally, it is because the mappings are not at the phonemic level of representation that sub-lexical mappings do not develop; thus, the ability of these children to read words does not generalise to allow them to read words they have not encountered before, as usually assessed by non-word reading. In contrast, we hypothesise that the milder phonological deficits seen in children with surface dyslexia indicate that their phonological representations are better specified. Thus, they can set up their reading system in the normal way although its development is delayed. A similar suggestion has been made by Manis et al. (1996) from a large-scale study of individual differences in dyslexia.

Thus, there need be no paradox between unitary theories of dyslexia and theories that posit sub-types of dyslexia. The most parsimonious theory to date is that the core deficit in dyslexia is in phonology. We propose that the manifestations of this phonological deficit vary as a function of its severity: children with severe phonological deficits will develop coarse mappings between orthography and phonology and therefore resemble phonological dyslexics. Conversely, children with milder phonological deficits create more adequate mappings between orthography and phonology (though they are still delayed in this respect). These children might therefore be described as 'surface' dyslexics. However, it is important to emphasise that, in our view, there is no clear distinction between the patterns described as phonological dyslexia or surface dyslexia. In our study, most of the children could not be classified as showing either pattern. Our view is essentially a unidimensional one with those children having the most severe phonological deficits also being more likely to display a phonological dyslexic pattern.

Learning to Read with Poor Phonology

Our discussion so far predicts that children with spoken-language impairments that encompass phonology will be at greater at risk of reading difficulties (cf. Tallal, this volume). However, an apparent paradox exists with regard to the reading skills of children with spoken-language impairments; these children do not inevitably become poor readers. Catts (1993) reported that children with specific speech-articulation difficulties in kindergarten do not develop reading difficulties in first grade whilst those with more widespread language impairments, encompassing difficulties with semantics and syntax, do. Similar results have been reported by Magnusson and Naucler (1990) and Stackhouse (1982).

In one of the largest prospective studies of children with pre-school specific language impairments, Bishop and Adams (1990) also reported that reading developed normally in the early school years. Those children with good prognosis, whose spoken language difficulties had resolved by 5:6 years, showed normal reading accuracy and comprehension at 8 years, and also performed within normal limits on tests of non-word reading and spelling. In contrast, children still exhibiting specific language impairments at 5:6 had reading problems at 8 years. Interestingly, their difficulties were not primarily with decoding but with reading comprehension.

Recently, we have followed up the children from the original Bishop studies, and have assessed 71 of them at 15 years of age. The results of this follow-up study are presented elsewhere (Stothard et al., submitted). However, with regard to their reading performance, outcomes were variable. Broadly, the children who had a good prognosis at 5:6 and normal reading skills at 8 years, were found to be performing worse than controls at 15 years in terms of reading accuracy. They also had problems with non-word reading and non-word spelling although their word spelling and reading comprehension skills were within the normal range.

These findings are difficult to interpret. It seems clear that the course of reading development can be shaped by a child's language skills. However, the causal relationships among language and reading skills may change over time. The results of this longitudinal study show that, even if children make a good start in learning to read, their decoding skills may develop slowly if phonological resources are reduced. This we believe to be the case in children with specific language impairments whose spoken language difficulties resolve. It is interesting that the children in the good prognosis group showed phonological processing difficulties at 15 years, including impairments of non-word repetition, sentence repetition and phonological awareness, although their other more general language skills were in the normal range.

The reading skills of the children with a poor spoken-language prognosis had also changed over time. At 8 years, they exhibited reading comprehension difficulties, yet at 15 years they had problems not only with reading comprehension but also with reading accuracy. Clearly, if children have difficulty understanding spoken language they are likely to have considerable difficulty comprehending text. A knock-on effect of this is that reading experience fails to facilitate growth in vocabulary or general knowledge, factors that are known to fuel further increases in comprehension. We also suggest that limited comprehension and impoverished vocabulary knowledge may constrain the development of reading accuracy skills. To illustrate this point, consider the difficulty facing children learning to read words such as *chaos*, *enough* or *unique*, if they have little understanding of their meanings. Thus, there is clearly more to reading than decoding and more to the prediction of reading skills than phonology.

The Use of Context by Readers Varying in Comprehension Skill

In order to elucidate how different language skills are related to different forms of reading difficulty, we have been investigating the use of contextual cues when reading by dyslexic children, poor comprehenders and normal readers, equated for reading accuracy (Nation & Snowling, submitted). In this experiment, children were presented with a printed word, either in isolation or following a spoken context. The contexts comprised sentence frames created to constrain the possible final word but not to be so predictive that the word could be guessed. In fact, preliminary work allowed us to select sentences which, in fewer than 10% of instances, allowed the target word to be guessed correctly.

We measured the accuracy of the children's responses to target words both in isolation and in context, and also their speed of response. There was a significant effect of context; all children's reading improved when context was available to them. However, there was also an important group-by-context interaction. This interaction revealed that, for accuracy, the context effect was greatest for the dyslexic poor readers and smallest for the poor comprehenders, with controls benefiting to an intermediate degree. For speed, the facilitation effect was far greater for the dyslexic readers than the other two groups.

The findings of this experiment underline the fact that there is more to reading than decoding. To focus on the dyslexic children: in the face of deficits in decoding, they benefited from context more than younger, normal readers matched for Reading Age. Importantly, the benefits that accrued were not just because the availability of context allowed them to guess; our materials were constructed to rule out this possibility. Rather, the availability of semantic and syntactic information from the sentence frame allowed the children to modify their incomplete or inaccurate pronunciations of target words to bring them in line with context. This 'self-teaching' device provides one plausible explanation for how many dyslexic children eventually attain reasonable levels of word-reading accuracy, despite persisting difficulties with phonological processing and non-word reading. The corollary of this is that children with language deficits extending beyond phonology (encompassing problems with semantics or grammar for example) will have difficulty in using context to decipher unfamiliar words; this may account for relative declines in reading skill over time in children with language problems who are forced to rely on their (typically weak) decoding skills, without the benefit of semantic and syntactic back-up. It also accounts for their poor reading comprehension.

We turn finally to discuss the critical variables that predict the ease with which children can use context. We examined this in a large-scale study assessing children's performance on a battery of tests of language and cognitive skills, and relating this to their susceptibility to the context effect. We found that the context effect was predicted by measures of language processing that appear to tap semantic skills. These tests included tests of synonym judgement, semantic fluency, listening and reading comprehension. The context effect did not correlate with phonological measures such as rhyme judgement, rhyme fluency or non-word reading.

Thus, just as individual differences in phonological processing predict individual differences in reading–decoding skill, individual differences in semantic processing predict a separate source of variance in reading skill, namely differences in the use of context and in reading comprehension. Dyslexic children, by definition, have normal semantic skills and they can use these to good effect to promote their reading development. However, children with impairments of spoken language vary in the extent to which processing is impaired in different language sub-systems; heterogeneity of their reading disorders is therefore to be anticipated.

Returning to the connectionist view outlined earlier, the same framework can be modified to explain how strengths and weaknesses in different aspects of language are related to reading performance. Recently, Plaut et al. (1996) have implemented a model of word recognition that incorporates knowledge of semantics alongside mappings between phonology and orthography. To summarise their results very briefly, the addition of semantic input influenced the mappings between orthography and phonology such that the network as a whole learned more efficiently, and resembled skilled reading more closely, than networks trained without semantic input. In short, the development of reading depends on interacting phonological and semantic pathways. It is reasonable to assume, therefore, that individual differences in both phonology and semantics will be related to individual differences in reading ability. As we outlined previously, dyslexic children's poorly specified phonological representations place limitations on how well they can set up mappings between orthography and phonology. As a result, they may come to rely heavily on semantic support when reading. For those children with more general language problems, however, inadequately specified semantic representations will also constrain the development of mappings between semantics, orthography and phonology, leading to more pervasive reading difficulties.

Conclusions

There is still much work to be done to clarify the relationship between spoken and written language impairments. From the evidence presented here, it is clearly important to think of the relationship as one that changes with development. Studies of pre-school children at risk of dyslexia suggest these children suffer delayed phonological development in the context of slow vocabulary acquisition. It can be assumed that, at the point when these children come to learn to read, their phonological representations of speech are poorly specified and, at the least, their acquisition of reading will be slow. However, the course of reading development they follow will be determined not only by the nature and severity of the phonological processing problem they have, but also by their other language skills. Dyslexic children who have good semantic skills are likely to follow an atypical course of development. Their word recognition may improve in the face of decoding deficits because they rely heavily on context. However, should they have poor language skills, their reading development will be slow and, in the longer term, deficits of both decoding and comprehension may follow.

Acknowledgements

The research reported in this paper was supported by grants from the Medical Research Council, the Economic and Social Research Council of Great Britain and The Wellcome Trust.

References

Bishop, D. V. M. & Adams, C. (1990). A prospective study of the relationship between specific language impairment, physiological disorders and reading retardation. *Journal of Child Psychology* **31**, 1027–1050.

Bradley, L. & Bryant P.E. (1983). Categorising sounds and learning to read: A casual connection. *Nature* **301**, 419–421.

Bruck, M. (1992). Persistence of dyslexics' phonological awareness deficits. *Developmental Psychology* **28**, 874–886.

Castles, A. & Coltheart, M. (1993). Varieties of developmental dyslexia. *Cognition* **47**, 149–180.

Catts, H. W. (1993). The relationship between speech–language impairments and reading disabilities. *Journal of Speech and Hearing Research* **36**, 948–958.

Ehri, L. C. (1992). Reconceptualizing the development of sight word reading and its relationship to decoding. In P. B. Gough, L. C. Ehri & R. Treiman (Eds.) *Reading Acquisition*. Hillsdale, NJ: Erlbaum.

Gallagher, A., Frith, U. & Snowling, M. (submitted). Language processing skills in pre-schoolers at risk of developmental dyslexia.

Gallagher, A., Laxon, V., Armstrong, E. & Frith, U. (1996) Phonological difficulties in high functioning dyslexics. *Reading and Writing* **8**, 499–509.

Goswami, U. (1990). A special link between rhyming skills and the use of orthographic analogies by beginning readers. *Journal of Child Psychology and Psychiatry* **31**, 301–311.

Gough, P. B., & Tunmer, W. E. (1986). Decoding, reading and reading disability. *Remedial and Special Education* **7**, 6-10.

Hatcher, P., Hulme, C. & Ellis, A. W. (1994). Ameliorating early reading failure by integrating the teaching of reading and phonological skills: The phonological linkage hypothesis. *Child Development* **65**, 41–57.

Hulme, C. & Snowling, M. (1992). Deficits in output phonology: An explanation of reading failure? *Cognitive Neuropsychology* **9**, 47–72.

Hulme, C., Snowling, M. & Quinlan, P. T. (1991). Connectionism and learning to read: steps towards a psychologically plausible model. *Reading and Writing* **3**, 159–168.

Lundberg, I., Frost, J. & Peterson, O. P. (1988). Effects of an extensive programme for stimulating phonological awareness in pre-school children. *Reading Research Quarterly* **33**, 263–284.

Magnusson, E. & Naucler, K. (1990). Reading and spelling in language disordered children – linguistic and metalinguistic prerequisites: Report on a longitudinal study. *Clinical Linguistics and Phonetics* **4**, 49–61.

Manis, F. R., Seidenberg, M. S., Doi, L. M., McBride-Chang & Petersen, A. (1996). On the basis of two subtypes of developmental dyslexia. *Cognition* **58.**, 157–195.

Morton, J. & Frith, U. (1995). Causal modelling: A structural approach to developmental psychopathology. In D. Cicchetti and D. J. Cohen (Eds.) *Manual of Developmental Psychopathology*. New York: Wiley.

Muter, V, Hulme, C. & Snowling M. (in press). Segmentation, not rhyming, predicts early progress in learning to read. *Journal of Experimental Child Psychology*.

Nation, K. & Snowling, M. (in press). Assessing reading difficulties: The validity and utility of current measures of reading skill. *British Journal of Educational Psychology*.

Nation, K., & Snowling, M. (submitted). Contextual facilitation of word recognition: evidence from dyslexia and poor reading comprehension.

Paulesu, E., Frith, U., Snowling, M., Gallagher, A., Morton, J., Frackowiak, R.S.J. & Frith, C.D. (1996). Is developmental dyslexia a disconnection syndrome? Evidence from PET scanning. *Brain* **119**, 143–157

Pennington, B. F., Van Orden, G. C., Smith, S. D., Green, P. A., & Haith, M. M. (1990). Phonological processing skills and deficits in adult dyslexic children. *Child Development* **61**, 1753-1778.

Plaut, D., McClelland, J. L., Seidenberg, M. S. & Patterson, K. E. (1996). Understanding normal and impaired reading: Computational principles in a quasi-irregular domains. *Psychological Review* **103**, 56–115.

Rack, J. P., Snowling, M. J. & Olson, R. K. (1992). The nonword reading deficit in dyslexia: a review. *Reading Research Quarterly* **27**, 29–53.

Rack, J.P., Hulme, C., Snowling, M. & Wightman, J (1994) The role of phonology in young children's learning of sight words: The direct mapping hypothesis. *Journal of Experimental Child Psychology* **57**, 42–71.

Scarborough, H.S. (1990). Very early language deficits in dyslexic children. *Child Development* **61**, 1728–1743.

Seidenberg, M. & McClelland, J. (1989). A distributed, developmental model of word recognition and naming. *Psychological Review* **96**, 523–568.

Seymour, P. H. K. (1986). *Cognitive Analysis of Dyslexia*. London: Routledge & Kegan Paul.

Share, D. L. (1995). Phonological recoding and self-teaching: *sine qua non* of reading acquisition. *Cognition* **55**, 151–218.

Snowling, M. (1995). Phonological processing and developmental dyslexia. *Journal of Research in Reading* **18**, 132–138.

Snowling, M., & Hulme, C. (1994). The development of phonological skills. *Transactions of the Royal Society B* **346**, 21–28.

Snowling, M., Bryant, P. & Hulme, C. (1996). Theoretical and methodological pitfalls in making comparisons between developmental and acquired dyslexia: Some comments on Castles & Coltheart (1993). *Reading and Writing* **8**, 443–451.

Snowling, M., Goulandris, N. & Defty, N. (in press). A longitudinal study of reading development in dyslexic children. *Journal of Educational Psychology*.

Snowling, M., Goulandris, N. & Stackhouse, J. (1994a). Phonological constraints on learning to read. In C. Hulme & M. Snowling (Eds.) *Reading Development and Dyslexia*. London: Whurr Publishers.

Snowling, M., Hulme, C. & Goulandris, N. (1994b). Word recognition and development: a connectionist interpretation. *Quarterly Journal of Experimental Psychology* **47A**, 895–916.

Snowling, M., Nation, K., Moxham, P., Gallagher, A. & Frith, U. (1997). Phonological processing skills of dyslexic students in higher education: A preliminary report. *Journal of Research in Reading* **20**, 31–41.

Stackhouse, J. (1982). An investigation of reading and spelling performance in speech disordered children. *British Journal of Disorders of Communication* **17**, 53–60.

Stanovich, K. E. (1988). Explaining the differences between the dyslexic and the garden-variety poor reader: The phonological-core variable-difference model. *Journal of Learning Disabilities* **21**, 590–612.

Stanovich, K. E. & Siegel, L. S. (1994). The phenotypic performance profile of reading-disabled children: A regression-based test of the phonological-core variable-difference model. *Journal of Educational Psychology* **86**, 1–30.

Stein, J. & Fowler, M.S. (1985). Effect of monocular occlusion on visuomotor perception and reading in dyslexic children. *Lancet* **ii**, 69–73.

Stothard, S. E., Snowling, M. J., Bishop, D. V. M., Chipchase, B. & Kaplan, C. (submitted). Preschoolers with language impairment: A follow-up in adolescence.

Tunmer, W. E. (1994). Phonological processing skills and reading remediation. In C. Hulme & M. Snowling (Eds.) *Reading Development and Dyslexia*. London: Whurr Publishers.

Vellutino, F. (1979). *Dyslexia: Research and Theory*. Cambridge, MA: MIT Press.

Chapter 10
Academic Outcomes of Language Impaired Children

PAULA TALLAL, LEE ALLARD, STEVE MILLER AND
SUSAN CURTISS

Epidemiological studies have demonstrated that approximately 8% of all pre-school aged children have a developmental language impairment (LI), depending on how impairment is defined (Beitchman et al., 1986; Silva, 1980; Tomblin, personal communication; see Tallal, 1988, for review). Specific developmental language impairment is usually defined as a deficit in expressive and/or receptive language that cannot be attributed to general developmental delay, hearing impairment, frank neurological disorders (cerebral palsy, seizure disorders, hemiplegia), or emotional disturbance (Tallal, 1988). The eventual outcome of children with pre-school impairments in language development is still a matter of debate. Some evidence suggests that the language impairment resolves across time, in at least some children, whilst other evidence indicates that many of these children remain impaired. Another issue of importance concerns whether language impairment overlaps with other developmental disabilities, especially disorders in academic skills (specifically dyslexia), attention deficit disorder, and/or behavioural–emotional disturbance. This is a critically important question, as the answer influences the diagnostic categories applied to these children and therefore the delivery of services.

A number of studies have provided evidence that, as a group, LI children experience academic difficulties. Hall and Tomblin (1978) examined the academic performance, from grades 3 to 12, of 18 children diagnosed as LI, using 18 children with only articulation difficulties as controls. Results of standardised tests administered in school were used to determine academic performance. The authors reported that, as a group, the LI children showed academic deficits across all grades, especially in reading. Differences between LI children and controls increased from grades 3 to 5, then declined gradually from grades 5 to 8. Silva, McGee & Williams (1983) examined the reading performance of 68 7-year-old children diagnosed as LI at age 3. At age 7, 28 of these children showed evidence of a reading disability. Stark et al. (1984) followed-up 29 children diagnosed as LI between the ages of 4 and 8 years. The follow-up, done four years later, when the children were between the ages of 8 and 12, indicated that 23 of these children were at least two grade levels behind in reading vocabulary and comprehension. Aram, Ekelman & Nation (1984) performed a 10-year follow-up of 20 children diagnosed as LI between the ages of 3 and 6. The follow-up indicated that 50% of the LI children scored below the 25th percentile on a standardised reading test; for spelling and mathematics, the respective figures were 56% and 75%.

Taken together, these studies converge on the finding that a substantial number of LI children experience academic difficulties. It is not clear, however, whether these difficulties are primarily in the area of language-related academic areas (reading/spelling) or operate across all subject areas. Also, the change in academic status of LI children across time is not clear. Hall and Tomblin (1978) found increasing deficits, relative to controls, from grades 3 to 5, followed by a gradual decline. The other studies did not look at the time course of academic growth in LI children. Of utmost importance in evaluating outcomes in academic achievement is the fact that various studies differ in the criteria used to initially diagnose language impairment and subsequently to determine academic deficits. Several of the studies reviewed included children who were highly variable in terms of age as well as physical and intellectual abilities. Hence, the effects of language impairment *per se* on academic achievement cannot be specifically determined.

As part of a broad-based prospective longitudinal study, we evaluated the outcomes of specific language-impaired children diagnosed at age 4 years and matched control children. These children were assessed annually for five years from the age of 4 years to 8 years. We will focus here on the development of academic skills in this well-defined group of specifically language-impaired and normal matched control children. The following research questions were addressed:

1. Do children with pre-school language impairment subsequently demonstrate deficits in pre-reading skills and in academic achievement?
2. If so, what is the extent and severity of these deficits?
3. Do academic deficits, if found, occur in all subject areas or only certain language-related subject areas, especially reading?
4. What is the time course of academic growth for LI children? Is it similar to that of normal children? More specifically, do LI children, with time, catch up with or fall further behind their normal counterparts?

The Longitudinal Study

The children who took part in the present study had all been diagnosed as specifically language impaired (SLI) at age 4. The 67 participating children were from an initial cohort of 89 LI children, diagnosed at age 4 years, who completed all five years of the San Diego Longitudinal Study. Strict subject-selection criteria were used and are described in detail elsewhere (Tallal, Dukette & Curtiss, 1989). In brief, children had to meet the following criteria to be included in the study:

1. non-verbal IQ of at least 85;
2. mean language age at least one year below performance mental age and chronological age;
3. normal hearing, and no motor handicaps or oral structural impairments;
4. English only language spoken in home;
5. not autistic;
6. no known neurological disorders.

The control group consisted of 54 of the original 66 normally developing children who completed all five years of the study and were matched to the LI children on the basis of chronological age, race and non-verbal IQ. In order to be included as controls, children had to meet the following criteria:

1. Non-verbal IQ of at least 85;
2. mean language age within six months of chronological age;
3. speech articulation age within six months of chronological age;
4. normal hearing, and no motor handicaps or oral structural impairments;
5. English only language spoken in home;
6. no known emotional or neurological problems.

All subjects were tested annually over a period of five years. Table 10.1 provides mean values, at the time of induction into the longitudinal study at age 4 years, for chronological age, Leiter Nonverbal IQ, and scores on the following standardised language tests: the Sequenced Inventory of Communication Development (SICD; Hedrick, Prather & Tobin, 1979); the Northwestern Syntax Screening Test (NSST; Lee, 1971); the Carrow Elicited Language Inventory (CELIE; Carrow, 1974); and the Children's Token Test (DiSimoni, 1970).

The children were tested annually from ages 4 to 8 years. A large battery of tests assessing perceptual, motor, cognitive, linguistic, social–emotional and academic performance were administered. A detailed description of all measures and testing procedures used in the San

Table 10.1 Performance of language-impaired (LI) and normally developing (N) children at age 4, on standardised tests

Variable	N Mean	LI Mean	t-score	value
Age	4.4	4.3	0.99	ns
Leiter IQ	111.8	109.4	1.35	ns
SICD-rec	90.7	81.1	3.88	0.0002
SICD-exp	108.4	91.7	13.74	0.0001
NSST-rec	25.9	18.4	9.84	0.0001
NSST-exp	24.8	6.1	19.57	0.0001
CELIE	57.9	5.2	26.05	0.0001
Token Test	36.2	12.8	11.32	0.0001

Note: SICD: The Sequenced Inventory of Communication Development (Hedrick et al., 1979); NSST = The Northwestern Syntax Screening Test (Lee, 1971); CELIE = The Carrow Elicited Language Inventory (Carrow, 1974); rec = receptive language; exp = expressive language.

Diego Longitudinal Study has been reported elsewhere (Tallal, Curtiss & Kaplan, 1988). Because the present study focused on academic achievement outcomes, both pre-reading and academic attainment tests were given. The pre-academic tests included the visual discrimination (VD), letter form (LF) and letter sound (LS) sub-tests from the Comprehensive Test of Basic Skills (CTBS; 1973). The academic tests used included the Gates MacGinitie Reading Test (Gates & MacGinitie, 1972), the Gates-McKillop Phonics Test (Gates & McKillop, 1966), and the CTBS. Five academic domains were assessed including decoding, reading vocabulary, reading comprehension, mathematical computation and spelling.

Each of the academic tests used has several levels, each level intended for a particular grade. To reduce floor and ceiling effects, subjects were, where appropriate, given a level of a test below or above the level corresponding to the child's actual grade. To move to the next level of a given test, a child had to achieve a criterion of 80% correct. Because the LI children may not have been in a grade appropriate for their age, standardised grade equivalent scores could not be used. Thus, for the purpose of the analyses used in this study, for each test, raw scores were standardised to a scale of 0 to 100, with 100 corresponding to the highest score achieved by any child in the sample (normal or LI). However, because the distribution of scores differed for each test, these standardised scores are not directly comparable. For example, a score of 70 on the decoding test would not necessarily be equivalent to a score of 70 on the mathematics test.

Normal vs LI children: pre-reading measures

The three pre-reading measures were given annually at ages 5 to 8. However, statistical comparison of scores was performed only at age 5, as by age 6 ceiling effects began to occur in the control group. Mean values at age 5 showed that scores for the normal group were consistently higher than for the LI group on the Visual Discrimination (VD) sub-test, the Letter Form (LF) sub-test, and on the Letter Sound (LS) sub-test. A multivariate analysis of variance was used to compare scores for normal and LI children, using scores on these three CTBS sub-tests as dependent variables and group (normal vs LI) as a between-subjects effect. This analysis confirmed that the overall performance of the LI group was significantly poorer than that of the control group; follow-up testing revealed significant effects for the Letter Sound and Letter Form tests, but not for Visual Discrimination.

The second stage of analysis compared the percentage of LI and normal children achieving competent performance for each sub-test at ages 6 to 8, where competent performance was defined as a score within one point of the maximum (which ranged from 18 to 21 points) for each sub-test. For the Visual Discrimination sub-test, between group differences were significant at age 6, age 7 and age 8. For the Letter Form sub-test, differences were significant only at age 6. For the Letter Sound sub-test, differences were significant at age 6 and age 7, but not at age 8. These data indicate that the LI children were slower than the normal children to acquire pre-reading skills, but by age 8 most had done so. On the Visual Discrimination sub-test, however, many LI children and some normal children were continuing to acquire these visual processing skills even at age 8.

Normal vs LI children: academic domains

Each of the five academic domains (decoding, reading vocabulary, reading comprehension, spelling and mathematical computation) was assessed at ages 6, 7 and 8. The results revealed that, across the five domains, the LI children performed more poorly than the controls. Moreover, a significant interaction between group and age indicated that the LI children were developing at a different rate over the years, as compared with the control children. To better evaluate group differences, each academic domain was evaluated separately. For all five academic domains, there were highly significant main effects for group and age, and for the interaction of group by age. Furthermore, differences between normal and LI children increased from age 6 to age 8 for all academic domains; for certain measures, (notably decoding and reading vocabulary), the rate of improvement from age 6 to age 8 was very rapid for controls, whereas the same profile was not seen for the LI children.

These results suggest that rather than catching up, the LI children are actually falling further behind their unimpaired classmates in the early elementary school years, at least in some domains. To further examine this possibility, the LI children's scores in all academic domains at all ages were converted to standard deviations from the normal means. These data, given in Table 10.2, demonstrate that the magnitude of the standard deviation scores of the LI children are increasing from age 6 to age 7, indicating that they are indeed falling even further behind. From age 7 to age 8 the standard deviation scores indicate that these children's deficit remains the same across all academic domains assessed. This finding clearly indicates that no improvement or 'catching up' has occurred.

Individual patterns of performance

The main effects of the group in the above analyses indicate that, in terms of mean test scores, the LI children show deficits in all academic areas assessed, at all ages tested. However, as mean data can obscure individual patterns of performance, the data were examined in more detail. Tables 10.3 and 10.4 give the results of individual subjects' performance for approximately the first one-third of children completing the five-year longitudinal study (Table 10.3 for the LI children and Table 10.4 for the controls). The first two columns list the non-verbal IQ scores for year 1 of the study at induction at age 4 and for year 5 of the study when the subjects were 8 years old.

It will be recalled that, at age 4, all subjects met the study entry criteria requiring a non-verbal IQ of 85 or above and the LI and control groups were matched for IQ. By the fifth year of the study the IQ of 11 of the first 18 LI subjects completing the study had dropped by more than 10 points. However, a similar trend was also seen in the control group with 6 of the first 18 subjects showing an IQ score at age 8 more than 10 points below their age 4 score. This indicates that the Leiter test may score higher for a 4-year-old than for an 8-year-old child. Of concern, however, is that whereas none of the control children failed to reach the study criterion of an IQ of 85 or above at age 8, several LI children showed IQs in ranges lower than 85 by age 8, at least as measured by the Leiter. Thus, some children who clearly met the criteria as SLI at age 4, no longer did at age 8. Have these children changed from

Table 10.2 Mean performance of LI children expressed as standard deviations from normal means

Domain	Age 6	Age 7	Age 8
Spelling	−0.5	−0.8	−0.8
Math	−0.4	−0.9	−0.7
Decoding	−0.4	−0.7	−0.7
Vocabulary	−0.7	−1.1	−1.1
Comprehension	−0.6	−0.9	−1.0

Table 10.3 Performance of language impaired children

Nonverbal IQ		CYCLE[1]		Attainments			
				VOC[2]	COMP[3]	SPELL	MATH
YR 1	YR 5	Receptive Age level	Expressive Age level	%ile	%ile	%ile	%ile
91	68	3	3	<1	<1	<1	<1
93	72	5	3	<1	<1	<1	<1
98	73	3	3	<1	<1	1	<1
90	107	7	5	<1	<1	<1	8
96	113	4	5	<1	<1	<1	49
104	91	4	3	<1	<1	<1	<1
106	85	4	5	7	<1	21	38
116	100	7	5	<1	<1	1	97
125	118	5	3	<1	<1	2	<1
115	79	6	5	<1	<1	<1	<1
94	102	6	5	<1	<1	<1	3
109	94	7	7	<1	<1	2	<1
111	87	3	5	<1	<1	6	2
111	104	7	5	<1	<1	1	4
104	89	5	7	<1	<1	<1	1
120	101	7	5	<1	<1	26	8
104	103	4	5	<1	<1	23	22
102	103	7	5	<1	<1	61	<1

1. Curtiss, Yamada Comprehensive Language Evaluation
2. Reading Vocabulary
3. Reading Comprehension

Table 10.4. Performance of normally developing children

Nonverbal IQ		CYCLE[1]		Attainments			
				VOC[2]	COMP[3]	SPELL	MATH
YR 1	YR 5	Receptive Age level	Expressive Age level	%ile	%ile	%ile	%ile
113	124	8	9	98	79	89	97
96	112	7	9	98	98	89	97
123	97	7	9	<1	<1	<1	6
104	108	7	8	<1	<1	1	33
114	112	6	8	<1	<1	2	33
118	110	9	9	98	98	89	97
118	89	9	9	76	62	80	38
116	109	89	9	73	79	92	97
124	103	8	9	<1	<1	2	<1
123	129	7	9	<1	<1	<1	4
122	95	9	9	62	50	24	36
116	130	9	9	99	98	97	72
123	121	9	9	62	79	97	72
120	110	9	9	79	79	92	79
109	119	8	9	92	50	72	73
102	110	6	6	86	76	52	97
110	95	7	9	79	86	11	39
111	86	7	9	99	99	95	97

1.Curtiss, Yamada Comprehensive Language Evaluation   N=18
2.Reading Vocabulary
3.Reading Comprehension

SLI to more generally mentally retarded? Was the initial diagnosis incorrect for these children? Are the Leiter and other IQ tests stable enough across ages to base important diagnostic decisions on them for LI children? These are important concerns raised by these data which require further study.

It is also interesting to note that the drop in IQ score does not seem to be directly related to language or reading outcomes for either the LI or control children. Some of the control children with the largest IQ decrements nonetheless have relatively good language and reading outcomes, whereas others do not. The same pattern is true for the LIs. Thus, change in IQ does not seem to relate to language or academic achievement outcomes in this study.

Language outcomes in the fifth year of the longitudinal study when the subjects were between the age of 8 and 9 years are also shown for the Curtiss, Yamada Comprehensive Language Evaluation (CYCLE). These are given as the highest level reached in terms of age-equivalent scores. For example, a score of 4 indicates that 80% of 4-year-old normal children pass this level. As can be seen, the highest receptive language level and the highest expressive language level on the CYCLE for the controls ranged from 6 to 9 years with the mean score approximately 8 years, which is what would be expected for 8- to 9-year-old control children. The language outcome scores for the LI subjects are considerably lower, ranging from 3 to 7 years. Not one of the LI children scored in an age-appropriate range in either receptive or expressive language, indicating that all of these children diagnosed at age 4 as SLI have remained significantly language impaired at age 8.

Reading vocabulary, comprehension and spelling outcomes are also clearly dismal for these LI children, with virtually all of these LI children being non-readers throughout the third grade. Although mathematics scores are somewhat higher for several LI children, they are, nonetheless, impaired for the majority of children. As expected, the control children show a normal distribution of scores in academic achievement measures. These data show that the majority of LI children appear to have global deficits in all academic areas assessed rather than a specific deficit in language-based academic areas (i.e., reading and spelling).

We next investigated whether LI children were more likely to show specific deficits in reading, as opposed to more global academic achievement deficits. Each child was defined as having a specific reading deficit at age 8 if the following criteria were met:

1. reading scores more than 0.5 standard deviations below the normal mean;
2. maths scores within 0.5 standard deviations of the normal mean;
3. reading scores at least 0.5 standard deviations below maths scores.

A specific mathematics deficit was defined similarly. Recall that only mathematical computation (not word problems) was assessed in an attempt to limit the impact of verbal deficiencies on mathematical concepts. Using these criteria, 11 of the 67 LI children could be defined as having a specific reading deficit, whilst only one had a specific math deficit. Of the 54 controls, five showed a specific reading deficit whilst one met the criteria for a specific math deficit. Thus, although the majority of LI children showed severe academic achievement deficits during the early elementary school years assessed in this longitudinal study, few showed deficits specific to reading. For both LI and normal children, specific reading disabilities were more common than specific math disabilities, which were very infrequent, at least in the lower grades.

In order to assess individual differences in rate of development of academic skills, the number of LI children showing a change in relative performance across time was examined. Of particular interest were two groups of children: those showing a significant decline in performance across time (in either mathematics or total reading scores), and those showing a significant improvement. A significant decline was coded if the following criteria were met:

1. a decline of at least 0.5 standard deviations from age 6 to age 8;
2. age 8 scores at least 0.5 standard deviations below the normal mean.

A significant improvement was coded if the following criteria were met:

1. age 6 scores at least 0.5 standard deviations below the normal mean;
2. an increase of at least 0.5 standard deviations from age 6 to age 8.

Results showed that LI children were much more likely than normal children to show a significant decline, from age 6 to age 8, both in reading and in mathematical performance. Also, LI children were somewhat less likely than normal children to show a significant improvement in reading (one LI, six normal) and to a lesser degree in mathematics (six LI, eight normal), although these differences were not significant.

Correlations between and within academic domains

As a final way of looking at the data, correlational analyses were completed. Correlations among the five academic domains were all highly significant, and the patterns of correlations were quite similar for LI and normal children at age 6 and age 8 (see Table 10.5). Correlations between mathematical and other academic skills ranged from 0.48 to 0.77, with higher correlations at age 8 than at age 6 years. Correlations between language-based academic skills, decoding, reading and spelling were higher, ranging from 0.52 to 0.95. These correlations were generally higher at age 6 than at age 8. The lowest correlations occurred between decoding and other academic skills at age 8, especially for the LI children.

Table 10.5 Correlations Between Academic Domains for Normally Developing (ND) and Language Impaired (LI) Children.

	Age 6		Age 8	
Domains	N	LI	N	LI
Math/Spelling	.47	.51	.68	.71
Decoding	.53	64	.64	.46
Vocabulary	.67	.59	.75	.77
Comprehension	.49	.52	.77	.77
Spelling/Decoding	.75	.67	.64	.60
Vocabulary	.80	.95	.77	.89
Comprehension	.81	.85	.69	.82
Decoding/Vocabulary	.68	.75	.70	.52
Comprehension	.63	.68	.67	.55
Vocabulary/Comprehension	.93	.91	.86	.89

Table 10.6 Within group correlations of academic achievement scores across time (age 6 and age 8)

Variable	Normal	LI
Math	0.64	0.66
Spelling	0.63	0.60
Decoding	0.62	0.62
Vocabulary	0.70	0.64
Comprehension	0.68	0.68

Within each academic domain, age 6 scores were correlated with age 8 scores, separately for each group. Table 10.6 shows that again all correlations were highly significant, and that patterns of correlations were very similar for LI and normal subjects. The strength of the correlations was very similar across academic domains for both groups, ranging from 0.60 to 0.70.

Assessing the Evidence

Academic outcomes of LI children

The first and second questions addressed in the present study focused on whether children with pre-school language impairments experience difficulties in developing pre-reading and academic skills, and if so, on the extent and severity of those difficulties. Three conventional pre-reading measures (visual discrimination, letter forms and letter sounds) were administered to LI and normal children at ages 5 to 8 years. Results indicated that LI children performed more poorly than their normal counterparts on each measure at age five. Furthermore, although most normal children had reached ceiling performance on these measures by age 8, a substantial number of LI children had still not reached ceiling performance by this age. These results indicate that many LI children experience difficulties performing a number of basic skills, presumed to be prerequisite for reading success, before entering school, and that some LI children remain deficient in these skill areas even well after school entry.

At ages 6 to 8 (generally corresponding to grades 1 to 3), performance in five academic domains (mathematics, spelling, decoding, reading vocabulary and comprehension) was tested. Results indicated that LI children showed marked deficits in all academic domains across all years of the longitudinal study. These data clearly indicate that preschool language impairments are predictive of later academic difficulty.

Examination of individual patterns of performance generally confirmed the above findings. Although there was some overlap between normal and LI children in range of scores, the LI children were clearly concentrated at the lower end of the continuum.

Global vs specific academic deficits

The third question addressed in the present study was whether LI children show global deficits in all subject areas, or, rather, selective deficits in language-related areas, especially reading. This question was addressed in several ways. First, results of an analysis of variance indicated that LI children showed highly significant deficits in all domains tested, including mathematics. It is important to recall that only mathematical computation was assessed to keep the evaluation of mathematical skills as 'language-free' as possible. Nonetheless, the LI subjects clearly demonstrated deficits in mathematical computation. Second, correlational analyses indicated strong correlations between maths scores and reading vocabulary and comprehension scores, suggesting that children who showed deficits in one domain were likely to show deficits in the other. Third, examination of individual patterns of performance indicated that specific reading deficits were infrequent in LI children, although they were considerably more frequent than specific maths deficits, and more frequent in LI than in control children. It should be noted that LI children were more likely than normal children to show a significant decline in academic performance across time; this was especially the case for reading. Thus, it may be the case that LI children's deficits become more specific to reading over time. In order to determine this it will be necessary to follow language-impaired children over a more protracted period of development.

Change in academic performance across time

The fourth research question concerned changes in academic performance across time. Results of an analysis of variance revealed a significant interaction between group and age, indicating that LI children were
not showing the same rate of change as normal children. Closer examination of this interaction showed that differences between LI and
normal children were increasing from age 6 to age 7, and stabilised from
age 7 to age 8. Another level of analysis focused on individual patterns
of performance. These analyses indicated that a substantial number of
LI children showed significant declines in performance in both reading
and mathematics. Very few LI children, in contrast, showed significant
improvement. In sum, these results suggest that at least some LI
children may show increasing academic difficulties throughout their
school years.

Conclusions from the Longitudinal Study

The results of this longitudinal study of the development of pre-reading
and academic achievement skills in normally developing and specifically
language-impaired children clearly demonstrate that children ascertained in pre-school with developmental language disorders are at high
risk for developing deficits in academic skills in the early elementary
school years. These deficits appear to be global in nature, affecting
reading as well as other academic areas, for most of the language-
impaired children assessed. However, some children show specific
reading deficits. Little evidence supporting a hypothesis of developmental delay was found in this longitudinal study, at least for the time-
course under investigation (4 to 8 years old). That is, few of the LI
children showed evidence of delayed onset of either language or academic skills, with subsequent performance approaching normal limits.
On the contrary, the performance of the language-impaired children as
a group showed decline in comparison with their normal matched
controls, and a similar trend was found in examining individual subject
data.

What is the relationship between SLI and dyslexia?

Studies of children with specific developmental reading deficits
(dyslexia) have demonstrated that these children have significant
impairments on oral language tasks requiring phonological awareness,
and are impaired in their ability to name objects and process speech in
noise (Liberman, 1973; Liberman, et al., 1974). Thus, children with
reading disabilities have been shown to have difficulty on oral-language
as well as written-language tasks. Similarly, studies with dyslexic

children have demonstrated that they also have non-verbal perceptual and motor deficits, specifically in areas which require information to be perceived or produced rapidly in time, similar to those shown to characterise SLI children (Tallal & Stark, 1982). Tallal (1988) has suggested that a basic deficit in processing and producing information in rapid succession may underlie the phonological problems of reading-impaired children, by interfering with the discrimination and production of brief and rapidly changing cues within speech. This in turn would compromise phonological awareness and memory storage.

In an attempt to understand the possible relationship between developmental disorders of oral and written language, Stark and Tallal (1988) studied children with reading disability with or without concomitant oral language deficits. Results showed a clear relationship between the temporal perceptual-motor profiles of children with specific language impairment and the sub-group of dyslexic children who demonstrated oral phonological discrimination and language difficulties, as well as reading decoding deficits. Importantly, no relationship was found for dyslexics who demonstrated normal performance on tests of oral language or reading decoding. These studies suggested that there may be a developmental continuum between early language disorders and phonologically based reading disorders, both of which may be related to basic non-verbal temporal processing deficits. In other words, this basic processing constraint may disrupt the normal development of phonological processes differently across the age range, affecting oral language development in the early years and subsequent reading development in the school years.

The results of the present longitudinal study add additional support to the hypothesis that early language disorders predispose the child to subsequent deficits in academic achievement. The current study demonstrates that the majority of children with oral language deficits in preschool will have reading deficits in early elementary school. This study also indicates that the academic deficits may be both more global and less transient than previously thought, affecting mathematical as well as language-based skills.

Longitudinal studies have concurred in demonstrating a clear relationship between developmental language and reading disorders in the same child, across different ages. Nonetheless, these disorders continue, for the most part, to be defined, diagnosed, conceptualised and treated as distinct clinical and research entities. The results of this prospective longitudinal study, taken together with previous reports, suggest that, at least for children with developmental language impairment, it may be primarily the *age* of the child that differentiates developmental language from developmental reading impairment, as well as deficits in acquiring other academic skills (see Stackhouse & Wells, this volume). Thus, we may be observing the developmental course of a single deficit rather than two distinct syndromes in this group of children. That is not to suggest that all reading-impaired children also have oral language impairments or that early language impairment is the only route to reading impairment. However, empirical data from every prospective longitudinal study to date have demonstrated a clear relationship between developmental language and reading disorders. SLI children are clearly at great risk for global academic deficits, including reading and spelling.

There is now increasing evidence that a large percentage of children diagnosed as reading impaired also have a variety of oral language deficits including, but not limited to, the areas of phonological processing and awareness (see Snowling & Nation, this volume). There is also considerable overlap between the sensory, perceptual, motor and cognitive deficiencies that have been reported for SLI and reading-impaired children (see Stark & Tallal, 1988 for review). As such, it appears that at least a sub-group of children experiencing academic achievement deficits show a longitudinal profile beginning in the pre-school years as specific oral language disorder and manifesting itself in the early elementary school years as reading and other academic achievement deficits. For these children, therapeutic intervention needs to recognise the ongoing, yet changing nature of their basic language learning disability and focus on a more integrative approach to ameliorating their oral as well as written language-processing deficits as they proceed through the school years.

References

Aram, D.A., Ekelman, B. L. & Nation, J. E. (1984). Preschoolers with language disorders: 10 years later. *Journal of Speech and Hearing Research* 27, 232–244.

Beitchman, J. H., Nair, R., Ferguson, M. & Patel, P. G. (1986). Prevalence in psychiatric disorders in children with speech and language disorders. *Journal of the American Academy of Child Psychiatry* 24, 528-535.

Carrow, E. (1974). *Carrow Elicited Language Inventory*. Boston, MA: Teaching Resources.

Comprehensive Test of Basic Skills (1973). New York: McGraw Hill.

DiSimoni, F. (1970). *The Children's Token Test*. Allen, TX: Teaching Resources.

Gates, A. I., & MacGinitie, W. H. (1972). *Gates–MacGinitie Reading Tests*. New York: Teachers College Press.

Gates, A. I. & McKillop, A. (1966). *Phonics Tests*. New York: Columbia University Press.

Hall, P. K. & Tomblin, J. B. (1978). A follow-up study of children with articulation and language disorders. *Journal of Speech and Hearing Disorders* 43, 227–241.

Hedrick, D. E., Prather, E. M. & Tobin, A. R. (1979). *Sequenced Inventory of Communication Development*. Seattle, WA: University of Washington Press.

Lee, L. (1971). *Northwestern Syntax Screening Test (NSST)*. Evanston, IL: Northwestern University Press.

Liberman, I. Y. (1973). Segmentation of the spoken word and reading acquisition. *Bulletin of the Orton Society* 23, 65–77.

Liberman, I. Y., Shankweiler, D., Fischer, F. W. & Carter, B. (1974). Explicit syllable and phoneme segmentation in the young child. *Journal of Experimental Child Psychology* **18**, 201–212.

Silva, P. A. (1980). The prevalence, stability and significance of developmental language delay in preschool children. *Developmental Medicine and Child Neurology* **22**, 768–777.

Silva, P. A., McGee, R. & Williams, S. M. (1983). Developmental language delay from three to seven years and its significance for low intelligence and reading difficulties at age seven. *Developmental Medicine and Child Neurology* **25**, 783–793.

Stark, R. E. & Tallal, P. (1988). *Language, Speech, and Reading Disorders in Children: Neuropsychological Studies*, Ed. R. J. McCauley. Boston, MA: College-Hill Press.

Stark, R. E., Bernstein, L. E., Condino, R., Bender, M., Tallal, P. & Catts, H. (1984). Four-year follow-up study of language impaired children. *Annals of Dyslexia* **34**, 49–68.

Tallal, P. (1988). Developmental language disorders. In J. F. Kavanaugh & T. J. Truss, Jr. (Eds.) *Learning Disabilities: Proceedings from the National Conference.* Parkton, MD: York Press.

Tallal, P. & Stark, R. E. (1982). Perceptual/motor profiles of reading impaired children with or without concomitant oral language deficits. *Annals of Dyslexia* **32**, 163–176.

Tallal, P., Curtiss, S. & Kaplan, R. (1988). The San Diego Longitudinal Study: Evaluating the outcomes of preschool impairments in language development. In S. E. Gerber & G. T. Mencher (Eds.) *International Perspectives on Communication Disorders*. Washington, DC: Gallaudet University Press.

Tallal, P., Dukette, D. & Curtiss, S. (1989). Behavioral/emotional profiles of preschool language-impaired children. *Developmental and Psychopathology* **1**, 51–67.

Chapter 11
How do Speech and Language Problems affect Literacy Development?

JOY STACKHOUSE AND BILL WELLS

When normally developing children begin school at around the age of 5 years, they already have a well-developed speech processing system for spoken language. This chapter will examine this speech processing system and how it is the foundation for both speech and literacy development. It will be argued that phonological awareness comprises a range of speech-processing skills and is the vehicle through which children apply their knowledge about spoken language to literacy. Children with persisting speech difficulties may perform poorly on phonological awareness tasks and may be at risk for literacy problems because their speech processing system is underdeveloped. To illustrate how this might be the case the chapter will present a speech processing perspective on phonological awareness and literacy development, and the relationship between speech and literacy will be explored by comparing developmental phase models for both.

The Speech-Processing System

The speech processing system comprises input systems for receiving spoken information (mainly auditory information, but visual information is also important for processing facial expression and lip-reading cues) and output systems for selecting and producing spoken words and sentences. In addition, the child needs to store linguistic information about spoken language in a variety of representations (a means for keeping information about words) within the lexicon (a store of word knowledge). Figure 11.1 illustrates the basic essentials of such a psycholinguistic model of speech processing.

On the left of the model in Figure 11.1 there is a channel for the input of information via the ear/eye and on the right a channel for the output of information through the mouth. At the top of the model there are the lexical representations which store previously processed

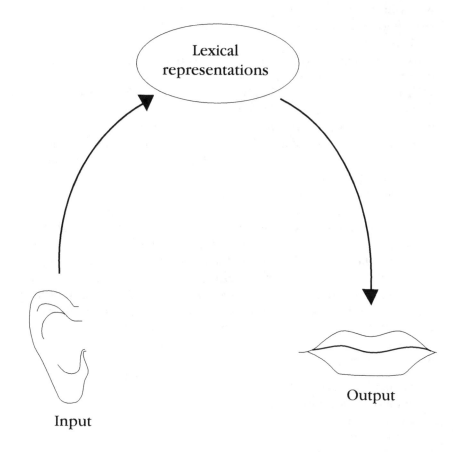

Figure 11.1 The basic structure of the speech-processing system

information, whilst at the bottom there is no such store. Within this model, *top-down* processing refers to when previously stored information (i.e. in the lexical representations) is used. A *bottom-up* processing activity is less dependent on stored linguistic knowledge and may be completed without accessing the lexical representations.

What are Lexical Representations?

Storing accurate information about words is part of the normal development of spoken language. To reflect on what a child has to learn about words, consider what you know about the word *cat*.

One of the first things you might have noted is what the word means – you have a *semantic representation* for this word which stores information about the attributes of a cat (e.g. small furry domestic animal with whiskers) and you may have classified it along with similar animals (e.g. dog), or other cats (e.g. tame versus wild). You can discriminate the spoken word from other similarly sounding words (e.g. *cat ~ cap*), and can detect speech errors made in that word (e.g. *tat* for *cat*). You therefore have a *phonological representation* for *cat*, which stores enough information to allow a word to be identified on the basis of auditory and visual (e.g. lip reading) cues. You also know how to say the word *cat*; you do not have to work this out every time you want to produce the word. This stored set of instructions for the pronunciation of the word is the *motor programme*. However, you do not produce this word in isolation very often. It is more likely to be put into a sentence structure, e.g. 'Have you fed the cat?'. Part of your knowledge of *cat* is that it belongs to a certain class of word (i.e. nouns), which can be used in some positions in the sentence but not others, and which has a plural form (i.e. *cats*) that can be derived by rule. Such knowledge is stored in your *grammatical representation* for the word *cat*. Finally, you have no trouble recognising the printed form of this word and do not have to assemble letters one by one when you want to spell it. You have therefore stored information about what this word looks like in its printed form and this is held in your *orthographic representation*. In summary, information about a word is stored in the following representations within the lexicon:

- semantic representation;
- phonological representation;
- motor programme;
- grammatical representation;
- orthographic representation.

By developing this speech-processing system for the purpose of spoken communication, children develop awareness of the sounds and structure of their language. This allows them to match spoken output with the written form, e.g. through letter knowledge and orthographic experience. This speech-processing system, developed primarily to deal with spoken language, is therefore also the foundation for written language development.

A Speech-processing Perspective on Reading and Spelling

Intact input processing skills are necessary for the child to discriminate and understand spoken and written language. Reading comprehension is underpinned by the child's existing verbal language comprehension skills (Stothard, 1996). When reading, however, processing words for meaning does not always happen. It is quite possible for skilled adult readers to read text silently or out loud perfectly well but have no recollection or understanding of what has been read! This may also be the case for young readers who have learned how to decode words written on a page into a spoken form but may not understand the vocabulary or sentence structure being used in the text. This is not construed as a problem as it is through reading that children can develop their vocabulary and grammatical knowledge. In normal development top-down and bottom-up skills are associated. However, in atypical development a *hyperlexic* condition may arise where language comprehension – a top-down processing skill – is not developing in line with bottom-up decoding skills (i.e. converting the written form to spoken words) and a *dissociation* or lack of connection occurs between bottom-up decoding skills and top-down comprehension skills. Hyperlexia has been reported in children with autism who may read aloud perfectly well and be able to decode unfamiliar words but who do not have any understanding of what they have read. Thus, when reading for comprehension, whether single words or continuous text, top-down processing has to be involved because prior linguistic knowledge is necessary for understanding; this prior knowledge is stored in the semantic and grammatical representations.

Some children described as dyslexic may have the opposite dissociation. Their bottom-up decoding difficulties are out of line with their verbal comprehension skills and prevent them accessing intact but separate semantic representations. Subtle auditory discrimination problems can lead to difficulties in speech and spelling in particular. Children who cannot detect the differences between similar sounds (e.g.'p' ~ 'b'; 's' ~ 'sh'; 'f' ~ 'th', or 'w' ~ 'r'), or sequences of sounds in clusters (e.g. 'st' ~ 'ts' as in *lots* ~ *lost*), will lay down imprecise or 'fuzzy' phonological representations of words containing these sounds and clusters. For example, if a child cannot discriminate between *pin* and *bin* the phonological representation for these two words may be the same, i.e. only one phonological representation for both words instead of two separate ones. The child may however have two semantic representations for these items if he or she knows their meaning and recognises visually both items as distinct.

This was the case for Zoe; a girl aged 5;11 with speech difficulties (Stackhouse & Wells, 1993). She was unable to discriminate between minimal pair words containing the voicing contrast on the *Auditory Discrimination and Attention Test* (Morgan-Barry, 1988) even though she recognised the items: *pear~bear, fan~van, coat~goat, lock~log*. This was reflected in her early spellings and was still a problem for her when she was followed up at 9 years of age:

C.A. 5;11		C.A. 9;8	
Target	*Spelling*	*Target*	*Spelling*
pet	bt	sink	sing
cap	cb	desk	disg
trap	tb	pyjamas	beg

Similarly, Thomas aged 8;6 had difficulties discriminating between frica-tive sounds (e.g. f, s, sh, th) at the beginning and ends of words. He also had difficulties with these sounds in speech and spelling, for example 'sh' was pronounced as 'th' and transcribed as <ch>:

Target	*Speech*	*Spelling*
shadow	thadow	chadow
membership	memberthip	memberchip

and 'sh' and 'ch' were transcribed as <s>:

Target	*Spelling*
refreshment	refresment
adventure	edvenser

Thomas's speech and language therapist targeted these sounds in audi-tory phonological awareness and speech output activities. This resulted in spontaneous improvement in his spelling skills and by 9 years of age he had no difficulties in producing or transcribing fricative sounds (Stackhouse, 1996).

On the output side of the model, reading aloud single familiar words is normally a top-down activity because the child can utilise stored ortho-graphic representations and read words 'automatically'. Reading aloud new and therefore unfamiliar words is a bottom-up activity because there is no stored orthographic representation and therefore the word needs to be decoded by using letter-to-sound conversion rules (e.g., the letter b is pronounced [b]). When these sounds have been abstracted from the letters they can be blended together to form the new word. An alterna-tive strategy for reading new words which is both bottom-up and top-down is to read the word by analogy with a known and similar word (top-down) but then make the necessary changes via applying bottom-up skills. For example, if a child can read the word *cat* and is asked to read a new word, mat, he or she can recognise that the new word has *at* as in *cat* (top-down) but that the new word has a different first letter, i.e. m. By decoding (bottom-up) this as the sound [m] and attaching it to the segmented and familiar at he or she can produce the new word mat.

Correct spelling requires knowledge of the conventions for how words are formed in a particular language. When spelling familiar words children draw on stored spellings in their orthographic representations.

This top-down approach to spelling may be described as 'automatic' spelling in that children can output quickly words with which they are familiar and for which they already have a stored spelling programme.

Sometimes a child will be asked or will want to write familiar words (i.e. words already in his or her vocabulary) for which he or she has not yet developed an orthographic representation. If the word is in the child's *spoken* vocabulary, there will be a stored motor programme for speaking the word that can be used as a basis for spelling. If the word is in the child's *receptive* vocabulary only, i.e. the child can recognise it as distinct from other words but does not use it in speech output, then there will be a stored phonological representation from which a motor programme can be derived and used to support spelling.

However, a child may be asked to spell a word that he or she has never heard or seen before. In this case there are no stored representations to draw on. The child will therefore need to hold on to the word in a temporary store in order to segment it into its components and allocate appropriate letters. One way of doing this is to assemble a new motor programme from the temporary auditory image so that the word can be rehearsed verbally (this may be sub-vocally, i.e. not necessarily out loud) which gives the child an opportunity to reflect on the word's structure. For example, a common strategy children use when they are trying to work out the components of a word is to elongate it or emphasise different aspects of it such as its beginning or end. Once a child has worked out the segments that make up the new word, he or she is in a good position to assign corresponding letters. Spelling can therefore take place by decoding the word heard into its segments and allocating the appropriate graphemes. This bottom-up approach to spelling is typical of beginner spellers who may be quite happy to output clearly segmented units that are incorrect in terms of conventional spelling rules but logical in terms of their components, (e.g. the spelling of *Giraffe* as <jrarf>, from a child with a Southern British English accent). However, experienced spellers will use top-down processing as well, checking their output for spelling conventions or making analogies with the spellings of known similar words stored in their orthographic representations.

Children with speech output difficulties are disadvantaged when it comes to rehearsing words prior to spelling them. Children described as having phonological impairments or verbal dyspraxia are particularly vulnerable. These children may not be able to pronounce a word in the same way on different occasions. For example if asked to pronounce *buttercup* three times in succession a child with dyspraxia may say: 'butterpuk, tupperbuk, bukertup'. This makes it impossible to segment the word into its components prior to allocating the appropriate graphemes to the segments. Such was the case for Keith who at age 14 announced:

If I can't say it I can't split it up! (Stackhouse, 1992a).

He had difficulty spelling longer words, particularly if they contained clusters or a sequence of sounds comprising two or more of w, r, l, y, for example:

Target	*Spelling*
mysterious	mistreriles
familiar	ferminiler
amateur	aminayture

Adopting this speech-processing perspective on reading and spelling illustrates how a child's literacy development is dependent on intact speech input and output skills as well as accurate phonological representations. Phonological awareness skills are also a product of this speech-processing system and are essential for connecting speech and literacy development (Stackhouse, 1997).

A Speech-processing Perspective on Phonological Awareness Skills

Phonological awareness refers to the ability to reflect on and manipulate the structure of an utterance as distinct from its meaning. It is tested by a range of tasks which include rhyme knowledge, syllable or sound segmentation and manipulation, and blending (Lewkowicz, 1980). Children need to develop this awareness in order to make sense of an alphabetic script, such as English, when learning to read and to spell. For example, children have to learn that the segments (the consonants and vowels) in a word can be represented by a written form – letters. When spelling a new word, children have to be able to divide the word into its segments before they can attach the appropriate letters. When reading an unfamiliar word, they have to be able to decode it by converting the printed letters into segments and blending them together to form the word.

The development of phonological awareness is dependent on the speech processing system presented in Figure 11.1 being intact. Tests of phonological awareness are important because they tap the integrity of this underlying speech-processing system. Children with poor phonological awareness have a faulty or immature speech-processing system, and therefore have a weak foundation for the development of literacy skills. It is not surprising that children with problems of phonological awareness often have associated speech and literacy problems as all depend upon the child's speech-processing system. Figure 11.2 illustrates the relationship between speech, literacy and phonological awareness and how all three behaviours are dependent on the speech-processing system. However, currently popular phonological awareness tests rarely make this connection explicit and children's phonological awareness skills are often assessed in isolation from their speech skills.

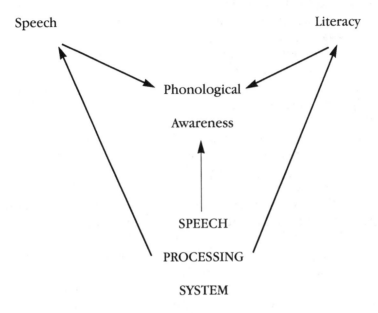

Figure 11.2 The connection between speech and literacy development

Let us examine some popular phonological awareness tasks (rhyme, sound segmentation, blending and spoonerisms) from this speech-processing perspective.

Rhyme

Rhyme tasks are widely used in assessment and teaching (Bradley & Bryant, 1983; Catts & Vartiainen, 1993; Frederikson, 1995; Hatcher, 1994; Layton & Deeney, 1996; Stackhouse, 1992b). Rhyme ability is an important measure of a child's speech-processing skills and can be observed at quite a young age. To understand the concept of rhyme, children need to detect what it is that rhyming words have in common and also how they differ from each other. For example, the words *cat*, *mat*, *brat*, *splat* all have the same *rime*: i.e. the vowel and any conso-nant(s) following the vowel (in this case: at), but differ in their *onsets*, i.e. any consonant(s) preceding the vowel (in this case: c, m, br, spl). Rhyme skills therefore reflect an understanding of the syllable structure onset/rime.

Children begin to develop their rhyme knowledge through exposure to nursery rhymes and songs. This experience can then be mapped on to increasing exposure to letters and the printed word. Having developed the ability to segment onsets from rimes (e.g. c/at, m/at, br/at, spl/at), children are in a good position to match what they see in the written form to what they hear spoken. The ability to segment onset and rime in words facilitates reading and spelling by analogy with known words (Goswami, 1994; Muter, 1996). For example, when confronted by the printed word *hat* for the first time, a child who can already read (or spell) *cat* and *mat* will recognise the rime *at* as a chunk [at] from known words but detect that the new word has a different onset. Through letter knowledge, the child can read the onset as [h] and then blend [h] + [at] to read the new word *hat*. When spelling, he or she may already have a motor programme for writing at which can be utilised. This is much more economical than having to segment every bit of a new word and blend it together, as in [h] [a] [t] → *hat* when reading, or allocating letters to each bit when spelling.

Without the understanding that syllables can be divided into an onset/rime structure, each word in the rhyme string *cat, mat, hat, fat, sat, rat, bat, flat, brat, splat, sprat* would have to be learned as a separate item rather than being incorporated into an existing sound family of -*at* words. Children with speech and literacy problems have specific difficulties developing these rhyme connections and are consequently disadvantaged when learning to read and spell (Bird & Bishop 1992; Marion, Sussman & Marquardt, 1993; Wells, Stackhouse & Vance, 1996). It is therefore important to assess rhyme skills routinely as part of a psycholinguistic investigation because this assessment can uncover speech-processing problems that may alert us to actual or potential literacy problems.

There is a range of rhyme tasks available which can be used to tap different levels of speech processing in children. Broadly, these can be divided into (a) *rhyme judgement* – deciding whether two items rhyme or not, e.g. *fan~van, fan~fin*; (b) *rhyme detection* – deciding which items in a sequence of items rhyme and which do not, e.g. *fan van pin*; and (c) *rhyme production* – producing verbally a word or a string of words that rhyme with a given target. Stimulus items can be presented verbally by the tester or visually via pictures. If a picture presentation is used for (a) and (b) above, the child can respond silently by pointing to the picture(s) he or she believes to be the correct response or by naming the correct picture. If a verbal presentation is given, non-word items can be used as well as words.

Our rhyme test battery includes the following five tasks (from Vance, Stackhouse & Wells, 1994):

1. Rhyme judgement of words (spoken/auditory presentation and no pictures), e.g. Do these rhyme?: *cat hat*; Do these rhyme? *cat shoe*. The child has to respond 'yes' or 'no'.
2. Rhyme judgement of non-words (spoken/auditory presentation),

e.g. Do these rhyme?: lat dat; Do these rhyme? lat foo. The child responds 'yes' or 'no' as in Task 1 above.

3. Rhyme detection – auditory presentation (no pictures), e.g. Tester presents three finger puppets. Each one says a word. The child points to the two puppets which said the rhyming words in the following: *shell*, *bell*, sea; *bear*, boy, *chair*.

4. Rhyme detection – picture presentation (no auditory presentation), e.g. Point to which two pictures rhyme: *spoon*, *moon*, knife; *house*, horse, *mouse*.

5. Rhyme string production, e.g., Tell me as many words as you can that rhyme with (a) *cat*; (b) *tea*; (c) *goat*.

This range of rhyme tasks taps both input and output channels, as well as lexical representations. The speech-processing properties of these tests can be identified by answering the following three simple questions about each of the above (Stackhouse & Wells, 1997).

1. *Is this an input or an output test?* If the task requires the child to produce a verbal response (for example as in producing rhyming words) then it is an output task. If the verbal response required is merely 'yes' or 'no' this does not constitute an output task as the response could be made non-verbally by nodding or shaking the head, or pointing. If the child's response is non-verbal or silent, then the task is an input one.

2. *Does the child have lexical representations for the stimuli used in this task?* If the answer to this question is *No* (for example in a task using non-word stimuli), then the task will be less dependent on existing lexical representations than tasks where the answer is *yes*. If the answer is *Yes*, then a third question is posed.

3. *Does the child* have *to access these lexical representations in order to complete the task?* If the answer to this question is *Yes*, as for example in a task that uses picture rather than spoken stimuli, then the child will not be able to complete the task without accessing his or her own lexical representations and performance will be dependent on the precision of these representations.

By answering these questions about the five rhyme tasks above, it is possible to plot their location on the speech-processing model presented in Figure 11.1 to illustrate the psycholinguistic demands made by each task (see Figure11.3).

Rhyme judgement: words

Rhyme judgement (Task 1) is an input task because the verbal response required is minimal and could be replaced by a nod or shake of the

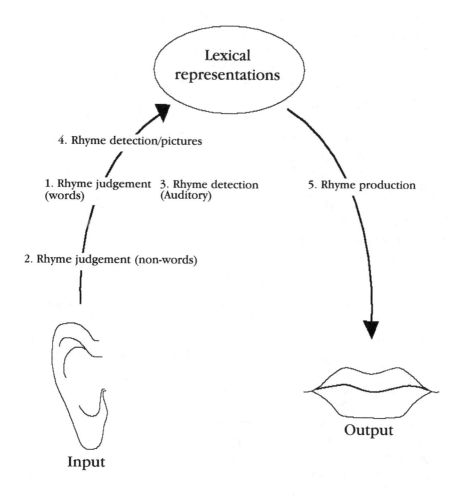

Figure 11.3 Location of rhyme tasks in the speech-processing model

head. In order to judge whether two words rhyme or not, the child has to detect the difference in the onsets and the commonality of the rime. The rhyme judgement task involving words can be completed without reference to the representations, i.e. the child does not have to know the meaning of the words to succeed on this task. The child may, however, use top-down processing to help him or her complete the task. This task has therefore been placed halfway between the ear and the representations.

Rhyme judgement: non-words

Rhyme judgement of non-words (Task 2) is also an input task but in contrast with Task 1 the child does not have lexical representations for the test items. This task has therefore been located around halfway between the ear and word rhyme judgement to mark that Tasks 1 and 2 may be treated differently by a child because top-down processing may be more helpful in the word task. Normally developing children perform equally well on these tasks. However, some children with speech and literacy difficulties may find the non-word task more difficult because they rely on top-down skills to compensate for weaker bottom-up skills.

Rhyme detection: auditory presentation – no pictures

Rhyme detection of auditorily presented words (Task 3) is another input task and involves the same skills as judging whether two words rhyme or not (Task 1); the only difference is that there are more words to remember. A choice has to be made about which word is different from two other words on the basis of its rhyme. Rhyme detection of real words has therefore been placed on the same level as rhyme judgement, but to the side, indicating that it is a more challenging task. This distinction is important as a child who succeeds on rhyme judgement tasks shows that he or she understands what is involved in rhyme, even if unable to do rhyme detection. In this case, his or her capacity for doing the task may be overloaded so that performance will break down even though the child has the basic skills to perform the task. A child with this profile will need a different focus in his or her remediation programme from one who cannot perform tasks of either rhyme judgement or detection because he or she does not understand the task. Here, the concept of rhyme needs to be introduced and developed.

Rhyme detection – picture presentation

Rhyme detection from picture presentation is another input task. Because the tester is not naming any of the pictures for the child, the child *has* to access his or her own representations in order to perform this task. First, the pictures have to be identified via the semantic representation before the child can conjure up the spoken form of the words to reflect on their structure and make a decision about which two rhyme. The rhyme detection from pictures task is therefore located high up on the left-hand side of the model to show that success on this task will depend on the child's ability not only to access his or her own representations but also the accuracy of those representations.

Although this task is meant to be 'silent' in that the child is not required to produce any rhyming words, normally developing children often name the pictures out loud as a means of rehearsal when carrying out the task. The importance of this verbal rehearsal strategy for at least some children is evident in the following response from a normally developing 4-year-old girl who, when asked if two pictures rhymed, replied:

> I don't think so yet, cos I haven't talked!

Vance et al. (1994) reported a developmental trend in this use of verbal rehearsal in their investigation of rhyme skills in a group of 100 children in the age range of 3–7 years. Verbal rehearsal was particularly apparent in 4-, 5- and 6-year-olds but declined in the 7-year-olds, who, were at ceiling (i.e., very successful) on the picture rhyme detection task. The smallest percentage of verbal rehearsal occurred in the group of 3-year-olds, who were struggling on this task and only performed at chance level (i.e. often just guessing the response). These findings suggest that verbal rehearsal is important when children are striving to perform the task but that it declines once children become proficient.

Clearly, this has implications for children with speech output difficulties who could be disadvantaged in the use of this rehearsal strategy. If accurate verbal rehearsal is, if not a prerequisite, at least a great help in learning to segment words in one's lexicon into onset and rime, then the inability to perform accurate rehearsal might be expected to have a negative effect on the development of onset-rhyme segmentation (Wells et al., 1996).

Rhyme production

Rhyme production is clearly an output task and it should therefore be located on the right-hand side of the model between the lexical representations and the mouth – but where? It is not purely a low-level articulatory task because awareness of the structure of words is needed. It would be easy to assume that children generate all their rhyme response from their lexicon by somehow connecting all the rhyming words they already know and producing them in a string. However, the finding that young normally developing children produce a mixture of word and non-word rhyme responses indicates that not all rhyme production responses are the result of such a lexical search (Vance et al., 1994). The non-words that children produce cannot be stored in the lexical representations, so must be being assembled at a level lower than the lexicon.

To generate rhymes there is a finite number of consonants that can go in the onset slot. Older children (and adults) can produce rhymes by changing the onsets by systematically working through the alphabet, dropping a different letter into the onset slot. For example, for what rhymes with *cat*, they may respond: 'At Bat Dat, Fat, Gat, Hat Jat, Lat', rejecting items that do not rhyme, e.g. Eat or Iat. This rhyme string inevitably includes non-words (Dat Gat Jat Lat) which may be rejected if only 'real' words have been requested by the tester.

There may therefore be more than one strategy for producing rhyming words. One approach to the task is to generate a rhyme string that has been stored in the lexicon. Some words have a large rhyme pool and are popular targets for rhyme tasks (e.g., *cat*) whereas others have small rhyme pools (e.g., *cup*) and therefore a restricted number of word responses. However, even when dealing with words from large rhyme pools, the length of a child's rhyme production string will be restricted by the extent of his or her vocabulary development and how efficiently rhyming words have been linked together within the lexicon. Unfortunately, a child with speech and literacy difficulties may have trouble setting up such connections within the lexicon and may need to adopt an alternative strategy.

This alternative strategy may be to generate rhyming words by filling in the onset slot through a sound or letter strategy as described above. Children can check their responses against their own representations and reject any non-words if only 'real' words have been requested. Children with speech and literacy difficulties also have difficulty with this strategy which may explain their persisting difficulty with rhyme production tasks (Bird & Bishop, 1992; Marion et al., 1993; Stackhouse & Snowling, 1992a; Stackhouse & Wells, 1991); both of the strategies normally employed to complete rhyme production tasks are problematic for them. In contrast, children without speech and literacy difficulties are able to employ both strategies; in fact, rhyme production skills are typically in advance of rhyme detection skills in normally developing children (Chaney, 1992; Reid et al., 1993; Vance et al., 1994).

Rhyme production is therefore located high up on the right-hand side of the model because performance on this task is facilitated by intact and well-connected lexical entries. However, it is not placed right at the top because it is not completely dependent on the lexical representations. In contrast with naming pictures, for example, which can only be derived from the child's lexical representations, for rhyme production there is an alternative lower level strategy of mechanically filling in the onset slot.

Examining rhyme tasks in this way shows how they can tell us more about the integrity of a child's underlying speech-processing system. The pattern of a child's performance on these tasks will indicate where difficulties are arising within his or her speech-processing system. We can classify other popular phonological awareness tasks in the same way to extend our assessment of a child's speech-processing skills, for example onset/coda knowledge (often referred to as 'sound segmentation'), blending and spoonerisms.

Onset/Coda Knowledge

The ability to detect the beginnings and ends of words and syllables is important when storing words and producing them in speech and spelling. In the description of rhyme tasks, we described the *rime* as the part of the syllable that includes the vowel and any following consonants. The consonants (or consonant) that follow the vowel are referred to as the *coda*, whilst the consonant or consonants preceding the rime are known as the *onset*. Thus, in the word *cat*, the onset/rime division is c/at, and the coda is *t*. Confusing sounds in onset or coda positions can lead to misunderstanding as well as errors in speech and spelling, for example if a child cannot discriminate between *cat* and *hat* or *cat* and *cap* (see the cases of Zoe and Thomas described above).

Blending

An assessment and teaching activity often used with school-age children is syllable and sound blending. This is when a child is presented with elements of a word, e.g. the syllables in *computer* (com-pu-ter) or the segments in *fish* (f-i-sh), and is asked to put them together to produce the word. The ability to do this correlates well with reading achievement and is a good predictor of reading performance (Fox & Routh, 1984; Perfetti, Beck, Bell & Hughes, 1987). The sound blending sub-test of the *Aston Index* (Newton & Thomson, 1982) comprises both word and non-word test items, e.g., p-o-t, d-i-nn-er, d-u-p, t-i-s-e-k. The same task is also referred to as auditory synthesis (cf. the *Fullerton Test of Adolescent Language*, Thorum, 1986), and is used in teaching programmes (e.g. Hatcher, 1994, 1996).

Children with speech and literacy problems have particular difficulties with sound-blending tasks. However, an isolated test result like this provides insufficient evidence to conclude that the child *cannot* blend the elements correctly; the problem may be that he or she is physically *unable* to produce the response verbally. An important principle of psycholinguistic assessment is that a minimum of two tasks, normally one silent and one involving some production, need to be administered to identify with any precision the difficulty the child is having.

Silent blending tests have been devised where the child is asked to point to the picture (Chaney, 1992; Counsel, 1993) or written word (Stackhouse, 1989) which represents the spoken target item. Here, unlike in production tasks, the child does not have to produce the word verbally. The finding that some children can succeed on such 'silent' tasks, even though they may have failed production blending tests, is encouraging, and for such a child this strength can be used when planning his or her remediation programme.

Spoonerisms

Spoonerisms are fun for older children who enjoy metalinguistic games. The process involves transposing onsets of initial syllables, e.g., Bill Wells

→ Will Bells; Joy Stackhouse → Stoy Jackhouse. The ability to perform spoonerisms is an advanced metalinguistic skill. Spoonerisms can therefore be a useful assessment tool for older children who can perform well on simpler phonological awareness tasks, such as rhyme or onset/coda tasks. It would seem that there are at least two general ways of tackling a spoonerism task. Feedback from normally developing children and adults suggests that many conjure up the orthographic image of the word (its spelling) and then visually transpose the first letter of the two words in order to read back the response. It is therefore not surprising that Perin (1983) found a strong correlation between the ability to perform a spoonerism task and the spelling skills of young teenagers. The second approach, as reported by unimpaired adults, is to deal with the whole process phonologically without any conscious recourse to the orthography.

Let us now classify other phonological awareness tasks in the same way as we did the rhyme tasks in Figure 11.3 by answering the same three questions (listed above) about the following sound segmentation tasks and plotting their location on our speech-processing model (see Figure 11.4).

1. Silent blending – Point to the picture of what I am saying: m-ou-se. Picture choice: *house cat mouse* (the three pictures per item are not exposed to the child until the segmented target word has been completed by the tester, from Counsel, 1993).
2. Silent coda detection – Point to the two pictures which end with the same sound: *tap, mop, dish*; *pen, watch, spoon*.
3. Phoneme supply – Child looks at a picture, e.g. a *fish*, but the tester does not name it. Child is asked to produce what the tester misses out when he or she produces the name of the picture, e.g. tester says '*fi_*'. The child should answer '*sh*' (from Muter, Snowling & Taylor, 1994).
4. Spoonerisms – Exchange the first sounds of the following: *cold tap, fat bear* (from Vint, 1993);.
5. Alliteration production – The child is asked to produce as many words as possible that begin with /k/ (e.g., Alliteration fluency subtest from the Phonological Assessment battery – PhAB – Frederikson, 1995).
6. Spoken blending of real words – Child produces the target word from the segments spoken by the tester: *sh-o-p, b-a-by* (from the *Aston Index*, Newton & Thomson, 1982).

Silent blending

The silent blending task (Task 1) is located high up on the left-hand side because it cannot be performed without accessing lexical representations. To do this task, a child has to take in the segments spoken and hold them in a temporary store while they are blended together to form a word. He or she then has to recognise the word and its meaning, which involves accessing both its phonological and semantic representations, in order to match it to a picture.

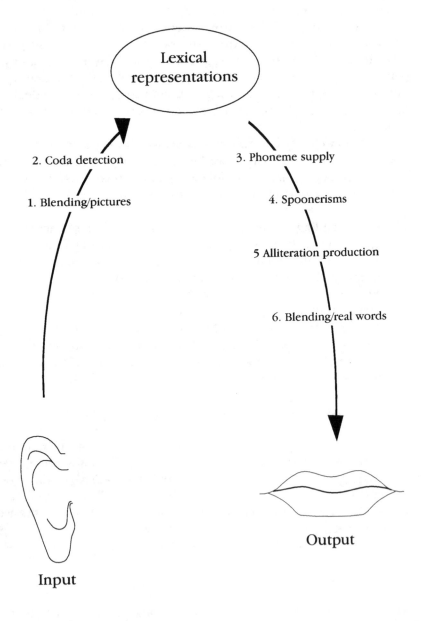

Figure 11.4 Location of phonological awareness tasks in the speech-processing model

Silent coda detection

This task (Task 2) is also located at the top left-hand side of the model around the same place as rhyme detection from pictures (compare Figure 11.3). These two tests cluster together because both rhyme detection from pictures and coda (or onset) detection from pictures are testing the child's awareness of the syllable structure of words they have had to access from their own representations. They are placed slightly above Task 1 (silent blending) because the child does not hear the target spoken by the tester in any form and is therefore totally reliant on his or her own representations.

Phoneme supply

Task 3 involves supplying the missing coda (last sound) and is therefore an output task. To perform this task, the child *has* to access his or her own representations via a picture in order to supply the coda (last sound) that has been omitted by the tester. It has therefore been placed at the highest level on the output side of the model as in order for the child to supply the correct coda he or she must have stored an accurate motor programme for the word.

Spoonerisms

Spoonerisms are located on the top right-hand side but beneath Task 3 (phoneme supply). Accessing the orthographic representation of the word can facilitate performance on this task. However, this may not be the case for those who report performing the task at an auditory level. For them it does not matter if the stimuli are words or not: they merely move the sounds around in a mechanical way. Spoonerisms could therefore be located at two places in the model: one at the top right and the other halfway down. This reminds us that among normally developing children (and adults) there is evidence of more than one way to complete a task; there is no reason why this should not be the case in atypical development too. It is also a reminder that when assessing a child, it can be helpful to ask him or her to describe how he or she completed the task. This can reveal, first, whether the child has any insight into what he or she is doing ('meta' skills), and, second, what strategies he or she is finding helpful which might be incorporated more explicitly into a remediation programme. Conversely, the child may have adopted strategies which limit performance and which may need to be eliminated or changed.

Alliteration production

This output task is similar to the rhyme production task discussed above (compare Figure 11.3). This time, however, the child has to focus on the onset of the word and change the rime. Rime and alliteration (onset) production are therefore both about manipulating phonological units and are located at the same position on the speech-processing model.

Spoken blending of words

This task is located halfway between the lexical representations and mouth on the output side of the model because although it might help to access the representations for this task, the child does not have to access them in order to complete it. In fact, normally developing children will often produce a correct response out loud and then show surprise that what they have said is a real word – one that they know. The opposite can occur in children with specific speech and literacy difficulties. When Michael aged 14;6 was asked to produce the word *pr-a-m*, he was unable to do so. He replied 'prom, promp .... we call it a pushchair!' (Stackhouse, 1993). Clearly, he had blended the segments sufficiently in his head to recognise and access the meaning of the word. His difficulty was in assembling the segments for production of the word. This was confirmed when he was 100% correct on a silent test of blending (like Task 1 but using printed words instead of pictures) but scored 0% on a blending production task. The case of Michael illustrates why one test result in isolation can be misleading and should not be used as a basis for a remediation programme.

Figures 11.3 and 11.4 illustrate how phonological awareness is not a separate entity in a child's development but an integral part of the speech-processing system. It is made up of auditory and speech production tasks which are dependent to varying degrees on stored lexical representations. Thus, the speech-processing system presented in Figure 11.1 is the foundation for the development of children's speech and phonological awareness skills. Children with speech problems have difficulties at one or more points somewhere in this speech-processing model. The locus/loci of difficulty also affects their ability to develop phonological awareness skills. In turn, problems with developing phonological awareness skills will be reflected in associated literacy problems. The precise location(s) of the levels of deficit will influence the type of reading and spelling problems manifested (Snowling et al., 1986; Stackhouse & Wells, 1997). Phonological awareness is therefore a product of the speech-processing system and connects speech and literacy development by making explicit the relationship between spoken and written language (see Figure 11.2). Without phonological awareness children cannot decode words when reading or segment words into syllables and sounds for spelling.

Problems with reading and spelling therefore result from a failure to develop proficient speech and phonological awareness skills. To understand how this arises, it is helpful to take a developmental perspective on speech and literacy problems.

A Developmental Perspective on Speech and Literacy

A phase model for speech development

Speech develops through an ordered series of phases that are dependent on increasing articulatory and phonological sophistication. One such phase model of speech development has been presented by Stackhouse and Wells (1997). In this model children pass through five phases before they begin school, as follows (the ages assigned to each stage will overlap and are for guidance only):

- Prelexical (1st year);
- Whole Word (2nd year);
- Systematic Simplification (3rd year);
- Assembly (4th year);
- Metaphonological (5th year).

Prelexical phase

The neonate is able to respond to sound and even detect phonetic differences between syllables, e.g. [ba] vs [da] (e.g. Eimas et al., 1971). Motor execution skills exist for feeding and crying, but the kinds of sounds produced do not resemble speech. Between the ages of the 6 to 9 months period, the baby begins to form phonological and semantic representations of familiar words as perceptual gestalts (e.g. *teddy*, *mummy*). There is no evidence of any kind of segmental analysis at this stage. On the output side, babble strings are programmed and produced by the articulators. Around the age of 9 months, babble sequences become more like the language of the environment (see Vihman, 1996).

Even at this early stage of speech development, a number of warning signs indicate the presence of a future speech disorder (Oller et al., 1994). Children with learning difficulties may be slow to move through this stage. In contrast, children with hearing loss may begin to babble but progress differently from normally developing babies (Eilers & Oller, 1994). Children with verbal dyspraxia are reported not to babble or readily engage in sound play at this stage (Milloy & Morgan-Barry, 1990).

Whole word phase

Usually around 12 months of age, the first spoken words begin to emerge. The first 50 words or so appear to be learned and stored as wholes or gestalts (Ingram, 1989). It is hypothesised that each phonological representation is unsegmented and consists of the most acoustically salient features, which allows it to be differentiated from other words (Juszcyk, 1992; Waterson, 1987). Similarly, the motor programme or scheme for each word consists of a gestalt of gestures.

As vocabulary size increases throughout the second year, there is a corresponding increase in the variability of how words are produced (Ferguson & Farwell, 1975; Studdert-Kennedy & Whitney-Goodell, 1995). This variability occurs as the child attempts to reproduce the phonetic features of the word. Phonetic parameters rather than linear order of segments dominate their productions. For example, Laura at the age of 18 months produced *Muffin* (a cat's name) as [m m̊ᶠ]. The response had the correct number of syllables and showed that she had abstracted the correct phonetic features of nasality ([m]), friction ([f]), place of articulation (lip for [m]) and voicing of the vowels and nasal sounds, but all these were collapsed together so that the utterance sounded like two voiced 'm' sounds being produced from her nose! Gradually, a more precise temporal alignment of these features developed and her utterance of the target word was recognised more easily.

The speech of normally developing 1-year-olds therefore has many of the signs associated with developmental verbal dyspraxia: inconsistent and variable output, sequencing problems, and phonetic distortion (Stackhouse, 1992). It is as though children described as having verbal dyspraxia do not move easily into the next phase of speech development.

Systematic simplification phase

This next phase of speech development is characterised by simplifying processes such as fronting, stopping, cluster reduction and phonological mapping rules (Grunwell, 1987; Ingram, 1989). Children become more systematic and consistent in their speech output at this stage. As yet *explicit* phonological awareness has not developed, but many children will begin to remember and sing nursery rhymes and enjoy sound games around 3 years of age.

Children delayed in their speech development may reach this stage after 3 years of age and are often referred for speech and language therapy because the persisting use of simplifying processes renders their speech unintelligible beyond the accepted age. If they have moved through the previous stages smoothly, their problems may resolve following appropriate intervention or through maturation. Other children may reach this stage, but continue to use simplifying processes for longer than expected. Children who are still in this stage at the point they begin school (at around 5 years of age) are likely to have phonological awareness problems and associated literacy difficulties (Bishop & Adams, 1990; Bird, Bishop & Freeman, 1995).

The assembly stage

Having successfully passed through the previous stages, which focus on single word intelligibility, the child is faced with what happens to words when they are joined together. For example, compare the different pronunciations of the final [t] in great in the following: *great elephant, great tiger, great cat.* Morphological issues need to be tackled. For example, learning that 'a pear' is appropriate but 'a apple' is not. Junction between words is a complex business. Children who have had the diagnosis of verbal dyspraxia or phonological disorder may have particular difficulties at this stage and have persisting speech problems around the junction between words in connected speech (Wells, 1994).

There are also still some tricky pronunciations to sort out, such as the acoustically close f~th, r~w distinction and the articulation of words with complex clusters (e.g. *scrape, splatter*) and increasing syllable length (e.g. *hippopotamus*). Children with specific reading impairment (dyslexia) often have persisting difficulties with this phase of speech development (Stackhouse, 1996; Stackhouse & Wells, 1991).

Metaphonological phase

Children enter the metaphonological stage when they can apply their speech-processing skills, developed in the earlier stages for storing and producing speech, to phonological awareness tasks such as rhyme and syllable or sound segmentation. Normally developing children have reached this stage by around 5 years of age, at a point when they can take advantage of reading instruction offered at school. In turn, literacy instruction accelerates metaphonological awareness which becomes more explicit as the child's orthographic experience increases.

Inevitably, these stages overlap and are not as clear-cut as presented here. An advantage of adopting a developmental perspective on children's speech development and difficulties is that it allows the unfolding nature of speech problems to be charted. The phase model also makes explicit how phonological awareness is related to normal speech development.

A phase model of literacy development

In 1985, Uta Frith presented a three-phase model of literacy development in which the child moves from an initial *logographic* or visual whole-word recognition strategy of reading, on to an *alphabetic* phase utilising letter–sound correspondences and finally to an *orthographic* phase dependent on segmentation of larger units: morphemes.

Logographic phase

In the first phase, children's reading is limited by the extent of their orthographic lexicon (their store of written words). They can only recognise words that they know and are not able to decode unfamiliar words. When spelling, children may have some learnt programmes for familiar words such as their own name, but in general, spelling is *non-phonetic* in this stage and does not show sound–letter correspondences. For example, a normally developing 5-year-old spelt *orange* as <oearasrie>. This was quite typical for children of her age. She had segmented the first sound of the word correctly and shown an awareness of letter forms and word length. The incidence of this type of spelling soon diminishes in young normally developing children (Stackhouse, 1989) but it persists in children with a history of speech difficulties (Clarke-Klein & Hodson, 1995; Dodd et al., 1995).

Alphabetic phase

Breakthrough to the alphabetic phase occurs when the child can apply letter–sound rules to decode new words. When reading, the child may sound out letters in the word and then blend them together to produce the target (e.g. [f - ɪ - ʃ] → *fish*). At the beginning of this stage, *semi-phonetic* spelling occurs. Vowels are often not transcribed, and letter sounds might be used to represent syllables, e.g., *burglar* → bgl; sounded out as [bəgələ] to represent the three segmented syllables in the word. Gradually, the child learns how to fill in the gaps. Vowel names are helpful (e.g. *boat* → bot) where the letter o is used to represent the sound used for the letter name, i.e. [əʊ], and spelling becomes more logical or *phonetic*. Targets are recognisable even if the spelling is not conventionally correct (e.g. *orange* → orinj), indicating that phonological awareness skills are developing normally. The child is segmenting the word successfully and applying letter knowledge, but has not yet learned (or been taught) the conventions of English spelling.

Orthographic phase

Finally, in the orthographic stage, the child is able to recognise larger chunks of words such as prefixes and suffixes (e.g., *addition*), and to read more efficiently by analogy with known words. Once the child has the skills to perform at each stage, the most appropriate strategy for the task can be adopted depending on the different kinds of words presented for reading or spelling.

Frith (1985) suggested that it is the failure to progress through these stages that is characteristic of children with literacy problems. Children with *delayed* development may progress through these stages albeit at

a slower rate than their peer group. Children with *specific* literacy difficulties, however, (i.e. unexpected reading and spelling problems given
their cognitive abilities), may be unable to progress through the normal
stages outlined above and need to develop compensatory strategies or
ways round barriers to their literacy development. These children are
often called *dyslexic* (see Snowling, 1996 for further discussion of this
term).

A particularly severe form of dyslexia which occurs when a child's
development is arrested at the logographic stage of literacy development is known as *phonological dyslexia*. This is characterised by a
particular difficulty with applying speech-processing skills to literacy.
Children with phonological dyslexia have poor phonological awareness
skills, limited memory for phonological information, and poor verbal
repetition and naming skills. A consequence of these deficits is that they
are unable to break through to the alphabetic phase of literacy development. They are unable to read new words because they cannot decode
letters into sounds and blend them together to produce the word.
Further, their spellings may be predominantly non-phonetic, particularly in longer and more complex words (Snowling, Goulandris &
Stackhouse, 1994 and see Goulandris, 1996 for further discussion of
how to assess spelling skills).

It is not a coincidence that the most severe forms of phonological
dyslexia have been reported in children with serious and persisting
speech difficulties, in particular in those diagnosed as having developmental verbal dyspraxia (Stackhouse, 1982; Stackhouse & Snowling,
1992a). If we compare the two phase models we can see why this might
be so.

The developmental relationship between speech and literacy

The two phase models show that for both speech and literacy development, children move from whole-word processing phases where
segmentation skills are not developed (Prelexical and Whole Word
Phases in speech; and Logographic Phase in literacy) through to phases
where segmentation skills are an increasingly dominant feature
(Systematic Simplification, Assembly and Metaphonological Phases in
speech development; and Alphabetic and Orthographic Phases in
literacy development.)

Children with developmental verbal dyspraxia are arrested at the
Whole Word Phase of speech development (Stackhouse & Snowling,
1992b; Stackhouse, 1993). Their speech is characterised by unsystem-
atic sequencing errors and a lack of the normal simplifying processes
typical of the next phase of speech development. Their literacy development is also arrested at the whole-word level. Reading and spelling is
typical of children at the Logographic Phase of literacy development;

their reading contains predominantly visual errors, they are unable to apply letter–sound rules, and spelling is non-phonetic (Stackhouse & Snowling, 1992a).

Breakthrough to the Systematic Simplification Phase of speech development is a necessary prerequisite for the development of phonological awareness skills which, in turn, is necessary for the breakthrough to the Alphabetic Phase of literacy development. By moving through the phases of speech development smoothly and at the appropriate time children reach the Metaphonological Phase of speech development by the time they start school and are ready to take advantage of the literacy instruction offered. Children who have phonological delay or impairments may be slow moving through the phases and be disadvantaged when they begin school.

The relationship between the two phase models is presented in Figure 11.5. By taking this developmental perspective on speech and literacy problems we can explain why children with verbal dyspraxia are

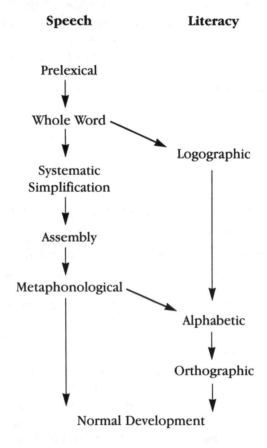

Figure 11.5 The relationship between the phases of speech and literacy development

most at risk for serious literacy problems. Their difficulties arise prior to the Systematic Simplification Phase and they therefore do not acquire the phonological skills necessary for developing phonological awareness. This developmental perspective also explains why children who have persisting speech problems beyond the age of 5;6 are at risk for literacy problems (Bishop & Adams, 1990); for whatever reason they have not moved into the Metaphonological Phase in time to take full advantage of the literacy instruction offered at school. For some this means a slow start to their literacy development following which satisfactory progress will be made; for others the slow start is followed by slow or atypical progress and associated educational problems.

Summary and Conclusions

This chapter has presented a speech-processing view of literacy to show the relationship between speech and literacy skills. Speech-processing skills play a major role in the development of reading and spelling. Without intact input skills children cannot process what they hear. Auditory processing problems will have a knock-on effect to how words are stored in a child's lexicon. An inaccurate or imprecise phonological representation of a word will be particularly problematic when a child wants to spell or name that word, as the phonological representation is the basis for spontaneous written or spoken production. Consistently accurate output skills are particularly important for rehearsing and remembering verbal material and for reflecting on the structure of words in preparation for speech, spelling and learning new vocabulary. Without this verbal rehearsal children find it difficult to segment utterances into their components – a necessary prerequisite for storing words in the lexicon and for allocating letters to sounds to form spellings of new words. Success in acquiring literacy is therefore dependent on coupling speech processing skills at the input, representation and output levels with alphabetic knowledge gained through orthographic experience.

The chapter has also illustrated how phonological awareness tasks can be interpreted within a simple speech-processing model. This interpretation shows that phonological awareness is not a separate area of children's development but rather an extension of their speech-processing skills. As a result any difficulty a child has in the basic speech-processing system will result not only in speech difficulties but also in phonological awareness problems which in turn will lead to literacy problems. The precise nature of the speech and literacy problems will depend on the location of the deficit(s) in the speech-processing system.

By analysing a range of phonological awareness tasks from a speech processing perspective, it is clear that both top-down and bottom-up skills are necessary for reading and spelling to develop normally. Deficits in top-down and/or bottom-up processing will impact on a child's literacy development in different ways. Identification of a child's processing skills is therefore necessary for understanding literacy difficulties and for targeting intervention appropriately. The process of identifying these skills constitutes a psycholinguistic investigation (Stackhouse & Wells, 1997).

Finally, the chapter took a developmental perspective by comparing two phase models: one for speech and one for literacy. Both models emphasised the move in normal development from the whole-word level of functioning to being able to detect, segment and produce smaller units such as syllables and sounds. Atypical development in both speech and literacy occurs if a child is unable to move through the phases at the normal time or, in severe cases, if a child's development is arrested at a particular phase. Problems prior to the Systematic Simplification Phase of speech development will inevitably lead to serious problems with literacy development because children need to pass through this phase in order to be able to deal with units smaller than the whole word.

This speech-processing view of literacy development and difficulties has implications for the assessment and management of children with literacy problems. Although it is not the case that *all* children with literacy problems have underlying speech-processing problems, it is likely that there is a higher incidence of 'hidden' speech problems in the population described as dyslexic than has been uncovered in the past. Adopting this speech-processing view ensures that a balanced investigation of a child's speech input, representation and output skills is carried out and that results from phonological awareness tests are interpreted within the same speech-processing framework (see Stackhouse & Wells, 1997 for further discussion of this assessment framework). By drawing up a child's speech-processing profile from the assessment findings we can ensure that the subsequent intervention programme is utilising a child's strengths when targeting their weaknesses. Finally, this approach helps to clarify how speech and language therapists can work in collaboration with teachers on children's literacy skills:

> The role of the speech and language therapist does not include *teaching* reading and spelling which is traditionally and rightly the teacher's domain. Rather, the role is one of identification and promoting the underlying skills that contribute to literacy development. (Snowling & Stackhouse, 1996, p. 240)

This chapter has focused on these underlying skills.

Acknowledgement

This chapter includes extracts from Stackhouse, J. & Wells, B. (1997). *Children's Speech and Literacy Difficulties: A Psycholinguistic Framework*. London: Whurr Publishers.

References

Bird, J. & Bishop, D.V.M. (1992). Perception and awareness of phonemes in phonologically impaired children. *European Journal of Disorders of Communication*, **27**, 289–3 11.

Bird, J., Bishop D.V.M. & Freeman, N.H. (1995). Phonological awareness and literacy development in children with expressive phonological impairments. *Journal of Speech and Hearing Research* **38**, 446–462.

Bishop, D.V.M. & Adams, C. (1990). A prospective study of the relationship between specific language impairment, phonological disorders and reading retardation. *Journal of Child Psychology and Psychiatry*, **31**, 1027–1050.

Bradley, L. & Bryant, P. (1983). Categorising sounds and learning to read: A causal connection. *Nature* **301**: 419.

Catts, H. & Vartiainen, T. (1993). *Sounds Abound*. East Moline, IL: Linguisystems.

Chaney, C. (1992). Language development, metalinguistic skills and print awareness in 3-year-old children. *Applied Psycholinguistics*. **13**, 485–514.

Clarke-Klein, S. & Hodson, B. (1995). A phonologically based analysis of misspellings by third graders with disordered-phonology histories. *Journal of Speech and Hearing Research* **38**: 839–849.

Counsel, J. (1993). *Oral Language Deficits in Reading Impaired Children*. M.Sc Thesis. Department of Human Communication Science. University College London.

Dodd, B., Gillon, G., Oerlemans, M., Russell, T., Syrmis, M. & Wilson, H. (1995). Phonological disorder and the acquisition of literacy. In B. Dodd, *Differential Diagnosis and Treatment of Children with Speech Disorder*. London: Whurr Publishers.

Eilers, R.E. & Oller, D.K. (1994). Infant vocalizations and the early diagnosis of severe hearing impairment. *Journal of Pediatrics*, **124**: 199–203.

Eimas, P., Siqueland, E., Jusczyk, P. & Vigorito, J. (1971). Speech perception in infants. *Science* **171**: 303–306.

Ferguson, C.A. & Farwell, C. B. (1975). Words and sounds in early language acquisition. *Language* **51**: 419–439.

Fox, B. & Routh, D.K. (1984). Phonemic analysis and synthesis as word attack skills: Revisited. *Journal of Educational Psychology*, **76, 6**: 1059–1064.

Frederikson. N. (Ed.) (1996). *Phonological Awareness Battery (PhAB)*. Windsor: NFER-Nelson.

Frith, U. (1985). Beneath the surface of developmental dyslexia. In K.E. Patterson, J.C. Marshall and M. Coltheart (Eds.) *Surface Dyslexia*. London: Routledge and Kegan Paul.

Goswami, U. (1994). The role of analogies in reading development. *Support For Learning* **9**, 22–25.

Goulandris, N. (1996). Assessing reading and spelling skills. In M. Snowling & J. Stackhouse (Eds.) *Dyslexia, Speech and Language: A Practitioner's Handbook*. London: Whurr Publishers.

Grunwell, P. (1987). *Clinical Phonology* (2nd ed.). London: Croom Helm

Hatcher, P.J. (1994). *Sound Linkage: An Integrated Programme for Overcoming Reading Difficulties*. London: Whurr.

Hatcher, P. J. (1996). Practising sound links in reading intervention with the school age child. In M. Snowling & J. Stackhouse (Eds.) *Dyslexia, Speech and Language: A Practitioner's Handbook*. London: Whurr Publishers

Ingram, D. (1989). *First Language Acquisition: Method, Description and Explanation*. Cambridge: Cambridge University Press.

Juszcyk, P.W. (1992). Developing phonological categories from the speech signal. In C.A. Ferguson, L. Menn & C. Stoel-Gammon (Eds.) *Phonological Development: Models, Re.search, Implications*. Timonium, MD: York Press.

Layton, L. & Deeney, K. (1996). Promoting phonological awareness in preschool children. In M. Snowling & J. Stackhouse (Eds.) *Dyslexia, Speech and Language: A Practitioner's Handbook*. London: Whurr Publishers.

Lewkowicz, N.K. (1980). Phonemic awareness training: What to teach and how to teach it. *Journal of Educational Psychology*. **72. 5**: 686–700.

Marion, M.J., Sussman, H.M. & Marquardt, T.P. (1993). The perception and production of rhyme in normal and developmentally apraxic children. *Journal of Communication Disorders*, 26, 129–160.

Milloy, N. & Morgan-Barry, R. (1990). Developmental neurological disorders. In P. Grunwell (Ed.) *Developmental Speech Disorders*. London: Whurr Publishers.

Morgan-Barry, R. (1988). *The Auditory Discrimination and Attention Test* Windsor: NFER-Nelson.

Muter, V. (1996). Predicting children's reading and spelling difficulties. In M. Snowling & J. Stackhouse (Eds.) *Dyslexia, Speech and Language: A Practitioner's Handbook*. London: Whurr Publishers.

Newton, M. & Thomson, M. (1982). *Aston Index*. Wisbech, Cambs.: LDA.

Oller, D.K., Eilers, R.E., Steffens, M.L., Lynch, M.P. & Urbano, R. (1994). Speech like vocalizations in infancy: An evaluation of potential risk factors. *Journal of Child Language* **21**: 33–58.

Perfetti, C.A., Beck, I., Bell, L.C. & Hughes, C. (1987). Phonemic knowledge and learning to read are reciprocal: A longitudinal study of first grade children. *Merrill Palmer Quarterly*. **33**: 283–219.

Perin, D. (1983). Phonemic segmentation and spelling. *British Journal of Psychology* **74**: 129–144.

Reid, J., Grieve, R., Dean, E.C., Donaldson, M.L. & Howell, J. (1993). Linguistic awareness in young children. In J. Clibbens (Ed.) *Proceedings of the Child Language Seminar*, University of Plymouth.

Snowling, M. (1996). Developmental dyslexia: An introduction and theoretical overview. In M. Snowling & J. Stackhouse (Eds.) *Dyslexia, Speech and Language: A Practitioner's Handbook*. London: Whurr Publishers.

Snowling, M., Goulandris, N., & Stackhouse, J. (1994). Phonological constraints on learning to read: Evidence from single case studies of reading difficulty. In C. Hulme & M. Snowling (Eds.) *Reading Development and Dyslexia*. London: Whurr Publishers.

Snowling, M. & Stackhouse, J. (1996). Epilogue: Current themes and future directions. In M. Snowling & J. Stackhouse (Eds.) *Dyslexia, Speech and Language: A Practitioner's Handbook*. London: Whurr Publishers.

Snowling, M., Stackhouse, J. & Rack, J. (1986). Phonological dyslexia and dysgraphia - a developmental analysis. *Cognitive Neuropsychology* **3.3**: 309–340

Stackhouse, J. (1982). An investigation of reading and spelling performance in speech disordered children. *British Journal of Disorders of Communication* **17.2**: 53–60.

Stackhouse, J. (1989). *Phonological Dyslexia in Children with Developmental Verbal Dyspraxia*. PhD Thesis, Psychology Department, University College London.

Stackhouse, J. (1992a). Developmental verbal dyspraxia: A longitudinal case study. In R. Campbell (Ed.) *Mental Lives: Case Studies in Cognition*. London: Blackwell.

Stackhouse, J. (1992b). Promoting reading and spelling skills through speech therapy. In P Fletcher & D Hall (Eds.) *Specific Speech and Language Disorders in Childlren*, London: Whurr Publishers Ltd.

Stackhouse, J. (1993). Phonological disorder and lexical development: Two case studies. *Child Language, Teaching & Therapy* 9.3: 230–241.

Stackhouse, J. (1996). Speech, Spelling and Reading: Who is at risk and why? In M. Snowling & J. Stackhouse (Eds.) *Dyslexia, Speech and Language: A Practitioner's Handbook*. London: Whurr Publishers.

Stackhouse, J. (1997). Phonological awareness: Connecting speech and literacy problems. In B. Hodson & M.L. Edwards (Eds.) *Perspectives in Applied Phonology* Maryland: Aspen Publishers.

Stackhouse, J. & Snowling, M. (1992a). Barriers to literacy development in two cases of developmental verbal dyspraxia. *Cognitive Neuropsychology* 9.4: 272–299.

Stackhouse, J. & Snowling, M. (1992b). Developmental verbal dyspraxia II: A developmental perspective. *European Journal of Disorders of Communication* 27: 3–54.

Stackhouse, J. & Wells, B. (1991). Dyslexia: The obvious and hidden speech & language disorder. In M. Snowling & J. Stackhouse (Eds.) *Dyslexia: Integrating Theory & Practice*. London: Whurr Publishers.

Stackhouse, J. & Wells, B. (1993). Psycholinguistic assessment of developmental speech disorders. *European Journal of Disorders of Communication* 28: 331–348.

Stackhouse, J. & Wells, B. (1997). *Children's Speech and Literacy Difficulties: A Psycholinguistic Framework*. London: Whurr Publishers.

Stothard, S. (1996). Assessing Reading Comprehension. In M. Snowling & J. Stackhouse (Eds.) *Dyslexia, Speech and Language: A Practitioner's Handbook*. London: Whurr Publishers.

Studdert-Kennedy, M. & Whitney Goodell, E. (1995). Gestures, features and segments in early child speech. In B. de Gelder & J. Morais (Eds.) *Speech and Reading: A Comparative Approach*. London. Taylor & Francis.

Thorum, A.R. (1986). *The Fullerton Language Test For Adolescents*. Consulting Psychologists Press, Inc., California.

Vance, M., Stackhouse. J., and Wells, B. (1994) "Sock the wock the pit-pat-pock" Children's responses to measures of rhyming ability, 3-7 years. Department of Human Communication Science (formerly the National Hospital's College of Speech Sciences): *Work in Progress*, 4 171–185. University College London.

Vihman, M.M. (1996). *Phonological Development: The Origins of Language in the Child*. London: Blackwell Publishers.

Vint, D. (1993). *Spoonerisms: A Study of the Development of Phonological Awareness in Older Children*. B.Sc project. Department of Human Communication Science, University College London.

Waterson, N. (1987). *Prosodic Phonology: The Theory and its Application to Language Acquisiton and Speech Processing*. Newcastle upon Tyne: Grevatt & Grevatt.

Wells, B. (1994). Junction in developmental speech disorder: A case study. *Clinical Linguistics & Phonetics* 8: 1–25.

Wells, B., Stackhouse, J., & Vance, M. (1996). A specific deficit in onset-rhyme assembly in a 9-year-old child with speech and literacy difficulties. In T.W. Powell, (Ed.) *Pathology of Speech and Language: Contributions of Clinical Phonetics and Linguistics*. New Orleans, LA:ICPLA.

Chapter 12
Achieving Competence in Language and Literacy by Training in Phonemic Awareness, Concept Imagery and Comparator Function

PATRICIA LINDAMOOD, NANCI BELL and
PHYLLIS LINDAMOOD

Introduction

Independent, competent language processing consists of a hierarchy of lower-level skills required for higher-level processing. In this chapter we focus on three primary sensory-cognitive skills that are critical in this hierarchy of lower- to higher-level language processing: phonemic awareness, concept imagery and comparator function. Phonemic awareness refers to the ability to identify individual sounds and their order within words – to divide a whole word into its parts. Concept imagery refers to a complementary skill, the ability to create an imaged gestalt – to construct a whole from its parts. Comparator function refers to a feedback and analysis process that constantly computes the match or mismatch between incoming sensory information, prior information and/or information from other senses. We will show, through a review of the instructional techniques we have pioneered, that developing these sensory-cognitive functions can move a child or adult towards becoming an independent language processor.

Confident, automatic language processing requires that all levels in the hierarchy function well. When any level in the hierarchy is missing or inadequately developed, the end result is incomplete processing. Top-down processes or compensatory methods may come into play, attempting to fill the spot left by the missing or incomplete part, but automaticity will not be developed. In the hierarchy of lower- to higher-level skills required, phonemic awareness is a key factor in decoding and spelling, whilst concept imagery is a key factor in oral and written language comprehension. Self-correction is enabled in these processes by the monitoring provided through comparator function and the conscious processing and integration of sensory feedback. These functions are both primary and basic to competence in language and literacy.

Powers (1973), in *Behavior: The Control of Perception*, provides a wealth of theory and research, as relevant now as it was then, regarding the neural structure of human feedback control, 'in which higher-order systems perceive and control an environment composed of lower-order systems'. He specifically calls attention to the importance of distinguishing *conscious perception* from *perception*, and emphasises the lower to higher cumulative action of the levels as what enables the final conscious perception to occur for self-correction.

Missing Lower Levels

Independent, competent language processing – the ability to comprehend and express in both oral and written language – requires the missing parts. The whole requires the parts, each is necessary, one affecting the other. But the field of education has missed identifying all the cognitive levels involved. Much effort has been focused in the arena of written language; especially in the area of decoding. However, despite years of effort the struggle has primarily led to errors in philosophy and instruction and a lack of desired results. Errors in instruction such as teaching to a strength, or starting immediately with contextual reading, miss the concept of lower-order cognitive processes required for higher-order cognitive processing in the final complex act of accurately reading and critically comprehending what is read.

In the history of reading instruction, because the cognitive parts required to develop fluent decoding were not all identified, different schemes and procedures emerged that addressed parts of the process and ignored others. Some worked better with some students, some with others, depending on which processing levels students already had in place. The dogma 'nothing works for everyone' emerged because no reading instruction method addressed all levels needed. The question of why some children and adults could *easily* learn to decode accurately and quickly, while others struggled, was a many-decades-long puzzle. Why could some bright individuals *not* decode as well as others less bright? Why did some seem to figure out the alphabetic system automatically and others remain baffled by what appeared to be an unsolved mystery for them? What were the underpinnings of decoding accuracy?

Phonemic awareness

Instruction in phonics was not the answer. Some attained decoding accuracy and fluency with phonics sound/letter instruction and some did not, even though they learned all the rules. Instruction in sight words only was not the answer. Some attained decoding accuracy and fluency from memorising a lot of words, and independently acquired the ability to process unfamiliar words phonetically, but some did not and were left trying to add more and more words to an overloaded memory bank, with no way to attack new, unfamiliar words. Some even attained decoding accuracy with neither phonics nor sight word instruction, and just seemed to learn to read through exposure to print. Taught a whole language approach of contextual hypothesising, they miraculously learned to attack new unfamiliar words (even without background or contextual constraints) and achieved decoding automaticity. Decoding was not a mystery for them, even without being taught a systematic approach to the alphabet system. But others, many others, could *not* learn to decode simply by exposure or contextual guessing. In all those scenarios, the many individuals who did not reach independence and competence had a missing *primary sensory-cognitive function* – a missing part that is a much needed lower-level skill required for a higher-level task. That missing function is *phonemic awareness – the ability to identify individual sounds and their order within words*.

As in the search for a missing primary part in decoding, the same search has been under way for a missing primary part in language comprehension, both oral and written. Why is it that some children and adults easily learn to comprehend oral language? They quickly and automatically understand conversation, get the point, make inferences, reason. But others seem unable to follow conversation and lectures, miss the point, ask and re-ask questions, and are unable to reason and think critically despite much instruction and encouragement from parents and teachers. Why can they not get it automatically? Why does the same pattern emerge with written language? Why do some children and adults have an easy time recalling, understanding and interpreting what they read? They easily get the main idea, make inferences, draw conclusions and reason as they process written language. But others read words that literally seem to go in one ear and out the other, with a few parts sticking, but no gestalt? Reading the words may be easy for them, but getting the point or recalling and reasoning with the information is very difficult. Why can some individuals interpret language and others not?

Concept imagery

Instruction in decoding has not been the answer. Seductive ways to teach decoding have not always resulted in improved reading comprehension. Some individuals can be taught to decode and then their reading comprehension improves correspondingly, whilst others can decode both lists of words or words in paragraphs, but their comprehension remains significantly lower than their decoding. Also, instruction in vocabulary development has not been the answer. Some individuals have better comprehension when their vocabulary is increased, but others have a very high understanding of the meaning of each isolated word, yet when the words come together to form concepts these individuals get lost or confused, and cannot recall or interpret from the concepts presented. Instruction in contextual hypothesising and background information has not been the answer, either. Some individuals can self-correct a word from the *sentence syntax* or *sentence semantics*, but they cannot get the concept presented in the paragraph. They cannot bring the parts to a whole. In short, as in decoding, being able to comprehend oral and written language has been a mystery to some individuals. As a college graduate with difficulty comprehending said, 'I used to watch other students easily get information they heard or read and I couldn't understand how they did it. What did they have in their cognitive tool kit that I didn't have?' An answer is a missing *primary sensory-cognitive function* necessary in higher level skills. That missing function is *concept imagery – the ability to create an imaged gestalt (whole) for language concepts*.

The Processing Hierarchy

To examine the role of phonemic awareness, concept imagery and comparator function in language processing, we begin by examining the component skills that contribute to competent performance. We start at the end of the process and work backwards through the parts.

Independence

The goal in language processing is *independence*. Decoding independence is being able to read accurately and confidently, without needing someone else to tell you if you have the word right or wrong. It is *knowing* that you have said or read a word accurately. Comprehension independence is being able to receive language, in oral or written form, and *know* you understand it. It is the ability to interpret it without confusion, without mystery. Independent language comprehension is the highest skill, the end result of all levels in the processing hierarchy working together.

Self-correction

But the ability to be independent has a lower level process beneath it – *self-correction*. You cannot be independent without the ability to self-correct. In decoding this means you can judge the error, tell how you read a word wrong or said a word wrong, and fix it. In comprehension, it means you can tell how you were off in your reasoning, were not thinking it through from the parts to the whole. In independent decoding and comprehension *you* find your errors, and fix them, not someone else. But how do you know to self-correct? How do you know when you have made an error in decoding or thinking? What mechanisms are at work in the sensory system?

Monitoring

The ability to self-correct has yet another process beneath it – *the monitoring of sensory feedback through comparator function*. You can self-correct your decoding error *only* because you can monitor your response. For example, if you look at the word *stream* and say 'steam' you can *notice* that you have left out the /r/. You can monitor your response by *comparing* what you said with what you saw. This is comparator function: holding one sensory input and comparing it with another. Your sensory system gets jolted in the process of comparing and you self-correct. No one has to help you. Your sensory feedback loop is operating. You are independent because you can self-correct; you can self-correct because you can monitor; you can monitor because your sensory system has access to phonemic awareness; phonemic awareness enables you to compare what you said with what you saw. Comparator function closes this feedback loop and signals you to self-correct if there is a mismatch.

In comprehension monitoring, comparator function acts in the same way, enabling you to monitor, judge an error in your reasoning and self-correct. You can say to yourself, 'Yes, that is the right inference because that matches the whole.' Or, you can say, 'No, that can't be the right conclusion because that earlier statement (part) changed the whole, and now this doesn't match.' You hold and compare your imagery with the language, or your older images with new images, or parts of images with the whole. Again, no one has to help you or correct you. You think and reason in this way because your sensory system has access to concept imagery; and concept imagery enables you to compare your images and the language. This sensory feedback loop and comparator function enables you to self-correct your comprehension.

Sensory input and perception

The ability to monitor, then self-correct, then reach independence, has another cognitive prerequisite – *sensory input*. You are able to monitor because your brain has received information from your sensory system, which you perceived and are able to process, thus the term sensorycognitive. Sensory input bombards our senses constantly; however, to make sense of this chaos, perception and comparator function need to organise the information. Though you started processing written language by trying to decode words and then comprehend a paragraph, your sensory system was activated far back in the hierarchy of processing to enable you to do those seemingly simple tasks. Your sensory system received information that you *consciously* perceived and compared with other sensory information, and you developed the primary sensory-cognitive functions of phonemic awareness and concept imagery.

Phonemic awareness is the ability to judge the relationship of sounds *within* words, receive the whole and identify the parts. Concept imagery is the ability to create an *imaged gestalt*, receive the parts and create the whole. One sensory-cognitive function enables you to process the parts and the other sensory-cognitive function enables you to process the whole. These functions and comparator function are needed for independence in spoken and written language-processing competence.

Dyslexia and Phonemic Awareness: Processing the Parts

A significant gap between oral and written language skills, called dyslexia, is usually related to difficulty in the encoding and decoding aspects of literacy. It has a primary cause. The cause has been documented through a mounting body of worldwide research as a lack of phonemic awareness. A lack of this oral judgement for sound segments in words means there is no basis for grasping the logic of an alphabetic system which uses letters to represent these sound segments. This neurophysiological processing problem has been called *lack of auditory conceptual function*, *phonological awareness* and *phonemic awareness* by various researchers, (Calfee, Lindamood & Lindamood, 1973; Liberman & Shankweiler, 1985; Lundberg, Frost & Peterson, 1988; Olsen et al., 1994; Wagner, Torgesen & Rashotte, 1994; Torgesen, Wagner & Rashotte, 1996).

Assessment

The Lindamoods' early research on lack of phonemic awareness resulted in a test for its assessment, the Lindamood® Auditory Conceptualization (LAC) Test (Lindamood & Lindamood, 1971, 1979). The number, sameness/difference and order of phonemes in the stimulus patterns are represented by coloured blocks. This avoids the need for prior learning such as would be required if letter symbols were used, which could then in itself affect performance. Research in a kindergarten up to twelfth-grade population revealed high correlations at every grade level (range 0.66–0.81, average 0.73) between performance on the LAC Test and an at-or-above versus below grade combined reading/spelling score on the Wide Range Achievement Test (Calfee et al., 1973).

A particular feature of the LAC Test is the involvement of comparator function on the syllable part of the test (see Figure 12.1). A metalinguistic task is presented which requires comparison and indication of how one syllable differs from another as a single phoneme is added, omitted, substituted, repeated, or two phonemes are reversed in their order. Subjects are not simply asked to show how many phonemes are in a given word, but are asked to compare two words and represent precisely how they differ. This assessment of comparator function in respect of phonemes may be one of the most significant contributions of this test, as it is measuring one of the important mechanisms necessary for encoding/decoding self-correction and independence. The neuropsychology division at Bowman Gray Medical School has used the LAC Test for over 10 years in dyslexia research. They hold that its cognitive load is more similar to the cognitive load in reading than other phonemic awareness measures (R. Felton, personal communication).

We anticipate extending the complexity in an LAC Test-R to increase the similarity to the cognitive load of reading. At present the syllables on

STIMULUS	RESPONSE	
Show me / i /	☐	one phoneme—one block
if that says / i / show me / ip /	☐ ■	a phoneme is *added*— a block is added
if that says / ip / show me / pi /	■ ☐	the phonemes are *reversed*—the blocks are reversed
if that says / pi / show me / pip /	■ ☐ ■	the first phoneme is *repeated*—the first block is repeated
if that says / pip / show me / ip /	☐ ■	the first phoneme is *omitted*—the first block is omitted
if that says / ip / show me / op /	▨ ■	the first phoneme is *substituted*—the first block is substituted

Figure 12.1 Examples of the lowest level of comparator function tasks, conceptualizing five types of phoneme contrast, in Category II of the LAC Test

the test are composed of one to four sounds; older individuals face decoding words far more complex than four sounds, so some individuals may 'pass' the LAC Test and not actually have enough phonemic awareness for the decoding demands they face. Clinical use of the extended version into syllables of five sounds and also into multisyllable patterns reveals that more sensitive diagnoses are possible with this more subtle level of assessment.

In the multisyllable extension, four-inch coloured squares are used in Category III A to conceptualise the number of syllables in spoken pseudo-words, and then in III B to conceptualise the nature of the change as a syllable is added, substituted, or omitted from a pseudo-word (see Figure 12.2). Category III C becomes more complex, requiring comparator function in conceptualising a syllable *or* a phoneme addition, substitution or omission in pseudowords with two to five syllables.

Awareness of the segmental structure of words, as an oral language skill, is critically related to acquiring an understanding of the alphabetic principle: how letters can be used to represent words on the printed page. Although various studies have shown traditional phonics training to be effective in helping some students to understand the alphabetic principle and develop independent word-reading skills (Adams, 1990; Ball & Blachman, 1991), a common problem with many of the training procedures reported in the research is that they may not be powerful enough to aid students who are most at risk for the development of reading difficulties. For example, Torgesen, Morgan & Davis (1992) and Lundberg (1988) found that a significant number (20–30%) of students were unable to profit from phonics training procedures. This is because typical phonics activities assume that the ability to say a word indicates the ability to identify its individual sounds. The reality is that 20–30% of

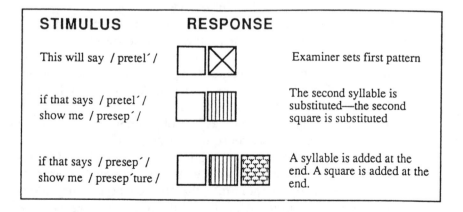

Figure 12.2 Examples of multisyllable comparator function tasks in Category III B of the LAC Test-R

the population lack adequate development of this sensory-cognitive function (Calfee et al., 1973; Shankweiler & Liberman, 1989). Although research shows this lack of phonological awareness to be a genetically transmitted tendency (De Fries, Fulkes & LaBuda, 1987; see also, Chapter 2 of this volume) it can be developed through appropriate intervention (Lindamood, 1985; Alexander et al., 1991; Truch, 1994).

Phonics instruction can be expected to be ineffective for students with severe weakness in phonemic awareness. Those students need to *acquire* phonemic awareness, not just exercise and better use an already existing level. Most phonics activities are either below or above the level of *development* of phonemic awareness. For example, teachers may have the student practice isolated sound/letter associations and assume those exercises will develop the ability to judge sounds within words. Teachers may try rhyming activities and be frustrated or puzzled by a few students who never understand how rhyming works. Or they may assume phonemic awareness is in place and say to the student, '*Listen* to the sounds in the word.' No matter how many ways teachers ask that, or what incentives are offered, students cannot perform if the phonemic awareness they need is missing.

Stimulating Phonemic Awareness through Articulatory Feedback

So, how do we develop phonemic awareness for those individuals for whom it is not naturally occurring? What are some individuals not noticing about phonemes that prevents them from perceiving those parts within the whole even after exhaustive practice with consonant and vowel sounds in isolation? Speech perception research shows that the *acoustic* features of phonemes are not constant from one syllable to another: you may think the /p/ in /pat/ sounds just like the /p/ in /slips/, but acoustic spectrographs measure them as two very different patterns. From this information has arisen the motor theory of speech perception (Liberman & Mattingly, 1985), which says that the critical articulatory features of phonemes are the constants that gives us categorical perception in spite of widely disparate acoustic signals. We 'know' phonemes by how they are made, not by how they sound.

It is our premise that the motor aspect of phonemes needs to be brought to a conscious level for those with weak phonemic awareness. There is evidence from research (Montgomery, 1981) and clinical observation that those individuals with naturally strong phonemic awareness process articulatory feedback more fully than those who lack phonemic awareness; and so development of phonemic awareness may best be achieved by directly stimulating that processing of articulatory feedback. The Auditory Discrimination in Depth (ADD) Program (Lindamood &

Lindamood, 1969, 1975, 1997) directly develops awareness of articulatory feedback in the process of stimulating phonemic awareness. Stetson (1951) also directs attention to the principle that the study of phonemes should not be separated from the oral-motor movements that produce them, because the motor activity involved is what allows phoneme segments to be verified. He stated, 'Speech is rather a set of movements made audible than a set of sounds produced by movements.'

Consonants

The ADD Program is different from traditional phonics procedures – even those that include some attention to articulatory feedback – in several ways. It is both more basic and more extensive in developing awareness of articulatory feedback as a means of perceiving phonemes within words. It begins with sensory feedback from the mouth rather than with print as phonics programmes do. Students are helped to discover they can categorise and classify our 24 consonant sounds in eight unvoiced/voiced pairs, plus three other groups, by *place and manner of articulation*. Questions are asked to stimulate awareness of this articulatory feedback; labels are given which conceptualise the articulatory action; and pictures are chosen which categorise and make concrete the distinctive features of the sensory feedback involved. The alphabet symbols that need to be associated with these phonemes then have a reality to represent (see Figure 12.3 for examples of some of the consonant pairs and their labels. The simple, high-imagery labels are versions of scientific terms such as bilabial plosives /p,b/, lingua-alveolar plosives /t,d/, etc.).

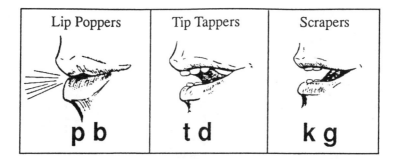

Figure 12.3 Labels used, mouth pictures chosen and graphemes associated *after* discovery of the motor features that categorise the consonants forming the first three cognate pairs

Vowels

Students also discover that instead of identifying vowels as 'long' or 'short', 11 of the vowels can be configured in a half-circle, relative to the essential tongue position that produces them (toward the front, toward the bottom, toward the back of the mouth), or require a sliding action that involves two positions (the diphthongs). Second, within those place of articulation references, the vowels can also be categorised and classified by manner of articulation related to mouth shape involved (smile, open, round and sliders.) This brings order out of what otherwise can seem like chaos for many students (see Figure 12.4). Again, the alphabet symbols that need to be associated with these vowel phonemes can represent physical realities. English orthographic conventions regarding vowels can then be perceived more readily.

Tracking

Most important, once students are able to compare phonemes by articulatory features, the articulatory feedback is used to *track* and *verify* the identity, number and order of phonemes in words, and the mouth pictures and coloured blocks are used to code syllables more concretely,

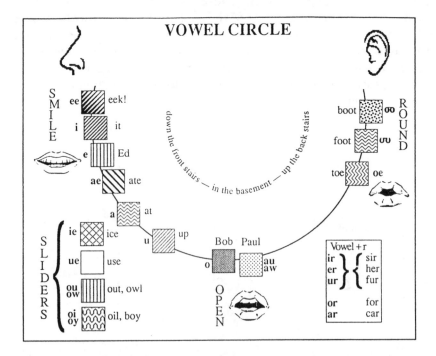

Figure 12.4 The configuration and labelling of vowels in a half-circle relationship, with diphthongs and vowel + r units related adjacently to the circle

before letter symbols are used to code syllables in spelling and reading. The tracking activity *directly develops* phonemic awareness in a carefully structured progression from simple to complex one syllable words of two to five sounds, into multisyllable words of two to five syllables.

Spelling and reading

The processing competence developed in phoneme tracking is directly applied to spelling (encoding) and reading (decoding). As tracking is developed at the simple syllable level, an overlap is made to spelling and reading simple syllables and words. The same overlapping progression at the complex and multisyllable levels assures success in spelling and reading because students are never 'lost' through too sudden an increase in phonological complexity.

'Respond to the response' error handling

The ADD Program uses a discovery format with Socratic questioning techniques and a special 'respond to the response' procedure. This procedure feeds back an error response and puts it in relationship to something that enables the error to be perceived and corrected. This error-handling technique is a core element in the instructional interaction throughout the ADD Program. It involves the principle discovered by quantum physics, cited by Wheatley (1992), that *relationship* is the key determiner of what is observed...*that particles come into being and are observed only in relationship to something else*. If we substitute *phonemes* for *particles*, the statement also applies to the structural units of language and literacy. This quantum physics principle helps us understand why the 'respond to the response' error-handling procedure of the ADD Program is so important in developing phonemic awareness and comparator function for self-correction.

In reading, the error-handling procedure requires the phonemes involved in the error to be put into a relationship in which they 'come into being and are observed'. For example:

> If the student makes the reading error 'The fox went into the *den*', when the word was *pen*, the instructor covers the word and responds, 'When you say /den/, what do you feel first?' The student checks oral-motor feedback and responds, 'A tip tapper'. The instructor uncovers the word, points to the *p* and asks, 'What do you need to feel?' The student answers 'A lip popper!' and reads the word correctly.

If the student's error is in the interior of the word, as in 'The shirt has a *band* on it', when the word was *brand*, the instructor covers the word and questions to an interior relationship. 'When you say /bænd/, what do you feel right after the lip popper?' The student checks oral-motor feedback and responds 'A smile sound'. The instructor uncovers the word, points to the *a* and says, 'We do need a smile sound – do you need to feel it right after the popper, or do you need to feel something else there?' The student answers, 'Oh. There's a back lifter' (the label for an /r/ sound because the tongue lifts toward the back to produce it) and reads the word correctly.

Ultimately, through the problem-solving experiences provided, the brain spontaneously connects this feedback loop of sensory information and self-corrects without intervention from the instructor. This is how decoding and encoding automaticity and independence can be assisted to come into being.

Prevention and Remediation

At the preventive level we suggest that it is unnecessary to test and diagnose which children should receive direct stimulation of phonemic awareness. Classroom research indicates that it is productive for all children to receive this stimulation. For many students it further refines phonemic awareness and the use of comparator function, and accelerates reading/spelling development significantly beyond the norms indicated on standardised tests. At the same time it develops a conceptual base and prevents reading failure for students who are at risk. At the remedial level, however, it is very helpful in diagnosis and prognosis to know the student's performance on the LAC Test. It indicates the conceptual base an individual has for functioning with the alphabetic code in reading and spelling, and how much needs to be developed.

Two preventive studies have shown that, applied in regular kindergarten or first-grade classrooms with all of the children, the ADD Program has a very substantial impact not only on the acquisition of beginning reading skills but also on the continued development of superior levels of skill. In a study with first graders (Lindamood, 1985), the experimental class received only the ADD Program during language arts instruction until January, when virtually all of the class could self-correct encoding and decoding errors in CVC syllables and words. They were then phased into the district's reading curriculum. The control class received the district's reading curriculum with a phonics strand starting in September. There was no significant difference between the classes in September pre-testing. In the May post-testing, the experimental class receiving the ADD Program was superior to the control class on four individually given measures: phonological awareness, word recognition, word attack and spelling. This superiority was still present in a follow-up study in fifth grade. On the Stanford Achievement Test measures of Reading Comprehension, Word Study Skills, Spelling and Total Reading, the mean percentile rankings of the 19 remaining experimental students ranged from 63.6 to 81.7, and there was no overlap in performance with the 66 fifth graders who had not received the ADD Program. Their mean percentile rankings ranged from 39.4 to 56.5, and this population included the school's gifted students.

In an eleven-year longitudinal study reported in a doctoral dissertation, Howard (1986) noted that the ADD Program's oral-motor approach to beginning reading instruction trains kindergarten and first-grade children in segmentation and blending skills associating awareness of oral-proprioceptive qualities of phoneme production with auditory and visual properties of speech. Research examined programme effects on first-grade entry and exit reading scores, as measured by the Woodcock Reading Mastery Tests and the Reading sub-test from the Iowa Tests of Basic Skills (ITBS). Analyses of covariance with the pre-test as the covariate indicated that first-grade students trained in the ADD Program techniques made greater gains in word attack and reading achievement in first grade and had higher reading scores in subsequent grades (second to eighth) than students not receiving such training; that kindergarten children trained in ADD Program techniques entered first grade with higher word attack skills than students not receiving such training; and that boys and girls perform equally well on word attack or reading achievement after receiving ADD Program training.

In a recent remedial study (Alexander et al., 1991), the ADD Program was used with a group of severely reading-disabled students averaging 10;9 years, who had not benefited from extensive previous remedial instruction. After 65 hours of one-on-one training, this group of 10 students improved from an average standard score of 77 on a measure of alphabetic reading skills to an average of 98.4 (standard score mean = 100). The poorest reader in the group improved from a score of 62 to 92, which placed him in the average range. This group of students had begun treatment with an average score on the LAC Test of 57.9 (minimum score recommended for their age and grade = 86), and had improved to an average score of 99.9 (total score possible = 100) following treatment.

In a larger remedial study, with 281 individuals, school-age to adult, Truch (1994) also reported powerful effects with the ADD Program procedures. Results indicate that 80 hours of intensive individual instruction, four hours daily, five days per week, produced highly significant gains on measures of phonological awareness, sound/symbol associations, word identification, word attack, spelling and decoding in context.

Concept Imagery: Processing the Whole

Just as phonemic awareness cannot be assumed, language comprehension cannot be assumed, and seems to be diminishing as is noted in numerous recent studies. For example, in the United States, the National Assessment of Educational Progress (NAEP) findings have shown particular deficiencies in higher-order reasoning skills, including those necessary for advanced reading comprehension (Healy, 1990). 'Reading instruction at all levels must be restructured to ensure that students learn to reason more effectively about what they have read', states the report. As comprehension scores have been declining and more and more children are labelled *hyperlexic* or *attention deficit*, the field of education has recognised the need for better diagnosis and instruction in reading comprehension, oral language comprehension and following directions.

Imagery has been linked to language processing, cognition, critical thinking, creativity and reading comprehension. There is strong historical evidence regarding the role of imagery in cognition, and this role has been discussed since Aristotle. He theorized that it is impossible to even think without a mental picture. Jean Piaget (1936, cited by Bleasdale, 1983) wrote, 'Thinking is concerned with the objects and events of the world we know....When the objects are not physically present, they are represented indirectly by what we remember and know of them. In what shape do memory and knowledge deliver the needed facts? In the shape of memory images, we answer most simply. Experiences deposit images.' Continuing in the 1960s, Allan Paivio (1969), who has written extensively on imagery and cognition, stated, 'As every psychologist knows, imagery once played a prominent role in the interpretation of associative meaning, mediation, and memory. It was widely regarded as the mental representative of meaning – or of concrete meaning at least.'

The 1970s brought further illumination from Paivio (1971). He had been attempting to demonstrate the way in which imagery can affect the acquisition, transformation, or retrieval of different classes of information. His Dual Coding Theory (DCT) for cognition defines imagery as one of the two types of cognitive coding. The other type is verbal coding. Paivio suggested that linguistic competence and performance are based on a substrate of imagery. Kosslyn (1976) conducted a developmental study on the effects and role of imagery in retrieving information from long-term memory. He reported that imagery provided significantly more opportunity for retrieval.

Linden and Wittrock (1981) stated, in a study with fourth graders, 'The generation of verbal and imaginal relations or associations between the text and experience increased comprehension approximately by fifty percent.' Further research by Oliver (1982), in three experiments to determine whether an instructional set for visual imagery would facilitate reading comprehension in elementary school children, concluded, 'These findings indicate that teachers should try to help children develop the metacognitive skills of visual imagery as a strategy for improving comprehension....Visualization enhances comprehension.'

Paivio (1986) indicated that cognition is proportional to the extent that language and mental representations (imagery) are integrated. The research of Long, Winograd & Bridge in 1989 provided further evidence regarding the role of imagery in reading:

'Our results suggest that imagery may be involved in the reading process in a number of ways. First, imagery may increase the capacity of working memory during reading by assimilating details and propositions into chunks which are carried along during reading. Second, imagery seems to be involved in making comparisons or analogies – that is, in matching schematic and textual information. Third, imagery seems to function as an organizational tool for coding and storing meaning gained from reading.'

As is evident, theories and research regarding the relationship of imagery to thinking have been held and proved repeatedly throughout history. The 1990s have produced further research to support the role of imagery in cognition and reading. 'Imaginative processes, including imagery and emotional responses, are necessary to breathe life into the reading experience.' (Sadoski, 1992). Sadoski, in researching DCT, reading theory and reading efficiency, showed that imagery is directly related to reading comprehension and recall by carefully proving that the more reading concepts are imaged the better they will be comprehended, the longer they will be recalled, and the more interesting they will be to the reader.

The concept of mental representation has become increasingly important in theories advanced to account for mechanisms of brain activity (Rumbelhart & Norman, 1988; Kosslyn & Koenig, 1992). Using positron emission tomography (PET), a current sensitive technique for investigating human functional neuroanatomy (Posner, 1993), Kosslyn reported that an area located near the primary visual area was more activated when subjects created a mental image of a letter on a perceived grid than when they actually saw the letter on the grid (Kosslyn et al., 1993).

Denis (1995) states:

'Representations are now viewed as psychological entities resulting from subject's interactions with the external world, and standing for absent or distant objects. Some representations are highly symbolic by nature, as is the case for linguistic or conceptual representations, whereas others preserve features as well as the internal structure of perceptual events in a highly analog fashion.'

Despite the importance of imagery to cognition, a significant percentage of children and adults may not be able to form adequate mental images for the language concepts presented with words. Imagery that empowers comprehension is vivid, relevant and forms a gestalt; it is not vague or isolated glimpses. Imagery weakness can occur with words presented orally or in writing, and it is not just that these individuals cannot form mental images, it is that they cannot bring the images to a gestalt (whole). If the sensory-cognitive function of concept imagery – the ability to create an imaged gestalt – is not available, then good decoding skills or good vocabulary or good contextual anticipation for a single word may not result in good language comprehension. The lower-level weakness in concept imagery may result in individuals being able to get only scattered parts, details, a few facts, a few names, a few dates, and weakness in bringing parts to a whole. This then results in weakness in the higher-order thinking skills of main idea, conclusion, inference, prediction, evaluation. Without a whole from which to process, those interpretive skills cannot be developed, and individuals are not able to monitor, self-correct and be independent in reasoning and thinking skills for either oral or written language. Without the sensory-cognitive function of concept imagery to bring parts to a whole, accurate decoding will not ensure reading comprehension. Individuals in this situation are left puzzled by the mystery of the reasoning ability that others possess.

Will 'reading and answering questions' develop concept imagery?

Why may having students read and answer questions, the most popular way to teach comprehension, not be effective? Educators have thought that comprehension can be developed in this way. Books entitled 'Getting the Main Idea' or 'Making an Inference' are used where students read the language and then answer questions. However, when students are wrong, it is common to ask them to read the paragraph again, or read the question again. Will simply re-reading language actually stimulate comprehension, or will it just give the student enough input to finally guess? Will asking higher-order thinking questions stimulate comprehension? Assuming comprehension, teachers may think the student is not trying or is not paying attention. Will encouragement such as 'Think when you read', 'Pay attention', 'Listen again' develop comprehension? No matter how many ways such things are said, or how many incentives are offered or penalties bestowed, students cannot perform if the lower level cognitive function of concept imagery is missing. Even attempts to bolster imagery with experiences to fill in background information may be ineffective with students who lack imagery ability, because that ability is needed to store the experiences for later reference, compare the experiences with what they read, and generalise.

Stimulating Dual Coding for Language Comprehension

How, then, do we develop concept imagery for those individuals who do not tend to naturally image a gestalt? The sensory system *can* be taught to image a gestalt and dual code, but the stimulation must be more basic yet more extensive than popular imagery exercises used for relaxation techniques. Teachers may believe they are stimulating imagery by telling students to 'Picture it in your head' or by leading guided imagery. And, in every classroom some students may be wondering, 'What do you mean? I see nothing', and may also be wondering what the people around them are doing. A teacher's suggestion to 'Picture that' can bring confusion or frustration to students who have not yet learned to image.

Paivio (1996) referred to the theory and steps of the Visualizing and Verbalizing for Language Comprehension and Thinking (V/V) Program, (Bell, 1991b) as the *methodology* of DCT: imagery and language...visualising and verbalising... dual coding. The goal of the V/V Program is to develop an imaged gestalt which will consciously be used to develop higher-order thinking skills. The integration of imagery and language moves in a carefully sequenced series of steps beginning at the *Verbalizing* level. Students describe a given picture prior to describing an imaged picture, and use Structure Words such as *what, color, size, shape, movement, number, background, mood, when*, and *sound* to add detail to the verbalising. The questioning interaction between the student and teacher develops and refines sequential, specific verbalising skills. As this is developing, the student is overlapped to verbalising about one word – a *Known Noun*. Using the Structure Words to stimulate detail, the goal is to develop vivid imagery for the smallest unit of language – a word – prior to moving to the next step of imaging a sentence and then combining sentences to form an imaged gestalt.

As imagery develops at the word level, the student is overlapped to the *Sentence-by-Sentence* step. Receiving a sentence and placing a coloured summary square to anchor the sentence imagery, the student again uses the Structure Words to stimulate detailed imagery. Continuing to image and place coloured summary squares, the student begins the integration of imagery with language, dual coding, by touching each coloured square and giving a *Picture Summary*, sequentially verbalising the imagery designated by each square. After completion of the picture summary, where the student has been able to describe his or her imagery in detail, the coloured squares are picked up and the student gives a *Word Summary, paraphrasing the overall gestalt of the paragraph*. Then as this imaged gestalt is developing, the stimulation is extended to the development of higher-order thinking skills of main idea, conclusion, inference, prediction and evaluation. For example, the student answers a main idea question by recalling what most of the images were about in the paragraph. The steps extend from low- to high-level content and from *Sentence-by-Sentence* to *Multiple Sentences, Paragraphs* and *Pages* of concepts and content – always with higher-order thinking questions imaged and verbalised – dual coded. As with the ADD Program, the instruction is delivered in a questioning format to stimulate comparator function and judgements of parts/ wholes relationships.

The V/V theoretical and instructional model is supported by Paivio's Dual Coding Theory and Sadoski's research: (1) the use of Structure Words to add detailed imagery for enhancing the vividness of the mental representations concretises the imagery and language, (2) the coloured summary squares for each sentence serve as the 'conceptual pegs' described by Paivio, and (3) the use of the Picture Summary for verbalising imagery enhances verbal recall from imagery prior to the Word Summary for paraphrasing or retelling.

Findings with the V/V Program indicate that ability to image the gestalt can be stimulated, with a corresponding gain in reading comprehension. Bell (1991a) reports on 45 individuals who received only V/V intervention in a clinical setting. They ranged in age from 9 to 57, including 22 males and 23 females. Pre-testing showed that they were performing poorly in reading comprehension, but receptive and expressive oral vocabulary were at the upper end of the normal range, as were phonemic awareness, word attack and word recognition. After an average treatment time of 47.26 hours, with a range of 16 to 110 hours, retesting indicated all had made significant improvement in reading comprehension. The pre-testing indicated a percentile mean for reading comprehension on the Gray Oral Reading Test-Revised (GORT-R) of 43.94 and at post-test, a percentile mean of 75.55.

Truch (1996) reports on using the V/V Program with 59 subjects in 80 hours of instruction. Subjects were of different ages and ability levels. Overall, 60% were in the age group 6–12; another 25% were from ages 13–17, and the remaining 15% were adults aged 18 and over. The majority met the traditional criteria for 'learning disabilities' and some met the criteria for 'attention deficit disorder.' The average age was 21 years, with 37 males and 22 females. After only V/V instruction, the gains in comprehension scores on the Gray Oral Reading Test (GORT) were highly significant with an average gain of four years in reading comprehension. Word reading did not account for weak reading comprehension and nor did poor vocabulary.

A 1995 study in a public school setting using the V/V Program with an entire fourth-grade class from February to May revealed significant improvement in reading comprehension with the V/V experimental group compared with the control group. With approximately 40 hours of instruction, there was a significant improvement in reading comprehension, as measured by the Gray Oral Reading Test-3 (GORT-3), despite no significant improvement in oral vocabulary and a modest decline in decoding accuracy (Bell & Torgesen, in preparation).

Conclusions

Independent, competent oral and written language involves lower-level skills required for higher level processing. In this chapter we focused on lower-level sensory-cognitive functions that are critical: *phonemic awareness, concept imagery*, and *comparator function*. Phonemic awareness – the ability to identify individual sounds and their order within words – enables the perception of parts within the whole. Concept imagery – the ability to create an imaged gestalt (whole) – enables the creation of a whole from the parts. Phonemic awareness is a key factor in decoding and spelling, whilst concept imagery is a key factor in oral and written language comprehension. Though these are not the only cognitive functions needed in processing language, they are primary and basic to competence.

A third critical aspect of neural functioning, comparator function, needs to be involved at every level from sensory input to perception, to monitoring, to self-correction, if independence is the goal. Comparator function is the ability to hold one sensory input and compare it with another, to note specific differences in errors in the parts and wholes involved. The sensory system gets jolted in the process of comparing, and self-corrects, enabling independent, competent processing.

Traditional instruction tends to assume conscious awareness of sensory input, perception, and access to comparator function, if there are no peripheral impairments such as faulty vision or hearing. It also tends to teach concepts, rather than questioning to facilitate their emergence, and then is disappointed in the degree of storage, retrieval and generalisation that occurs. What will it take to change this situation in respect of the current concerns about literacy deficiencies and the lowering of critical thinking skills in our populations?

Research helps answer this question. Findings indicate the effectiveness of directing *conscious* attention to *sensory input/perception and comparator function to establish phoneme awareness, concept imagery and judgements of parts/wholes relationships*. Sensory-cognitive process-based instruction enables concepts regarding encoding/decoding and language comprehension to emerge for learners because they discover how and what to attend to, and at what level to attend, to get the information they need. When concepts are acquired through this process, learners know *how* they know, *why* they know, *what* they know, and storage, retrieval and generalisation within the language and literacy systems are specifically facilitated. Learners have a complete cognitive tool kit with which to function independently to their full potential.

References

Adams, M. (1990). *Beginning to Read: Thinking and Learning about Print*. Cambridge, MA: MIT Press.

Alexander, A., Anderson, H., Heilman, P., Voeller, K. & Torgesen, J. (1991). Phonological awareness training and remediation of analytic decoding deficits in a group of severe dyslexics. *Annals of Dyslexia* 41, 193–206.

Ball, E. & Blachman, B. (1991). Does phoneme awareness training in kindergarten make a difference in early word recognition and developmental spelling? *Reading Research Quarterly* 26, 49–66.

Bell, N. (1991a). Gestalt imagery: A critical factor in language comprehension. *Annals of Dyslexia* 41, 246–260.

Bell, N. (1991b). *Visualizing and Verbalizing for Language Comprehension and Thinking*. San Luis Obispo, CA: NBI Publishing.

Bell, N. & Torgesen, J. (1996). The role of imagery in reading comprehension: Results of a classroom study. (in press).

Bleasdale, F. (1983). Paivio's dual-coding model of meaning revisited. In J.C. Yuille (Ed.), *Imagery, Memory and Cognition: Essays in Honor of Allan Paivio* (p.184). Hilladale, NJ: Lawrence Erlbaum.

Calfee, R., Lindamood, C. & Lindamood, P. (1973). Acoustic-phonetic skills and reading-kindergarten through twelfth grade. *Journal of Educational Psychology* 64, 293–298.

DeFries, J., Fulkes, D. & LaBuda, M. (1987). Reading disability in twins: Evidence for a genetic etiology. *Nature* 329, 537–539.

Denis, M. (1995). A positron emission tomography study of visual and mental spatial exploration. *Journal of Cognitive Neuroscience* 7, 433–445.

Healy, J. (1990). *Endangered Minds: Why our Children don't Think* (p.25). New York: Simon & Schuster.

Howard, M. (1986). Effects of pre-reading training in auditory conceptualization on subsequent reading achievement. PhD dissertation, Salt Lake City, UT: Brigham Young University.

Kosslyn, S. (1976). Using imagery to retrieve semantic information: A developmental study. *Child Development* 47, 434–444.

Kosslyn, S., Alpert, N., Thomson, W., Maljkovic, V., Weise, S., Chabris, C., Hamilton, S., Rauch, S. & Buonanno, S. (1993). Visual mental imagery activates topographically organized visual cortex: PET investigations. *Journal of Cognitive Neuroscience* 5,263–267.

Kosslyn, S. & Koenig, O. (1992). *Wet Mind: The Cognitive Neuroscience*. New York: Free Press.

Liberman, A. & Mattingly, I. (1985). The motor theory of speech perception revisited. *Cognition* 21, 1–36.

Liberman, I. & Shankweiler, D. (1985). Phonology and the problems of learning to read and write. *Remedial and Special Education* 6, 8–17.

Lindamood, P. (1985). Cognitively developed phonemic awareness as a base for literacy. Paper presented at the National Reading Conference, San Diego, CA, December 1985.

Lindamood, P. (1994). Issues in researching the link between phonological awareness, learning disabilities, and spelling. In G.R. Lyon (Ed.), *Frames of Reference for the Assessment of Learning Disabilities* (pp. 351–372). Baltimore, MD: Brookes Publishing.

Lindamood, C. & Lindamood, P. (1997). *Auditory Discrimination in Depth*. Austin, TX: Pro-Ed.

Lindamood, C. & Lindamood, P. (1979). *Lindamood® Auditory Conceptualization (LAC) Test*. Austin, TX: PRO-ED.

Linden, M. & Wittrock, M. (1981). The teaching of reading comprehension according to the model of generative learning. *Reading Research Quarterly* 17, 44–57.

Long, S., Winograd, P. & Bridge, C. (1989). The effects of reader and text characteristics on reports of imagery during and after reading. *Reading Research Quarterly* 19, 353–372.

Lundberg, I. (1988). Preschool prevention of reading failure: does training in phonological awareness work: In R.L. Masland & M.W. Masland (Eds.) *Prevention of Reading Failure* (pp. 163–176) Parkton, MD: York Press.

Lundberg, I., Frost, J. & Peterson, O. (1988). Effects of an extensive program for stimulating phonological awareness in pre-school children. *Reading Research Quarterly* 23, 263–284.

Montgomery, D. (1981). Do dyslexics have difficulty accessing articulatory information? *Psychological Research* 43, 235–243.

Oliver, M.E. (1982). Improving comprehension with mental imagery. Paper read at the annual Meeting of the Washington Organization for Reading Development of the International Reading Association, Seattle, WA: March 1982.

Olson, R., Forsberg, H., Wise, B. & Rack, J. (1994) Measurement of word recognition, orthographic, and phonological skills. In G.R. Lyon (Ed.) *Frames of Reference for the Assessment of Learning Disabilities* (pp. 243–277). Baltimore, MD: Brookes Publishing.

Paivio, A. (1969). Mental imagery in associative learning and memory. *Psychological Review* 76, 241–263.

Paivio, A. (1971). *Imagery and Verbal Processes*. New York: Holt, Rinehart & Winston. [Reprinted 1979. Hillsdale NJ: Lawrence Erlbaum]

Paivio, A. (1986). *Mental Representations: A Dual Coding Approach*. New York: Oxford University Press.

Paivio, A. (1996). Presentation at the National Lindamood-Bell Research and Training Conference, San Francisco, CA: March 1996.

Posner, M.I. (1993). Seeing the mind. *Science* 262, 673–674.

Powers, W. (1973). *Behavior: The Control of Perception*. Chicago, IL: Aldine.

Rumbelhart, D. E. & Norman, D. A. (1988). Representation in memory. In R. C. Atkinson, R. J. Herrnstein, G. Lindzey & R. D. Luce (Eds.) *Stevens Handbook of Experimental Psychology* . New York: Wiley.

Sadoski, M. (1992). An exploratory study of the relationship between reported imagery and the comprehension and recall of a story. *Reading Research Quarterly* 19,110–123.

Shankweiler, D. & Liberman, I.Y. (1989). *Phonology and Reading Disability*. Ann Arbor, MI: University of Michigan Press.

Stetson, R. (1951). *Motor Phonetics: A Study of Speech Movements in Action*. Amsterdam, The Netherlands: New Holland.

Torgesen, J., Morgan, S. & Davis, C. (1992). The effects of two types of phonological awareness training on word learning in kindergarten children. *Journal of Educational Psychology* 84, 364–370.

Torgesen, J., Wagner, B. & Rashotte, C. (1996). Approaches to the prevention and remediation of phonologically based reading disabilities. In B. Blachman (Ed.)

Cognitive and Linguistic Foundations of Reading Acquisition: Implications for Intervention Research. Hillsdale, NJ: Erlbaum.

Truch, S. (1994). Stimulating basic reading processes using Auditory Discrimination in Depth. *Annals of Dyslexia* 44, 60–80.

Truch, S. (1996). Stimulating basic recall using the Visualizing/Verbalizing Program (in preparation).

Wagner, R.K., Torgesen, J.K. & Rashotte, C.A. (1994). The development of reading-related phonological processing abilities: New evidence of bi-directional causality from a latent variable longitudinal study. *Developmental Psychology* 30,73–87.

Wheatley, M. (1992). *Leadership and the New Science.* San Francisco, CA: Berrett-Koehler.

Chapter 13
Prevention of Dyslexia in Kindergarten: Effects of Phoneme Awareness Training with Children of Dyslexic Parents

INA BORSTRØM and CARSTEN ELBRO

Introduction

It is well documented that reading problems run in families. Children of dyslexic parents are at greatly increased risk of the disorder. Estimates of the risk of a dyslexic parent having a dyslexic child indicate at least a fourfold increase compared with the risk in control families (Cardon et al., 1994; Gilger, Pennington & DeFries, 1991; Scarborough, 1990). An obvious target for dyslexia research is therefore the prediction and prevention of reading disabilities in children of dyslexic families. This chapter reports an attempt to prevent the development of dyslexia by pre-school intervention.

It is quite clear that many children and adults with reading problems have poor phonological recoding skills (see surveys in Fowler & Scarborough, 1993; Lyon, 1995; Rack, Snowling & Olson, 1992): they are poor at making use of the systematic relationships between letters and speech sounds, and between strings of letters and strings of sounds (Vandervelden & Siegel, 1995). In other words, many problems in reading may be referred back to fundamental difficulties in making use of the alphabetic principle (Elbro, 1990). These difficulties are seen in a variety of ways, but one of the clearest and best documented is a difficulty in non-word reading. Deficits in such phonological recoding have been found in poor readers across a wide range of general cognitive abilities (e.g. Siegel, 1988; Stanovich & Siegel, 1994), and are characteristic of adults with a school history of difficulties in learning to read (e.g. Bruck, 1990; Elbro, Nielsen & Petersen, 1994). Even adults who appear to have overcome their early reading difficulties ('compensated dyslexics') show signs of phonological recoding problems (Pennington et al., 1987). It also appears that such difficulties in decoding may be a significant cause of reading comprehension problems (Shankweiler, 1989; Share, 1995; Stanovich, 1986).

The present study focused on dyslexia (defined as a decoding deficit related to problems with phonological processing). In a recent study we found that adults with a history of difficulties in learning to read were quite clearly separated from a control group of adults by poor phonological recoding in reading (Elbro et al., 1994; Elbro, submitted). The central questions addressed by the present study were how, and to what extent, similar problems could be prevented in the children of these adults.

Phoneme Awareness as a Target for Early Intervention

One of the most important causes of decoding difficulties seems to be a lack of sensitivity to, and awareness of, phoneme-sized speech segments (for surveys see Elbro, 1996; Lundberg, 1994; Mattingly, 1972; Stanovich, 1986). In this chapter the term *phonological awareness* is used to refer to the general ability to shift attention from word meaning to the phonological form of spoken words (Mattingly, 1972; Tornéus, 1984). This shift may be required when children are asked to make judgements about spoken words based on, for instance, their length, shared rhymes, number of syllables, or initial sounds. The term *phoneme awareness* is used in a narrower sense to denote conscious access to and ability to manipulate phoneme-sized segments of spoken words. Whilst most children develop many aspects of phonological awareness long before learning to read – for example, most young children appreciate nursery rhymes (e.g. Bryant, Maclean & Bradley, 1990; Chaney, 1992) – phoneme awareness normally develops during the pre-school years and during initial reading instruction (Bowey & Francis, 1991).

There is no doubt that initial reading instruction is an efficient way to train phoneme awareness. During the first grade children normally take a much bigger leap forward in awareness of phonemes than during the preceding kindergarten year (Bentin, Hammar & Cahan, 1991; Bowey & Francis, 1991). On the other hand, children with poor access to segments of spoken words in kindergarten are at risk of developing reading difficulties – even when differences in letter knowledge and emergent word reading skills are accounted for (Elbro Borstrøm & Petersen, forthcoming; Wagner, Torgesen & Rashotte, 1994) and compensated dyslexic adults still perform more poorly than reading-matched controls on phoneme segmentation and phoneme manipulation tasks (Pennington et al., 1987).

The influence of early phoneme awareness on reading development has been verified by many training studies with unselected children in kindergarten (e.g. Ball & Blachman, 1991; Brady et al., 1994; Byrne & Fielding-Barnsley, 1993, 1995; Cunningham, 1990; Lundberg, Frost & Petersen, 1988; Schneider & Näslund, in press; Uhry & Shepherd, 1993; Vellutino & Scanlon, 1987). Although the effects of phonological awareness training (including phoneme awareness) appear to be strongest when letters are introduced simultaneously with the sounds (e.g. Bradley & Bryant, 1985; Tangel & Blachman, 1995), significant effects have also been reported from a training study which did not introduce letters (Lundberg et al., 1988). Furthermore, two studies by Cary and Verhaeghe (1994) indicated that, in order to help children develop phoneme awareness, training must focus the children's attention on phonemes. A focus on higher linguistic levels (e.g. rimes and syllables) does not lead to improved phoneme analysis in children; but phoneme awareness training may lead to improved skills with syllables.

Schneider and Näslund (in press) replicated the study of Lundberg et al. (1988) with German kindergarten children. The German study comprised 22 training groups, but only nine of the kindergarten teachers used the training programme consistently. The other 13 kindergarten classes fell behind schedule and did not spend as much time as planned on phoneme analysis and synthesis. The children in the nine consistently trained groups outperformed children in a control group on four out of six measures of phonological awareness. No differences were found between the inconsistently trained children and the control group. These results suggest that the quality of the training and the amount of time spent on it may be critical determinants of its effectiveness.

The least successful studies of phoneme awareness training appear to be those with (older) students who have already been diagnosed as dyslexic. As pointed out by Olson et al. (1996, in press), phoneme awareness training may transfer to accuracy in phonological recoding but with little or no apparent effect on the reading of familiar words or on reading comprehension (as in the case of the studies by Lovett et al., 1994 and Wise & Olson, 1995). Whilst the causes of such a lack of transfer are yet unknown, these problems clearly underline the importance of early intervention.

Another approach, taken by a few studies, is to identify children at risk of reading difficulties on the basis of low pre-school scores on phonological awareness (and other predictors of reading difficulties). Lundberg (1994) analysed the reading development of the children who had the lowest scores in phonological awareness in the Lundberg et al. study (1988). He then compared the reading development of the 25 poorest children in the experimental and control groups. Whilst the at-risk children in the experimental group reached a normal reading level in grade three (i.e. the average reading level of the untrained control group), the at-risk children in the control group were clearly lagging behind their peers in grade three. However, even in the experimental group some of the children remained quite poor readers.

Positive effects of phonological awareness training were also reported by Torgesen, Wagner & Rashotte, (1994). Sixty at-risk children with poor phonological awareness in kindergarten were given a phonological training programme in small groups (with three or four children) during 20-minute sessions four times a week for a period of 12 weeks. The trained group far outperformed an untrained comparison group of 40 other at-risk children on a segmentation task. However, this result covers a substantial variability in response to the training: even after training, about 30% of the children in the trained group were practically unable to segment words.

The only intervention study reported so far with children of dyslexic families involved 54 children in kindergarten (Byrne et al., in press). Preliminary results have been obtained from 40 of these children who have been taught phoneme awareness (using the programme of Byrne & Fielding-Barnsley, 1991) for one 40-minute session per week. After 16 to 20 weeks of training in small groups (one to six children) 32% of the children showed no growth in phoneme awareness, and a further 20% of the children showed only partial improvement. These numbers are much higher than the corresponding numbers reported previously from a random sample of children (of 5% and 2%, respectively). However, it is too early to know whether the results for reading and spelling development will be equally variable.

Reading and Phonological Awareness in Danish Kindergarten Classes

Kindergarten attendance is not mandatory in Denmark, but about 98% of children enter kindergarten in the year they become six years of age. The adults who take care of the children in kindergarten are not educated as teachers, and they are not supposed to teach the children academic skills. Neither are children usually taught to read at home before the first grade, which means that the vast majority of children spend their first year in school before they receive any formal or informal instruction in reading. These factors make Danish kindergarten classes well suited for intervention studies of phoneme awareness (cf. Lundberg et al., 1988): the children cannot read, yet they are old enough to understand some formal properties of their language (e.g. in a context of language games) and they spend a full year in school before being taught to read.

The linguistic awareness programme of Lundberg et al. (1988) has been a vehicle for the introduction of the concept of 'linguistic awareness' to almost all kindergarten teachers in Denmark. Linguistic awareness is often taught in the form of nursery rhymes, syllable games, rhyming games and other activities which help children develop a feeling for some of the segments in spoken utterances and words. In many cases, however, these linguistic awareness programmes do *not* include activities to develop phoneme awareness, even though it now seems evident that this level of language awareness is especially important for learning to read. For instance, 73 of the 77 Danish kindergarten teachers in the study reported below said that they taught (or played with) rhymes in their classes, whereas only 37 of 77 teachers said that they included activities with speech sounds of phoneme size, and only 25 said that they taught their children the alphabet and initial letters.

Aims of the Study

The intervention study reported here was part of a longitudinal study of the linguistic abilities underlying individual differences in early reading development. The study followed children from their entry into kindergarten until the beginning of the second grade (with a planned follow-up one year later). The general aim of the longitudinal study was to investigate the relative strengths of a range of theoretically motivated predictors of dyslexia (see Elbro, 1996; Elbro, et al., forthcoming). This aim was pursued by means of a combination of longitudinal and intervention methods. A specific aim of the intervention reported here was to study the preventive effects of phoneme awareness training in children of dyslexic parents. We had two main hypotheses:

1. It would be possible to train phoneme awareness during the kindergarten grade even in at-risk children of dyslexic parents.
2. Phoneme awareness training should reduce the incidence of dyslexia in the at-risk children.

Method

Design

The study comprised three groups of pre-school children: a group of 36 children of dyslexic parents participated in an extended programme designed to help them develop phoneme awareness during the kindergarten grade, whilst another 52 children of dyslexic parents served as one control group, and a third group of 48 children of normally reading parents formed a second control group. For brevity, the children of dyslexic parents will be referred to as 'at-risk' children here. The at-risk children in the experimental condition received phoneme awareness training in their regular kindergarten classrooms (27 different ones) provided by their own teachers, whilst the at-risk control children (from 44 classes) and the non-at-risk control children (from six classes) participated in the ordinary activities of their classes. The two control groups did in fact receive some instruction in linguistic awareness because most kindergarten teachers know about the value of such instruction for reading development. At the onset of the study the kindergarten teachers reported that they spent an average of 16 minutes a day on language games and activities with their classes; this was the same amount across all three groups in the study. Some teachers also said that they spent time on phoneme awareness activities. However the intensity and highly structured nature of our training programme, and its clear focus on phoneme-sized segments, distinguished it from the control conditions. The development of several reading-related language abilities was measured before and after training (at the beginning of the kindergarten year, and one year later), whilst the initial reading development of the children was assessed at the beginning of grade two.

Participants

In the present study we defined at-risk children as children with at least one dyslexic parent. Dyslexia in adults was defined as a self-reported history of long-lasting difficulties in learning to read – in addition to an objectively measured difficulty in decoding. Decoding was measured by tests of oral non-word reading and pseudo-homophone recognition (which is a homophone of a real word: *rane, pame, saip, warld? (rane = rain* is the expected answer). Adults were classified as dyslexic if they had scores one standard deviation below the mean of a group of adults with reportedly normal reading development, whilst a few adults with reading difficulties were excluded owing to poor receptive vocabulary (below the 10th percentile) (for details see Elbro et al., 1994, with further discussion in Elbro, submitted). Children were excluded if two (or more) languages were spoken regularly at home or if Danish was not the first language of the child. We also excluded children with uncorrected sensory impairments or clear signs of general learning disabilities.

Most of the children of dyslexic families were referred to the study by their parents a year before the children entered kindergarten. The families were recruited by TV, radio, newspaper and magazine advertisements. A group of normal control children and a few additional at-risk children were included from randomly selected schools. The teachers of the at-risk children were randomly assigned to the experimental and the control conditions.

The two groups of at-risk children did not differ on any of our measures (Table 1). Neither did the at-risk children taken as a single

Table 13.1 Characteristics of the three groups of participants

Characteristic	At-risk children		Normal children
	Experimental	Control 1	Control 2
Boys/girls (n)	20/16	22/30	23/25
Age (y:m)	6:2 (0:4)	6:3 (0:4)	6:4 (0:4)
Raven (raw score)	17.0 (4.7)	18.3 (4.1)	19.0 (4.1)
Mother's education (years)	12.0 (2.6)	12.1 (2.5)	13.1 (2.9)
Father's education (years)	10.6 (3.0)	10.1 (2.1)	13.7 (3.2)
Home reading to child (hours/week)	2.2 (1.4)	2.6 (1.5)	2.8 (1.4)

group differ from the normal children with regard to age, IQ (as measured by Raven's coloured matrices, Raven, 1990) or in terms of how much they were read to by their parents at home. The Raven raw scores of the three groups correspond to the 58th, 69th, and 75th percentiles (according to the 1982 standardisation): for the experimental, control group 1 and control group 2, respectively. However, both mothers and fathers from families without reading difficulties had been educated for longer on average than mothers and fathers from families with reading difficulties.

The training programme

The training programme was specially prepared for this study (Borstrøm & Petersen, 1996) and designed to meet the needs of children with relatively poor language abilities. Unlike many similar programmes, it does not include an introduction with general listening games, word and syllable segmentation, and play with rhymes. Instead, it focuses on single speech sounds right from the start, but progresses very slowly with only two new consonants per week, and with repetition every other week of the sounds covered so far. The vowels are introduced during the first two weeks of the programme. Each consonant is introduced in many different ways:

First, the children are given a semantic cue to the sound and asked to pronounce it, e.g. [m] is the 'taste-good' sound. They are shown the corresponding letter and told its name. Then the sound is introduced by means of a spoken rhyme (a children's poem) with many words beginning with the sound, and the children are asked to find the words beginning with the sound. The children are also encouraged to find other words and names which begin with the sound. Finally, the children are told how to articulate the sound, e.g. 'When you say [m:], your mouth is closed. The air comes out of your nose rather than out of your mouth. This is why you can say [m:] even if you put a hand over your mouth (try that). If you hold your hand under your nose you can feel the air coming out of your nose. When you say [m:] you do not have to do anything with your tongue. The tongue can just relax while you say [m:]. We call [m:] a nose sound.' The two sounds introduced the same week are chosen so that they differ widely in articulation. For instance, [m] is introduced with [s]: [m] and [s] are the first consonants of the programme because they are easy to pronounce in isolation.

Second, the identity and significance of the sounds in whole words are taught without written words. The division into onset and rime is introduced by means of pictures; for instance, the teacher draws an ice cream on the blackboard and then adds an initial [m] to get *mice*. The children are told that *ice* and *mice* sound very much the same. The only difference is that *mice* begins with a [m] while *ice* does not. The distinctive significance of the two sounds of the week is illustrated by means of minimal pairs, e.g. *may*, *say*. Next, the children are taught how to add a consonant to a non-word (visualised by a box). For example, the children are shown a box drawn on the blackboard and told that it contains [1][eɪl]. This is not a word, the children are told, but if they put [m] before [1][eɪl] they get a real word (*mail*). If instead they say [s] before [1][eɪl] they get another word (*sail*). Again the teacher points out to the child that the words *mail* and *sail* sound alike; the [s] and [m] sounds make the difference. The final step in blending is to build a word with an initial consonant cluster, e.g. [s] + [m] + [2][aɪl] yields *smile*.

During weeks of repetition, all the sounds covered so far are practised together in language games (e.g. 'Find the pair of pictures which begin with the same sound') and in articulatory exercises where sounds articulated in the same place are to be grouped as a part of a game; e.g. lip sounds (m, p, b) in contrast with front tongue sounds (n, d, t). The distinctions covered by the programme include rounding (vowels), place of articulation (six positions) and manner of articulation (only nasal).

The programme includes all initial consonants in Danish. It was designed to take about 30 minutes every school day for 17 weeks. This time was taken from other of the play-like activities in the participating kindergarten classes.

Administration of the Training Programme

All teaching was administered to whole kindergarten classes by their own teachers – even though in most cases only one of the children in a class participated in the study. This was undoubtedly less efficient than teaching in small groups (e.g. Byrne & Fielding-Barnsley, 1993, 1995) and the teachers were not highly trained. However, the approach was in line with long-lasting Danish teaching traditions, and it has high ecological validity. The experimental teachers were given a 15-hour introduction to phonetics and phonology at the University of Copenhagen. The course also introduced the phoneme awareness programme.

Early Kindergarten and Early Grade 1 Measures

Measures of emergent reading abilities, of a variety of phonological and morphological skills together with a vocabulary measure were taken at the beginning of kindergarten grade and again at the beginning of first grade. At the beginning of second grade, several measures of reading abilities were administered to the children. In this report we focus on the trained measures (on which we expected to see group differences), and on a few control measures. We expected to see effects of training on measures of phoneme awareness and on letter knowledge, because letters were included as a vehicle for phoneme awareness training. We also expected training to have some impact on awareness of syllables. But we did not expect the training to influence lexical knowledge such as receptive vocabulary. As to reading, we anticipated that training would enhance decoding and hence reduce the risk of dyslexia. The measures are presented in further detail in Elbro et al. (in press). All tests were administered individually. In the language-awareness tasks, corrective feedback was given with all items, and testing was discontinued if a child made four errors in a row.

Letter naming: The child was shown all the 29 letters in Danish randomly arranged and printed in upper case. The child was asked to name the letters one by one.

Word decoding: Children who were able to name at least six letters of the alphabet were given a short version of a standardised silent word reading test (OS 400, Søegård & Petersen, 1974). The short version contained the first 36 items of the original 400 items. Each item consists of a printed word and a choice of four pictures; the child is asked to mark the correct one.

Phoneme deletion: The child was simply asked to say a word without a particular sound, e.g. '*mice* – if you say *mice* and then take away /m/, what is left then?' (*ice*). The expected reply was a word for all items. The idea of the task was introduced and illustrated using syllables with picture cards: the experimenter told the child that if one says *football* and then takes away *foot*, then there is only *ball* left (using pictures to visualise the operation). There were two practice items and nine test items.

Phoneme identification: The child was presented with single phonemes spoken by the experimenter in isolation and in a model word and for each phoneme asked to identify the word beginning with this phoneme (pre-test). The child was asked to point to the correct picture from a selection of six pictures, e.g. '[m:] is the first sound in *milk* – point to the word which begins with [m:]' (*mouse*). There were two practice items and eight test items.

Syllable deletion: This task with syllables was administered in complete analogy with (and immediately before) the phoneme subtraction task. It has six items.

Syllable identification: This task was similar to the phoneme identification task, except that the target was a syllable rather than a phoneme. There were eight items.

Receptive Vocabulary (PPVT-R, Dunn & Dunn, 1981): The Peabody Picture Vocabulary Test was used in a Danish translation to assess receptive vocabulary. The Danish version of the test has not yet been standardised, so raw scores were used.

Grade 2 measures of reading

Two tests were selected to measure the children's abilities to decode written words. The tests were easy versions of the tests which were used to help confirm the presence of dyslexia in the parents. A very poor score (zero or only a few correct responses) in these tests after a year of conventional reading instruction was taken as an indication of possible dyslexia. In addition to these tests, the full version of the word decoding test with 400 items was also administered at the beginning of the second grade.

Non-word reading: Thirty non-words were presented in three graded lists beginning with four CV words. The child was told that the words were not real words but that it was possible to read them aloud anyway. Five practice words were given with corrective feedback. No corrective feedback was given with the test words. If a child hesitated for more than 10 seconds, he or she was encouraged to continue with the next word. Testing was discontinued when a child failed to read any of the words correctly in a list. The score was number correct.

Identification of pseudo-homophones: The child's task was to identify pseudo-words which could be homophones of real words. Each item contained four pronounceable non-words (e.g. *bote, boaf, beal, hote*) and a picture (e.g. a boat), and the child was told that the words were written by a girl who tried to spell only by ear because she had not quite learned to spell yet. She had only been successful once in each line, whilst the other three attempts did not sound like the word in the picture. The task was to find the successful attempt which sounded right. After three practice items with feedback on all four non-words of each item, the child was given five minutes to solve as many items as possible out of a total of 48 items.

Results

Effects of training on reading-related language abilities during kindergarten

Individual gains on each of the language measures were calculated as lod-scores (the logarithm of the quotients between the odd-transformed scores at each testing occasion, see Allerup & Elbro, 1990; submitted). The gains in the three groups of participants were then compared by means of the non-parametric Mann-Whitney U-test. This procedure was chosen because many of the scores were not normally distributed. Group comparisons indicated that the experimental group gained significantly more than the at-risk control group in *letter naming*, *word reading* and *phoneme deletion*. The experimental group also progressed significantly more than the at-risk controls on a simple sum score from the two measures of phonemic awareness (see Figure 13.1).

Phoneme awareness (total of 17)

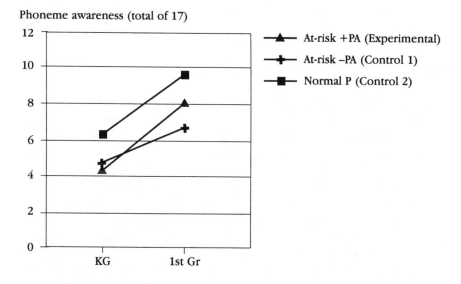

Figure 13.1 Development in phoneme awareness measured as an unweighted sum of the two phoneme awareness tasks in each of the three groups (maximum score on both test occasions was 17)

The experimental group gained as much as the normal controls in phoneme awareness over the kindergarten year, whereas the untrained at-risk group tended to lag behind the untrained normal controls, though this difference was not significant.

There were no significant differences between groups in terms of gains in syllable awareness or receptive vocabulary (PPVT) (see Figure 13.2).

Syllable awareness (total)

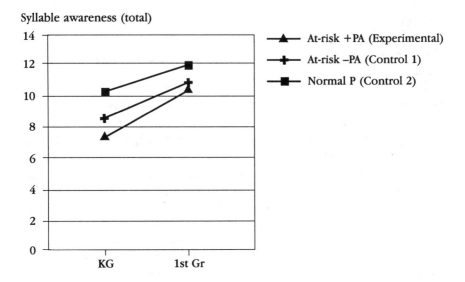

Figure 13.2 Development of syllable awareness measured as an unweighted sum of the two syllable awareness tasks in each of the three groups (maximum score is 14 on both testing occasions)

Effects of training on early reading development

The reading data from early in grade 2 are given in Table 13.2. Non-parametric comparisons of group means indicated that the experimental group outperformed the untrained at-risk children on pseudo-homophones and on word decoding. The experimental group also outperformed the at-risk controls on a combined measure of the pseudo-homophone task and the oral non-word reading task (average standardised scores on the two tasks were used). The untrained at-risk children were behind the normal controls on all reading measures.

In order to study the effects of training on the incidence of dyslexia, we selected a simple cut-off criterion for poor phonological recoding which yielded 8% (four of 48) poor readers in the normal control group. The measure of phonological recoding was the average of the standardised (z) scores on the two reading measures. This measure corresponds closely to the measure used to define dyslexia in adults (Elbro et al., 1994; Elbro, submitted). The cut-off point was selected at a fairly low reading level to make sure that children included in the group with possible dyslexia would be quite likely to experience fairly severe reading problems. Table 13.3 shows the distribution of possibly dyslexic and normally achieving children in the three groups of participants.

The prevalence of possible dyslexia was much higher in the two groups of at-risk children (27 out of 88 = 31%) than in the normal controls (four out of 48 = 8%), corresponding to an odds ratio of roughly 5.2. Significantly more of the at-risk children were categorised

Table 13.2 Reading abilities at the beginning of the 2nd grade. Average scores (and standard deviations in brackets) on two measures of phonological recoding in reading and on a measure of silent decoding of real words. Statistics of group differences are displayed in the last three columns (z values from Mann-Whitney U-test)

Beginning 2nd Gr	At-risk children		Normal	Group differences (z)		
	Experimental	Control 1	Control 2	E-C1	E-C2	C1-C2
Phonological recoding in reading						
Non-words	9.7	7.9	13.9	< 1	2.29*	3.76***
(max 30)	(8.3)	(7.2)	(8.1)			
Pseudo-homophones	16.8	11.7	19.3	3.06**	< 1	3.96***
(max 48)	(8.3)	(7.1)	(11.7)			
Combined (z score)	0.01	−0.37	0.39	2.17*	1.75	4.12***
	(0.87)	(0.76)	(1.01)			
Word decoding						
Real word reading	64.2	51.3	84.6	2.08*	1.10	3.37***
(max 400)	(36.9)	(35.3)	(60.7)			

Note: * = $p < 0.05$, ** = $p < 0.01$, *** = $p < 0.001$

as possibly dyslexic than of the normal control children. The training programme appeared to reduce the prevalence of dyslexia in the at-risk group: whilst 21 of 52 (40%) untrained at-risk children were classified as possibly dyslexic, only six of 36 (17%) were classified as such among the trained at-risk children. This difference between the two at-risk groups was significant. Furthermore, whilst the prevalence of dyslexia was much higher in the untrained at-risk group than in the normal control group, there was no significant difference between the occurrence of dyslexia in the trained at-risk children and the normal controls.

Finally, the effect of phoneme awareness training was assessed by means of a stepwise logistic regression analysis. In this analysis,

Table 13.3 Number of children in each of three groups identified in the beginning of second grade as either normal or possibly dyslexic (i.e. with low scores in phonological recoding, below 10th percentile in the normal control group).

Reading status at the beginning of grade 2	At-risk children		Normal
	Experimental	Control 1	Control 2
Possibly dyslexic	6	21	4
Possibly normal	30	31	44

linguistic predictors of dyslexia were entered at the first step, and training condition was entered at the second step. The analysis was carried out in the following way. A previous study of a (largely untrained) sub-group of the participants in the present study indicated that possible dyslexia in grade two was predicted quite well by three sets of language abilities at the beginning of kindergarten: letter naming, phonological awareness (phoneme deletion and phoneme identification), and quality of phonological representations (pronunciation accuracy and distinctness of vowel segments) (Elbro et al., in press). Consequently, as a first step, a logistic regression analysis was performed in the two groups of at-risk children ($n = 88$). Possible dyslexia was entered as dependent variable (with the cut-off point used above) and the five predictors as independent variables. The resulting model gave a good fit to the data and an overall prediction rate of 79.3%. At the second step, training condition (training or not) was entered as the sixth predictor. The addition of training condition as a predictor significantly improved the model confirming that the risk of dyslexia was decreased by training. The estimated coefficient corresponds to a 0.28 decrease of the odds for possible dyslexia. This means that the risk of 40% of the phonologically untrained sample becoming dyslexic (the untrained at-risk group) would theoretically be expected to decrease to 16% with training –in a sample of children with the same level of language abilities. This figure of 16% is not much different from the 17% we found in the trained at-risk group.

Discussion

Recently Torgesen et al. (1994) have reported that it is not as easy as generally believed to help children at risk of reading disabilities to improve their awareness of phonemes and Byrne et al. (in press) have provided evidence that phoneme awareness training in small groups is more effective than classroom teaching. Despite this, our findings show that it *is* possible to teach phoneme awareness successfully in a whole-classroom setting to children of dyslexic parents. Furthermore this training programme improves the reading-related language skills of a group of children at risk for dyslexia to a level indistinguishable from that of a normal control group. The specificity of the training was demonstrated, however, by its lack of effect on vocabulary and morphology development. The children in the experimental group outperformed the at-risk controls in basic decoding skills at the beginning of second grade. Like other studies of the reading development of children from dyslexic families (e.g. Gilger et al., 1991), many more of the at-risk children than the normal controls in this study experienced difficulties in the acquisition of the alphabetic principle in reading.

However, significantly fewer children could be classified as possibly dyslexic in the trained at-risk group than in the control at-risk group. However, the trained at-risk group was still worse than the normal control group in oral non-word reading but this was not surprising given the advantages of the normal controls in almost all areas of reading-related language abilities on both testing occasions. As a whole, the results of the present study corroborate the results of the Lundberg et al. (1988) study, particularly with regard to children who enter kindergarten with poor linguistic awareness (Lundberg, 1994).

The simple principle that children tend to learn what they are taught applies well to this study. However, possible indications of transfer of training were found in the comparisons of the experimental and normal control groups. The experimental group did not gain more than the control groups on measures of syllable awareness. So there was no transfer of linguistic awareness training from lower levels (phonemes) towards higher levels (syllables), as was reported by Cary and Verhaeghe (1994). Our effect is quite small in any case, and this may also suggest that transfer is less likely in at-risk children than in normal children.

Cursory comparisons suggest that the present study was more successful than previous ones in helping many at-risk children develop phoneme awareness. The proportion of children who did not seem to improve at all over the kindergarten year was lower in this than in the studies reported by Byrne et al. (in press) and by Torgesen et al. (1994). Whilst this difference may be attributable to the more intensive instruction in the present study than in previous ones, floor effects in the previous studies may also have contributed to this difference. The criterion of unresponsiveness was a score of less than two items correct at post-test in the study referred by Torgesen et al. (1994). This suggests a marked floor effect. Similarly, Byrne et al. report that their at-risk children as a group scored just above chance level on a phoneme identification measure at pre-test. Such low scores may be predictive of later difficulties in reading acquisition, and they may be important in this respect. However, such floor effects prevent an accurate assessment of the extent to which phoneme awareness has developed as a result of training. We would assume that the proportion of unresponsive children would have been somewhat smaller in the previous studies if they had included easier tasks (such as those used by Chaney, 1992).

A limitation of this study is inherent in its relative brevity. We do not yet know about the possible long-term effects of our training on word reading and reading comprehension. Immediately after the training and a year later, significant training effects were found on real-word reading. These effects are not as trivial as they might appear as training did not include fully written words, but combined initial letters with pictures and boxes representing the rime of the syllables. However, it still remains to be seen whether the improvements in decoding achieved give the children a smoother start in reading real words and with reading comprehension.

Finally, one important implication for teaching should be mentioned. Many Danish kindergarten teachers acknowledge the importance of linguistic awareness for reading development. Language games and other 'metalinguistic' activities are now part of the daily routines in many kindergarten classes in Denmark. However, from the present study it is obvious that children of dyslexic parents do not benefit much from current practices. The untrained controls clearly lagged behind their normal peers. A lesson to learn from the training is that similar at-risk children were in fact able to acquire phoneme awareness at a fairly normal rate – but this required an intense and phonemically based programme.

Acknowledgements

The research reported here was supported by grants to the second author from The Danish Research Council (5-25-98-85) and from the Rebekka foundation. The authors are highly indebted to Dorthe Klint Petersen for collaboration on all phases of the project including the training programme, data collection and the development of many of the measures. Data collection and scoring was also done by Kikki F. Christensen, Thora H. Fjeldgren, T. Henriksen, Knud Larsen, Mette Pedersen and Line Petersen. We are very grateful for the collaboration and enthusiasm of the teachers, the children and their families.

References

Allerup, P. & Elbro, C. (1990). Comparing differences: The use of log odds in calculation of individual differences in reading accuracy with two word lists. In C. Elbro (Ed.) *Differences in Dyslexia. A Study of Reading Strategies and Deficits in a Linguistic Perspective* (pp. 222–233). Copenhagen: Munksgaard.

Allerup, P. & Elbro, C. (submitted). Comparing individual differences: The use of log odds in calculation of individual differences in scores on two related tests.

Ball, E. W. & Blachman, B. A. (1991). Does phoneme awareness training in kindergarten make a difference in early word recognition and developmental spelling? *Reading Research Quarterly* 26, 49–66.

Bentin, S., Hammar, R. & Cahan, S. (1991). The effects of ageing and first grade schooling on the development of phonological awareness. *Psychological Science* 2, 271–273.

Borstrøm, I. & Petersen, D. K. (1996). *På vej til den første læsning. Fonologisk opmærksomhed* [*Towards initial reading. Phonological awareness*]. Copenhagen: Alinea.

Bowey, J. A. & Francis, J. (1991). Phonological analysis as a function of age and exposure to reading instruction. *Applied Psycholinguistics* 12, 91–121.

Bradley, L. & Bryant, P. (1985). *Rhyme and Reason in Reading and Spelling*. Ann Arbor, MI: International Academy for Research in Learning Disabilities/University of Michigan Press.

Brady, S., Fowler, A., Stone, B. & Winbury, N. (1994). Training phonological awareness: a study with inner-city kindergarten children. *Annals of Dyslexia* 44, 26–59.

Bruck, M. (1990). Word recognition skills of adults with childhood diagnoses of dyslexia. *Developmental Psychology* 26, 439–454.

Bryant, P., MacLean, M. & Bradley, L. (1990). Rhyme, language, and children's reading. *Applied Psycholinguistics* 11, 237–252.

Byrne, B. & Fielding-Barnsley, R. (1991). Evaluation of a program to teach phonemic awareness to young children. *Journal of Educational Psychology* 83, 451–455.

Byrne, B. & Fielding-Barnsley, R. (1993). Evaluation of a program to teach phonemic awareness to young children: a one year follow-up. *Journal of Educational Psychology* 85, 104–111.

Byrne, B. & Fielding-Barnsley, R. (1995). Evaluation of a program to teach phonemic awareness to young children: a 2- and 3-year follow-up and a new pre-school trial. *Journal of Educational Psychology* 87, 488–503.

Byrne, B., Fielding-Barnsley, R., Ashley, L. & Larsen, K. (in press). Assessing the child's and the environment's contribution to reading acquisition: what we know and what we don't know. In B. Blachman (Ed.), *Foundations of Reading Acquisition and Dyslexia: Implications for Early Intervention*. Mahwah, NJ: Lawrence Erlbaum.

Cardon, L. R., Smith, S. D., Fulker, D. W., Kimberling, W. J., Pennington, B. F. & DeFries, J. C. (1994). Quantitative trait locus for reading disability on Chromosome 6. *Science* 266, 276–279.

Cary, L. & Verhaeghe, A. (1994). Promoting phonemic analysis ability among kindergartners: Effects of different training programs. *Reading and Writing: An Interdisciplinary Journal* 6, 251–278.

Chaney, C. (1992). Language development, metalinguistic skills, and print awareness in 3-year-old children. *Applied Psycholinguistics* 13, 485–514.

Cunningham, A. E. (1990). Explicit versus implicit instruction in phonemic awareness. *Journal of Experimental Child Psychology* 50, 429–444.

Dunn, L. M. & Dunn, L. M. (1981). *Peabody Picture Vocabulary Test – Revised*. Circle Pines, MN: American Guidance Service.

Elbro, C. (1990). *Differences in Dyslexia. A Study of Reading Strategies and Deficits in a Linguistic Perspective*. Copenhagen: Munksgaard.

Elbro, C. (1996), Early linguistic abilities and reading development: A review and a hypothesis. *Reading and Writing: An interdisciplinary Journal* 8, 453–485.

Elbro, C. (submitted). Reading-listening discrepancy definitions of dyslexia. Paper submitted to P. Reitsma & L. Verhoeven (Eds.) *Problems and Interventions in Literacy Development*. Amsterdam: Vrije Universitet.

Elbro, C., Borstrøm, I. & Petersen, D. K. (in press). Predicting dyslexia from kindergarten. The importance of distinctness of phonological representations of lexical items. *Reading Research Quarterly*.

Elbro, C., Nielsen, I. & Petersen, D. K. (1994). Dyslexia in adults: Evidence for deficits in nonword reading and in the phonological representation of lexical items. *Annals of Dyslexia* 44, 205–226.

Fowler, A. E. & Scarborough, H. S. (1993). *Should Reading-disabled Adults be Distinguished from Other Adults Seeking Literacy Instruction? A Review of Theory and Research, Technical Report TR93-7*. Philadelphia, PA: National Center on Literacy.

Gilger, J. W., Pennington, B. F. & DeFries, J. C. (1991). 'Risk for reading disability as a function of parental history in three family studies'. *Reading and Writing: An Interdisciplinary Journal* 3, 205–217.

Lovett, M. W., Borden, S. L., DeLuca, T., Lacerenza, L., Benson, N. J. & Brackstone, D. (1994). Treating the core deficits of developmental dyslexia: Evidence of transfer of learning after phonologically- and strategy-based reading training programs. *Developmental Psychology* 30, 805–822.

Lundberg, I. (1994). Reading difficulties can be predicted and prevented: A Scandinavian perspective on phonological awareness and reading. In C. Hulme & M. Snowling (Eds.) *Reading Development and Dyslexia* (pp. 180–199). London: Whurr Publishers.

Lundberg, I., Frost, J. & Petersen, O.-P. (1988). Effects of an extensive program for stimulating phonological awareness in pre-school children. *Reading Research Quarterly* 23, 263–284.

Lyon, G. R. (1995) Toward a definition of dyslexia. *Annals of Dyslexia* 45, 3–27.

Mattingly, I.G. (1972). Reading, the linguistic process, and linguistic awareness. In J.F. Kavanagh & I.G. Mattingly (Eds), *Language by Ear and by Eye. The Relationships between Speech and Reading* (pp. 133–148). Cambridge, MA: MIT Press.

Olson, R. K., Wise, B., Johnston, M. & Ring, J. (in press). The etiology and remediation of phonologically based word recognition and spelling disabilities: are phonological deficits the 'hole' story? In B. Blachman (Ed.), *Foundations of Reading Acquisition*. Mahwah, NJ: Lawrence Erlbaum.

Pennington, B. F., Lefly, D. L., Van Orden, G. C., Bookman, M. O. & Smith, S. D. (1987). Is phonology bypassed in normal or dyslexic development? *Annals of Dyslexia* 35, 62–89.

Rack, J. P., Snowling, M. J. & Olson, R. K. (1992). The nonword reading deficit in developmental dyslexia: A review. *Reading Research Quarterly* 27, 28–53.

Raven, J. C. (1990). *Coloured Progressive Matrices. Sets A, AB, B*, Manual. Oxford: Oxford Psychologists Press.

Scarborough, H. S. (1990). Very early language deficits in dyslexic children. *Child Development* 61, 1728–1743.

Schneider, W. & Näslund, J. C. (in press). The impact of early phonological processing skills on reading and spelling in school: evidence from the Munich longitudinal study. In F. E. Weinert & W. Schneider (Eds), *Individual Development from 3 to 12: Findings from the Munich Longitudinal Study*. Cambridge: Cambridge University Press.

Shankweiler, D. (1989). How problems of comprehension are related to difficulties in decoding. In D. Shankweiler & I.Y. Liberman (Eds), *Phonology and Reading Disability: Solving the Reading Puzzle*, IARLD Monograph Series. Ann Arbor, MI: University of Michigan Press.

Share, D. L. (1995). Phonological recoding and self-teaching: *sine qua non* of reading acquisition. *Cognition* 55, 151–218.

Siegel, L. S. (1988). Evidence that IQ scores are irrelevant to the definition and analysis of reading disability. *Canadian Journal of Psychology* 42, 201–215.

Søegård, A. & Petersen, S. P. B. (1974). *Ordstillelæsningsprøve OS400 [Silent word decoding test with 400 items]*. Copenhagen: Dansk Psykologisk Forlag.

Stanovich, K. E. (1986). Matthew effects in reading: some consequences of individual differences in the acquisition of literacy. *Reading Research Quarterly* 21, 360–407.

Stanovich, K. E. & Siegel, L. S. (1994). Phenotypic performance profile of children with reading disabilities: a regression-based test of the phonological-core variable-difference model. *Journal of Educational Psychology* **86**, 24–53.

Tangel, D. M. & Blachman, B. (1995). Effect of phoneme awareness instruction on the invented spelling of first-grade children: a one-year follow-up. *Journal of Reading Behavior* **27**, 153–185.

Torgesen, J. K., Wagner, R. K. & Rashotte, C. A. (1994). Longitudinal studies of phonological processing and reading. *Journal of Learning Disabilities* **27**, 276–286.

Tornéus, M. (1984). *Rim eller reson. Språklig medvetenhet och läsning.* Stockholm: Psykologiförlaget.

Uhry, J. K. & Shepherd, M. J. (1993). Segmentation/spelling instruction as part of a first-grade reading program: effects on several measures of reading. *Reading Research Quarterly* **28**, 219–233.

Vandervelden, M. C. & Siegel, L. S. (1995). Phonological recoding and phoneme awareness in early literacy: a developmental approach. *Reading Research Quarterly* **30**, 854–875.

Vellutino, F. R. & Scanlon, D. M. (1987). Phonological coding, phonological awareness and reading ability: evidence from a longitudinal and experimental study. *Merrill-Palmer Quarterly* **33**, 321–363.

Wagner, R. K., Torgesen, J. K. & Rashotte, C. A. (1994). Development of reading-related phonological processing abilities: new evidence of bidirectional causality from a latent variable longitudinal study. *Developmental Psychology* **30**, 73–87.

Wise, B. W. & Olson, R. K. (1995) Computer-based phonological awareness and reading instruction. *Annals of Dyslexia* **45**, 99–122.

Chapter 14
Teaching Phonological Awareness With and Without the Computer

BARBARA W. WISE, RICHARD K. OLSON and JERRY RING

Introduction

During the last 25 years, strong evidence has accrued which suggests that children with dyslexia have primary deficits in analytic language skills that are the underlying causes for their difficulties in reading and spelling words (Lyon, 1995). The deficient language skills include *phoneme awareness*: the awareness of sounds within spoken syllables, often measured by deleting or manipulating sounds within spoken syllables. They also include *phonological decoding*, the ability to translate print into sound, frequently measured by reading pronounceable non-words (e.g. 'niss', 'framble'). Evidence supporting the causal nature of these deficits converges from at least five sources, including studies of: behaviour genetics, neurobiology, predictors of reading ability, reading-level match designs and training studies (Wise, 1991).

The opening section of this chapter briefly discusses this background evidence, which guided our own training studies using talking computers. Our early training studies examined gains in reading and phonological decoding when children with reading disabilities read stories with accurate high-quality speech and decoding support for difficult words in context. These were our early ROSS studies, for Reading with Orthographic and Speech Support.

The following two-year study examined whether small-group and individualised computer instruction could improve phoneme awareness and phonological decoding prior to and concurrent with the ROSS story reading, and whether these improving skills would enhance the benefits of reading with the speech and orthographic support. We compared the training in phonological analysis to equivalent amounts of small-group instruction in comprehension strategies. Each of these interventions was given for equivalent amounts of time in small-group and individualised computer-based lessons. In both interventions the reading of stories on the computer provided decoding support for difficult words.

Our current studies now focus on which aspects of phonological analysis training, both on and off the computer, will prove most beneficial for children with different initial profiles of skills. The chapter will conclude by trying to clarify what our studies suggest for teachers who want to know how current research findings may inform their own teaching.

The Causal Nature of Phonological Deficits

In this chapter, the terms *dyslexia* and *Specific Reading Disability* (SRD) are used to describe the same children as in the recent NIH working definition of dyslexia (Lyon, 1995). While children with dyslexia certainly do have problems comprehending text, these problems are secondary to their primary problems of slow and inaccurate word recognition. Their poor word recognition hinders comprehension in many ways. First of all, the meaning of a story is lost when too many words are misidentified. Also, a child who struggles with many words has few resources left over for comprehension, even if he or she eventually identifies the words correctly. Finally, comprehension over the long haul will suffer if students with dyslexia lag in vocabulary development and in familiarity with text structures, as a result of diminished reading experience.

Many lines of evidence suggest that deficient analytic language skills underlie the primary deficits in word recognition of children with dyslexia. Behaviour genetic studies of dyslexia show that on average individual differences in word recognition skills are due about half to inherited and half to environmental factors (Olson, Forsberg & Wise, 1994). Group deficits in non-word reading and phoneme awareness show strong heritability in these studies of fraternal and identical twins with and without dyslexia, and path analyses suggest they cause the problems in word recognition (Conners & Olson, 1990). Neuropsychological studies of Magnetic Resonance Imaging and PET scans have revealed differences in areas of the brain that relate to analytic language, when comparing people with dyslexia with people who read normally. Specifically, investigators have found that normal readers tend to have the left larger than the right in certain structures related to language processing, such as the planum temporale and the insular region. On the other hand, people with dyslexia tend to have symmetrical plana or asymmetries with the right larger than the left (Hynd, Semrud-Clikeman & Lyytinen, 1991; Hynd et al. this volume; Larsen et al., 1989). Also, blood flow to the language areas during reading is less for people with reading disabilities (and not with attention deficit disorders) than for normal readers (Felton & Wood, 1989).

Correlational analyses have also pointed to phoneme awareness as the strongest predictor of reading ability through the elementary school years (Calfee, Lindamood & Lindamood, 1973).

Reading-level match studies add evidence suggesting that deficits in analytic language skills cause the word recognition problems of children with dyslexia. When older children with dyslexia are compared with average readers of the same age, they score lower than these controls on many measures (Olson et al., 1989), due in part to their reduced reading experience and to their frustration with school. In order to infer which measures might reflect a causal role, researchers sometimes instead match children on their word recognition reading level (RL) rather than on age, thus matching older children with dyslexia to younger average readers who read real words at the same level. The older dyslexic children score higher on vocabulary, listening comprehension and reading comprehension than their younger RL matched controls (Conners & Olson, 1990). Their higher-level thinking skills and greater experience with story structures and context lead to this advantage. This suggests that word recognition difficulties cause problems in reading comprehension for dyslexic children, rather than comprehension deficits causing problems in word recognition. Perfetti (1985) presented other evidence about the causal nature of word recognition difficulties for reading comprehension.

In contrast, older dyslexic children tend to score lower in non-word reading and in phoneme awareness tasks, compared with their younger RL matched controls (who read real words at the same level). This suggests that these analytic language skills are causing the problems in word recognition for the dyslexic children (Olson, et al., 1989; Olson et al., 1994; Rack, Snowling, & Olson, 1992; Wise, 1991).

The most hopeful of the lines of evidence that suggest a causal role for phoneme awareness in reading disabilities comes from training studies. Many studies have demonstrated that training to improve phoneme awareness and phonological analysis prior to and concurrent with reading instruction can improve later reading and spelling in both early and remedial readers (Ball & Blachman, 1991; Bradley & Bryant, 1983; Byrne & Fielding-Barnsley, 1993; Hatcher, Hulme & Ellis,1994; Lundberg, Frost & Petersen, 1988). Thus, even though the evidence reported above suggests an organic basis for deficits in phoneme awareness and phonological decoding in many children, training studies suggest that they can be improved with interventions specifically designed to remedy them.

Reading with Orthographic and Speech Support (ROSS)

When high-quality synthetic speech (our studies use DECtalk) became available, 'talking computers' provided a powerful new way to conduct remediation research. One typical problem in most training studies is control of method; a good teacher modifies methods according to what he or she thinks is best for the child. While this is effective for teaching, it makes methodological research difficult. Using computer-assisted instruction can address this methodological problem. A computer program will continue to deliver a method as long as it is programmed to do so, so one can compare benefits unconfounded by teachers' preferences or inconsistencies.

In our first study with talking computers, children did their word decoding in the context of stories, with no isolated skills work (Olson & Wise, 1992). We called our program ROSS, for Reading with Orthographic and Speech Support. The point of the early ROSS research was to see whether reading in context with immediate speech and decoding support would improve children's word recognition and phonological decoding. The study also compared different kinds of decoding support: whole words, syllables or sub-syllables of 'onset and rime' (e.g., pl/ant). When students targeted a word with a mouse, the computer first highlighted the segments sequentially in reverse video, and then highlighted and pronounced the segments. We hypothesised that support with syllable or onset-rime segments would benefit decoding skills more than support with whole words.

Teachers referred second- to fifth-grade students they thought were in the lower 10% of the class for reading word recognition; screening with the Wide Range Achievement Test (Jastak & Jastak, 1978) confirmed the difficulty. All students had normal intelligence, English as first language, and no sensory or emotional problems. Children were pre- and post-tested on word recognition, non-word reading, phoneme awareness and reading comprehension.

The children came to the computer room for 30 minutes per day during reading or language arts time, to keep reading instruction time equivalent for experimental subjects as for matched untrained controls in the same class. Trained students read with the computer for three or four days a week, for one semester. Students selected stories from reading-grade-level directories (primer to sixth grade, based on word length). Students read silently when reading independently, and orally when with a trainer. When a student encountered a word he or she found difficult, he or she targeted that word by clicking on it with a mouse, and the ROSS program segmented the word and pronounced the segments. If the student reached the end of a sentence without targeting a misread word, the trainer pointed to the word and asked the child to target it. At logical breaks in the story, the program asked a multiple-choice comprehension question, and at the end of the session, the program tested the student on 15 of the words targeted that day, or filled in with long words from that day's reading if less than 15 words had been targeted. Trainers were present only two days per week, and on the other days students were asked to read independently.

One hundred and eighty-four students read for one semester each (Olson & Wise, 1992). At the end of each semester, students had read for 10 to 14 hours with the computer. ROSS students averaged about twice the gains in word recognition compared with the controls who spent that time back in the classroom, 0.6 compared with 0.3 grade levels gain, on the Peabody Individualised Achievement Test (PIAT, Dunn & Markwardt, 1970). They gained about four times as much on our test of non-word reading as the untrained controls, about 10 compared with 2.5 percentage points. However, no reliable differences occurred between the segmentation conditions: children with whole-word support gained as much in real and non-word reading as those who had received speech support for word segments.

In all training conditions, children's initial skill and their gains in real and non-word reading correlated positively with their initial skill in phoneme awareness. That is, children with lower initial phonemic awareness started lower and also gained less than students who started with relatively higher awareness. This is the typical 'Matthew effect' (Stanovich, 1986) found in most training studies: children who start with the lowest abilities in reading do not just lag behind the others; they gain less and continue to fall further behind. Our next studies aimed at improving phoneme awareness, to see whether this deficit could be reduced and whether this would affect benefits of reading with ROSS.

Phonological vs Comprehension Strategy Training

We compared two very different supplemental strategies that we hoped would aid different aspects of reading: an experimental phonological analysis (PA) training condition and a control comprehension strategy condition (CS). Detailed descriptions of the training methods follow a brief overview of the structure of the study. The PA children spent almost two-thirds of their time on structured and sequenced work to improve phoneme awareness, some in small group instruction (7 hours) and some in computer-assisted exercises to improve phoneme awareness and phonological decoding by manipulating sounds in isolated words and non-words (10 hours). They spent the other third of their time reading ROSS stories with decoding support (8.4 hours). Small-group instruction sessions were interspersed with independent practice on the computer.

The children in our CS comparison group received equivalent amounts of time in small group instruction (7 hours), where they learned the comprehension strategies while reading stories on and off the computer. Their individualised computer time was spent entirely on reading ROSS stories with decoding support (18.4 hours). Thus this group spent about twice as much time reading in context as did the children doing the phonological analysis work.

Children attended in sets of three, with the trainer present every day. When working with the computer, all children worked independently for two of the three days, and worked with the trainer on the third day. We balanced conditions for ability, by matching sets of three students on age, word recognition and non-word reading, and then randomly assigning the sets to training condition. One important aspect of this study relative to most other training studies is that we could control both trainer and school effects. We did this by having both methods taught in each school and by each trainer, so that method, trainer and school effects would not confound each other.

The training methods had many planned similarities. Both methods had theoretical and research support (Lyon, 1995; Montgomery, 1981; Palinscar & Brown, 1984; Wise et al., 1993). Both used a guided discovery, or teaching by questioning, approach. Finally, both methods were expected to improve children's error detection. In our previous studies, children often did not recognise their errors. We had used much training effort to get them to target words even half as frequently when they read independently as when they read with a trainer.

For story reading for both conditions, the computer showed targeted words with segments written against blue and green backgrounds, and children in both conditions were asked to attempt to pronounce each segment before clicking the mouse again to hear the speech support. One-syllable words were segmented as onsets and rimes (e.g. pl/ant), and multisyllable words were segmented as syllables (e.g. bas/ket). Main-idea comprehension questions occurred at logical breaks in the story, and children were tested at the end of the session on 15 of the words that they had targeted that day. Forty of these tested words were retested at the end of each month, and at the end of the training period. Children were also tested on non-words constructed by the program which were analogous to words from the child's monthly and year-end tests. Onsets and rimes of items were swapped to create the non-words (e.g. *farmer* and *plant* yield *fant* and *plarmer*).

The Phonological Analysis (PA) condition included initial work in articulatory awareness concepts from the Auditory Discrimination in Depth Program (ADD, Lindamood & Lindamood, 1975; see also Chapter 12 this volume). It continued with other programs designed in our laboratory in Colorado to encourage manipulation and comparison of sounds in word and non-word reading and spelling exercises. In the ADD programs, the teacher selected items for the children to practice. The Colorado exercises automatically increased or decreased in difficulty depending on the child's performance.

We chose the ADD method for the initial work partly because of its theoretical base. The ADD program begins by training awareness of the articulations made in producing speech sounds, to provide a concrete foundation with which children can notice and compare the order of sounds in syllables. Much research points to the importance of awareness of articulatory gestures in perceiving phonemes (Liberman et al., 1989), and other research has shown that children with dyslexia have greater problems than normal readers associating pictures of articulatory movements with speech sounds (Montgomery, 1981). We also chose it because of a reanalysis we did of data from a study of first-grade reading by the Lindamood-Bell Learning Resources Center. Our analysis suggested that children with especially low phoneme awareness gained at least as much from this program as children who had started with higher phonological skills (Wise et al., 1993). Finally, the ADD method had appeared to help children who had failed to succeed with other methods, in reports of evidence from reading clinics without control group comparisons (Alexander et al., 1991; Truch, 1994).

In the PA small-group instruction, children learned to feel the articulatory movements that produced different sounds, and associated the feelings with sounds, pictures, labels and letters to help them analyse and compare sounds as in the ADD program (Lindamood & Lindamood, 1975). For instance, children used mirrors to help them discover that their lips popped apart to make the 'brother pair' sounds of /p/ and /b/. They associated these feelings with the labels 'quiet and noisy lip poppers' and with a picture of mouth with two lips together with a puff of air. They learned to distinguish the 'quiet from the noisy brother' by feeling their vocal cords vibrating, and/or by covering their ears to compare the sounds. They learned feelings, pictures, labels and letters for all consonant sounds. They also learned to use mouth feelings to distinguish and compare vowel sounds, organising these sounds into a 'vowel circle' representing mouth shape and tongue position in the mouth. Small-group instruction was interspersed with computer exercises with programs under development at Lindamood-Bell Learning Processes (Lindamood-Bell CD-Rom Software: Lindamood-Bell Learning Resources, 416 Higuera Street, San Luis Obispo, CA), where the children practised associating the pictures, sounds, letters and labels.

When children were about 80% successful with the consonant concepts and had at least three vowels sounds 'ee' [i]; 'ar' [a], and 'oo' [u], they practised in small groups manipulating mouth pictures to represent changes in simple two- and three-phoneme syllables (e.g. The trainer said, 'If this is 'op', show me 'pop', and the child added a picture of a lip popper at the front of a picture of an open vowel followed by a lip popper). Students then started working individually with programs developed at Colorado with synthetic speech support for analysing and manipulating sounds within syllables, which were designed to be compatible with the ADD concepts and methods.

The PAL (Phonological Analysis with Letters) program asked children to build a simple syllable, and then to change single sounds to match changes that the program said (e.g. 'Show me 'eef'. The child found the appropriate letter-symbols, and compared how the program pronounced them with how it pronounced what they were supposed to spell. Then the program said, 'If that says 'eef', show me 'meef'', and the child made changes to match the changes made by the program. Letter-symbols matched those taught in the ADD program. The PAL program advanced and retreated from consonant–vowel (CV) levels up to levels that contained up to three-consonant clusters (CCCVCCC).

Children also used another program (Non) designed in our lab where they chose one of four non-words to match one pronounced by the program. The non-words used regular English orthographic patterns, as opposed to the Lindamood symbols. Words were pronounced and scored as the children chose them, and children received more points for choosing the correct non-word on the first try. The Non program automatically advanced and retreated in difficulty depending on the child's performance from CV to multisyllable levels.

When children were 80% successful at a Consonant–Vowel–Consonant (CVC) level with the PAL program, they started spending about half their daily computer time reading stories as in the earlier ROSS studies, and the other half on the phonological analysis programs described above. After success at the next CVC level which included more vowels, a spelling exploration program was introduced (Spello: Wise & Olson, 1992), where children could manipulate letters and sounds to explore real English spelling patterns. Spello also advanced and retreated in difficulty from CVC to multisyllable words, according to the child's performance.

Computer decoding support in stories was the same in the PA condition as in the CS condition. Children in both conditions were trained to use the colours to help sound out the word whenever they encountered a word that was difficult or that they were unsure of. However, teacher support differed for the two conditions when a child failed to target a misread word. If a child in the PA condition reached the end of a sentence without targeting a misread word, the trainer asked the child to compare his or her pronunciation with what was on the page, by first covering the word and asking 'Now, when you say [the error as the child pronounced it], what do you feel [at the point of contrast with the correct pronunciation of the word on the page]?' Then the trainer let the child see the word and make an attempt at correction, and the child then listened to the speech to confirm the word. This feedback resembles that used in Lindamood training to encourage self-correction. When a child in the CS condition failed to target a misread word, the trainer pointed to that word and asked the child to use the colours to help sound out the word.

The Comprehension Strategy Treatment

The trained control condition used a Comprehension Strategy (CS) approach based on reciprocal teaching (Palincsar & Brown, 1984). Children began with small-group instruction, learning the strategies that good readers use: predicting, generating questions, clarifying and summarising. The trainer discussed how and why children would learn to be their own teachers, and that they would learn how and when to apply the above strategies in reading. They discussed why they would be trading the role of teacher, so children could learn to use the strategies in their independent reading. Later they defined and explained how to use a strategy like prediction, for instance by discussing what a prediction is and why and when we make predictions, in real life and in reading. Then they modelled leading the group using this strategy, and later traded the role of discussion leader, guiding the children as they learned to lead discussions using the strategy. The other strategies were gradually introduced and integrated, and the children practised leading discussions of group story-reading first of stories on paper and then on the computer. The student leader chose readers and asked students in the group to use particular strategies and to justify why a particular strategy might best be used at different times to aid comprehension.

We used a wooden 'teaching apple' to designate who was acting as leader of the group, to help suit the method of work to our small groups or one-on-one reading. When reading one-on-one with the trainer, the teacher and child would trade the apple to be clear who was in charge of leading the discussion about the text. Children enjoyed trading roles, and discussions were often quite lively, although the method was harder to use with some second-grade groups than with the older children, probably due both to the children's immaturity and the simplistic content of the primer and first-grade stories. When reading independently with the computer, students marked a chart to show places they used the strategies.

Results of the Phonological vs Comprehension Strategy Study

A total of 201 second- to fifth-grade students participated in the strategy study from eight different schools, during two years. Students were selected and screened as being in the lower 10% on word recognition (see Table 14.1 for subject characteristics). Students were pre-tested in the fall and completed training and were post-tested at the start of May. The next year, a new contingent of four schools was pre-tested, trained and post-tested, and the first year's groups were given one-year follow-up testing.

Table 14.1 Subject characteristics in the phonological studies
Phonological analysis (PA) vs comprehension strategy (CS):

Group	CS	PA	
n	91 (36F)	110 (46 F)	
Age (at pre-test)	8.9	8.9	
Grade	3.2	3.2	
Severity of deficit*	0.74	0.73	

Articulatory (Art) vs non-articulatory (Non) phonological awareness

Group	NonPA	ArtPA	
n	17 (2F)	24 (3F)	
Age (at pre-test)	9.0	9.6	$p < 0.05$
Grade	3.4	4.1	$p < 0.05$
Severity of deficit*	0.61	0.58	

Note: * Severity of deficit is calculated as the ratio of grade equivalent on the PIAT word recognition test over the expected grade equivalent. Normally achieving students in Boulder score at about 1.4 on this ratio.

Across both years, both groups made larger gains in non- and real-word reading and in comprehension than in the earlier ROSS study (see Table 14.2). The PA training led to very large gains in non-word reading, as evidenced by our measure of phonological decoding (see Table 14.2). Even the CS students gained a few percentage points more than in the previous studies, probably due to increased engagement and training time. But the PA students gained more than twice as much as the earlier students and as the CS students, on three different measures of non-word reading where all students read the same non-words, and on the individualised tests of non-words created by the program to be analogous to words they had studied (see Table 14.3).

PA students also made substantial and significant gains in phoneme awareness relative to the CS students. Phoneme awareness gains were measured by the Lindamood Auditory Conceptualization (LAC) Test (Lindamood & Lindamood, 1979), which uses coloured blocks to represent sound changes and by a phoneme deletion task. We use the raw score on the second half of the LAC test, as this is the only part that has to do with the ability to be aware of sounds within syllables. The LAC test has a slight confound in our study, because many students noticed that the task is quite similar to our PAL letter–sound manipulation program (although no blocks are used in our training). However, the phoneme deletion task did not resemble anything done in training, and the PA children made substantially and significantly stronger gains on this test than the CS children.

Table 14.2 Pre-test and gain scores following Phonological (PA) or Comprehension (CS) Training

Group	CS		PA		
	pre-test	gain	pre-test	gain	
Phoneme awareness					
LACii[1] No. correct	5.0	1.8	5.1	4.5	$p < 0.001$
Phoneme Deletion (%)	32.7	7.0	31.4	19.1	$p < 0.001$
Non-word (%)	25.8	12.6	26.4	26.3	$p < 0.001$
Word recognition untimed					
PIAT (Grade Equiv)	2.4	0.9	2.4	1.1	$p < 0.1$
WRAT (Grade Equiv)	2.5	0.9	2.5	1.1	$p < 0.05$
Word recognition timed					
No. correct	23.5	15.8	23.5	12.9	$p < 0.05$

Note: [1]LACii indicates the second half of the LAC test.

Table 14.3 PA/CS strategies: daily reading behaviour

Training group	CS	PA	
Target ratio	65%	69%	$p < 0.05$
Daily monitored word checks	80%	88%	$p < 0.05$
Monthly word check	61%	73%	$p < 0.05$
Monitored comprehension	95%	93%	$p < 0.05$
Independent comprehension	87%	88%	
End-of-year:			
Studied words	76%	83%	$p < 0.05$
Non-word analogues	47%	60%	$p < 0.05$

Differences in the gains in word recognition between the PA and CS conditions were not as strong as the differences in the gains in phonological skills. The PA children scored significantly higher than the CS children when the Wide Range Achievement Test (WRAT, Jastak and Jastak, 1978) and the PIAT (Dunn & Markwardt, 1976) were combined into one measure. The PA children also outperformed the CS children, by significant and fairly substantial amounts on the daily, monthly and end-of-year tests of words studied in the stories (see Table 14.3). In contrast, the CS students, who had more time decoding words in context, actually scored significantly higher on the test of time-limited word recognition (see Table 14.2).

There were no differences between the groups on any standardised reading comprehension measures, nor on measures of comprehension in independent daily reading. However, on the days that the children read with the trainer, children in the CS condition scored significantly higher on comprehension questions than children in the PA condition (see Table 14.3). Children in the CS condition were often prompted to use their comprehension strategies while reading with their trainer.

Discussion of the Phonological vs Comprehension Strategy Study

Children in this study made greater gains than children in the previously discussed ROSS study. Besides their greater gains in word recognition and non-word reading, the students themselves, their teachers and their parents enthusiastically reported gains in reading far more than they had in the earlier study. These differences were probably due to a combination of improvements in this study compared with the relatively passive use of computer support in the earlier ROSS study. These improvements included the social setting of three children and part-time small-group training, the longer training times, the daily presence of a trainer, as well as increased engagement by the students while using the strategies.

Comparing the training groups within the study, PA children made much larger gains in all tests of phonological skills than CS children. They also performed better in all tests of untimed word recognition both of words studied on the computer, and on the standardised measures of untimed word recognition. Yet they showed a disadvantage on tests of time-limited word recognition.

Why might the PA children have shown lesser benefits on standard-ised tests than on our computerised tests of words from the stories? For one thing, the tests of words from the stories were never timed, and children were encouraged to use the same strategies, in the same computer context, that they had used in reading. Thus the generalisa-tion of context probably encouraged transfer of the analytic techniques to these tests. Also, the PA students probably had spent more time and energy while studying the words in context than the CS students had, because of applying the strategies they had learned.

And why might the CS students have shown a small but significant advantage on time-limited word recognition? Our test of time-limited word recognition apparently did not allow our PA students to use their relatively slow but strong decoding skills to the same advantage as they showed on the untimed tests. Their analytic skills actually worked to their disadvantage.

Perhaps the PA students' improved phonological skill needed more time to transfer into independent, time-limited word recognition. A follow-up of the children trained in the first year of this study, after one year showed that PA students maintained their advantage in non-word reading and phoneme awareness, and caught up to the CS children in untimed word recognition (Olson et al., in press). But no differences remained on the PIAT test of untimed word recognition. The children's rate of gain in all skills was much less when they no longer received the small-group and individualised computer instruction.

Larger gains in non-word reading and yet smaller or non-significant gains over trained controls in word recognition are also being found in other recent studies that use intensive phonological training. Torgesen and his colleagues (Torgesen et al., in press) reported this pattern of results in their one-year training study which used the full version of the ADD program. Lovett et al. (1995) also reported a similar pattern of results (relative to their trained controls): a small but significant differential word recognition gain only on tests of words created to be like those used in training and on the WRAT reading test. Lovett's trained children did better in word recognition relative to controls who received less reading instruction, as we also found with the untrained controls in the ROSS study.

What all these studies have shown thus far is still very important. We, Lovett et al., and Torgesen et al. have shown that intensive training, which includes dealing with sounds in syllables and teaching regularities of English orthography and phonology, can improve deficient phoneme awareness and phonological decoding in children with dyslexia. All three studies are notable and unusual for two reasons: (1) they successfully trained children who had demonstrated phonological deficits, and (2) they compared two good training methods, not just comparing a carefully designed treatment with untrained controls. Our study adds two more contributions: (1) we demonstrated that computer instruction can help support and extend work on phonological skills and reading, and (2) in our study, training method was not confounded by differences in schools or trainers. This does not deny the results of studies where different methods are taught by different teachers, or in different schools, but it is important to have a study to confirm these results in an unconfounded situation.

Our study was designed to find out whether phoneme awareness and phonological decoding could be improved substantially and to see how that would affect reading progress; it did not aim to provide a complete reading and writing program. Some of our future studies aim to demonstrate how to extend these gains more strongly into word recognition. We hypothesise that further explicit training in how to predict and be flexible about vowel sounds in words, and explicit training in sight words and in automaticity, will strengthen the gains in fluent word recognition especially for the children with improved phonological awareness. Note that during our training period, most children had still not achieved grade-level skills or strong self-correction abilities. We also believe that more students will retain their skills and achieve continuing rates of growth more similar to their classmates if we can continue their training until they are self-correcting their errors while reading at or above their grade level.

Comparing Different Types of Phonological Training

Although we do want to examine how to extend our students' gains into more fluent and flexible word recognition, we have been pleased with the PA students' consistent gains in phoneme awareness, phonological decoding and untimed word recognition, especially given that only 25 hours of training were given. When we planned this training, we included many aspects of good phonological awareness training in our treatment, including both articulatory awareness and the manipulation of sounds. (We also taught 'phonics', letter–sound correspondences, and practising applying all the skills while reading stories). A pilot study conducted last year (Wise et al., in press), and our current study, are both designed to examine which parts of our phonological training are most helpful for children with different initial levels of skill.

Uhry and Shepherd (1993) have previously demonstrated the importance of activities like spelling and manipulation of sounds for the improvement of phonological awareness in early readers, and Lundberg et al. (1988) and Ball and Blachman (1991) used similar activities in their programmes. We hypothesised that children with the most severe phonological deficits might benefit the most from the solid grounding in articulatory awareness. We also thought that students with relatively less severe phonological deficits might benefit as much from a program that involved simpler phonological awareness training which would allow more time to be spent on the programs manipulating sounds in spelling and non-word reading.

We piloted a study of this last year in only one school, owing to temporary disruption of our funding. We had some help from the special education teachers in the school, so we increased the size of our training sets to about five students each, so we could train more students. Twenty-four students received the same articulatory-based phonological analysis training (Articulatory PA) described earlier (see Table 14.1 for subject characteristics). The other 17 subjects (NonArticulatory PA) learned to manipulate syllables, rimes and phonemes in small-group instruction, instead of doing the work on articulatory awareness. For example, they counted, manipulated and deleted syllables, they played rhyming games and learned to 'Balk Tackwards' using coloured strips and squares to manipulate onsets and rimes, and they manipulated coloured squares to represent phoneme changes in syllables as in Ball and Blachman (1991), Elkonin (1973), and in Lindamood and Lindamood (1975) (see Wise, Olson & Ring, in press, for a fuller description of the non-articulatory phonological awareness method). They also learned all the phonic rules that the Articulatory PA group learned. The non-articulatory group used a Keyword chart for vowel sounds (five saying their names A, E, I, O, U, and apple, Ed, It, octopus, up; and oil, owl, awesome, boo, hook). They never learned any articulatory concepts nor did they use mirrors. They were encouraged to listen to and to notice sound changes in words, whilst the articulatory group was encouraged to use their mirrors to help them see and feel and compare the actions that accompanied sound changes in words. Computer practice for the non-articulatory group included about an hour's practice on games of rhyming and vowel-matching from Lexia (Lexia Learning Systems, PO Box 466, Lincoln, MA 01773), nine hours in small-group instruction, and about 21 hours practising with the computers.

Students in the pilot study generally made somewhat stronger gains and performed slightly better on measures of words from the stories compared with students in the PA/CS study (see Tables 14.2 and 14.3, and 14.4 and 14.5), probably because of their slightly longer training time. We were surprised that, in general, both groups made equivalently strong gains. Most trends and the few significant differences actually favoured the non-articulatory phonological awareness training. These children spent more small-group time practising phoneme manipulation than the Articulatory group did and they spent more time with the computer programs that manipulated sounds. Perhaps this led to their surprisingly strong gains and their significant advantage in phoneme deletion at post-testing time.

We have begun to examine the gains of the lowest scoring children in both groups. Unfortunately, whilst the smaller non-articulatory group generally matched the articulatory group on pre-test scores, it had no students as extremely low or as extremely high as in the larger articulatory group. However, it is interesting that the trainer and the special education teachers all thought that the three lowest-scoring students in

Table 14.4 Pre-test and gain scores following training in articulatory phonological analysis (Art PA) and phonological analysis without articulation (Non PA)

Group	Non-articulatory PA		Articulatory PA		
	pre-test	gain	pre-test	gain	
Phoneme awareness					
LACii[1] No. correct	4.7	5.8	5.2	4.5	
Phoneme Deletion (%)	29.1	31.0	31.6	16.0	$p < 0.02$
Non-word (%)	23.4	28.2	28.0	25.1	
Word recognition untimed					
PIAT (Grade Equiv)	2.3	1.3	2.4	1.1	
WRAT (Grade Equiv)	2.3	1.4	2.5	1.1	
Timed					
No. correct	18.9	17.5	23.6	15.1	

Note: [1]LACii indicates the second half of the LAC test.

Table 14.5 ArtPA/NonPA: daily reading behaviour

Group	Non-articulatory PA	Articulatory PA	
Target ratio	92%	150%	$p < 0.05$
Words monitored	87%	90%	
Monthly word check	70%	70%	
Monitored comprehension	95%	93%	
Independant comprehension	87%	88%	
End-of-year:			
Studied words	82%	79%	
Non-word analogues	63%	57%	

the non-articulatory group were handicapped by their lack of training in articulatory awareness.

We selected the four lowest-scoring students and the four highest-scoring students in the non-articulatory PA group. We based this choice on a factor score derived from their initial, age-partialled scores in phonological awareness tests. We matched these children on the factor score to eight students from the articulatory awareness groups, and tested whether effects for these small groups differed in ways we expected. With such a small sample, we were looking only for trends at this point. In general, all the children made gains. Trends suggested that the children who began with the lowest initial phonological awareness skills gained less than those who started with higher skills (this trend was nearly significant only for WRAT untimed word recognition). Only one approached significance, and it did so in the direction we expected. The lowest four children in the Nonarticulatory PA group gained only 13.6% in non-word reading, whereas the highest four children in that group gained 39.2%. In contrast, the matched low-scoring children in the Articulatory PA group gained 35.8% in non-word reading, whereas the matched higher scoring children in that group gained 23.3%. This result lends some support to our hypothesis that children with especially low skills in phonological awareness may need the articulatory awareness training more than students who begin with relatively higher skills (and perhaps that children who begin with relatively higher skills might do as well or better with the non-articulatory training, which allowed the children to spend more of their time in manipulation of sounds and letters).

These pilot results are certainly not strong enough to answer the question of which students are more likely to benefit from which kind of phonological training. But the question is of such strong theoretical and practical interest that we are continuing to study it in a larger and better controlled study this year. We spent the whole summer intensely training five trainers in three training methods and in principles of experimental control. We are now comparing three combinations of phonological training, with 140 second- to fifth-graders in five schools. All students are learning the same phonic rules, and all are reading stories with ROSS with decoding support for difficult words. It is the supplementary training that differs for the three groups. One-third of the students are receiving PA training that includes both articulatory awareness and the manipulation of sounds in the PAL, Non and Spello programs, as in the original PA study. Another group is receiving training in manipulation of sounds in small groups and in PAL, Non and Spello, but is receiving no training in articulatory awareness, as in the non-articulatory PA group from the pilot study. A third group, different from the pilot study, is receiving all the training in articulatory awareness (and in phonics and in ROSS reading), but none in the manipulation of sounds, either in small group or on the computer. With this design, we hope to be able to tease out the benefits of training in both articulatory awareness and in manipulation of sounds.

We think this work is important theoretically, to understand how and whether these deficits can be remedied. It may have practical importance as well, if only certain children require the most intensive training. Teaching all teachers how to lead children in games that manipulate syllables, rimes and phonemes would be much easier than to teach them all to help children discover the concepts of articulatory phonetics. Yet this research may support the idea of providing intensely trained teachers to help the children who really need it.

Summary

We have now studied the remediation of dyslexia using talking computers for 10 years. We have found that children enjoy the computers, and that they benefit from reading stories with accurate speech feedback for difficult words. These gains are made much stronger with intensive training in phonological awareness, taught by teachers using guided discovery activities off the computer, and practised by the children on the computers. While we have succeeded in substantially improving students' phoneme awareness, phonological decoding and untimed word recognition, we still have more work to do to demonstrate in a controlled study how to extend these gains into even stronger, more fluent and flexible reading. Currently we are also examining which aspects of our phonological training will prove most helpful for children with varying degrees of dyslexia: the articulatory awareness, the manipulation of sounds in syllables, or their combination.

What does the work so far suggest to teachers? The most important finding for concerned teachers converges from our own and other studies (Ball & Blachman, 1991; Hatcher et al., 1994; Lovett et al., 1995;

Torgesen et al., in press; Truch, 1994; Wise & Olson, 1995): children who are struggling in word recognition and spelling can improve their deficient phonological skills. They do benefit from intensive training that is designed to get them to discover the structure of the English sound and spelling system and to pay attention to and to manipulate the order of sounds in syllables, to learn about letter–sound correspondences, and to practice applying the strategies in reading in context. Exactly which kind of phonological awareness work will be the most beneficial for different children has not yet been demonstrated. Not surprisingly, the same research also suggests that phonological awareness and decoding work will not sufficient by itself. Exactly how to extend the improved phonological skills into equally strong and fluent reading has also not yet been demonstrated in carefully controlled research studies, but teachers of reading know many of the likely techniques that can be used once the children's underlying deficits have been improved. Students with reading disabilities will probably need direct instruction and much practice on automaticity, on learning to be flexible with vowel sounds and stress in sounding out words, and on spelling, writing and reading for understanding to have all these skills transfer into strong and successful reading and writing.

Sometimes it is frustrating how long it takes to do a good, controlled training study, and how many questions remain at the end of it. It is difficult to measure all important aspects of how best to train children to read well. It will take large groups of children in many well-controlled studies to ever be able to understand exactly which aspects of programmes are the most crucial for different children. But it is exciting to work at a time when so much theoretical and training research and so much evidence from clinical practitioners is converging on such a hopeful picture: that children with dyslexia can improve their underlying deficits and become good readers.

Acknowledgements

We thank principals, staff and students of 10 schools in the Boulder Valley Schools for the studies summarised in this chapter. We thank our other graduate student Mina Johnson, our trainers Heather Burke, Robyn Mason, Sue Parette, Luanne Sessions and Joanna Stewart; our previous trainers Heidi Gilman, John Green, Sally Moody, Beverly Peterson, Laura Rogan, Joanne Trombley and Kate Wise; our programmer Jennifer Restrepo; and research assistants Laura Kriho, Bonnie Houkal and Laurie Toeppen. We thank consultants Pat Lindamood and Beverly Peterson for help with ADD training, and Leigh Kirkland and Michael Meloth for help with Reciprocal Teaching. We thank NICHD for supporting the research with grants No. HD 11683 and HD 22223 to Richard K. Olson and Barbara Wise.

References

Alexander, A., Anderson, H., Voeller, K. & Torgesen, J. (1991). Phonological awareness training and remediation of analytic coding deficits in a group of severe dyslexics. *Annals of Dyslexia* **31**, 193–207.

Ball, E. & Blachman, B.A. (1991). Does phoneme awareness training in kindergarten make a difference in early word recognition and developmental spelling? *Reading Research Quarterly* **26**, 49–66.

Bradley, L. & Bryant, P. (1983). Categorizing sounds and learning to read: A causal connection. *Nature* **301**, 419–421.

Byrne, B. & Fielding-Barnsley, R. (1993). Evaluation of a program to teach phoneme awareness to young children: A 1-year follow-up. *Journal of Educational Psychology* **85**, 104–111.

Calfee, R., Lindamood, P. & Lindamood, C. (1973). Acoustic-phonetic skills and reading: kindergarten through twelfth grade. *Journal of Educational Psychology* **64**, 293–298.

Conners, F. & Olson, R.K. (1990). Reading comprehension in dyslexic and normal readers: a component skills analysis. In D.A. Balota, G.B. Flores díArcais & K. Rayner (Eds.) *Comprehension Processes in Reading*. Hillsdale, NJ: Erlbaum.

Dunn, L.M. & Markwardt, F.C. (1976). *Peabody Individual Achievement Test*. Circle Pines, MN: American Guidance Service.

Elkonin, D.B. (1973). USSR. In J. Downing (Ed.), *Comparative Reading* (pp. 551–580). New York: Macmillan.

Felton, R. & Wood, F. (1989). Cognitive deficits in reading disability and attention deficit disorder. *Journal of Learning Disabilities* **22**, 3–13.

Hatcher, P.J., Hulme, C. & Ellis, A.W. (1994). Ameliorating early reading failure by integrating the teaching of reading and phonological skills: The phonological linkage hypothesis. *Child Development* **65**, 41–57.

Hynd, G., Semrud-Clikeman, M. & Lyytinen, H. (1991). Brain imaging in learning disabilities. In J. Obrzut & G. Hynd (Eds), *Neuropsychological Foundations of Learning Disabilities*. New York: Academic Press.

Jastak, J. & Jastak, S. (1978). *The Wide Range Achievement Test – Revised*. Wilmington, DE: Jastak Associates.

Larsen, J., Hoien, T., Lundberg, I. & Odegaard, H. (1989). *MRI Evaluation of the Size and Symmetry of the Planum Temporale in Adolescents with Developmental Syslexia*. Stavanger, Norway: Center for Reading Research.

Liberman, I.Y., Shankweiler, D. & Liberman, A.M. (1989) The alphabetic principle and learning to read. In I.Y. Liberman & D. Shankweiler (Eds.) *Phonology and Learning to Read*. Ann Arbor, MI: University of Michigan Press.

Lindamood, C. & Lindamood, P. (1975). *Auditory Discrimination in Depth*. Columbus: OH: Science Research Associates Division, Macmillan/McGraw Hill.

Lindamood, C. & Lindamood, P. (1979). *Lindamood Auditory Conceptualization Test (LAC)*. Hingham, MA: Teaching Resources Corporation.

Lovett, M., Borden, S., DeLuca, T., Lacerenza, L., Benson, N. & Brackstone (1995). Treating the core deficits of developmental dyslexia: evidence of transfer-of-learning following strategy and phonologically-based reading training programs. *Developmental Psychology* **30**, 805–822.

Lundberg, I, Frost, J. & Peterson, O. (1988). Effects of an extensive program for stimulating phonological awareness. *Reading Research Quarterly* **23**, 263–284.

Lyon, G.R. (1995). Toward a definition of dyslexia. *Annals of Dyslexia* **15**, 3–30.

Montgomery, D. (1981). Do dyslexics have difficulty accessing articulatory information? *Psychological Research* **43**, 235–243.

Olson, R.K. & Wise, B.W. (1992). Reading on the computer with orthographic and speech feedback. *Reading and Writing* 4,107–144.

Olson, R.K., Forsberg, H. & Wise, B.W. (1994). Genes, environment, and the development of orthographic skills. In V. Berninger (Ed.) *The Varieties of Orthographic Knowledge, I: Theoretical and Developmental Issues.* Dordrecht, The Netherlands: Kluwer.

Olson, R.K., Wise, B.W., Ring, J. & Johnson, M. (in press). Computer-based remedial training in phoneme awareness and phonological decoding: Effects on the post-training development of word recognition. *Scientific Studies of Reading.*

Olson, R.K., Wise, B.W., Conners, F., Rack, J. & Fulker, D. (1989). Specific deficits in component reading and language skills: Genetic and environmental influences. *Journal of Learning Disabilities* 22, 339–348.

Palincsar, A.S. & Brown, A.L. (1984). Reciprocal teaching of comprehension-fostering and comprehension-monitoring activity. *Cognition and Instruction* 2, 117–175.

Perfetti, C. (1985). *Reading Ability.* New York: Oxford University Press.

Rack, J., Snowling, M. & Olson, R. (1992). The nonword reading deficit in developmental dyslexia: A review. *Reading Research Quarterly* 27, 28–53.

Stanovich, K. (1986). Matthew effects in reading: some consequences of individual differences in acquisition of literacy. *Remedial and Special Education* 5, 11–19.

Torgesen, J.K., Wagner, R.K., Rashotte, C.A., Alexander, A.W. & Conway, T. (in press). Preventive and remedial interventions for children with severe reading disabilities. *Learning Disabilities: A Multidisciplinary Journal.*

Truch, S. (1994). Stimulating basic reading processes using Auditory Discrimination in Depth. *Annals of Dyslexia* 24, 218–233.

Uhry, J. & Shepherd, M. (1993). Segmentation/spelling instruction as part of a first-grade reading program: Effects on several measures of reading. *Reading Research Quarterly* 28, 218–233.

Wise, B. (1991). What reading disabled children need: What is known and how to talk about it. *Learning & Individual Differences* 3, 307–321.

Wise, B.W. & Olson, R.K.(1992). Spelling exploration with a talking computer improves phonological coding. *Reading and Writing* 4,145–156.

Wise, B. W. & Olson, R. K. (1995). Computer-based phonological awareness and reading instruction. *Annals of Dyslexia* 45, 99–122.

Wise, B., Olson, R. & Lindamood, P. (April, 1993). Training phonemic awareness: why and how in computerized instruction. Paper delivered at the annual meeting of the American Educational Research Association, Atlanta, GA.

Wise, B. W., Olson, R. K. & Ring, J. (in press). Investigating different aspects of phonological awareness training for children with reading disabilities. *Learning Disabilities Quarterly.*

Subject Index

Author Index